RETRIEVING THE CRIP OUTSIDER

RETRIEVING THE CRIP OUTSIDER

Representations of Disability in Literature and Culture

Edited by

Someshwar Sati

B L O O M S B U R Y

NEW DELHI • LONDON • OXFORD • NEW YORK • SYDNEY

BLOOMSBURY INDIA
Bloomsbury Publishing India Pvt. Ltd
Second Floor, LSC Building No. 4, DDA Complex, Pocket C – 6 & 7,
Vasant Kunj, New Delhi, 110070

BLOOMSBURY, BLOOMSBURY ACADEMIC INDIA and the Diana logo are
trademarks of Bloomsbury Publishing Plc

First published in India 2024
This export edition published 2024

Bloomsbury Academic India
An imprint of Bloomsbury Publishing Plc

ISBN: HB: 978-93-56402-88-1; eBook: 978-93-56402-89-8
2 4 6 8 10 9 7 5 3 1

Typeset by Manipal Technologies Limited
Printed and bound in India by Replika Press Pvt. Ltd.

To find out more about our authors and books visit www.bloomsbury.com and sign
up for our newsletters

To my parents, Professor Rameshwar and Dr Uma Sati, my wife, Arti, and son, Praneel

CONTENTS

ACKNOWLEDGEMENTS

This book has been in the making for quite some time now. Its genesis can be traced to the Oceanvale Workshop on Representations of Disability in Literature and Culture: Text and Context organised by Kirori Mal College's Department of English in October 2019. Out of the 13 chapters that comprise this volume, eight grew out of presentations made at this workshop: three had their origins in lectures delivered at the event by resource persons, mainly Shilpaa Anand, Karuna Rajeev and me. The other five were papers presented by Smriti Verma, Tayyaba Rizwan, Malvika Jayakumar, Deepak Kumar Gupta and Sanket Sakar, all participants in the workshop.

The Oceanvale programme has been instituted in memory of Ravi Singh, a former student of English at Kirori Mal College. Ravi intended to devote himself to the art and craft of writing but his early demise meant that *Oceanvale*, published in 1995, remains his first and last published novel. I would like to take this opportunity to thank the then principal of the college, Vibha Singh Chauhan, and the late Ravi's elder sister, Jawa Singh, for having instituted this programme and for their constant support during and after the workshop. To be honest, this book is a product of Professor Chauhan's visionary zeal. It was, in fact, her inspiring leadership that made me persevere through Covid and beyond. She has this uncanny ability to rekindle the inner flames of one's resolve when they seem to flicker low and I would like to thank her for making both the workshop and this book a reality. I would also like to thank my departmental colleagues Rudrashish Chakraborty, Dhananjay Kapse, Saloni Sharma, Nivedita Basu and Sunjay Sharma for their invaluable contribution in hosting and conducting the workshop. Like true colleagues, they were ever available, and without their support, this workshop and by extension this book would not have been possible. I also need to express my deep sense of gratitude to colleagues from other colleges of the University of Delhi—Debjani Sengupta, Rina Ramdev, Ruchi Sharma and Srinjoyee Dutta. They along with my departmental colleagues mentioned above and the resource persons for the workshop, Shilpaa Anand, Karuna Rajeev and Shubhangi Vaidya, reviewed the papers presented at the workshop, giving insightful comments and suggestions to all the participants. The participants benefited immensely from their feedback, which went a long way in shaping five of the 13 chapters anthologised here.

Three of the articles collected in this volume emerged out of papers presented at various International IDSC Conferences. The Indian Disability Studies Collective, or IDSC, is an association of disability studies scholars from across the country who, on 5 May 2019, came together in the seminar room of Kirori Mal College to establish an academic organisation that would promote scholastic engagement with the experience of disablement within Indian academia. While the chapter by Shilpa Das had its genesis in a plenary lecture delivered at the inaugural International IDSC conference hosted by the Department of English and Modern European Languages, University of Lucknow, in October 2019, the origins of the article by Rimjhim Bhattacherjee and the chapter jointly written by Kaustabh Kashyap and Rakhee Kalita Moral are to be traced to the 2021 International IDSC conference organised by the Centre for Disability Research and Training, Kirori Mal College in collaboration with Guru Angad Dev Teaching Learning Centre, SGTB Khalsa College, University of Delhi. I would like to express my profound sense of gratitude to IDSC, particularly to Ranu Uniyal and Ritwick Bhattacharjee for hosting these conferences.

Finally, the chapters by Priyam Sinha and Mansi Grover are revised versions of the lectures they had delivered at Drishtikon 2.0, a workshop on Disability and Hindi Cinema, organised by the Centre for Disability Research and Training (CDRT), Kirori Mal College, in July 2022. Formally launched in September 2021, CDRT is perhaps the first centre of its kind in a college in India. The primary objective of this centre is to popularise disability studies across the country, particularly amongst undergraduate and postgraduate students. The centre believes that it is necessary to introduce disability studies as a discipline early in a student's academic life. At present, students in India are generally exposed to the discipline quite late in their careers. By then they have already made decisions about the course of their academic journey. As a result, disability studies becomes incidental and peripheral to their scholarly pursuits. By introducing disability studies early in their academic lives, the centre hopes that, in the future, students will take up disability as a legitimate field of academic enquiry. Even the Oceanvale workshop of October 2019 was organised with a similar objective in mind and so is this volume.

This volume would never have been a reality had it not been for the tireless efforts of well-meaning friends. Himani Wadhwa, Ishita Mehta, Anukriti Bajpai and Malvika Jayakumar have all spent endless hours corresponding with contributors and publishers, editing and proofreading the manuscript and undertaking other tasks that are integral to the process of producing a book. Last but not least, thanks are due to Chandra Sekhar, the Publisher from Bloomsbury.

I know I have tested his patience by transgressing deadlines several times but he has always responded with ample generosity and understanding.

I'm glad that this book is finally seeing the light of the day. I may be the editor of the volume but as it is evident, the book belongs to all who play an invaluable part in bringing it to fruition and I shall cherish the contribution made by everyone for years to come.

Someshwar Sati
12 August 2023

INTRODUCTION

Someshwar Sati

If we give you a page scripted in Braille, will you be able to read it? Perhaps not. Would you then be called disabled? Obviously not. Why, then, are blind people who cannot read print and use Braille instead labelled as disabled? Why are those who adopt different ways of doing the same thing branded as 'deviant' and 'abnormal'? Why can we not embrace and celebrate alternative modes of 'being' and 'living' as a manifestation of human diversity? This book is an invitation to reflect on these questions and revisit the way we perceive and respond to disability and disabled people.

A vast majority of the human population has never experienced disability firsthand. Nor have they ever encountered a disabled person. Yet, whenever they are called to speak on the subject of disability, they never seem to find themselves short of words. Their prolonged pronouncements are full of sympathy and never-ending advice as if they were experts on the subject. I find this paradox quite peculiar, a little intriguing and somewhat baffling. I often sit back, pondering over it; there is one thing that I can state with utmost conviction:

Given that a vast majority of the nondisabled population have had no firsthand experience of disability, they have conjured their understanding of disability through second-hand sources, primarily, stories replete with normative stereotypes of disability that tend to flatten out the various complex nuances of the experience of disablement putting forward a rather simplistic objectified image of the disabled that bolsters the identity of the nondisabled collective. For this reason, the nondisabled world feels that disability is a simple phenomenon, a phenomenon easy to grasp. For them, disability is a fact of nature, it is the medical condition of 'a human body gone wrong'. They feel that you need to just imagine or simulate the inability to move or see or hear and one would have arrived at a comprehensive understanding of the experience of disablement. This, however, is to grossly simplify and understate the complex nature of this phenomenon. One should not forget that disability is primarily a social stigma that breeds prejudice, contempt and discrimination; it is a form of inequality and social oppression. Disabled people have been socially, culturally, economically and politically marginalised from mainstream society on account of their corporeal differences. One should also remember that disability is also an 'epistemology of inclusion', an issue, an idea, a metaphor, a phenomenon, a culture and a construction. It is a social and cultural manifestation of human diversity. The articles collected in this volume all endeavour to explore and unveil the experience of disablement in its manifold complexities.

The Changing Discourse of Disability

The discourse on disability has constantly changed and shifted over time. Prior to the emergence of the age of modernity, disability was primarily conceived within a religious register that perceived the phenomenon as a divine punishment inflicted on disabled people for a misdemeanour committed by them or by their forbearers in the present birth or previous reincarnation. But with the advent of modernity and the emergence of medical and clinical practices, the semantic underpinnings of this phenomenon underwent a sea change. Medicine saw disability as a clinically diagnosed corporeal or cognitive ailment, a physical or mental deficit, in need of medical attention.

Before the 1960s, intellectual engagement with disability, even within the discipline of social sciences, displayed a marked tendency to medicalise and individualise the experience of disablement, tracing the genesis of the phenomenon to the abnormality of an individual's body. The standard professional and academic protocol at the time was to respond, manage and rectify this abnormality through care and rehabilitation. The 1970s and 1980s, however, saw disability scholarship move away from the individualistic language of medicine in which it had hitherto been couched and embrace what Michael Oliver calls the 'social model of disability'. Conceptually embedded in a theory of social oppression and politically structured by a distinct Marxist ideological orientation, this model traced the genealogy of the experience of disablement not to the medical condition of an individual's body but rather to the systemic insufficiencies and social structures of an uncaring and unjust disabling society. The exponents of this school of thought position disability as a form of social inequality and discrimination, and disabled people as an oppressed community excluded from the mainstream of society. They also believe that it is the responsibility of society to remove the obstacles, the 'barriers', that prevent disabled people from realising the fullness of their potential. Accordingly, they are intent on dismantling these oppressive social and political structures. For this purpose, they sought to establish a pragmatic link between a critical exposition of the experience of disablement and a political praxis with a well-defined transformative agenda, namely, 'the removal of barriers' and the 'individual and collective empowerment of disabled people'. The social model, in this sense, provided the political movements of disability rights with a rigorous intellectual framework to further their protest against discrimination in the name of social justice. In this sense, the conceptual framework of this model neatly dovetailed with the human rights approach to disability. This model believes that disability as a social problem can be solved by promulgating and effectively implementing rights-based policies that would promote the accessibility, participation and mainstreaming of disabled people.

The contribution that the social and human rights model has made to the political movement for disability rights across the globe is undeniable. But both these models tend to gloss over the role that culture—as a form of social practice that conditions the collective consciousness of society— plays in shaping the normative perceptions of disability by attributing a widely accepted meaning and significance to the experience of disablement. Predictably, many disability studies scholars feel that the social model has today become 'a little dusty' (Waldschmidt 2017). Even Colin Barnes, a leading proponent of the social model of disability, acknowledges the importance that culture plays in shaping the experience of disability in today's world:

> Disabling stereotypes which medicalise, patronise, criminalise and dehumanise disabled people abound in books, films, on television, and in the press. They form the bedrock on which the attitudes towards, assumptions about and expectations of disabled people are based. They are fundamental to the discrimination and exploitation which disabled people encounter daily and contribute significantly to their systematic exclusion from mainstream community life. (Barnes 1992)

Barnes's observation puts to rest any speculation against the value of a cultural approach to disability. After all, the attitudes towards assumptions about and expectations of disabled people that condition and define the way society responds to them are reproduced and disseminated in and through culture. The cultural model, therefore, perceives disability as not just an effect of social discrimination and exclusion. Its main objective is to explore the experience of disablement as the inevitable outcome of a wide range of social practices and their relation with symbolic knowledge systems, institutionalisation and labelling processes, their consequences for both the disabled and the nondisabled populations, their social status and the ways their subjectivities are constituted, and the materiality of their day-to-day existence.

The present volume, therefore, seeks to probe deeper into 'the social meanings attached to ... disability identity and asks how they relate to enforced systems of exclusion and expression' (Siebers 2008). In other words, this book belongs to the school of disability studies that believes in incorporating culture within its disciplinary purview as an analytical tool. In this sense, it traces its academic lineage to a tradition of Tom Shakespeare, Lennard J. Davis, Rosemarie Garland-Thomson, Sharon L. Snyder, David T. Mitchell, Robert McRuer, David Bolt, Margrit Shildrick, Tobin Siebers and others—all of whom, through their pioneering work, have demonstrated the usefulness of using literature and culture as an effective theoretical framework for understanding disability. Their works inevitably reveal that a critical analysis of culture enhances our understanding of disability and our exegesis of disability furthers our comprehension of culture. But before outlining the cultural approach to disability in greater detail, it would be well in order to unravel the meaning of disability and trace the contours of the emergence and development of disability studies as an academic discipline.

Unveiling Disability

The very mention of the word disability evokes in popular imagination countless images of the human body 'gone wrong'—images of fractured and fragmented limbs, unseeing eyes, unhearing ears and unstable minds. There appears in society at large an almost instinctive impulse to relate disability with a sub-human mode of existence. But why are disabled people always perceived in terms of lack and inadequacy? The answer to this question is fairly simple. It is because of the way we use the term in common parlance. In our day-to-day conversation, the word 'disability' is used generally to connote a clinically diagnosed physical or mental deficit that hinders and incapacitates the individual from performing normative life functions. What is discernable here is the tendency to medicalise and individualise the phenomena and trace the genesis of the experience of disablement to an individual's body. But is the experience of disablement to be exclusively associated with the condition of the human body?

Let us ponder this question by contemplating the 'predicament' of a wheelchair user confronted with a flight of steps. When wheelchair users come face to face with a staircase, they are unable to ascend or descend the different levels of a building and, in a sense, find themselves 'disabled'. But when the very same wheelchair users are provided with a ramp or an elevator, they are immediately able to negotiate the different floors of a premise with consummate ease. In a sense they cease to be 'disabled'. If this is the case, should the experience of disablement be exclusively traced to the condition of the human body? Or does disability have something to do with the disability-unfriendly and hostile social environment that simply refuses to recognise the specific means of the disabled population, thus hindering and preventing them from realising their potential?

For this reason, disability studies seek to define disability by consciously going beyond the biological determinants of the phenomena, locating the experience of disablement firmly within the realms of the social, the cultural and the political. It believes that '[i]f we locate disability in the person, then we maintain a disabling status quo. In contrast, by viewing disability as a cultural and political phenomenon, we ask serious questions about the social world' (Goodley 2012). Therefore, any attempt to medicalise the phenomena is a concerted endeavour to exonerate society from any form of culpability in shaping the experience of disablement. Expressing disability in the language of medicine also tends to naturalise the phenomenon. But is disability a universal category of human experience? Historically, the experience of disablement has varied across different cultures both temporally and spatially. At one time, homosexuality, for example, was considered socially unacceptable across all cultures. Today, however, some countries like the UK, USA, Germany, Canada and Australia have legalised it and consider it to be a normal way of being, while Afghanistan, Pakistan, UAE, Sri Lanka, Singapore, and others continue to view it as a deviant and an unacceptable mode of sexual orientation. Society's attitude to homosexuality and by extension disability is thus culturally and ideologically diverse. More importantly, neither culture nor ideology are politically neutral categories. Disability, then, as Rosemarie Garland-Thomson aptly puts it 'is the attribution of corporeal deviance—not so much a property of bodies as a product of cultural rules about what bodies should be or do' (Garland-Thomson 1997). This statement is profound and has far-reaching consequences; it therefore needs to be unpacked at length.

H.G. Wells's short story, 'The Country of the Blind' (1904), provides us with an apt fictional illustration of the above dictum. The story focuses on Nunez, a sighted mountaineer, who, on an expedition to the Andes Mountains of Ecuador, lost his way and landed in a village whose inhabitants were all blind. On arriving in the village and seeing that everyone there could not see, Nunez was filled with the thought of becoming the chieftain of the village. 'In the country of the Blind the One-Eyed Man is King' is a refrain that recurs throughout the narrative. However, as the story unfolds, the authority of sight and Nunez's claimed superiority on its basis are repetitively undermined.

In the course of his stay in the village, he soon realises that the social and cultural processes that govern the day-to-day activities there have been scripted for the convenience of those who cannot see and without keeping him and his dependence on sight in mind. For example, in the country of the blind, the day is not divided into day and night in the manner that it is in the sighted world. The division of the day on these lines would not make sense to the blind inhabitants of the village. After all, blind people cannot detect the shift from light to dark. They, however, are able to sense the change in temperature as the day disappears into the night. While the day is warm and sultry, the nights are colder and more pleasant. For this reason, blind people prefer to work during the night rather than in the course of the day. The blind people of the village had thus scripted a timetable of their daily routine as per their needs and convenience. However, the same was not convenient for Nunez. Working during the night was simply unthinkable to him as he was too dependent on his eyes and light to carry out his daily activities. Consequently, he feels marginalised in the village becoming unproductive. Did Nunez's low productivity have anything to do with the corporeality of the sighted man? Or is his marginal status to be attributed to a social and cultural system that pays little heed to his needs and requirements?

As the plot gathers momentum, Nunez falls in love with and wants to marry a young woman from the village—the blind Medina-sarote. Her father Yakob, however, rejects the proposal of marriage as he is not in favour of his daughter marrying a man who is never in his senses. Nunez's repeated references to the colour of the sun, sky, trees, grass and other objects are to Yakob nothing but the gibberish of a madman, as they make sense neither to him nor any other villagers. The doctor of the village, after examining Nunez, diagnoses him as having the disease of sight and suggests that he could be cured if he has the two soft organs called eyes operated and removed. So, in the country of the blind, sight becomes a disease. The problem, one can safely agree with Lennard Davis, 'is not the person with disabilities: the problem is the way that normalcy is constructed to create the "problem" of the disabled person' (Davis 1995). For Davis, the primary task of a disability studies scholar is therefore to problematise the ideology of normalcy and find alternative ways of knowing and thinking about corporeal difference. It is to denaturalise disability by unpacking the relationship between '[disability] and the political, social, even spatial environment that places that [disability] in a matrix of meanings and significations' (Davis 1995). It is in this context that the present volume attains meaning and significance.

Evolution of Disability Studies

Prior to the 1960s, academic engagement with the experience of disablement was largely confined to the medical sciences and allied disciplines. Even within the realm of social sciences, intellectual deliberations on this experience were largely couched in the language of medicine, which perceived disability as a clinically diagnosed, unacceptable bodily deviation from the normal state of corporeal embodiment, a kind of corporeal ailment in need of care, rectification and cure. Talcott Parsons' functional analysis of the social role of medicine is perhaps a good example of this school of thought. Writing in 1951, the American sociologist, in his book, *The Social System*, declared that health is normal and sickness is not. What is discernible here is that Parson conceptualises sickness as a form of abnormality, a deviation from the normal (healthy) state of being. As a result, sick people are not able to perform the economic and social roles expected from a healthy individual and therefore they cannot associate themselves with a standard lifestyle. For this reason, it is the moral responsibility of the medical practitioner to respond to and manage this abnormality. The role of medicine, according to him, is to care for sick people and nurse them back to the state of health.

Though the knowledge produced within the domain of medical sciences and allied disciplines tends to govern the way that society at large looks at disabled people, the knowledge produced in these domains, strictly speaking, does not belong to the realm of disability studies. This is not to undermine the value and denigrate medical science and its allied disciplines; rather, the endeavour is to delineate the disciplinary boundaries of an academic discipline that goes by the name of disability studies.

Disability studies is a liberal arts-based interdisciplinary field of academic enquiry that seeks to examine and understand disability as a social, political and cultural phenomenon. While the language of medicine attempts to individualise the experience of disablement and treat it as a personal problem that needs to be cured and rectified, disability studies scholars perceive disability as a systemic condition of an uncaring and unjust disabling society and treat it as a manifestation of human diversity to evolve an epistemology of inclusion. The medicalisation of disability, on the other hand, leads to the pathologisation of difference breeding a divisive ethos of exclusion. It is to be noted here that the hospitalisation and rehabilitation of disabled people inevitably result in them being segregated from society.

Interestingly, the emergence of disability activism in the UK is historically linked to the protest campaigns by disabled people against their segregation into residential homes. It was felt at the time that these homes in the name of care and rehabilitation systematically excluded them from social and economic life, plunging them into a state of social isolation and abject poverty. This led to the politicisation of disability activism and the establishment in 1974 of the Union of the Physically Impaired Against Segregation (UPIAS). In fact, it was the UPIAS that, for the first time, outlined the experience of disablement as a socio-political phenomenon:

> Disability is something imposed on top of our impairments by the way we are unnecessarily isolated and excluded from society. Disabled people are therefore an oppressed group. It follows from this analysis that having low incomes, for example, is only one aspect of our oppression. It is a consequence of our isolation and segregation in every area of social life, such as education, work, mobility, housing etc. (UPIAS 1976)

What is discernable here is the UPIAS attempt to make a crucial distinction between impairment, the biological, and disability, the social.[1] If nothing else, the bifurcation of impairment and disability signalled a movement away from a focus on the physical limitations of disabled individuals to an engagement with the ways the physical and social environments impose limitations on disabled people (Oliver 1981). The social model stipulates that a person with an impairment is rendered disabled by an uncaring and unjust society. This was the big idea at the time and it deeply influenced academic discourse on disability across the world, particularly in the UK. In other words, during the 1970s and 1980s, the discourse on disability within British academia was governed by a social model perspective, that is, it was a reaction to the social processes of alienation that secluded disabled people from society. The research in the field at the time focused on the social and economic consequences of impairment and was primarily carried out within the disciplinary domain of social sciences. Its objective was to unearth the structural foundations of oppression and establish the factors that led to the social, economic and political isolation of disabled people. Scholars like Mike Oliver, Vic Finklestein and Colin Barnes, for example, used Marxist and Gramscian conceptual frameworks to analyse the various structural barriers experienced by disabled people in the spheres of work, education and community living. These theoretically nuanced studies inevitably politicised the phenomenon, providing disability activism with an intellectual framework that deeply influenced legislative discourses across the globe, including the UN Convention on the Rights of Persons with Disabilities.

But these studies simply ignored the ideological and cultural underpinnings of the experience of disablement. Reacting to the above criticism, Oliver seems to suggest that the study of culture could not be of significance so long as poverty and unemployment continue to govern the lives of disabled people (Oliver 1996). This, however, is not to suggest that Oliver has not discussed cultural representation at all. For example, in *The Politics of Disablement* (1990), he devotes two entire pages to an exegesis of cultural representation. But his discussion of culture is rather schematic and animated by a materialist understanding of the ideology which postulates that ideas about the disabled are the inevitable product of the material social relations between disabled and nondisabled people. Ideology, in this sense, comes across as systems of theoretical formulations that justifies and legitimises oppression and leaves no room for the critical analysis of culture as an autonomous space for constituting subjectivity (Shakespeare 1994). But people with disabilities are discriminated against not only on account of material relations and processes but also on account of prejudice and attitudes. This is why, Tom Shakespeare felt a strong need to reconceptualise the social model, go beyond it and advocate a cultural approach to disability studies.

The Cultural Turn

'The Social Model,' Shakespeare suggests, 'needs to be reconceptualized: people with impairment are disabled, not just by material discrimination, but also by prejudice. This prejudice is not just interpersonal, it is also implicit in cultural representation, in language and in socialization' (Shakespeare 1994). But, it is important to note that Shakespeare here is not advocating a wholesale rejection of the Marxist paradigm. His writing is marked by a continued engagement with Marxist principles, particularly those associated with the idea of the 'fetish'. He, however, blends these Marxist principles with insights from contemporary feminist discourse. Inspired by Simone de Beauvoir's incisive analysis in *The Second Sex* (1976) of the representation and objectification of women in culture, he argued that disabled people have and continue to be objectified in culture in a manner not too dissimilar to women, and gave a clarion call to disability scholars to pay attention to and problematise the cultural representation of disability.

Since then, disability scholars have been borrowing analytical tools from literary and cultural theory to bear on their analysis of disability and its representation in culture. Cultural disability studies is today already a widely flourishing and ingenious field of academic enquiry within the humanities across the globe. However, the first conscious attempt to institutionalise a cultural model within the disciplinary terrain of disability studies is to be found in Sharon Snyder and David Mitchell's *Cultural Location of Disability*. Writing in 2006, they poignantly observe that within the social model, '"disability" signifies only discriminatory encounters' (Snyder and Mitchell 2006). They, therefore, lay stress on the need to formulate a cultural model of understanding disability that would allow scholars to 'theorize a political act of renaming that designates disability as a site of resistance and a source of cultural agency previously suppressed [...]' (Snyder and Mitchell 2006). Snyder and Mitchell argue that disabled people are not just excluded from society but held in certain cultural locations that evoke 'sites of violence, restriction, confinement, and absence of liberty for people with disabilities' (10). These sites define disabled people, no doubt, but, at the same time, they also rely for their meaning and signification on the very disabled people they restrict and confine. Unpacking Snyder and Mitchell's concept, Tobin Siebers states that:

> disability confines affected individuals in social locations that carry negative meanings beyond those that the individuals are themselves capable of generating. Because disabled people do not cause the meanings attached to them, their confinement in particular social locations is often arbitrary, experienced as violent and existentially absurd but also as a spur to awaken new perceptions about society. (Siebers 2008, 119)

If Snyder and Mitchell build a case for evolving a cultural model that would explore the bodies of disabled people in relation to the society around them, Siebers puts forward a theory of complex embodiment that locates disability at the cusp of environmental and corporeal factors such as 'chronic pain, secondary health effects, and aging' (Siebers 2008) opening up a conceptual space that allows the disabled body to re-emerge as an integral component of the disability experience.

The 21st century saw disability studies embrace a host of different intellectual persuasions. While Tom Shakespeare advocated a return to the experiential realities of impairment as object(s) independent of knowledge (Shakespeare 2006), most other disability studies scholars have laid stress on the materiality of the disabled body to conceptualise the impaired body as a socio-cultural body. While Garland-Thomson sees disability as a cultural trope that interrogates the materiality of the body and the various normative epistemological formulations that are used to interpret corporeal difference (Garland-Thomson 1997), Margrit Shildrick dwells on the concept of an ambivalent and fluid social body that problematises any simple binarism between the biological and the social, transforming the body into a complex site of cultural production. The disabled body, she suggests, is a performative agent that simultaneously reproduces and rejects institutionalised standards of corporeality (Shildrick 2009). The simultaneous existence of multiple approaches to disability, in fact, has led Lennard Davis to describe the field of contemporary disability studies as 'dismodernist' and to see disabled people as the ultimate intersectional subjects through which various forms of exclusion and resistance can be understood and easily decoded.

As disabled bodies became complex and composite sites of cultural production, 'disabled bodies do matter' became a governing orthodoxy within the field of disability studies. While some of the articles collected in this volume ask the question—'why bodies of disabled people have been rendered invisible in traditional narratives of disability?'—others reveal how bodies do matter in a disability experience and how these bodies get materialised. Predictably, the volume opens with an article that endeavours to systematically deconstruct the ideological production of the figure of the disabled and problematise its dissemination in and through culture. Someshwar Sati, in 'Negotiating the Polemics of Intentional Evasion: The Nondisabled Imaginary, the Disabled Self and Academic Disability Activism', attempts to decode the working of the ideology of normalcy and its reproduction in and through the processes of othering. He explores the processes through which disabled people have been and continue to be objectified in culture and its impact on the constitution of disabled subjectivity. In the article, he poignantly observes that narratives of disability are seldom about the disabled character. In fact, in these narratives, disability comes across as an empty signifier, a metaphor endowed with pejorative connotations. He builds a case for the better treatment of disabled characters in cultural narratives and positions this as a preliminary prerequisite for effecting an attitudinal change in the ways the nondisabled population perceives and responds to disability and disabled people. In a sense, his article effectively blends literary criticism with disability activism in ways that foster the values and significance of a cultural approach to the understanding of disability.

The cultural approach to disability is first and foremost characterised by an intellectual endeavour to problematise the clear-cut division between impairment and disability that lies at the heart of the social model. The argument is simple: Both these categories, like the notion of normalcy, are discursively constituted in and through everyday discourses on disability that would include knowledge systems, social practices, the mass media and other modes of cultural production and therefore, the materiality of the body and for that matter, social identities cannot pre-exist or be separated from linguistic and cultural structures (Stiker 1999; Siebers 2008).

Building upon the above ideological premises, Shilpaa Anand, in 'Clinical Rescripts: Recovering the Affective Politics of Medicalising Women's Bodies', explores the social contours of medicine and dwells on its affective politics, that is, its impact on a woman's life and her domestic relations with spouses and parents. Through a nuanced reading of a female doctor's fictional account of women with small breasts, loose vaginas, infertile wombs and other bodily deviations from the desirable forms of female embodiment, she conclusively demonstrates that even impairment, like disability, is socially conditioned, in this case, by a discourse of biomedicine and a similar set of clinical practices. More importantly, she argues that the impairment affect is experienced by these women in and through relationships deeply affecting their perceptions of themselves. These women, however, use the clinical practices of biomedicine to their advantage in ways that boost their self-image and identity.

If Anand examines the sociality of medicine and dwells on the effect that the medicalisation of individuals produces, Shilpa Das takes the discussion on the constitution of the subjectivity of disabled women into the realm of social customs and religious festivals. Das, in 'Self-Concept, Embodiment, Sexuality and Disability: How Disabled Women Experience Navaratri and Gauri Vrat in Gujarat', examines cultural conceptualisations of femininity, sexuality and marriage worthiness by exploring a wide range of subjective accounts of how the experience of social customs and festivals have shaped disabled women's perceptions of themselves and their identity. Her essay explores the interplay between social factors and the lived experiences of disabled women in the city of Ahmedabad. It elaborates on disabled women's experiences and feelings as adolescents and young adults, and how they gradually come to terms with their bodies, especially with respect to two cultural ritualistic events or celebrations—the Navaratri festival and the Gauri Vrat. These women observe these rituals in ways that allow their bodies to at once reproduce and challenge normative ideas of the disabled gendered subject. In this sense, her essay is ideologically structured by a distinct phenomenological theoretical orientation that attests to the body's capacity to be a meaning-making agent that defines the interactions between self and society. Both Anand and Das address a pertinent question—in the course of a disability experience, where does the biomedical end and the socio-cultural begin? They suggest that the impaired/medical body is socio-cultural.

The above theoretical formulation allows the disability studies scholar to reinsert the disabled body back into the sociology of disablement, transforming it into a potent site where the self and society interact in novel, productive and liberating ways. This ideological manoeuvre gathers great significance, particularly in the context of the disabled body's potential to inflect and problematise normative perceptions of disability from its perspective.

The disabled body, with its variegated lived experiences, has a creative and meaning-making potential that can de-centre and even unsettle normative nondisabled perceptions of disability. In '(Re)defining Metaphorical Address: Female Disability, Embodiment and Agency in Jerry Pinto's *Em and the Big Hoom*', Smriti Verma unpacks the meaning-making potential of disabled people to define their identity and subjectivity by inflecting metaphorical expression from the perspective of their very own personal and embodied experiences and sees in this potential a mode of address that opens up normative nondisabled perceptions of disability to scrutiny. The novel, in her reading, pays testimony to a disabled woman's capacity to transform the material experience of her own body into a potent source for the discursive constitution of the self, in the process, disrupting ableist and patriarchal presumptions of her identity. Pinto, according to her, opens up discursive spaces wherein the disabled body can become the material ground that defines the contours of the interaction between the disabled self and society.

The materiality of disabled bodies, their lived experiences and their creative meaning-making potential do matter, or at least they must be made to matter if we are to evolve an epistemology of inclusion that can de-normalise the fundamental norms that structure the ableist society that we all inhabit. At the heart of this volume lie three fundamental questions: how do disabled bodies become materialised? How can the material disabled bodies find articulation? And, what is the impact of this articulation on the constitution of disabled subjectivity? All the contributors to this volume, each in their own respective way, comprehensively address one or more of the above questions and Tayyaba Rizwan is no different. Rizwan, in 'Dismembered Bodies in a Disabling Culture: Gendered Perception of Disability in Indian Myths', critically outlines the role that culturally internalised mythologies play in structuring the processes of meaning-making that shape and even condition the way we perceive and respond to the gendered disabled subject and conceptualise notions of disability/ non-disability, morality/immorality and beauty/grotesque. Drawing upon the stories of the treacherous, mentally deranged hunchback Manthara and the desexualised Surpanakha in the *Ramayana* and Kannagi in the *Silapaddikaram* with their respective dismembered nose and mutilated breast, she probes deep into and reconceptualises an ableist phallocentric ontology to create an emancipatory semiotic canvas that is at once empowering and liberating for a gender-disabled subject. Anand, Das, Verma and Rizwan all embark on a feminist investigation of the discursive constitution of the culturally normative figure of the gendered disabled subject and reveal how the constitution of this subject is deeply influenced by hegemonic medical, social and cultural discourses and how disabled women can and do insert their perspectives and experiences into these discourses to articulate a gendered disabled subjectivity that de-centres the normative. If their essays dwell on the intersectionalities between the categories of gender and disability, and patriarchy and ableism, for Malvika Jayakumar, the figure of the monster is the ultimate intersectional trope that collates the operations of various hierarchies of power, constituted along the axis of race, ethnicity and region.

In 'Overlapping Discourses of Monstrosity and Disability in India: Decoding Aryan–Dravidian Narratives in the *Ramayana* and Its Contemporary Iteration in Amish Tripathi's 'Shiva' Trilogy', Jayakumar's reading of the numerous narratives of monstrosity in the *Ramayana* inevitably reveals that the figure of the monster in the epic is for the Aryan race residing in northern India the most recurring image of the threatening, corporeally deviant other. Curiously though, these representations of monstrosity, she poignantly notes, are underpinned by subtexts of racial and spatial segregation, suggesting that the monster is not merely a diabolical figure but has also been appropriated to consider the racial and spatial other, the Dravadian race who inhabited the geographical locations beyond the Dandaka forests. The narratives of monstrosity in the epic form an integral part of an insidious process of Aryan self-fashioning which continues to be reproduced and disseminated even today. Disability, in Jayakumar's hands, becomes a complex intersectional, discursive space, a 'cultural trope' to mediate and meditate upon a host of racial, ethnic and regional issues that condition and even define our contemporary existence.

Even when disability is used in common parlance, it seldom appears to be about itself. It always comes across as a metaphorical stand-in for something else. Carrying this line of thought forward, Karuna Rajeev, in 'Disability, Discourse and Metaphor', poignantly observes that the nondisabled literary representations of disability are never about disability per se as they generally emerge from established conventions of a heteronormative ableist discourse that defines identity in terms of what a disabled person can/cannot do, should/should not do. Even the liberal rhetoric of inclusion that is being fostered in our academia today, particularly at the time of framing the syllabi of various courses, for that matter, is no different as it operates from the same hegemonic heteronormative location that imposes equivalences between distinct identities or, more specifically, between the experiences of disabled people and other identity groups, disregarding experiential frameworks and political histories.

Metaphorical evocations of disability seem to always gather meaning and significance from the perspective of the experiences of a nondisabled consciousness. Blindness, for example, has a generally used language in common parlance and literary narratives as a stand-in for the lack of understanding or insights. This is profoundly disturbing but what is even more unsettling is the consummate ease with which the nondisabled community accepts the naturalness of such arbitrary associations. This speaks volumes about the way disability is collectively lodged in an ableist consciousness. Deepak Kumar Gupta, in 'Blind Lives Matter: Metaphor and Materiality in Dharamvir Bharati's *Andha Yug*', problematises the working of this consciousness through an exploration of the metaphorical evocation of blindness in Dharamvir Bharati's play, *Andha Yug*.

Both Rajeev and Gupta, in their own respective ways, seem to suggest that the narrative of disability is, for the most part, never about the experience of a disabled person as in these narratives, disability is either deployed as a metaphor or rendered through a metaphorical association. Therefore, it would not be wrong to say that in an ableist cultural universe, there appears to exist an irrevocable bind between disability and its scripted cultural textuality. But more importantly, this bind is one that totally disregards the experiential reality of disabled people.

Sanket Sakar, in 'Disability, Textuality and the Hermeneutics of Distance in Sriram Raghavan's *Andhadhun*', critically unpacks this bind through an incisive reading of the representation and reception of blindness in the Sriram Raghavan movie, *Andhadhun*. The sighted protagonist of the film pretends to be blind but his act of simulation appears to be deeply embedded in the hegemonic socio-cultural scripts of blindness. The response of the other characters to this performance is no different, reducing and flattening the complexities of the lived realities of blind people and their embodiments to easily recognisable medical perceptions of the phenomenon. Despite the open-ended and indeterminate conclusion to the plot, the film, Sarkar argues, inevitably ends up recreating the stigma associated with disability in the audience's minds. The essay, however, eventually lays emphasis on the need to release the understanding of disability from the hegemonic sway of its deterministic socio-cultural manuals that interpret the phenomenon exclusively in medical terms and connect the perception of disability to its experiential realities and frameworks.

Priyam Sinha, in 'Sanjay Leela Bhansali's Disability Gaze: Lights, Camera and Sound! In *Black* and *Guzaarish*', is critical of the politics of disablement and peculiarities of disability characterisation popularised in contemporary Bollywood films. According to her, the culture of disablism prevalent in Bollywood has continued to emphasise the disabled character's ability to overcome the disability by overcompensating for it or complying with a tragic life that is devoid of companionship. Bollywood's disability representations could be, she argues, categorised within these two extremes. Her essay probes into the above proposition through a discourse analysis of Sanjay Leela Bhansali's *Black* (2005) and *Guzaarish* (2010) and explores how these films position the disabled body as a corporeal space located in a bleak and dark cinematic universe through an interplay of music, light and cinematography.

Bollywood, in fact, appears to speak from a hegemonic ableist cultural location, creating a meta narrative of deficiency and inadequacy around disability and in the process, projecting disabled people as unfit to take up societal roles and meet societal expectations. Mansi Grover's '"*Bezubaan*" or "*Humzubaan*": Problematising Deaf Identities through a Select Few Hindi Films' reflects upon the above statement through a study of the representation of deaf characters in Hindi films. She unpacks the significance of Deaf ontologies and Deaf epistemologies to understand Deaf bodies as linguistically diverse, wondering whether deafness should be categorised as a disability or not in an audist world. In Bollywood's representations of deafness, she laments that deaf ontologies and epistemologies are rarely granted understanding, denying the deaf characters any tangible form of sociality. Both Sinha and Grover seem to suggest that in Bollywood films disability becomes 'a master trope of human disqualification' (Mitchell and Snyder 2001).

At a time when first-person narratives by disabled people are generally dismissed in the critical establishments as disparaging narratives of overcoming, the last two essays in the volume appear to privilege the autobiographical mode of writing over third-person nondisabled narratives of disability. The intention is simply to evolve understandings of disability that are grounded in experiential realities and frameworks of disabled existence. Rimjhim Bhattacherjee, in 'From Cure to Healing: Comprehending Deafness through Madan Vasishta's *Deaf in Delhi*', underscores the radical potential of such narratives to disrupt the normative understanding of disability. According to her, such narratives function as antidotes to the third-person ableist opinions on disability. In a transgressive reading of Madan Vasishta's memoir, *Deaf in Delhi* (2006), she takes what in Deaf studies is called a 'deaf turn' and builds a case for transcending a strictly medical perception of deafness by challenging and reframing the normative ableist perceptions of the phenomenon. Her essay traces the journey of advantageously deaf Vasishta from the comprehension of deafness as an individual aberration—a medical 'condition' that alienates the deaf person from mainstream society by instilling in him a sense of abnormality—to the idea of a unique Deaf culture that creates value in the lives of Deaf people and helps them both challenge and resist debilitating preconceived notions and metaphors associated with deafness.

The volume concludes with an essay that attempts to establish an interdisciplinary dialogue between disability studies and medical humanities by laying stress on the corporeality of mental illness (depression) and placing the patient's experience at par with the doctor's diagnosis. Kaustabh Kashyap and Rakhee Kalita Moral, in 'Crossing Cultures in Storying Depression: *Shadows in the Sun* as Intersection and Dialogue between Disability Studies and Medical Humanities', use Gayathri Ramprasad's memoir, *Shadows in the Sun* (2014), to understand how these two disciplines can be brought together to arrive at a more nuanced, intersectional and holistic understanding of depression (or disability, for that matter). Disability studies is thus breaking boundaries between disciplines and moving towards inhabiting a transdisciplinary space, blurring the distinctions between professional experts and lay patients, overwriting traditional medicalised views of disability with socio-cultural notions of disablism.

Conclusion

The genesis of disability studies as an academic discipline can undoubtedly be traced to the political resistance of disabled people against their incarceration into care homes and their exclusion from social and economic activities. Accordingly, the discipline in its early days was primarily interested in accounting for the structural, social, and economic factors responsible for the above. At that point of time, disability scholars were primarily occupied in developing nuanced theoretical responses to the above and in politicising it. While the former intellectual orientation decolonised the traditional medical conceptions of disablement replacing it with a social understanding of disability, the latter led to the emergence of a human rights-based approach to the phenomena. However, the end of the 20th century saw disability studies go beyond the social and rights-based models of disability that are ideologically embedded in a Marxist account of the phenomena and embrace cultural discourses that draw heavily from feminist and postcolonial studies. The essays collected in this volume opens up the discipline of disability studies to a wide range of trans- and interdisciplinary influences, firmly locating the experience of disability within a material and discursive, intersectional space that enables us to think through a wide range of theoretical, political and practical issues relevant to both the disabled and nondisabled inhabitants of the world.

Note

1　According to the UPIAS, 'impairment' is 'lacking part or all of a limb, or having a defective limb or mechanism of the body' but 'disability is the disadvantage of restriction of activity caused by a contemporary social organisation which takes no or little account of people who have physical impairments and thus excludes them from participation in the mainstream of social activities' (UPIAS 1976).

References

Barnes, Colins. *Disabling Imagery and the Media: An Exploration of the Principles for Media Representations of Disabled People*. Halifax, Ryburn/British Council of Organisations of Disabled People, 1992.

Davis, Lennard J. *Enforcing Normalcy: Disability, Deafness, and the Body*. London and New York: Verso, 1995.

Garland-Thomson, Rosemarie. *Extraordinary Bodies: Figuring Physical Disability in American Culture and Literature*. New York: Columbia University Press, 1997.

Goodley, Dan. 'The Psychology of Disability'. In *Routledge Handbook of Disability Studies*, edited by Nick Watson, Alan Roulstone and Carol Thomas, 310–23. London and New York: Routledge, 2012.

Mitchell, David T. and Sharon L. Snyder. *Narrative Prosthesis: Disability and the Dependencies of Discourse*. Ann Arbor: University of Michigan Press, 2001.

Oliver, M. 'A New Model of the Social Work Role in Relation to Disability'. In *The Handicapped Person: A New Perspective for Social Workers*, edited by J. Campling, 19–32. London: RADAR, 1981.

———. *Understanding Disability. From Theory to Practice*. London: Palgrave, 1996.

Parsons, Talcott. *The Social System*. New York: Free Press, 1951.

Shakespeare, Tom. 'Cultural Representation of Disabled People: Dustbins for Disavowal?' *Disability & Society*, 9, no. 3 (February 1994): 283–99.

———. *Disability Rights and Wrongs*. London and New York: Routledge, 2006.

Shildrick, Margrit. *Dangerous Discourses of Disability, Subjectivity and Sexuality*. London: Palgrave Macmillan, 2009.

Siebers, Tobin. *Disability Theory*. Ann Arbor: University of Michigan Press, 2008.

———. 'Disability, Pain, and the Politics of Minority Identity.' In *Culture-Theory-Disability: Encounters between Disability Studies and Cultural Studies*, edited by Anne Waldschmidt, Hanjo Berressem and Moritz Ingwersen. Bielefeld: Transcript, 2017.

Snyder, Sharon L. and David T. Mitchell. *Cultural Locations of Disability*. Chicago: University of Chicago Press, 2006.

Stiker, Henri-Jacques. *A History of Disability*. Ann Arbor: University of Michigan Press, 1999.

Union of the Physically Impaired Against Segregation (UPIAS). *Fundamental Principles of Disability*. London: UPIAS, 1976.

Waldschmidt, Anne. 'Disability Goes Cultural: The Cultural Model of Disability as an Analytical Model.' In *Culture-Theory-Disability: Encounters between Disability Studies and Cultural Studies*, edited by Anne Waldschmidt, Hanjo Berressem and Moritz Ingwersen. Bielefeld: Transcript, 2017.

Wells, H.G. *The Country of the Blind and Other Stories by H. G. Wells—Delphi Classics (Illustrated)*. Delphi Classics, 2017.

1

NEGOTIATING THE POLEMICS OF INTENTIONAL EVASION: THE NONDISABLED IMAGINARY, THE DISABLED SELF AND ACADEMIC DISABILITY ACTIVISM

Someshwar Sati

I am blind and my neighbours generally tend to deliberately ignore my presence whenever they cross me in the corridors or run into me in the elevator. They, in fact, do not even bother to look at me, preferring instead to look through me as if I was simply not there. The experience of being consciously avoided by the nondisabled world has, in fact, become a matter of routine for a disabled person like me. It happens everywhere, whether it is while travelling in a metro or even while sitting in the staff room in one's very own college with so-called colleagues. My experiential knowledge of disability has taught me to understand and theorise the encounter between the nondisabled and the disabled people in terms of a dynamics of intentional evasion. What inevitably ensues is a disavowal of the disabled.[1] For example, when I used to visit a restaurant with my 10-year-old son, the waiters enthusiastically greeted us and asked my son what he would like to have. After taking down his orders, the waiter would once again look towards my son and, pointing towards me, would enquire, 'What about him?' To make matters worse, when we would be done with our meal, the waiter would hand over the bill to my son as if he would be the one making the payment.

Many may feel that disability is fundamentally a socio-economic phenomenon but my experience suggests otherwise. The process of marginalisation that I have experienced on account of being disabled comes across largely as a relational experience emerging in the routine day-to-day encounter between disabled and nondisabled people and one that manifests itself primarily on a psychological plane. Both the encounters that I have outlined made me feel as if I was being completely disembodied and literally rendered invisible.

While this may sound deeply unsettling, it is nevertheless what transpires with disabled people daily. But what is even more disturbing is the fact that both the dynamics of intentional evasion and the disavowal of the disabled is being routinely reproduced within the institutional space of an academia that prides itself on having a distinct liberal ideological orientation. Curiously, this so-called liberal academia has and continues to refrain from engaging with disability as a legitimate field of academic enquiry. Many of us have read, studied and even taught Charlotte Bronte's *Jane Eyre*. At the end of the story, the principal male protagonist of the novel, Sir Edward Rochester, becomes blind and crippled. Yet how many of us, whether inside or outside the classroom, have attempted to enter the plot of the novel and have read it from the perspective of Rochester's multiple disabilities? Even a casual look at previous years' question papers inevitably reveals that his physical condition has never been a subject of interest in the processes of evaluation. Whether it is our pedagogical practice or the way we examine our students, our academia has literally 'turned a blind eye' to disability and the phenomenon is yet to become a part of our academic consciousness.

Predictably, in a meeting of the syllabus review committee of the undergraduate courses of a distinguished Indian university, when we politely voiced the need to incorporate disability texts and perspectives within the undergraduate curriculum, even our so-called liberal colleagues who are never tired of flagging Marxist, feminist and postcolonial concerns met our humble suggestions with puzzled looks—looks that seemed to question the very state of our sanity. 'What is the point?' they seemed to suggest. What is the point indeed. The disabled population in India today numbers well over 26.8 million people and yet, 'what is the point'. We have an over three-thousand-year-old literary tradition of disability representation and yet, 'what is the point'. The line of demarcation between the disabled and the nondisabled people is extremely porous. The latter are, at best, temporarily able-bodied (Davis 1999) running the risk of becoming disabled as a result of a freak accident or advancing age and yet, 'what is the point'. Normalcy rests on shaky foundations. The nondisabled population of today is potentially the disabled population of tomorrow (Davis 1999) and yet, 'what is the point'.

As I sit down to write about the nondisabled imaginary, the constitution of disabled subjectivity within it, the identity of the disabled self and the role of disability activism within the academia, the troubling question—'what is the point?'—continues to haunt me and so do the dynamics of intentional evasion and disavowal of the disabled. At first sight, even the pioneering works of early literary disability studies appear to partake in this process of disavowal because they are characterised by a propensity to focus on the idea of normalcy rather than that of disability. In *Enforcing Normalcy*, for example, Lennard Davis defines disability about the normal. To him, the former was a state of negative difference defined in terms of deviation from the latter. 'When we think of bodies, in a society where the concept of the norm is operative,' Davis poignantly notes, 'then people with disabilities will be thought of as deviants.' Similarly, Rosemarie Garland-Thomson in *Extraordinary Bodies*, instead of focusing on the subject position of the disabled is more interested in exploring the subject position of the normate. Disability narrative, according to her, helps the normate to confirm their own sense of normality and normate sense of privilege. Extending this line of thought further, David Mitchell and Sharon Snyder argue in *Narrative Processes* that disability is used in literature as a narrative crux to both give the plot a narrative punch and to reaffirm the idea of normalcy.

All of these disability studies' scholars, in their own respective ways, reveal how narratives on disability tend to buttress the idea of normalcy. One begins to feel a deep sense of consolation when one realises that these scholars are not evading disability per se but rather underscoring the ideological tendencies of the nondisabled imaginary to evade disability. They seem to suggest that the figure of the disabled in these narratives is articulated through a divisive and demeaning process of othering that has real-life consequences for disabled people. Predictably, my subjectivity as a disabled person has been framed not only by my encounters with nondisabled people but also by how the nondisabled imaginary has objectified disabled people in and through culture. Both of these have deeply influenced my readings of the way disabled people have been represented in culture and even defined the course of the disability activism that I have embraced within academia.

Divided into six parts, this chapter stems from the need to counter the dynamics of intentional evasion and it is, in fact, a reflective account of the development of my personal and political consciousness of the experience of disablement and the constitution of my subjectivity, both as a blind person and a disabled academic. The first part is rooted in my understanding of how literature and cultural productions in general objectify the subjectivity of disabled people. While the second part is a contemplation on how this process of objectification affected my self-perception and my identity, part three dwells on my attempt to evolve strategies to negotiate and mitigate this influence. This is followed by a brief retrospective account of the development of my personal consciousness of disability. The fifth section traces the development of my political consciousness of disability in the context of my late realisation that disability is not just a medical condition but also a social, cultural and political phenomenon. The final part documents how the above realisation made me interact with academia in ways that would be best described as a form of academic disability activism.

This chapter is an attempt to understand the process of my growing up as a blind person in a predominantly sighted world culturally conditioned by a nondisabled imaginary. I briefly present a biographical outline of my life as a blind person to understand how the nondisabled imaginary influenced the constitution of my identity as a blind person and how I struggled to resist and negotiate this influence by turning my materially embodied self from a passive entity into an active site of cultural production. In what follows, I examine myself in terms of the social and discursive encounters that framed my subjectivity as a disabled person and the materiality of my very own existence that ceaselessly strove to problematise these encounters.

Objectified in Culture

Stories of bodies and minds make up literature; even more so, stories of abnormal bodies and unstable minds. This is particularly the case within the Indian literary tradition where characters with disabilities have populated the Indian creative imagination since the early days of our great epics. These characters have often dominated the story and quite often provided the plot with its principal narrative tension. We need to just think of the mentally deranged hunchback Manthara and the blind parents of Shravan Kumar in the *Ramayana*, or, for that matter, the blind king Dhritarashtra and his orthopaedically impaired brother-in-law Shakuni in the *Mahabharata*, to realise that this is true. But why do characters with some kind of disability reside at the very heart of the nondisabled imaginary? What ideological role and aesthetic function do they perform in these imaginaries and what do they tell us about the society in which they are produced and disseminated?

Let us open the discussion by stating a set of truisms. First, even though disability appears everywhere within the canonical contours of the Indian literary tradition, critical academic engagement with this tradition appears to have and continues to 'turn a blind eye' to disability representations. Never has a conference on the *Mahabharata* or the *Ramayana* addressed this aspect of the epics. Perhaps my acute awareness of the pervasive presence of disability in these narratives owes something to my subject position as a blind academic engaged in the discipline of disability studies. Second, disabled characters may figure everywhere in literature but they are allowed to inhabit only specific narrative spaces and perform only limited roles. The disabled characters in these narratives can figure mostly as the other of normal and it is only by virtue of being the other that they appear to legitimately occupy narrative space in the nondisabled imagination. Third, the very idea of normalcy is embedded in the divisive ethos of social exclusion because the constitution of the normal subject is premised on the othering of those whose corporeal embodiment does not fit into the idealised and standardised notion of the normal body. For this reason, the concept of normalcy is also oppressive in the extreme as it strikes at the very root of the humanity of those who have been othered. Finally, cultural representations of disability tend to depoliticise such discriminatory practises by individualising the experience of disablement and portraying it as a personal misfortune that is traced to the body of the individual rather than to socio-cultural systemic structures.

All the disabled characters mentioned so far in their own respective ways create a crisis within the nondisabled status quo. While mourning the death of their son, who was accidentally killed by King Dasharatha, the parents of Shravan Kumar curse the king, by pronouncing the wish that sometime in future, he too would have to pine for his son the same way that they had. This curse, in a way, foreshadows the series of events that ultimately leads to the banishment of Rama from Ayodhya for 14 years, leaving Dasharatha grieving for his son, and ultimately dying of sorrow. Manthara, by reminding Kaikeyi of the promise that her husband Dasharatha had made to her, sparks off the crises that lead to Rama's banishment. In the *Mahabharata*, Dhritarashtra, instigated by Shakuni, refuses to hand over the throne to the 'legitimate' heirs—his nephews the Pandavas—which leads to the battle of Kurukshetra.

In both, the *Ramayana* and the *Mahabharata*, the disabled characters come across as agents of disruption whose words and actions disturb the peace and tranquillity of a predominantly nondisabled society. For this reason, they are perceived within the narrative as a potential source of threat, having a demonic and diabolical dimension. After the battle of Kurukshetra, the Pandavas go to seek Dhritarashtra's blessings. But the wise Krishna is aware of the latter's concealed fury against Bhima, who killed his eldest son, Duryodhana. He warns Bhima to be careful and guard himself against Dhritarashtra who intends to avenge the death of his son. Suspicious of the blind king's machination, Krishna places an iron statue of Bhima before Dhritarashtra, who mistakes it for Bhima and embraces the statue with all his might, destroying it. Dhritarashtra, in this way, becomes an object to be feared.

What cannot escape the attention of a discerning, critical mind is the moral undertones of such representations. Dhritarashtra here is presented as the living embodiment of a constituent lack or rather a twin lack. While on the one hand, he is blind and he cannot see, on the other, he appears to lack moral fortitude. The parallel between the inability to see and the inability to behave rationally appears to be forced and arbitrary. However, the *Mahabharata*, through the depiction of the blind king's insane rage, tends to normalise the arbitrary association between disability and the diabolical. This kind of disability representation is quite widespread even today, particularly in cinematic representations, be it the evil genius Kaal in *Krrish 3* or the nefarious Bijjaladeva with his deformed left arm in *Baahubali*. The objectification of disabled people as the inevitable locus of the sinister, and, therefore, a source of threat and fear, is a stock feature of disability representation. It is a matter of little surprise that villainous characters in literary and cultural narratives down the ages have often been represented as having a bodily deformity, suggesting that a sound mind can only reside in a sound body.

While the nondisabled imaginary, on the one hand, through the representation of disability as a source of fear strikes at the very root of the humanity of the disabled population, on the other, it ceaselessly strikes to reconfirm the humanity of the nondisabled population by mobilising emotions of pity and compassion for the disabled. Entrances to temples, mosques and other places of worship are often crowded with beggars, most of whom are physically deformed. Devotees entering or leaving the religious shrine are expected to participate in the distribution of alms, the underlying assumption being that the lives of disabled people are defined by great suffering and such people are therefore deserving of sympathy and charity. It is the moral duty of decent people to be charitable and generous towards those with disabilities. Predictably, the nondisabled cultural imaginary is replete with extremely demeaning images of disabled people that apprehends them as tragic figures, turning them into an object of pity and pathos of the nondisabled gaze. The objectification of disabled people in charity advertisements is a case in point. The object of the charitable gaze in these advertisements is, in a sense, othered as it is the shoes that one does not want to be in.

The kinds of disability representations referred to above may not be wide-ranging; they are, nevertheless, the most recurring images of disability found in literature and culture. This is not an attempt to account for all kinds of disability representations in literature. The attempt is to identify certain recurring tropes of disability and consider the implications that they have on the constitution of disabled subjectivity.

The Affective Response

Forms of social inequality tend to institutionalise emotions of aversion and compassion towards the marginalised. This is particularly the case with persons with disabilities. This line of thinking would develop a kind of social ontology that would problematise the affective response of nondisabled people towards disabled populations. After all, emotions are, as phenomenologists would have it, the sources of 'pre-reflective judgement' and the means through which consciousness 'apprehends objects and attaches values to them' (Hughes 2012). The affective turn in literary studies teaches us to read the representations of disability, mentioned in the previous section, and the nondisabled responses to them in the following terms. While on the one hand disability is seen to have a negative affect response resulting in the emotions of fear, disgust and aversion, on the other, it is seen as producing an altruistic feeling in the nondisabled, both of which become, as we shall see, 'the emotional basis for discrimination and exclusion' (Hughes 2012).

Disabled characters were, in a sense, the ultimate embodiments of the non-conformist. For this reason, they are presented as the perpetual threat to the existing order of the average and normal. 'What we fear, we often stigmatize and shun and sometimes seek to destroy' (Longmore 1987). Both the *Ramayana* and the *Mahabharata* allude to these fears and attempt to address them obliquely as a way of seeking to reassure the nondisabled about themselves.

Fear of the disabled has often been read by disability scholars as a symptomatic expression of the nondisabled world's anxiety about the vulnerability of their own bodies. It is this fear of the disabled that lurks within the nondisabled imagination. Disabled people remind nondisabled people of their very own vulnerability. The latter are perpetually anxious to deny their mortality and the vulnerability of their physical body. Psychoanalysis would lead us to believe that the nondisabled would naturally refuse to acknowledge such anxieties and possibilities and therefore they would project this anxiety onto disabled entities. These anxieties and fears are expelled from the nondisabled self and projected onto the other, the disabled (Hughes 2012; Shildrick 2005). According to Susanne Mintz, the need for such a psychological manoeuvre 'emerges from fears about the fragility and unpredictability of embodied identity' (2002). It is not the corporeality of the disabled people that is at the heart of the issue; what lies at the centre is the nondisabled embodiment, their fears and anxieties.

Fear of the disabled can really manifest itself in emotions of aversion, leading to the segregation of disabled people and creating distance between the disabled and nondisabled. But more importantly, fear within the narrative of bodily deformity becomes a hierarchising emotion depicting enemies and outliers (Hughes 2012). The nondisabled world at large seems to digest the correlation between the two without questioning the logical basis of such an association. Disabled people become the living embodiment of our moral deficit that the nondisabled world definitely is not. Such sentiments depict an alterity that is evil, sinister, threatening, contemptible, repulsive and pitiable. All the moral deficits heaped on top of one another make up what the conceited 'we', most certainly, is not. Fear of the disabled strikes at the very root of the humanity of the disabled, reconfirming, in the process, the humanity of the nondisabled world.

Similarly, charity narratives are also strategically designed to restore the moral standing of the nondisabled. Disability is used in several narratives to test or enhance the ethical or moral standing of the nondisabled society. The purpose of the extremely demeaning and tragic images of disability that crowd the nondisabled imaginary is to evoke in the nondisabled population a deep sense of pity and sympathy towards the disabled and generate altruistic feelings in the nondisabled. By these demeaning images, nondisabled people can feel both powerful and generous. After all, 'pity is a hierarchizing emotion' that infuses a sense of 'superiority' in those who feel it and 'inferiority' in those for whom pity is felt (Hughes 2012).

Whether disabled people are represented as sinister and diabolical or whether they are projected as tragic figures and objects of pity, these representations tend to not only objectify disabled people but also simultaneously tend to reify the relationship between the disabled and nondisabled populations. In this sense, these images are what Karl Marx calls 'fetish'. While Marx uses the term to refer to how social relationships are reified as objects, Freud deploys the term to capture the projection of sexual drives into objects (Shakespeare 1994). Tom Shakespeare carries Freud's understanding of fetish to the sphere of disability and argues that 'disabled people within cultural representation are cyphers. Disabled people are objects, on which artists project particular emotions, or which are used to represent specific values or evils' (1994). He even goes to the extent of suggesting that disability representations are akin to pornography in the way they evoke a particular kind of emotion. He ingenuously suggests that the objectification of disabled people in cultural narratives parallels the objectification of women in pornography. In each case, there is an exaggerated focus on a particular part of the body: while pornography focuses its gaze on the sexual parts, disability representations focus on the flawed parts. The viewer is manipulated into an emotional response: desire, in the case of pornography, fear and pity in the case of disability representations.

Emotions of fear and pity are not the only affect responses of the nondisabled consciousness but they contain the two basic key responses that contribute to the distance between the disabled and nondisabled.

Both fear and pity are deeply entangled in the social construction of inequality. Both fear and pity are appropriated by the narrative in a pure act of othering. Both are multipliers of misery and have a life-denying effect.

These emotions inform the nondisabled imaginary and at the same time invalidate the disabled subjectivity. In addition to structural disablism, including the ubiquitous barriers to full social participation, disabled people experience the 'socially engendered undermining' of their 'psycho-emotional wellbeing' (Thomas 2007).

The Cultural Location of Disability

While reading disability narratives that produce the above affect response, I feel staggered and completely dislocated as, in them, I find little that I can relate to. Nothing in these narratives appears to correspond to my lived experiences of disability, nor is there in them anything that can correlate to the lived life experiences of any other disabled person I know.

What is discernible here is the complete lack of a causal connection between the corporeal embodiment of disabled characters and the ensemble of signification attributed to them by the narrative. The meaning and signification attributed to corporeal differences in these narratives do not reflect the realm of nature. The narrative, in fact, discursively constitutes a socially invested structure of meaning and interpretation around these differences to other and denigrate disabled people.

Strangely, disabled characters and even the world of the disabled are held up for judgement by those who have very little experience of disability or disabled people. In such representations, disabled characters have been deprived of the potential to create a self. They must accept definitions from outside the boundaries of their very own existence. They are the other and it is only as the other of the nondisabled that they occupy a space within the narrative. These representations are oppressive for disabled people as nondisabled narratives about disability are, in fact, not about disability at all. They are rather about the need to guarantee the privileged status of the nondisabled.

However, the crux of the matter is that these narratives generate a set of cultural myths about disability that deeply influence the constitution of the subjectivity of disabled people in day-to-day existence. The way disabled people are perceived in society is largely determined by the myths produced in these narratives. For this reason, these narratives are a kind of discursive oppression that disembodies the disabled subject.

How does one come to terms with one's very own disability in a world that fiercely stigmatises disabled people, in a world that perceives disabled people either as disruptive presences to be feared or as helpless victims of unfortunate circumstances?

We should not forget that the subjectivity of a disabled person constituted and objectified in culture is primarily discursive and saturated with pejorative connotations but subjectivity, and more importantly, identity is not just cognitive and immaterial as the cartesian dualism between mind and body would have us believe. It is rather based on a material linkage between the discursive self and the corporeally embodied existence. For this reason, the identity of a disabled person is primarily a function of the materiality of the body wherein the corporeally embodied experience of disablement becomes a potent site of cultural production and meaning-making. In fact, by transforming one's materially embodied lived experiences into a complex and fertile site of cultural and corporeal production (Shildrick 2012), disabled people can and should evolve a narrative of self-assertion. Such narratives would inevitably disrupt the epistemological authority of the dehumanising ideology that equates difference with lack and inadequacy, including those structured by ableist assumptions. This act of self-assertion also articulates a willingness to combat a long history which earlier in this chapter I called dynamics of intentional evasion and the politics of the disavowal of the disabled that lies at the heart of the nondisabled imaginative universe that has defined the processes of cultural objectification of disabled people.

It is with the view to negotiate this dynamic of intentional erasure and the politics of the disavowal of the disabled that I turn the materiality of my embodied existence into a site of cultural production. Drawing upon my materially embodied journey through life as a disabled person, I offer a detailed testimony of the experience of disablement with the objective of problematising and undermining the epistemological authority of nondisabled cultural narratives. Self-representation performs a radical and political function of declaring the self-worthy of being named.

Encountering Disability

My encounter with disability began at the very moment I gained consciousness. I was perhaps born with no light perception in my right eye and with the left having a moderate vision of 20/60. At the age of three, I was diagnosed as having progressive bilateral optic atrophy, with no hope of cure or even improvement. At least this was what the doctor told my parents. Even today, these medical nomenclatures and diagnoses seem to mean little to me. What seems to matter are faint memories of me as a four-year-old being surrounded by well-wishers expressing their concern about my squint in muffled whispers. They looked and stared at me as if I were an oddity. Their exclusionary gaze seemed to suggest that my sting squint was an instant subject of social censure. 'His looks are odd,' they said. 'They need to be rectified and corrected,' they unhesitatingly added. 'And this can be done through a simple operation,' they suggested in loud booming voices. It was not as if they were interested in improving my sight; the medical procedure they often referred to would have only accomplished a cosmetic function. Little did they seem to care about my limited vision. As I retrospectively reflect on these memories today, I realise that people stared at me not because I had a dysfunctional eye but because my very own stare deviated from the norm—the standard mode of seeing. It occurred to me that my oddity had little to do with my vision and more to do with a set of cultural rules about how one should see, look and stare.

Operated I was nevertheless and perhaps my squint was corrected, or at least, partially corrected. It ceased to invite unsolicited attention. But the ritualistic public censure of my squint left an indelible scar on my consciousness, one that never healed. I lived for the rest of my life traumatised by the fear of being the odd one out. The internalised pressure to conform and perform normally, the stigma of non-conforming, the burden of pejorative connotations and the dreadful negative associations that it carries more often than not force the disabled to adopt and mimic the dominant ways of the nondisabled, and I was no different. Since I could see a bit with the help of my left eye, I eventually learned to hide my impairment for fear of being stigmatised. I began to pass myself off as fully sighted. In class, I learnt huge chunks of text by heart in anticipation of being asked to read aloud. But my mimicry was soon brought to an abrupt end as my visual equity dropped to 20/200, and I was declared legally blind. But on a more pragmatic plane, I was rendered no longer capable of mimicking the ways of the dominant and camouflaging my disability. I began to accept and accommodate my failure of being unable to conform and perform normally.

I distinctly remember that once I stopped pretending that I was sighted, I began to use my other four senses to great effect—reaching out with my hand to find my way and things on the table, reading with the help of readers and audio recordings, dictating answers to scribes, and so on. This made me different in the eyes of my peers. My alternative ways of assessing the world through my remaining four senses appeared strange to them. They viewed it as a deviation from the normative ways of doing things. As I reached out with my hand to find things on my desk, I was mocked and referred to as *betaal*—a Hindi word for 'off-tuned'. The sighted world, obsessed as it is with oculus-centric modes of perception, fails to understand that the process of perceiving the world in which we live is malleable, in the sense that perception is multi-sensorial. While trying to masquerade as a sighted person, I was literally living on the border of sightedness and blindness, trying to be sighted while still being blind. But when I stopped concealing my disability and attuned my mode of being and living with the materiality of my corporeal embodiment, I began to experience a peculiar sense of freedom unleashed by the creative power of my impairment.

On a visit to Donna Paula in Goa, I realised the power of my other senses as I sucked the splendid environment through them with a great sense of joy. The sound of the sea hammering the rocks, the cool moist breeze gently stroking my whole body, tiny droplets of water caressing my face and moistening my lips with a salty flavour. This is an experience that I relish even today. But more importantly, as I look back on it, I realise that this apparently innocuous incident did indeed destabilise all stereotypes that tend to equate blindness with the inability to access the world. As I grew up, I was increasingly transforming my blindness into a multi-sensorial manner of seeing through touch, sound, smell and taste. And in many ways, I had become a 'whole bodied seer' (Hull 1990). The result was a new way of accessing the world and knowing it.

Nevertheless, my childhood attempt at passing gestured towards the nexus between ability and power that structured the encounter between the disabled and nondisabled worlds. This nexus manifested itself everywhere in our day-to-day existence. As a result, a blind person like me would inevitably end up nursing a sense of enfeeblement and deficiency. Retrospectively speaking, as I look back on my multiple acts of passing, I have come to realise that disabled people's experiences of a sense of lack and inadequacy in life are not an outcome of their personal limitations. It is, rather, a function of their social relations, which are largely conditioned by the ways disability has been objectified in culture.

As a blind person, growing up in a predominantly sighted society, I have experienced this firsthand. Elders talking about me in hushed voices, referring to me as '*bechara bacha*'—the poor boy—and wondering, '*yeh iss duniya mein kya kar sakega?*' (What will this poor boy be able to do in this world?') Others evoked the doctrine of *karma* to describe the state of my eyesight in terms of a punishment that I was given for the sins that I might have committed in the previous birth. I was also constantly referred to as a monster, *rakshasa*, an unsound body that hosts an unsound mind. This was a refrain that I was constantly made to hear and it relentlessly pierced my ears. All these experiences were indeed dehumanising. They played havoc with my psychology and deflated my sense of self-esteem, so much so, that as a six-year-old boy, before going to the doctor, I memorised the entire alphabet chart that is used to check one's eyesight. I did this because I was very scared of being branded a person with low vision. Blindness for me had become a form of social oppression, it had become a stigma that grew as I grew up, breeding into prejudice, contempt and discrimination. Even today, 'what will this poor boy do in the world', continues to resonate in my ears and my mind.

It was my mother who broke the distorted social mirror in which I used to look and see myself. The very next morning after I had lost my eyesight completely, she, as usual, woke me up at 7 in the morning and asked me to fetch the vegetables, which I had always done in the past. I hesitated and went promptly back to sleep, hoping that somebody else would do the job, but when I woke up three-and-a-half hours later, to my astonishment, there was no breakfast for me. In fact, nobody in the house had had their breakfast. 'How can cooking be done when there are no veggies at home?' said my mother. 'It is your responsibility to bring the veggies. If you don't bring them, there will be no cooking today.' I shook my head, picked up the shopping bag and went to the market. This small incident made me realise that there are no free lunches in life; that there were no concessions for me. 'Your only disability', my mother told me, 'is that you are not able to see your ability.' As I grew up and went through the journey of life, I realised that I was much more than just my eyes. After all, I was as normal and human as everybody else. Therefore, I could not commit the sacrilege of looking at myself reductively as the entire society did. I was human as any other human being, and I enjoyed the right to be happy, to get a proper education, to seek adequate employment and to get married and have children.

However, many people feel that blind people do not have these rights, and that joy and happiness do not come naturally to the blind. In this context, I would like to share a rather unsettling encounter with a bright and promising woman scholar. Nearly 30 years ago, I had met this scholar in Hyderabad. She was intrigued with the fact that I appeared to be happy and cheerful. 'How can you be so happy? After all, you are blind!' she enquired. 'I may be blind but I am happy and would like to enjoy life to the fullest,' I replied. She frowned at this and said, 'You're happy because you have no other choice; otherwise it is not possible for a blind person to be happy. When you say you are happy despite your blindness, you are suggesting to a young woman like me that if rape is inevitable, you better lay back and enjoy it.' Till today, I wonder, can blindness and rape be correlated? At least my experience in life does not seem to suggest so but strange are the ways of the world. Society at large tends to reduce the identity of a disabled person to their disability and view them through the prisons of ableist stereotypes. The following episode is a case in point.

I was brought up in Baghalpur, a small town in Bihar, and I regularly travelled by train to New Delhi, where I was doing my master's at Jawaharlal Nehru University. The Indian railways provided visually impaired people like me with a substantial concession on the ticket fare, and I often used this concession. It so happened that in one of the many journeys from Baghalpur to Delhi, the ticket collector approached me, asking for my ticket. As I was engaged in an animated conversation with my friends, I failed to notice and hear him. 'Where is your ticket?' he yelled. Perhaps the fact that I was talking in English had irritated him further. 'Where is your ticket?' he grunted again in a fit of anger. I politely turned towards him and handed him my ticket. After surveying it, the ticket collector howled, 'You cheat! You charlatan! How do you dare do this?' Surprised, my friends at once came to my rescue, 'What is the matter?'

'This boy is travelling on a blind concession!' the ticket collector triumphantly declared.

'But what is the problem? He is, after all, blind.'

'Blind?' the ticket collector wondered, 'How can he be blind? He is speaking in English.'

To this, I immediately replied that if speaking in English means that a person is not blind, then there would not be a single blind person in the US, Canada, UK, Australia and New Zealand. But jokes aside, the ticket collector was making a pertinent point. English is the language of education in India, and what the ticket collector was actually suggesting was how a blind person is educated and here I am today, having completed my master's, MPhil and PhD in English from a leading university in the country, a professor in English at a premier college in India, and writing an academic piece in English. This incident may have explored the normative conception of the relationship between sight and education but at the same time unsettled it. This is the power of my materially embodied journey through life.

I am often referred to as the young blind man who has overcome the limitations of his vision with education, determination, will power and commitment. The story of my life may conform to this image, yet this narrative is not meant or intended to claim equality with the nondisabled, nor is it directed to signal a triumph over disability. It is not a narrative of overcoming that celebrates the trouncing of my so-called limitations—the victory of my mind over my body and circumstances. Its prime objective is rather to complicate my relationship with the cultural terrain upon which dominant assumptions about disabled people are produced and to dislocate the cultural stereotypes that it generates.

My attempt to map out an autobiographical in this chapter is more an indictment of these stereotypes. The story of my material embodied existence is not a narrative that celebrates the triumph of an individual over cultural forces. Identity is, after all, produced in the very process of negotiating the stuff of culture. In my story, therefore, culture is not a secondary background against which my identity stands in sharp relief. Culture is rather the very material that needs to be negotiated, and it is only through this process of negotiation that an individual fashions his identity. Perhaps writing this chapter has made me truly disabled, that is, made me understand the true nature of my disability and my disabled identity, and reclaim it on my own terms. Now when I call myself disabled, I am not recapitulating or surrendering to the dominant stereotype produced in culture; rather, I am asserting the materiality of my very own existence and reclaiming my disabled identity on my own terms.

If the normative discursive universe of narrative provided me with the world's view of the nondisabled, my very own material embodied existence as a blind person furnished me with both my view of the world and my view of myself. My material embodied experience of disability is an integral part of the constitution of my identity, which is neither exclusively that of a victim nor of an achiever. It lies somewhere in between. It is a fluid identity that challenges the relationship between disability and any stable form of subjectivity/identity. This narrative, in fact, announces the authority of my multiple disjunctive selves.

The materiality of my body redefined my subjectivity in ways that allowed me to explore and problematise the normative discursive constitution of disabled subjectivity in and through culture, reshaping my relationship with the world which we all together inhabit from my perspective and the terms laid out by me.

Academic Awakening

My personal consciousness of experiencing disability may have begun quite early in life. However, my awareness of the political dimensions of this phenomenon dawned much later. It was only when I was introduced to disability studies that I realised that disability was not just a medical or bodily condition, it was much more. It was a stigma, a form of oppression, a kind of discrimination, and a socially, culturally and politically constituted experience.

My interest in disability as a field of academic enquiry came about pretty late in life, to be precise, when I was 44 years of age. As a postgraduate student and during my early academic career, I had never been exposed to the discipline of disability studies. Nor was I aware of the possibilities of engaging academically with the experience of disablement. During the 1990s postcolonial studies seemed to dominate the Indian academia. Perhaps this was an area of academic interest in which most Indian academics had a personal investment. They were vehemently challenging the way they had been portrayed in colonial and Western narratives. They believed that all talk of objective descriptions of the colonies handed down to them by Western scholars was, in fact, a subjective perception of the colonies that the Westerners had. The consensus was that if it was left up to the West to describe us, they would end up producing distorted and misleading images of the ex-colony and its inhabitants. This made it imperative for the postcolonial world to find a voice and represent itself. And I was no different. I spent most of my time like my contemporary academics, on the one hand, problematising the writings of Rudyard Kipling, E.M. Forster, Paul Scott and other Western canonical novelists, while on the other, I was swayed, as it were, by the subcontinent finding its voice through the novels of Salman Rushdie, Amitav Ghosh, Arundhati Roy and others. In both cases, I was engaged in dealing with the dynamics of racial othering and the question of marginalised identity in intersection with those of gender and class.

Interestingly, it was around this time, in 1995, that Western academic disability scholars were using similar theoretical paradigms to understand the way the disabled subject was constituted, objectified and othered in culture. These academics were completely focused on unsettling the normativity accorded to nondisabled accounts of disability and advocated the foregrounding of a wholly subjective account of the phenomena from the perspective of the disabled. However, as I had not been exposed to disability studies at that time, it never occurred to me that I could talk of my very own experience of being disabled through the prisms of not-too-dissimilar conceptual frameworks that I was using to analyse the representations of race, class and gender.

As I look back on those days, I feel quite perplexed and try to understand this inexplicable oversight. It was not as if I had not felt a deep sense of moral outrage at the way society had treated me. Little did I know that this was a collective experience of a particular community rather than an isolated experience of an individual. After all, in many cases, a blind person has no community experience of a blind collective. Unlike other marginal categories like caste, class, race, gender, ethnicity or religion, a blind person may have no filial or community ties with other blind people. And I was one such person. As a result, I hardly knew any other blind person from close quarters until I was 20 years of age. It was only when I shifted to a house overlooking a blind school that I, for the first time, had the opportunity to observe other blind students. To my horror, I saw them being ceaselessly maltreated, in the name of discipline and preparing them for their future, in ways that I could not have imagined. From the roof of my three-storey house that overlooked the school, I could hear the blind students being ceaselessly yelled at, caned and punished, and at times, even made to go without food for days. They were always forced to perform tasks in normative ableist ways according to the whims and fancies of sighted teachers and administrators. '*Andha kahin ka, koi kaam bhi theek se nahi kar sakta!*' ('You blind fool, you cannot even do things properly!') were refrains that constantly pierced my ears. As at the time, my thought processes were structured by the normative ways of the sighted world, I did not find anything unusual in such a mode of treatment. It appeared to me as normal, natural and a matter of fate. Despite having observed all this from a distance, it never occurred to me then that I could look at disability using the conceptual framework of marginal identity. It was only when I attended a conference on disability studies at the CSDS in Delhi in 2012 that my mind opened up to such a possibility. Mike Oliver, Colin Barnes, James Charlton, Lennard Davis, Rosemary Garland-Thomson, David Mitchell, Sharon Snyder, Nick Watson and others were names that I had heard for the first time. And what I heard at this conference proved to be quite revealing and life-changing. It was at the conference that it became clear to me that disability is a form of corporal deviation, a stigma that breeds prejudice, contempt and discrimination, as well as a minority identity rather than just a mere medical condition. The academic discourse on disability that I was introduced to at this conference had a far more profound impact on the development of my political consciousness than all the events or experiences of my life put together.

Coincidentally, around the same time, I was asked by the administration of my college to take up the charge of coordinator of its enabling unit. This unit was supposed to create a level playing field for the disabled students of the college and provide them with a wholesome inclusive educational experience. As the coordinator of the unit, I was expected to set up and supervise the running of a service-delivery mechanism that would be in constant touch with these students, identify their specific needs and provide them with customised solutions. This involvement embedded me into a network of relationships. On the one hand, it provided me with the unique opportunity to interact with disabled students and arrive at a better understanding of their experiences of disablement, on the other, it also brought me close to several well-intentioned nondisabled colleagues interested in establishing a support system for the disabled students of the college. Both these networks of relationships enriched my understanding of disability and opened up a new world before my eyes.

The growing interaction that I was having with disabled students consolidated my understanding of disability as a socio-cultural and political phenomenon. Their needs were not very different from mine when I was a student. However, thirty years ago, the institution did little to assist disabled students who were, for the most part, left to fend for themselves, and rely on personal contacts to create a support system. Readers and scribes, even assistive devices had to be procured by the students themselves. Though I felt outraged at the way the educational institutions treated me and my fellow disabled students, I never protested and viewed the matter as being personal. However, as the coordinator of the enabling unit, I understood that the problem, far from being individual, was a collective one. The students of today, unlike me, made demands in the name of their rights and followed it up with the administration as a group. I soon saw the value of collective action and that if the doors of opportunities for disabled students were to be kept open, such actions would have to be encouraged. During my days, disabled students were rarely visible on university campuses and a disabled collective was a far cry. For this reason, the connection between disability and politics was not easy for me to grasp. Till then it was as if they existed and operated in different cognitive spheres. My stint at the enabling unit taught me otherwise, fusing the two spheres and awakening my political consciousness.

But what staggered me was the way that my nondisabled colleagues went about creating a support structure for disabled students. They believed that disability was for the most part an individual condition and the best way to deal with it was to rehabilitate the individual. Their focus was largely on providing personal assistance to fix the individual, as it were, rather than changing the context and the system. Their approach was largely patronising and had little to do with the actual specific needs of disabled people. This left me convinced that only a subjective disability perspective could become the cornerstone of an effective service-delivery mechanism.

At disability conferences and other academic meetings, disability scholars lay great emphasis on the need to evolve a praxis of inclusion that would lead to restoring the dignity and humanity of disabled people by creating socio-cultural, educational economic spaces for them in an equitable society. But when I talked about these things to people outside the circle of a select few disability studies scholars, they hardly seemed to understand. Even several disability scholars, both disabled and nondisabled, seemed to pay scant attention to the need to fuse their academics with activism on the ground. It seemed as if they had trapped themselves into a kind of academic ghetto, exchanging ideas amongst themselves in an ivory tower, with little intention of engaging with the ground reality. It appeared as if disability scholars were becoming ever more comfortably settled into the academic world. I often wondered if, for them, disability was becoming just a field of study and disability studies a career, rather than an experiential material reality to be negotiated.

Such kinds of attitudes appeared to have domesticated the radical, political edge of disability studies. For this reason, I began to feel the need to move out of the academic ivory tower. My association with the enabling unit of the college was proving to, indeed, be a breath of fresh air but much more needed to be done in a process of context-changing rather than person-fixing. I strongly felt that to realise the above goal, the nondisabled community needed to be brought under the sway of disability studies–oriented thought processes and made to understand the subjective perspective of disabled persons. An occasional awareness/ sensitisation workshop or two was not the answer. It was necessary to draw them into a continuous, comprehensive and substantive process of engagement with the experience of disablement.

Towards a Praxis of Inclusion

In 2016, under the auspices of Jawaharlal Nehru Institute of Advanced Studies, New Delhi (JNIAS), we organised a national-level workshop on translating disability-centric short stories from various Indian languages into English. The prime objective of this workshop was to release disability from the enclosures of 'hospital hallways and therapeutic table' (Sati and Prasad 2020) and firmly relocate it within the realm of a socially and culturally constituted experience, thereby opening conceptual spaces from where we could offer from within the academia a resistance to the normative, ableist conception of the phenomena. After all, translation as an inter-linguistic exercise draws attention to the role that language and culture play in shaping our social relations. For this reason, translation can become a useful tool to make academics realise that disability is not exclusively a biomedical phenomenon but, rather, a socially and culturally constituted experience. For example, while translating Rabindranath Tagore's 'Subha', the story of a speech-impaired young woman, translators over the ages have traditionally translated the Bangla *boba*—a word which exclusively evokes the inability to speak—into the English 'dumb', which at once brings to mind the adjective 'stupid' along with speech impairment and conflate the two as if they were the same. However, in recent translations of the story, more enlightened translators have preferred to use the word 'mute' in place of dumb. Such a choice suggests that the speech-impaired person has been in fact on one level silenced by a society that refuses to acknowledge modes of articulation other than the normative verbal one, overlooking the language of the eyes and gestures. The choice of words we use, whether while speaking or writing, defines the way we perceive and constitute the world we all inhabit. The act of translation, therefore, is a form of academic social activism that opens up within the text discursive spaces for radical narrative transformation. This was something that every participant at the workshop realised.

Yet (as I have written elsewhere),[2] when we had first announced our plans to organise this workshop, even the so-called enlightened academics had greeted the announcement with a great deal of scepticism wondering whether such an enterprise would be academically viable and whether there were enough short stories within the Indian canon to merit such a workshop. These apprehensions made us approach the organisation of the event with a great deal of caution as they gestured towards a grim reality - disability is yet to become a part of our academic consciousness. But soon, to our pleasant surprise our inbox was buzzing with a large number of prospective participants and in no time we had a list of more than eighty disability short stories from twelve Indian languages. 'The abundant number of texts that the workshop uncovered was enough to silence the sceptics and put our worst apprehensions to rest' (Sati and Prasad 2020). But more importantly this made us aware of a simple fact that is often overlooked, that there are a number of scholars in different parts of India who are working on disability. We, however, are not aware of their endeavours, nor are they, for that matter, aware of each other's work. This made us realise the urgent need to create an institutional umbrella platform that could bring all these scholars in touch with each other. This undoubtedly had its own merit. In the first place, a pan-India association of this kind would not only enable disability scholars from different parts of the country to know, interact and network with each other but also get acquainted with each other's work. And on the other, it would also enhance the visibility of disability scholars as a group within the Indian Academia at large. This is a subject that I would return to slightly later in the article. For the time being, however, let us return to the translation workshop and how it, in many ways, proved to be an eye opener.

A number of participants at the workshop had confessed that the workshop had given them a unique opportunity to revisit a number of texts that they had translated earlier. They, however, admitted that while translating the texts on the previous occasion, it had never occurred to them that the text that they were translating was, in fact, a disability text. The workshop gave them a chance to approach the text from the fresh perspective of a disability narrative and provided them 'an alternative frame of reference of which they had until then been blissfully unaware'

(Sati and Prasad 2020). While such a confession was highly satisfying for us as organisers of the workshop, it also simultaneously raised a set of troubling questions. Despite their self-proclaimed liberal intellectual orientation towards matters pertaining to disability, one simply fails to understand why does it take a workshop on disability for them to be able to read a text from a disability perspective? Why are they unable to recognise and identify a disability text when they encounter one (Sati et al. 2022)? These questions gesture towards an uncomfortable truth—in the past, and even today, 'critical assumptions, ideological orientations, pedagogical practices and historical circumstances' (Sati et al. 2022) have been hostile to the idea of using disability as an academically acceptable theoretical paradigm for analysing literature. The question that automatically comes to a critically discerning mind is how can disability be made a part of our academic consciousness and what needs to be done to achieve this goal.

First and foremost, it was necessary to create a network of disability studies' scholars across the country so that they could routinely interact with each other and be aware of what other disability scholars in the country were doing. With this in mind, a number of disability studies scholars from different parts of India came together in the Seminar Room of Kirori Mal College, University of Delhi on 5 May 2019 to establish the Indian Disability Studies Collective (IDSC), an academic association that would promote and foster a scholastic engagement with the experience of disablement within the Indian academia. Its objective was to organise seminars and conferences in different universities and colleges in different parts of India and awaken faculty and students alike to the research possibilities that disability studies could offer. The inaugural International IDSC conference was hosted by the Department of English and Modern European Languages, University of Lucknow in October 2019. Since then, the IDSC has organised three international conferences and hopes to organise many more in the future.

Second, it was necessary to introduce disability studies as a discipline early in a student's academic life. At present, students in India are generally exposed to the discipline quite late in their careers. By then they have already made decisions about the course of their academic journey. As a result, disability studies becomes incidental and peripheral to their scholarly pursuits. To introduce disability studies early in their academic life, we began making concerted attempts to introduce an aspect of disability studies into the undergraduate and postgraduate curricula of various universities and colleges across the country. But more importantly, in May 2021, we established at Kirori Mal College the Centre for Disability Research and Training (CDRT), perhaps the first centre of its kind in a college in India. Its primary objective is to popularise disability studies across the country, particularly amongst undergraduate and postgraduate students. To begin with, we set up online certificate courses, faculty development programmes, seminars, conferences and a series of talks on disability; the response was overwhelming from all parts of the country. At the Centre, we also made attempts to organise a disability sensitisation workshop that would spread awareness about disability in society at large. We strove to put in place systemic structures to roll out inclusive education programmes that would create a level playing field for students with disability and provide them with a wholesome, inclusive educational experience. Today we have over hundred students with disability enrolled at Kirori Mal College and we endeavour to create within the campus a disability-friendly ecosystem, ranging from an effective service-delivery mechanism that provides them with human and technological support, to rolling out capacity-building programmes that would enhance their skills and facilitate their opening in the job market.

In this way, the Centre provided us with the perfect crucible to transform disability theory into disability praxis. We have made a small beginning and our professed goal is to assist other educational institutes to set up similar centres in their respective campuses. This is the only way through which we can evolve a strategy to resist the dynamics of intentional evasion and prevent the disavowal of the disabled.

Conclusion

The purpose of this chapter has been to link my understanding of the politics of disability representation and its effect on the constitution of the disabled subjectivity with my personal biography and academic practice in the hope of evolving a praxis of resistance to the dynamics of intentional evasion that structures the normative, nondisabled attitude towards disability and disabled people.

It is certainly true that my biography and academic practice have shaped my understanding of disability and my attempts to theorise it as a socio-cultural phenomenon. After all, as Wallace Balogh has put it in the context of emancipatory feminist theory, 'social theory, coming to terms with social life, means defining, describing, or naming our experience, our historical reality for ourselves rather than living with a definition imposed upon us' (1991). But to disseminate our understanding of these experiences amid society at large, we need to create a study collective and popularise it within academia and across the country. To achieve this goal, to quote Balogh again:

we must challenge the dominant, oppressive ... cultures of these institutions by creating a space ... a holding environment, in which we can come to terms with our social realities and their representations. The ... process of creating a holding environment for ourselves and each other, a social, intellectual space for political, intellectual sociability, for reflecting on our given 'realities' ... empowers us to address and challenge the oppressive ... nature of those realities and [their] representations. (Balogh 1991)

Notes

1 This chapter builds on Michael Bérubé's 'politics of disavowal' and David Bolt's concept of 'critical avoidance', both of which seem to condition and even define the social encounters between the nondisabled and the disabled people. While the politics of disavowal refers to the 'psychological distance most people put between themselves and disability' (Bérubé 1996), the notion of critical avoidance, which in many ways is an elaboration and extension of Erwin Goffman's theory of stigma and Rosemarie Garland-Thomson's theory of the normate, tries to decode the relationship between those with and without disability within a social context. The present chapter takes these concepts beyond the realm of the social and tries to grapple with them within the context of academia and culture. At the same time, it tries to evolve discursive and material strategies to negotiate both the politics of disavowal and the tendency of critical avoidance manifest in the normative, nondisabled attitudes towards disability and disabled people.

2 I have written at great length about our experience of organising the translation workshop under question. Please refer to the 'Introduction' to *Disability in Translation: The Indian Experience.* I have reproduced here many of the observations and arguments that I have made in that introduction.

References

Balogh, Wallach R. 'Learning from Feminism: Social Theory and Intellectual Vitality'. In *Intellectuals and Politics: Social Theory in a Changing World*, edited by C. Lemert. London: Sage Publications, 1991.

Bérubé, Michael. *Life as We Know It: A Father, a Family, an Exceptional Child.* New York: Pantheon, 1996.

Bolt, David. 'Social Encounters, Cultural Representation and Critical Avoidance'. In *Routledge Handbook of Disability Studies*, edited by N. Watson, A. Roulstone and C. Thomas, 283–93. Oxford: Routledge, 2013.

Davis, L.J. *Enforcing Normalcy: Disability, Deafness and the Body.* London: Verso, 1995.

Davis, L.J. 'Crips Strike Back: The Rise of Disability Studies.' *American Literary History,* 11, no. 3 (1999): 500–512.

Goffman, E. *Stigma: Notes on the Management of Spoiled Identity.* New York: Touchstone, 1963.

Goodley, Dan. 'Dis/entangling Critical Disability Studies.' In *Culture–Theory–Disability,* edited by A. Waldschmidt, H. Berresem and M. Ingwersen, 81–97. Bielefeld: Transcript Verlag, 2017.

Hughes, Bill. 'Fear, Pity and Disgust: Emotions and the Nondisabled Imaginary.' In *Routledge Handbook of Disability Studies,* edited by N. Watson, A. Roulstone and C. Thomas, 67–77. Oxford: Routledge, 2012.

Hull, J.M. *Touching the Rock: An Experience of Blindness.* London: SPCK, 1990.

Longmore, P.K. 'Screening Stereotypes, Images of Disabled People in Television and Motion Pictures.' In *Images of the Disabled, Disabling Images,* edited by A. Gartner and T. Joe. New York: Praeger, 1987.

Marx, K. *Capital, Vol. 1.* London: Penguin. 1867.

Mintz, S.B. 'Invisible Disability: Georgina Kleege's "Sight Unseen".' *NWSA Journal,* 14, no. 3 (2002): 155–77.

Mitchell, D.T. and S.L. Snyder. *Narrative Prosthesis: Disability and the Dependencies of Discourse.* Michigan: University of Michigan Press, 2000.

Oliver, M. *Understanding Disability: From Theory to Practice.* New York: St. Martin's Press, 1996.

Sati, S. and G.J.V. Prasad (eds). *Disability in Translation: the Indian Experience.* Oxford, New York: Routledge, 2020.

Sati, S., G.J.V. Prasad and R. Bhattacharjee (eds). *Reclaiming the Disabled Subject: Representing Disability in Short Fiction.* New Delhi: Bloomsbury, 2022.

Shakespeare, T. 'Cultural Representation of Disabled People: Dustbins for Disavowal?' *Disability and Society,* 9, no. 3 (1994): 283–99.

Shildrick, M. 'The Disabled Body, Genealogy and Undecidability', *Cultural Studies,* 19, no. 6 (2005): 755–70.

———. 'Critical Disability Studies: Rethinking the Conventions for the Age of Postmodernity.' In *Routledge Handbook of Disability Studies,* edited by Nick Watson, Alan Roulstone and Carol Thomas, 30–41. London: Routledge, 2012.

Siebers, T. 'Disability, Pain and the Politics of Minority Identity.' In *Culture–Theory–Disability,* edited by A. Waldschmidt, H. Berresem and M. Ingwersen, 111–21. Bielefeld: Transcript Verlag, 2017.

Thomas, C. *Sociologies of Disability and Illness: Contested Ideas in Disability Studies and Medical Sociology.* London: Palgrave, 2007.

Thomson, R.G. *Extraordinary Bodies: Figuring Physical Disability in American Culture and Literature.* New York: Columbia University Press, 1997.

Waldschmidt, A. 'Disability Goes Cultural: The Cultural Model of Disability as an Analytical Tool.' In *Culture–Theory–Disability,* edited by A. Waldschmidt, H. Berresem and M. Ingwersen, 19–28. Bielefeld: Transcript Verlag, 2017.

2

CLINICAL RESCRIPTS: RECOVERING THE AFFECTIVE POLITICS OF MEDICALISING WOMEN'S BODIES

Shilpaa Anand

Medical experiences are perhaps closer today than they ever were. Living through the pandemic has demonstrated that disease conditions and illness experiences lurk around every infected corner. Covid-19 has startled people into recognising themselves as medical entities, always only one sneeze away from being fully symptomatic even while they negotiate with the everyday as professionals, family members and in terms of our intersectional social identities. Moreover, the realisation that the world is constituted of public health inequalities has underscored access to medical diagnoses, facilities and treatment as political matters. Deaths due to delay or absence of medical care, other deaths caused by ancillary effects such as loss of employment, and distress caused to those left behind—all this has shown that access to medical awareness and resources is deeply tied to the reality of social inequalities. Against this backdrop, this chapter presents a discussion of the role that medicalisation plays in establishing normative ideas about corporeal aesthetics, and their affective impact on women's lives through a reading of fiction. Here is an attempt to explore an unpopular idea within disability studies—the contours of the medical model.

An under-explored potential of disability studies is its examination of the sociality that the medicalisation of individuals produces, something that goes beyond pathologisation. One such tool of analysis that the field offers is a critical interest in clinical practices and the production of subjectivities through the discourse and practice of medicine. What does medicine—all its approaches as knowledge and practice—enable? How does it constitute and interact with the social realities of its practitioners and patients? What kinds of affective relations inhabit the edges of medicalised bodyminds? In an attempt to examine the social contours of medicine—the institution and its impact on human life and relations—the present chapter makes observations about women's experiences when framed as medicalised bodyminds. Drawing on the departure of feminist disability studies from feminist theory, this chapter aims to investigate the politics of pain, illness and disablement. Additionally, the critique of the medical model that disability studies theory engages with is crucial here. The idea of the medical model does not merely entail notions of medicalised bodies but also captures the fact that disabled bodies are often individualised or that disability is individualised. Such individuation forecloses the possibility of transformative politics that identifies structural factors which animate a range of affective politics off and around differential embodiment.

Illness and disablement are at once excruciatingly familiar and robustly unfamiliar. Disability studies theory oddly exacerbates both the familiarity and unfamiliarity. At times, it appears to be constituting an object that has never been known, and at other moments, it startles one into realising that that object is oneself or that we were always it and in it. Both sets of narratives frame disability as a relatively new object. What often goes missing is the recognition of the potential of this seemingly new discourse to help us acknowledge the epistemic potential of that which has always been known, enabling us to think through familiar episodes and experiences in newer forms. Looking around at how we inhabit spaces and discourses may enable not so much a discovery but a recovery, an enterprise that Virginia Woolf outlines in her 1926 essay, 'On Being Ill'. Woolf was curious about the overt exclusion of illness from literature at a time when illness was ubiquitous and familiar to everyone. Reading literary instances of illness and disablement enable recognition and acknowledgement of the *always familiar* when writers like Audre Lorde share the survival of physiological pain and its affective counterpart, 'for use, that the pain not be wasted' (1997). In this light, this chapter offers a reading of short stories written by a medical and rehabilitation professional, Githanjali, who spotlights women's bodies and the pathologising that they are subject to within the space of their marital homes.

Institutional histories and disciplinary moorings have shaped disability as both familiar and unfamiliar by limiting our imagination. For instance, madness has a long history in literary studies as an object of study and probably a shorter recall within social science scholarship. The introduction of disability studies to literature students in India has followed an older social scientific thinking about disability where literary texts are treated as sociological data, holding the potential to uncover disability. Literary sources have been treated like qualitative data while staving off the more literary alternative to explore disability textually by attending to content and form. Young scholars are encouraged to believe that doing disability studies in literature requires one to extend such positivist approaches to the study of literary and cultural texts—their textual analysis has to prove that characters with different kinds of impairments are stigmatised by collecting evidence from the narrative, or that the medical model overwhelms a plot—the disabled character is a tragic hero. My exaggeration of facts is deliberate and brings with it the hope that newer research in literary disability studies may draw more convincingly on creative and critical analyses. While the emergent field of literary disability studies may be considered unfamiliar, it would be important to recognise that it does not bring with it unfamiliar objects. Adopting disability studies as an analytic toolkit would enable us to open up our familiar worlds to a newer scrutiny.

However, a brief sketch of what literary disability studies has enabled so far may not be out of place. As a field of enquiry, it studies the various aspects of the discourse of corporeal, cognitive and affective differences and the structures of responses they elicit. Scholars in the field have tacitly responded to this question by engaging with content and form. One axis has explored the manifestation of social stereotypes of disability in literary texts through the use of different impairments and metaphors of moral failings and social disruptions (Mitchell 2002; Quayson 2013; Donaldson 2018; Davidson 2008). Another axis explores disability as constitutive of the trope of melodrama, thus tapping into the affective resources of disability mimesis and diegesis (Holmes 2012). A third axis combines the two to examine the relations between narrative structures and popular conceptions of disablement (Mitchell 2002; Davis 1995). A fourth strand explores disability autobiographies and biographies of disabled achievers as a genre of writing (Couser 2002; Karah 2012; Kleege 2014). The dominant argumentative tropes in all of these ventures reflect on disability sociality and critically analyse issues related to disability representation. Departing from these trends, I choose to read a set of short stories for what they reveal about social and political actions and the ideologies that animate medical practices in the hope of recovering medicalised bodyminds as more complex than the otherwise customary dismissal of the medical model.

The Rock That Was Not

Githanjali's stories, collected in an anthology titled *The Rock That Was Not*, are populated with medical encounters experienced by women belonging to poor and middle-class families. She admits that these women, based on the people she met as patients in her professional life as a doctor and psychotherapist, offer vignettes of poor and middle-class families during their encounters with the medical complex. The women in these stories do not bear readily recognisable impairments but their bodyminds are rendered abnormal or pathological under the heterosexist rubrics of bodily perfection and affective sanism. It could be argued that the stories substantiate a long-standing idea within disability studies theory that impairments, and not just disabilities, are social, in that, their impairment effect is socially constituted. All the stories have at their centre women smashed physically and affectively by patriarchies that prescribe bodily and affective normativity. Commenting on the stories, the description printed on the dust jacket states that the women in the stories 'suffer the trauma of being treated as breasts, a vagina, a womb', referring to the characters' experiences of being objectified as sex toys or reproduction machines. Sexual politics within heteronormative marriages combines with socially backed reproductive imperatives to expose events in which women's embodiment is characterised as substandard, humiliated and subsequently shaped to fit men's desires. Disability, in these stories, subscribes to Alison Kafer's formulation of the relational model, whereby it 'is experienced in and through relationships' (2013). Furthermore, each story reveals the methods by which human social worlds are constituted by illness, medicine and psychiatry and their affective politics. Each story betrays the gendered nature of familial biopolitics as well as the ideological underpinnings of medical diagnoses and treatment alternatives.

Diagnostic categories and treatment regimens in a few stories selected for study enable patriarchal structures. In others, instances of supportive medical practitioners expose the ways in which an otherwise indifferent medical system is kinder to these women than the members of their marital homes. Every experience of physical and psychological domestic abuse bears the complex relations that women, caught in stifling patriarchal traps, have with clinical diagnosis and treatment as well as medical technology. Domestic relations, the stories reflect, are carved out of medico-psychiatric moments that erupt and control familial and romantic relations while the women are shackled in fetters of heteronormative expectations. They vouch for Lorde's claim that with fear comes knowledge.

Githanjali's stories are realist narratives that present women caught in everyday extraordinary circumstances that are unsettling. They disturb even as they expose women's subjugation in poor and middle-class families. Each one of the women negotiates a complex relationship with clinical diagnosis and treatment. Inviting readers to attend to the social contexts of every human-medical encounter, these stories provoke readers into observing and responding to situations that do not embrace happy endings. It is not surprising then, that Githanjali's Telugu title for the stories labels them as tragic. Nevertheless, her stories refrain from employing experiences of disablement and illness as techniques of defamiliarisation. Disablement in her stories does not remain as a literary device that carries metaphorical value while invoking sentimental affective responses; it is what the stories are about and dwell on the materiality of disablement experiences (Mitchell and Snyder 2002). Medical practice organises familial and romantic heteronormative relations in a wide range of manners in the different stories. Reading these stories helps us formulate questions that enable us to explore the contours of the medical: How do ordinary people engage with their bodies as medicalised ones? How are social realities brought into sharp focus when illness and medical interventions govern the lives of individuals and their families?

> Feminist disability theory offers a particularly trenchant analysis of how the female body has been medicalised in modernity. As I have already suggested, both women and the disabled have been imagined as medically abnormal—as the quintessential sick ones. Sickness is gendered feminine. This gendering of illness has entailed distinct consequences in everything from epidemiology and diagnosis to prophylaxis and therapeutics. (Garland-Thomson 2011)

What follows is a discussion of six stories as a response to Rosemarie Garland-Thomson's observation: '... both women and the disabled have been imagined as medically abnormal—as the quintessential sick ones. Sickness is gendered feminine' (2011). Three themes emerge from the stories to confirm and contest Garland-Thomson's view. In two stories, women victimised by their partners' sexual appetites are either coerced or volunteered to fix their bodies to suit their partners' desires. In both these stories, modern biomedicine's script is altered. A second theme highlights the high value attached to women's wombs as the sole organs that contain the potential and responsibility to produce male offspring. The third theme discussed in this chapter is a reinvestigation of the trope of the 'madwoman in the attic' through a close reading of two stories in the collection.

Changing Medicine's Script

> She should not have allowed them to fix the rocky liquid pouches in her body. Before the pouches were installed, the counsellor had said that cancer cannot be detected by mammography with the silicon

pouches in the breasts. How much she had wept, fearing something like that would happen to her! How much Ashok had scolded her! (*The Rock That Was Not*)

The first eponymous story in the collection, *The Rock That Was Not*, begins with Prathima dreaming of stars exploding into an outpouring of quartz particles that envelop her in a thick white liquid which finally fills her four breasts. The dream ends when she awakens from the searing dream pain of her breasts exploding into a fountain of molten rock and blood that flows down her body. This was a recurring dream that immobilised her with fear. Following her dream, the narrative asks, 'Was her identity merely her breasts sprouting from her headless trunk?' While the narrative focalises Prathima's tribulations and trauma as she is forced to surgically acquire silicone breast implants, the story's emplotment perhaps inadvertently succeeds in presenting the biography of a body part whose life is constituted affectively, medically and socially. As in other stories in the collection, in this one too the female protagonist and her oppressor-husband serve as stock figures that act as backdrops against which a female body part and the affective life it assumes are foregrounded. Prathima's femininity, sexuality, her wifeliness and her potential maternity all coalesce into a synecdochic characterisation of her breasts.

At one level, her breasts are pleasure-giving organs whose size can be enhanced based on the fancies of Ashok's desires. Before the surgical implantation, he refers to her breasts as 'empty' and ridicules her, referring to her as a pole. His affective corporeality, it appears, includes her breasts. Additionally, the story provides insights into Prathima's years in school and college when she had been made to feel conscious of the inadequate size of her breasts. Prathima was teased and called *chapatti*. The narrative moment set in the present in the story recounts the humiliation she faces in the college she teaches at because of the implants. She is surrounded by sniggers and has to leave the college and join a new one because of the humiliation.

Ashok's unbridled desire leads to Prathima's cosmetic surgery, which Audre Lorde, in the context of post-mastectomy prosthesis, refers to as 'prosthetic pretense' (1997). Prathima's synthetic breasts are created to fulfil Ashok's sexual urge, just as Suseela's vaginal stitches are created for her husband's pleasure. These prosthetic augmentations are as much affective extensions of the men's desiring bodyminds as they are physical attachments to the women's bodies. At the time that her cancer is detected, Prathima's breasts are hers alone—when the silicon pouch is removed for a biopsy to be conducted, Ashok's desire recoils. It is almost as if her newfound disease saves her. Her pathology, detected and treated by clinical intervention, restores her breasts to her mind and unites her sense of self. She finally reunites with her breasts and rids herself of the alienating prosthetics that in reality belonged to his desiring body. She hates and loves her breasts at the same time. He loves only her breasts.

Like Prathima, other women in Githanjali's stories attempt to solve their domestic dilemmas by modifying their bodies at the risk of grave harm to their lives. Garland-Thomson contends that the ideologies of normalcy and beauty not only objectify female and disabled bodies but make them 'pliable bodies' that are to be incessantly shaped and reshaped (2011). Prathima's breasts bear the burden of securing the necessary conjugality—they carry affective currency in relation to resolving and tying together bodily relations. We could say that the inherent logic of medical rationale appears to be stunned by such affective subversions. Or, could we consider that it is medical technology's ability to be moulded by sexist biases that is exhibited by these stories?

Suseela asked, 'What is an extra knot?'

> Sumathi looked at her sympathetically and said, 'Doesn't the vagina become wider after delivery? One extra knot is made so that it becomes tight and nice for the husband during sex.' ('The Husband Stitch')

In the story, 'The Husband Stitch', Suseela is troubled by the fact that her husband, whose second wife she is, does not have sex with her ever since she delivered their twin daughters. Vexed by his absence and desperate to have him back, she learns from her friend that women can get an additional vaginal suture after childbirth to tighten their vaginas and to continue to give pleasure to their husbands during sex. Seemingly empowered with this information, she seeks a medical procedure that will satiate her husband's desire even after being warned by the doctor that the surgery would not necessarily fulfil her need. Padmaja, the doctor, advises her not to get the vaginoplasty done. Indignant with her husband, the doctor scolds Suseela for being tortured in this manner by her husband's demands. She even recommends that exercises that would help tighten the vagina, be considered as a less intrusive option than the surgery. Uncaring about her high blood pressure, Suseela borrows money from relatives and friends to pay for the expensive vaginoplasty. Following the surgery, Suseela suffers sex with her husband—she bleeds and experiences excruciating pain but revels in the fact that her husband has returned to her for sex. Her joy at her husband being sexually active with her instead of the first wife to who he had returned ever since Suseela's body had stopped being a source of pleasure for him, supersedes her physical well-being. The vagina loosens in time and her husband abuses her for it, calling it her incapacity. She returns to the doctor who confirms that her vagina has loosened. On hearing this, Suseela's blood pressure shoots up and she collapses with a paralytic stroke.

Vaginoplasty, within the fictional world of the story, 'The Husband's Stitch', is rescripted as a bodily augmentation, a prosthesis that Suseela believes will save her marriage. It is very likely to be harmful to her health but its purpose is different; its usual clinical rationale of restoring physical health is subverted, and its rationale in this context, is relational (Kafer 2013). In seeking to save a conjugal relationship with such kind of medical intervention, Suseela appears to be subverting the very logic of medicine. Even as her action rescripts medical logic, it exposes the underlying ideology of medical knowledge and practice. Her social world, which is held in place by economic underprivilege and heteropatriarchy, provides her access to a kind of medical knowledge that is negotiated by women's needs to fulfil conjugal expectations. Medicine's role in the lives of women caught in unhappy marriages—like Suseela—seems to be a political one. Vaginas are pathologised for being loose and subsequently, a clinical remedy is presented as treatment and cure.

Githanjali's stories reveal that the privilege of being able-bodied is only available to and ascribed to male bodies. Such privilege makes them stand in judgement of their women's bodies and pronounce them as being inadequate, abnormal and unsatisfactory. Suseela does not accept any offer made by her doctor to counsel her husband. She even ignores her symptoms of hypertension in her singular pursuit of vaginal 'correction'. Kafer, while making a case for a political/relational model of disability, contends that 'medical framings of disability are embedded in economic realities and relations' (2013). As Suseela's situation makes explicit, the production of her loose vagina as impairment is deeply related to the politics of patriarchal notions of conjugality. Kafer further argues that 'medical beliefs and practices are not immune to or separate from cultural practices and ideologies' (2013).

Both Suseela and Prathima succumb to acquiring coercive prostheses to satisfy their husbands' desires. Lorde maintains that prosthetics such as breast implants are cosmetic shams and are deeply political. Referring to them as 'socially sanctioned prosthetics', Lorde calls for a rejection of normative notions of beauty and sexiness (1997).

Coercive Pregnancies and Toxic Births

Manjeera's body felt like a wound, with caesarean delivery, high blood pressure and two abortions in five years. She felt intimidated by the very word pregnancy. ('Murder!')

Manjeera's multiple failed pregnancies after the birth of a daughter don't serve as warnings to her husband Nagesh and his family. They remain undaunted by the fact that becoming pregnant again would be fatal for her. Her husband, Nagesh, insists on getting her pregnant in the family's pursuit of a male heir. The daughter they have is ignored. After an arduous pregnancy, a male child is born and grandly celebrated. However, a month after the delivery, Manjeera dies. Appropriately titled 'Murder', the story documents Manjeera's subjection to domestic torture in detail. The story centres on her coercive pregnancies and the overt control that her husband's family has over her reproductive abilities. Any small chance of a medical intervention to rescue her from her domestic misery is thwarted by the overarching need for the birth of a male child. When Manjeera's mother suggests that she should get a tubectomy to take care of her health and not submit to her husband's yearning for a male child, medical bureaucracy intervenes to prevent this. The need for a husband's signature at the hospital before the procedure is conducted makes it impossible for Manjeera to have any control over her reproductive health.

However, a striking aspect of the story is how medical knowledge and prescriptions are overpowered by a family's need for a male successor. The overwhelming need for the birth of a male child stands out in the story as a eugenic compulsion. The birthing of female children is pathologised. During a visit to the doctor, Nagesh asks her if Manjeera can be administered any treatment that would make her deliver a male child. The inability to bear a male offspring is treated as Manjeera's corporeal failure. In the absence of consent and reproductive justice, death offers Manjeera an escape.

> The doctor had night duty that day. She sat in her room thinking about Malanbi's refusal to get operated. Why did she say no? Why did she take such a risk when she had three children to look after? She wanted the tumour to be removed but the uterus to be retained, as if the uterus was a treasure trove of precious stones and as if her life would end if it were separated from the body. In fact, her life would end if it remained in her body. ('Offering')

Malanbi's strident defiance of medical procedures guides the narrative of the story, 'Offering'. She had given birth to daughters and her husband wanted a son. She had a tumour in her uterus and the only way of treating it was to remove the uterus surgically. Malanbi refused this medical solution. She feared that the surgical removal of her uterus, which would foreclose chances of reproduction, would drive her husband to marry another woman. Their conjugal relationship was held together by a thread of hope that she would one day birth a male offspring.

The story closely documents the doctor–patient relationship. Knowing that the tumour could become cancerous, the enraged doctor urges Malanbi to get the surgery done. Earlier, the doctor had chastised her for not taking care of her health and getting a CT scan done. Enraged at Malanbi's husband, the doctor asks her to bring her husband to the hospital so that he can be told that it is the man's chromosomal contribution that enables the birth of a male child and not a woman's. However, Malanbi, knowing that the doctor is aware of her circumstances and is still concerned about her health, begs to be spared the surgery. Tearily, she reminds the doctor of the time she had consumed poison when her husband had brought home another woman. She needed her uterus to keep their marriage alive and her affective logic defied all clinical logic that was oriented towards keeping her alive.

The story discloses matters related to women patient's choices and consent in medical decisions while also foregrounding the illusion of autonomy that shields women in situations like that of Malanbi's who are severely limited by socially accepted patriarchal expectations. Furthermore, the fear of knowing one's body through clinical lenses is also writ large in the story. Malanbi had refused to get a CT scan done for fear of finding out that something would be wrong with her. Resistance to clinical procedures and screenings is a common feature of women's lives and is indicative of two problems—one, the fear that diagnosis of a disease may disrupt everyday life that is filled with housework, informal labour or professional work; two, that medicine figures in their lives as an 'unknown devil' because of the poor access to knowledge of medical procedures and practices.

Aside from fearing clinical procedures, several stories in Githanjali's collection exhibit warm relations between women doctors and their women patients. The author's occupational position as a medico-rehabilitation practitioner perhaps inspired the characterisation of the medical staff as sympathetic and understanding of the women patients' circumstances. However, the doctors remain sympathetic bystanders in the denouement of their patients' lives. The stories, in rendering the doctors as helpless, underscore the failure of the clinician's inherent Hippocratic logic while additionally disclosing affective affinities these doctors feel towards their patients by an atavistic reasoning that they all share as women.

Denouncing the Attic

Literature has a long history of both embellishing and contesting the pathologising of women as mad/of unsound mind/hysterical. Adding to the ever-growing line of literary women, from Shakespeare's Lady

Macbeth to Brontë's Bertha Mason and from Charlotte Perkins Gilman's 'The Yellow Wallpaper's' (1892) Jane to Susanna Kaysen's *Girl, Interrupted*, Rudra and Arunakka expose systemic gender inequalities that compose normative notions of sanism. Their stories offer glimpses into the ways in which the practice of psychiatry betrays its commitment to enabling patriarchy.

Metaphorical and synecdochical meanings have accrued to the phenomenon of the attic. Signifying both banishment from the parts occupied by most people as well as exclusion from life itself, the attic has come to stand for women's experiences of distress caused by oppressive patriarchal structures and masculinist practices that inform psychiatry. However, Elizabeth Donaldson asserts that using madness as a feminist metaphor for women's rebellion erases the fact of mental illness (2018). Githanjali's stories resist the metaphorical notions of madness as rebellion and divulge the ways in which psychiatry pathologises women's need for independence from domestic oppression as devious and deviant. The stories of Rudra and Arunakka, diagnosed with nymphomania and obsessive-compulsive neurosis respectively, expose the ideological bases of clinical practices that read and pronounce women's actions as deviant.

> 'I'm not a sex maniac. I don't want these medicines.' I flung the medicines away. That was it—blows on my back. From then on, he tied up my legs and hands and made me swallow medicines. I searched the dictionary for the meaning of nymphomania. At one place, it said apsara (heavenly nymph). I was not an apsara anyway. When I continued to search, I found that nymphomania means a woman who is a sex maniac, a promiscuous woman who has an excessive sexual desire and sleeps with multiple men, a prostitute and a bitch. I had a black-out for a moment. My body trembled with rage and humiliation. ('Nymphomania')

In the story, 'Nymphomania', Rudra, who was caught in a loveless marriage, finds a lover who is kind to her and has a relationship with him. When her husband and children find out about the relationship, she is pathologised and hated. The psychiatric diagnosis she is assigned enables her family to detest and isolate her. When Rudra resists psychiatric medicines, she is verbally abused and forced to take it. Nagesh, her husband, is an artist and uses his studio to meet with many women and have sexual relations with them. Neither Rudra nor Nagesh acknowledges this regular phenomenon, resulting in her having to neglect her desire for sexual intimacy while he ensured that his desire thrived and was fulfilled as he pursued sexual relations with the women he had ostensibly invited to his studio to model for his art.

'Nymphomania' stands out in Githanjali's volume as a testimony of the unjust ways in which a woman's desire is pathologised and punished. The story is framed as a monologue that Rudra has with the profession of psychiatry whose patriarchal framework is unravelled as the narrative moves forward. Rudra's account documents the process of pathologising that is simultaneously moralising and criminalising; her need to have sexual intimacy with the stranger, Madhu is hastily labelled as a psychosexual disease and urgently treated with psychiatric medication. In time, Dr Manoja's, a marital therapist, services are sought and Rudra is absolved of the label of nymphomania, thanks to the professional intervention that deems that the roots of women's psychological problems are in the 'social and political institutions around us' (p. 56, 'Nymphomania'). The story ends with Rudra's husband and children counselled to the realisation that she did not have a psychological disease and that it was her family that had to bear the responsibility of causing her distress.

> Should women's creativity and intelligence burn to ashes in the kitchen? Men give different reasons to escape from housework and cooking. Who should tell these doctors that the patriarchal system controlled women? When would they understand that antidepressants were not the solution for women's psychological disorders? ('OCN')

Arunakka, a social activist, dies by setting herself on fire in a kitchen that had come to be her prison. During a visit to a counsellor, where she speaks of her inability to go on working in the kitchen to feed her family and activist-visitors, she is told to take a break and travel. She is diagnosed with 'obsessive compulsive neurosis', for her relentless thoughts about being stifled by domestic chores. Additionally, the counsellor tells her that it is women's responsibility to cook for everyone at home. On hearing this, Arunakka laughs at the irony—at the startling revelation that even therapists do not understand the oppression of household labour. For Arunakka, death is an escape from the idiomatic attic. In a domestic yet political re-enactment of Gayatri Chakravorty Spivak's exposition on the conundrum of the inability of subalterns to speak, Arunakka's suicide speaks eloquently of the oppression of women trapped in domesticity. However, the use of madness metaphorically in feminist literary discourse has entailed the tendency to discredit the lived experience of mental illnesses while purporting to glorify them as expressions of resistance. Githanjali's stories, by invoking specific diagnostic categories, draw attention to the material implications of attaching diagnostic labels that serve to pathologise them as ways of reinforcing docility and dispossessing them of legal and political capacity.

Tragic Plots and Their Political Potential

Literary disability studies scholars point to the problem of reinforcing negative stereotypes of disability by including disability as a standard tragic fall that the protagonist acquires. Studying aspects, such as Oedipus's and Rochester's blindness, Lady Macbeth's and King Lear's madness as well as Tiny Tim's sickness, scholars reason that these plotlines enable the conceptualisation of disability as personal or individual tragedy alone. However, the stories reviewed in this chapter suggest that tragic plots have a political potential and are therefore transformative. The women in these stories do not emerge as victors. Nevertheless, the pity they attract leads to a recognition of the deep structures of patriarchy that persistently render female bodies as pathological and abnormal. In doing so, they critically revise tragedy's potency to be political and subsequently enable a collective awakening. As Lorde reckons about what the medicalisation and rehabilitation of breast cancer reveals, Githanjali's stories too stand as an 'index of this society's attitudes towards women in general as decoration and externally defined sex objects' (1997).

Githanjali's stories are tragic and therefore deserve a recovery of their underlying politics. Medical and psychiatric practices embellish gender inequalities by pathologising women's bodies, minds and behaviour. Underscoring the variety of modes in which women's bodies are pathologised, the stories raise complex questions about ableist structures that contour women's lives—about normative standards of beauty, sexual attractiveness and of heteronormative familial expectations. What Alison Kafer refers to as a political/relational model best describes the consciousness that underlies Githanjali's stories that recognise the limitations of either rejecting or valorising medical intervention. Instead, the plots surrounding the women characters centre on the multiple modes in which 'representations, diagnoses, and treatments of bodily variation are imbued with ideological biases about what constitutes normalcy and deviance' (Kafer 2013).

Githanjali's stories use tragic emplotment to uncover complex affective relations that women have with medical knowledge. The absence of actual patient choice in determining one's treatment and consent to medical procedures is perspicuous in the stories. Her stories often end with the death of the female protagonist and while the tragic fall of the character is marked by the acquisition of a diagnosis or the failure of a clinical procedure, disablement is not merely a literary tool. These are tragedies in search of catharses, the kind that are healing, oriented towards rehabilitation and therefore, almost clinical.

References

Couser, Thomas. 'Signifying Bodies: Life Writing and Disability Studies'. In *Disability Studies: Enabling the Humanities*, edited by S.L. Snyder, B.J. Brueggemann and R. Garland-Thomson, 109–17. New York: The Modern Language Association of America, 2002.

Davidson, Michael. *Concerto for the Left Hand: Disability and the Defamiliar Body*. Ann Arbor: University of Michigan Press, 2008.

Davis, Lennard J. *Enforcing Normalcy: Disability, Deafness and the Body*. London: Verso, 1995.

Donaldson, Elizabeth J. *Literatures of Madness: Disability Studies and Mental Health*. Cham: Palgrave Macmillan, 2018.

Garland-Thomson, Rosemarie. 'Integrating Disability, Transforming Feminist Theory'. In *Feminist Disability Studies*, edited by Kim Q. Hall, 13–47. Bloomington: Indiana University Press, 2011.

Githanjali. *The Rock That Was Not and Other Stories*, translated by Suneetha Rani. Delhi: Ratna Books. 2019.

Holmes, Martha Stoddard. *Fictions of Affliction: Physical Disability in Victorian Culture*. Ann Arbor: University of Michigan Press, 2012.

Kafer, Alison. *Feminist, Queer, Crip*. Bloomington, Indianapolis: Indiana University Press, 2013.

Karah, Hemachandran. 'Blindness, Lockean Empiricism, and the Continent of Britain: An Examination of the Identities of Mr Spectator and Theseus in the Writings of Ved Mehta'. *Journal of Literary & Cultural Disability Studies*, 6, no. 3 (January 2012): 259–74.

Kleege, Georgina. *Blind Rage: Letters to Helen Keller*. Washington: Gallaudet University Press, 2014.

Lorde, Audre. *The Cancer Journals*. San Francisco: Aunt Lute Books, 1997.

Mitchell, David T. and Sharon L. Snyder, 'Narrative Prosthesis and the Materiality of Metaphor'. In *Disability Studies: Enabling the Humanities*, edited by S.L. Snyder, Brenda Jo Brueggemann and R. Garland-Thomson, 47–64. New York: The Modern Languages Association of America, 2002.

Quayson, Ato. 'Aesthetic Nervousness'. In *Disability Studies Reader*, 4th Ed., edited by L.J. Davis, 202–13. New York: Routledge, 2013.

Woolf, Virginia. *On Being Ill*. Musaicum Books, Kindle edition, 2017.

3

SELF-CONCEPT, EMBODIMENT, SEXUALITY AND DISABILITY: HOW DISABLED WOMEN EXPERIENCE NAVARATRI AND GAURI VRAT IN GUJARAT

Shilpa Das

Feminist disability theorists have written extensively on identity and embodiment, a concept borrowed from the phenomenological movement in philosophy. Embodiment pertains to the identification and description of the essential forms of human experience, beginning with the body as a site for sensation, perception and interaction (Merleau-Ponty 1962). These theorists have offered a rich variety of subjective accounts and analyses of the experience of disability and how it affected them and led them to form their identity of their selves, their body image and self-concept. Some write from the perspective of a lifelong disability identity (Morris 1996, 1998; Chib 2011), others describe their changeover into the world of disability and still others write about disability without having experienced disability firsthand (Fine and Asch 1988; Lonsdale 1990; Wendell 1996). Many of them create an account of disability identity that cautions against any kind of quintessential disabled identity and reformulates how disabled people differ from each other as well as from the nondisabled. This is significant because it helps to shed light on issues about identities shaped by other kinds of differences.

In India, feminist scholars have looked at embodiment in terms of caste, class and stages of national history and often sidelined the disabled body. Niranjana discusses this lapse:

> Focus on the body has been a symbolic one, where the body is perceived as sign or code, important to the extent that it is speaking about a social reality other than itself ... the question remains whether these perspectives can acknowledge the materiality of bodies, not merely as they are formed/represented in a culture, but how they constitute the lived reality of persons. (quoted in Ghai 2009)

Feminist disability studies in India also do not focus exclusively on identity formation and the body image of disabled women, though there are a few exceptions (Addlakha 1998, 2007; Ghai 2002, 2003; Mehrotra, 2004, 2006; Ghosh 2016, [quoted in Ghai] 2018).

A psychosocial perspective that is informed by the social model of disability is referred to in this study to understand how body image envelopes the self-concept of disabled people. 'Stigma' and 'otherness' are intrinsic aspects in this perspective. The social model of disability, Taleporos and McCabe note, infers that individuals with identical physical impairments are likely to vary in their feelings and attitudes towards their own bodies because of social factors such as education, social support and real or perceived social attitudes (cited in Addlakha 2009). The perspective entails examining the individual's experiences of the social world and societies' attitudes to them. Taleporos and McCabe urge for greater attention to and investigation of the body image of people with physical disabilities in the research literature (2009). Teal and Athelstan define body image as a psychological experience focused on feelings and attitudes towards one's own body (1975). Smith states that body image includes both conscious and unconscious feelings and that these may relate to the size, function, appearance and potential of one's body (1984). Slade accords primacy to the impact of environmental factors on body image. He defines it as a loose mental representation of body, shape, size and form that is influenced by a variety of historical, cultural, social, individual and biological factors which operate over varying timespans (1994). In light of these definitions, this study defines body image as the blend of an individual's psychological experiences, feelings and attitudes that relate to the form, function, appearance and desirability of his or her own body, which is influenced by individual and environmental factors. Linked to the body image is self-concept, which is defined as being 'based on accumulated perceptions throughout the lifespan and is strongly influenced by the interplay between their own actions, the reactions of others, and one's perceptions of the events and their surrounding behaviours and outcomes' (Davis-Kean and Sandler 2001). Thus, the body becomes a site for cultural inscription.

This chapter explores the interplay between social and cultural factors, and the lived experiences, of disabled women as adolescents and young adults in Gujarat with special reference to the festivals of Navaratri and Gauri Vrat or Goro as they relate to their self-concept. It examines the particularities of their bodily experience, their internalisation of socio-cultural constructions of the archetypal female body, how such constructions shape their perceptions and experiences of their bodies as they grow from childhood to adulthood, differences in their embodiment, their body image and the strategies of acceptance or resistance adopted by them. It also throws light on the cultural conceptualisations in Gujarat of femininity, sexuality and marriage worthiness, their social exclusion and how disabled women resist these and exercise agency for themselves. The materiality and the social construction of the disabled body render phenomenology a useful theoretical starting point to explore the lived experience of having a gendered disabled body. The lived and gendered narratives of disability are a useful starting point and perceptive locus to understand the complexity and politics of the socio-cultural world wherein the oppression of disability emerges and is perpetuated, and through which critical knowledge of bodily impairment, embodiment and disability are obtained.

Methodology

Qualitative data with a focus on the subject's or participant's frame of reference was collected for the study mainly through in-depth interviews, semi-structured interviews and focus-group discussions. The study sought to investigate the nature of discriminatory practices in the two celebrations of Navaratri and Goro, how young disabled women perceived these practices and how they shaped their self-concept concerning their sexuality. Personal experience occupies a position of central importance in this study. The disabled women respondents were between the ages of 18 and 30 as this is broadly observed to be the range for marriage. They were from lower-income or middle-income families. The study covered 30 women in three districts of Gujarat—Ahmedabad, Gandhinagar and Mahesana keeping in mind a rural–urban representation but ending up with about 85 per cent urban representation. The types of disabilities covered mainly included locomotor impairment, visual impairment, speech and hearing impairment and multiple disabilities. The participants in the study were selected through purposive sampling across the districts. Other stakeholders included parents, especially mothers, siblings of disabled young women, physiotherapists and college counsellors. Names used for the disabled women participants in this study are pseudonyms.

Sexuality and Self-Concept

This author's doctoral research earlier revealed that disabled women in Gujarat spend their childhoods in the loving care of their natal families, especially parents, and are caught in the mesh of doctors, physiotherapy, indigenous treatment and magico-religious rituals (to effect a 'cure' for disability), and going to school (Arvind et al. 2005; Das 2010; Das 2015). Adolescence or growing into adulthood, Steinberg feels, brings in a new 'set of transitions that unfold gradually in the context of their behaviour, development and relationships' and is marked by menarche or the onset of puberty (cited in Thapan 2009). As such, adolescence is a time when young men and women are acutely self-conscious of their bodies and the changes in them and rife with anxieties about the way they look. This is an age when clothing, fashion, music, media, friends, community activities, social events and school experiences assume greater significance in their lives (Addlakha 2013). Challenging parental values and social norms is commonplace. At this age, they are also easily susceptible to social and cultural stereotypes of the body and personhood and vulnerable to visual and print media. Young girls learn early in life that women are primarily defined by physical appearances and they begin to aspire to live up to those ideals of body type and beauty to be accepted in their peer group. Their self-concept as girls is significantly influenced by their body image. In fact, their self-concept is synonymous with their body image. Thapan explains that at this age, 'young women's self-images are essentially grounded in their embodiment' (2009). Embodiment involves individual's interactions with and through their bodies. The perspective of embodiment is important because, as Thapan says, 'a woman is undoubtedly located in a physical and psychological space as much as she is in the cultural and social domain' (2009). But body image determined by the messages women receive about how their bodies should look and behave is a gendered concept that is reinforced and legitimised by social institutions including the family and by the mass media, especially advertising and cinema. The dominant images of women perpetuated by these do not incorporate the diverse and individual characteristics of women, including disabled women, further alienating them. Moreover, the pattern of human response to its defined environment is through culture, its ubiquity and learned systems of meaning inherent in it. Culture, in the widest sense, may be said to be 'the whole complex of distinctive spiritual, material, intellectual and emotional features that characterise a society or social group. It includes the arts and letters, modes of life, the fundamental rights of the human being, value systems, traditions and beliefs' (Intergovernmental Conference on Cultural Policies for Development, Stockholm 1998). One way for culture to operate is by invoking sacred texts, historical precedents and the religious cosmology of mythology. With respect to disability, culture serves as a tightly controlled site of asymmetrical power relations that discipline the modes of perceiving and normalising selfhood and identity through select monolithic representations, articulations and internalisations. The high premium on a socially desirable, feminine and sexual self-ensures that women regulate their own bodies through an act of inner surveillance in order to fit that ideal.

How do disabled girls constitute their femininity in the face of their impairments? Addlakha says, 'The embodied female self of the disabled subject is primarily constructed through a formal allegiance to the sexual and aesthetic norms and values of the nondisabled patrifocal world' (2013). She underscores that 'disabled adolescent girls face the same physical changes in their bodies, emotional turmoil, social conflicts and sex drive that all adolescents face' at this age (Addlakha 2013). In the case of disabled girls, this situation gets compounded because they must also deal with their impaired bodies. In a patriarchal society that places substantial emphasis on 'feminine' attractiveness, endorses 'feminine' stereotypes and lays primacy on the ability to take care of one's bodily functions, disabled women are dealt a severe blow. Through the countless constructions, associations and representations of beauty that are all around them in their everyday lives, they internalise the notion that they must have a certain appearance to be admired and loved, particularly by men, which classifies them as 'marriage-worthy'. The premium attached to good looks corresponds directly to being able to find a good match in our system of arranged marriages. Besides, narratives of normalcy push disability into the disease narrative paradigm. Anything that differs from this perceived normalcy is considered 'abnormal', 'defective' or 'flawed'. Disabled women internalise such a differentiation from their childhood itself. Positive images of disabled women are rarely seen in the mass media which continue to perpetuate myths and stereotypes such as dependence, helplessness and so on and to project them as victims and objects of pity who need help. These representations are counterproductive in terms of the self-concept of disabled women, their families and society— in general anyone who internalises these depictions. This, in turn, stymies their opportunities to develop their capabilities and 'a damaged or distorted self-concept results' (Campling 1981).

Twenty-year-old Shaheen (who has polio in both legs, wears callipers and uses crutches) perceives the nondisabled world as 'normal' and herself as disabled in the sense of impaired. Her disability to her is a diminishing of her appearance, an absence of normalcy, of beauty, of attractiveness; an incomplete self—'there is something missing in us' ('*kuch kami hai*'), 'we are not "complete"' ('*poore nahi hain*'). This is a classic instance of internalising the labels that the nondisabled world imposes on the disabled identity. This heightened awareness of the 'lack' in her might be attributed to her young age and is perhaps the reason why she is always so conscious of how she comes across to other people. Her self-concept rests on this duality—this polarisation of her supreme self-confidence in terms of her career and her purpose in life that is driven by her work and her gauche hesitation that stems from the aesthetics of her impairment and how she perceives her body. She despairs, 'I know I can't do activities like running, or walking fast, or wearing certain kinds of clothes and saris. With my crutches, I can never look fashionable. No matter how well I dress, the difference between nondisabled women and me is inevitable.' So, Shaheen falls back on the imagined world inside her where she is not disabled, where she can dress and walk as the 'normal' do and where she can feel good that she looks as stylish as other young girls her age.

> When I see another girl, I imagine myself doing whatever she is doing. When she walks, I imagine I am walking like her. When we fall short in one thing, we make up for it in other things. When I wear a sari over my callipers, I cannot look as fashionable as normal women who wear saris. But when I see them, I think if I were well, and I wore a sari, I would look just like her. Then again, if I were to sit and pose for a photo there would be no difference, but in movement, the difference is discernible. They walk with style, and I think, if I were well (*acchhi*), I would walk just like her. In other's happiness, we can always find the happiness we are looking for ...

Finally, she succumbs to the despair that builds up in her when she realises that she can never match up, perhaps even in her imagination, when she judges or is impelled to judge herself by the aesthetic standards of the nondisabled world. 'I feel upset, "Why have I been made like this?" If He were to make one more as good as the others, what would He lose by it? But we cannot let others see us in such a depressed state.'

The feeling of inferiority in relation to nondisabled girls is exacerbated because she perceives that the nondisabled world has already rendered her an object with all the pity it can muster—a *bechaari* or unfortunate. It is interesting to counterpoint this sort of account with another kind, the account of young disabled women who dress well and with care, are acutely conscious of their appearance, and have been complimented on it often enough for it not to be such a pressing concern. This question of clothing is a recurring motif for disabled women, be it in the form of wearing a new dress on their birthday or a *chaniya-choli* for garba, which is discussed a little later in the chapter. The emphasis on clothing undercuts the widespread view held by people, including the families of disabled women, that functionality and not aesthetics should be a prime aspect of clothing for disabled people.

The other point that emerges from Shaheen's account is that the relationship between the use of prostheses by disabled women and their body image is a tenuous one. With the advancement of medical technology, claims of newer possibilities of 'rehabilitation' are welcomed by disabled people. But, the irony of the situation is that disabled women need and use it and yet are imbued with a negative sense of self; the un-aesthetic body that needs 'aid' is foregrounded. With very little attention given to the positive aspects of a person's appearance and a tendency to reduce the body to an asexual object, disabled women learn very early on that their bodies can be objects that are manipulated and controlled by others such as doctors, physiotherapists, prosthesis makers or their caregivers. If a woman loses respect for her own body and internalises the negative messages that are thrown her way, her body becomes a source of embarrassment, shame and pain. The shame is compounded and made more complex by culture laying primacy on conformity to its expressed ideals and expectations. This can subsequently lead her to believe that her body is beyond her control. A negative body image invariably leads to feelings of inferiority, worthlessness and inadequacy. Lonsdale mentions that in her reassessment of herself, the further a disabled woman perceives herself from society's standards, the more her self-concept is likely to suffer (1990). She also points out that the image of 'ideal womanhood' extends beyond the physical appearance to the traditional nurturance roles women are expected to fulfil as wives and mothers. Women who do not conform to acceptable notions of womanhood, disabled women for instance, face stigma and rejection and are deemed unfit as sexual partners and as mothers (Lonsdale 1990).

Addlakha highlights that the awareness of their differential status in terms of their bodies makes them acutely conscious of the physical appearance of the impaired limbs or their functioning. They are no longer comfortable with any display or visibility of the impaired body part (2013). They draw comparisons with their sisters at home and especially with their peers at school or in the neighbourhood, which has a deep impact on their self-concept. In fact, Thapan points out that the peer group at school is the most important group within which gender identity is validated and legitimised as the duration of school hours is long (2009).

Twenty-one-year-old Chitra, who has acute deafness and for whom hearing aids are of no use, speaks about name-calling at school where terms such as *body* (mute), *behrimoongi* and even *totdi* (stammerer) were hurled at her by people. 'Few had patience with me when I tried to express myself. Even when it was not overtly expressed, I could sense their exasperation lurking just below the surface of our conversation.' Intertwined with these aspects of physical beauty and self-esteem are notions of normality, plenitude and sexuality. The marking on the gauge of self-concept goes down on all these fronts.

Along with gender, class, caste, and sexual identity, sexuality is one among several axes of oppression. John and Nair state that sexuality must be seen not merely as signifying biological genitality, but as connoting 'a way of addressing sexual relations, their spheres of legitimacy or illegitimacy, through the institutions and practices, as well as the discourses and forms of representation, that have long been producing, framing, distributing and controlling the subject of 'sex' (cited in Menon 2007). Feminists have also considered sexuality as a domain in which women are disempowered and oppressed. At several times in the course of history, attempts and even force to constrain the sexuality and sexual agency of people and communities have been seen. Sexuality is a key aspect of people's lives and not an appendage to be tagged on once all other aspects are taken care of. Society seeks to establish, cultivate and naturalise a definition of normality and hence seeks to stigmatise as anomalous anything that is antithetical to it. Disability disrupts the stable and predictable schema of societal norms and must be contained. The disabled figure has also been equated with sexual delinquency and as inimical to the mores and values upheld by society.

Sexuality has been an area of considerable angst, exclusion and oppression for disabled women (Fine and Asch 1988; Morris 1996; Wendell 1996; Shildrick and Price 1999). There is pervasive de-sexualisation and 'rolelessness' of disabled women because of cultural ascriptions of passivity, weakness, illness or dependence on them, that is, disabled women are considered 'asexual and incapable of taking on sexual, reproductive and maternal roles' (Fine and Asch 1988). Their needs for affection, love, intimacy and having a sexual life are discounted in a culture like ours where even the discussion of sex is taboo. Sexual desire and sexuality in disabled women are not considered even as a remote possibility. Ghai states that 'the assumption that sexuality and disability are mutually exclusive denies that people with deviant bodies experience sexual desires ...' (2015). Chib foregrounds the stereotype of disabled women when she asserts that for men, disabled women can only be recipients of care, not subjects of sexual desire (2001). Chib further notes that women are seen as 'embodiments of sexuality', and having a disabled body is transgressive of the 'norms established and enforced by media stereotypes' (cited in Hans 2015). She states that disabled women 'hide behind a self-created brave front of denying that sex and their sexuality matters to them' and that a 'very important part of a woman's being—her sexual identity—is cruelly denied to a disabled woman' (2001).

The experience of being placed squarely outside the realm of possible sexual activity takes diverse forms for disabled women. The young disabled participants of this study speak about the social aspects of their growing up when they refer to 'emotional problems', 'sense of loneliness', 'suppressing my dreams and desires' and when they discuss relationships and marriage. Some of them speak about the loneliness they felt in their late teenage years and the trauma of those years when they felt buffeted on all sides by a society that refused to consider their looks as acceptable and continued to have allegiance with 'normalcy'.

In fact, I saw the greatest degree of emotionality in their subjective accounts when they were speaking about romantic relationships and their sexuality. 'Who can we go to discuss these issues?' is the refrain. Surbhi, who has low vision resulting from a skin condition that produces low melanin, mentions how her white hair, being considered ugly, fearful, 'whitewashed' and sometimes called *bhoot* (ghost) by other children (especially in case of a fight) bothered her and were a blow to her self-concept. Gradually, she started feeling depressed about the way she looked.

> My appearance used to really hurt … sometimes I used to ask my mother why I was the way I was. As I grew up, I developed more and more of an inferiority complex about my looks. I wanted to look good too and that's a very natural feeling for any teenage girl. It reflected in my behaviour in some way and I used to be really rebellious at home. I didn't know what I was doing and I wouldn't know why I was behaving like this. But I would do it because I thought it made me look better. Looks played so important a role in my life that I was forever struggling to be in tune with society, looking like one of everyone. It was a major struggle. More than my eyesight, it was that struggle that hindered my learning because everyone would dismiss me based on how I looked, ignore me or assume that I could do nothing. It was a vicious cycle. Since I had been ignored so much in my childhood I had very few friends. I felt I had to change my outlook in life because it had given me low confidence when talking to others. I started looking for someone who would pay me attention. So, at the age of 13, I had a relationship with a boy but the relationship did not last. It was very foolish of me because I didn't realise that the person was just taking advantage of me. The only good thing that came out of it was that I became more mature. I was able to cut myself off when I realised he was only fooling around with me and I outgrew the whole experience. After that, I became quite mature for my age. My friends started looking up to me for advice, which was really nice because I felt I was needed. Soon, an older cousin tried to take advantage of me sexually. I did manage to fend him off and my mechanism of understanding what happened was to write how I felt in diaries as a cathartic process. However, I continued to remain a very sensitive and emotional person with several complexes and getting affected deeply by almost everything. I was ignorant but was not aware of that. I was not very aware of myself as well. Somewhere, my disability was responsible for the mess in my life. I was still finding out things and was still having mixed feelings and hence, was very lonely overall.

The field of sexual desire for young disabled women in Gujarat is rife with contradictions and complexly embodied. College-going disabled women in Gujarat specifically have self-image issues because right from their childhoods, they have confronted dehumanising representations of themselves through social interactions. Many of the participants in this study who hail from small towns reside in special boarding schools or hostels in cities like Ahmedabad or Vadodara to pursue their college-level studies. When family members are unable to or do not visit them regularly, emotional issues and a sense of loneliness creep in. Young disabled women of this age group, who otherwise are confident and competent and moving towards building their careers, have low self-esteem and self-concept about their physical appearance as mentioned earlier. As such, traditional mores of Indian society frown upon sexual relations between men and women outside of marriage. Disabled women lack social opportunities to meet men and form a relationship. They go through emotional struggles, because as young women, they would like to have romantic relationships with boys their age, but for various reasons, stemming from disability they cannot. They see their nondisabled peers at college dating, having 'love interests' or boyfriends but realise early on that these are remote possibilities in their lives. They discover that even their male friends at college, social circle or neighbourhood are unlikely to develop a romantic interest in them because of their disability. When they are with their peer group, they have a heightened awareness of their 'non-aesthetic' and non-normative bodies. They feel trapped, as Wendell puts it, in the 'negative body' (1989). On the other hand, their disabled male friends are also not interested in them romantically or sexually. They are more interested in nondisabled women and it is also easier for them to forge such relationships. This rejection, even from disabled boys, is an additional blow to the body image and self-concept of young disabled women. In fact, the disabled women expressed that they were facing a conflict-ridden situation. On one hand, they find themselves battling with their needs for male attention, affection, love, sex and intimacy, and on the other, they are conscious of staying morally upright and doing nothing to invite salacious gossip, bring disrepute to their natal families or 'ruin their reputation' since their individual identities are closely tied to that of their families, kinship networks and communities. Thus, they regulate and police their own aspirations and desirous selves. But even as they inhabit this conflict-ridden space, they realise that what they perceived as a conflict had no basis at all because men are not romantically or physically attracted to them in the first place. The men perceive them as not being healthy, strong, appealing, beautiful or capable of caregiving. For all intents and purposes, disabled women are invisible to them. The young women, their experience of their own bodies mediated by ideological socio-cultural constructions, representations in the media, which is all-pervasive in their social environment, hesitate to make a move towards the boys because of their low self-confidence and fear of rejection or ridicule. Their diminished body image compounds the situation, leading to low sexual self-esteem. Disability scholars have also examined how the disabled body makes for a certain construction of identity (Wendell 1996; Morris 1998; Meekosha 1998). At that age, many disabled girls deliberately withdraw from the arena of sexuality by becoming social recluses and avoiding events such as college gatherings, dance parties, garba celebrations and any such function where their different bodies may be foregrounded or rendered conspicuous. They may, at most, passively watch the goings-on from the periphery as bystanders. This further seals them from social contact and they find themselves dealing with intense feelings of loneliness and isolation and what is termed by Addlakha as 'desexualised subjectivity' (2007). I was told about 'the sexual dalliance or affair' of one locomotor-impaired girl who went to a missionary college in Ahmedabad and lived in a hostel. Her counsellor and warden warned her repeatedly against such 'sexual rebellion', 'impetuous risk-taking' and of the 'undesirable consequences' that might follow from such a liaison. The manner of reportage of the sequence of events and its narrative texture became about 'boundaries' and the 'transgression of boundaries'. Reportedly, the girl paid no heed to their 'counsel' and was heard asking why she should deny herself the joy of being in such a relationship when such opportunities were not frequently likely to come her way and when it helped dispel some of the 'darkness of her loneliness'. Franco et al. state that such 'libidinal desire which is at odds with social sanctions and norms constitutes a mode of individual resistance, even if it remains at a latent level and is not expressed in action' and is a mode of self-assertion, and therefore, of agency (2007).

These sorts of life experiences are usually the reason for their acquiescence and willingness to go through several 'corrective' surgeries, painful physiotherapy and extensive rehabilitation measures at the behest of their families or elders. They hope for a better future where they will be as ordinarily 'normal' as nondisabled women and not only lead productive lives where they can shoulder their day-to-day domestic and other responsibilities but also, in some miraculous way, emerge out of the experience as nondisabled or nearly able-bodied and indeed as socially desirable and valued. Above all, such strategies seek to 'normalise' the disabled female body and elevate its feminine status. Everything must be endured to achieve this goal. No price is high enough to ensure the hegemony of the ideologies and practices for normalisation.

Navratri as a Site for the Foregrounding of Disability and
Its Contestation

In Gujarat, Navratri is an important Hindu festival where the Hindu goddess, Adi Shakti or Shakti, deemed the mother of the universe, is worshipped by her devotees as Amba mata or Ambema. The goddess with eight arms and holding multiple weapons rides a tiger and has a principal shrine to her name in north Gujarat. The nine nights of Navratri that fall sometime in September or October are a time when young and old all do the garba dance in reverence of Amba. In earlier times, the concept of '*sheri garba*' was popular, where each neighbourhood would organise its garba. As night would fall, women would themselves sing garba songs mostly addressed to Amba as they danced in a circle to the beat of a dhol around a framed picture or a symbolic pot lit up with lamps placed inside it. The dancing goes on for about four to five hours on average. Garbas are performed at any event or celebration of joy such as weddings and gatherings as a mark of merriment, celebration and revelry. They require a sense of timing, grace, speed and stamina. The ability to gracefully dance the garba is deemed a priori in Gujarat— expected, appreciated and looked at favourably in the young, especially in young women. It is an art and a craft to be perfected over time and meant to raise their attractiveness and femininity. Today, garba is a spectacle, with large-scale functions organised on party plots and clubs. It has now become a largely celebratory, almost cosmopolitan event, indulged in by young people of all faiths. In its current form, the strict religiosity of the festival has, by and large, taken on a broader cultural cosmology of community participation. It's a performance where one's heteronormative masculinity or femininity and its desirability is played out for the eyes of others.

During the nine days of the festival, girls wear new *chāniyā-choli*s (a traditional costume much like the *lehenga* of north India) and accessories such as faux silver costume jewellery (anklets, bangles, bracelets, necklaces and *maang tikka*s) while doing the garba dance. Disabled girls with visual or locomotor impairments, and among them especially those who cannot walk and therefore crawl, narrate instances of conscious or unconscious discrimination by their natal families and of being deprived of joys such as buying or getting new clothes and accessories during Navaratri. The rationale offered is that the clothes would most certainly get soiled by the act of crawling on the ground. One disabled woman with polio using callipers and crutches, mentioned that when she had expressed her desire to her mother for a new *chaniya-choli* like her sisters were wearing, was told, 'But where do you have to go wearing a *chaniya-choli*?' Disabled women are considered as not good-looking and as not needing to dress up or dress well. But, it is the iniquitous nature of their parents' behaviour vis-à-vis their sisters that is often more hurtful. 'Just because the body is impaired doesn't mean that we don't want to dress up like others,' says Tapini. She adds, 'They don't understand that we too have a heart, we may have desires (*umang*); we too may wish to wear new clothes. It is not as if parents neglect the disabled daughters at such festive times; they actually forget that we too may wish to dress up for the occasion.'

Indian families have a strong sense of cohesion, solidarity, responsibility and support among members. Mothers are the primary caregivers of disabled women. In this study, it must be said that mothers were often seen to treat disabled daughters the same as their nondisabled daughters, protecting them from discrediting experiences and identities. They were also sensitive to their feelings, which included buying new *chaniya-choli*s for the disabled daughter as well. In some cases, I observed that the mother is sympathetic towards her disabled daughter and understands her feelings, but the family's lower-income status may lead to her buying new chaniya choli and accessories for the nondisabled daughter at the exclusion of the disabled one. One mother said, 'How can we deny her sister a new chaniya choli simply because she (the disabled daughter) cannot dance? It would not be fair to her sister, would it?' Some mothers do discuss this situation with the disabled daughter. 'I asked Bela whether she would mind if this year I buy a new chaniya choli for Arti, her sister, and not for her. She would not be doing the garba anyway. Bela herself asked me to go ahead …' said Hemaben. The daughter, Bela, said,

> I was making it easy for my mother as she manages our middle-class household expenses on a tight budget. And yet, when they shopped for *chaniya-choli*s together, or when my mother was helping my sister dress up and doing her make-up, or when I saw the delight on her face when my sister was all prettily dressed up and ready to go to the garba function, I felt left out and sad. In other circumstances, she'd be dressing me up too. She would feel happy to see me look gorgeous too.

Other mothers find it uncomfortable to raise the topic or discuss not buying the *chaniya-choli* for their disabled daughter and yet others simply opt to remain silent in the hope that the daughter will understand why she has been deprived. 'Her (the mother's) silence sears my soul,' says Pooja, 'am I also not her daughter?'

In all the cases mentioned earlier, as a result of internalised ableist experiences, the young women with locomotor disabilities equated looking good in this context with the ability to walk straight and dance gracefully.

Their identities, by extension, get intertwined and associated with their bodies. It does not occur to them or they do not wish to consider that looking good may be associated with the manner in which they dress, their general personality, deportment, body language, personality, intelligence, self-confidence or attitude. 'What is the point of my personality, my academic performance at school, or my other abilities and skills if during Navaratri, I stand out in an incongruous (*vichitra*) manner and cannot participate with this community celebration?' The Navaratri celebrations, the dancing and the beauty imagery all become metaphorical of their aspirations and desires in terms of their femininity and appearance.

Young deaf women reported a different kind of experience during their participation in garba. Some mention that the unbearable decibel levels at which the music is often played by musical bands invited to the venues create problems for them, a fallout of wearing hearing aids, even leading to severe headaches. Others mention that the rapid dance movements or the sweat produced due to dancing for a prolonged time may lead to their hearing aids falling off. So, the usual recourse is to keep aside their hearing aids and try and match the dance steps and rhythm of their fellow dancers. Most mention a fair amount of success in this exercise and the support of friends, siblings, cousins, other family members or neighbours. However, a few report instances where, during the dance, they found themselves out of sync with the rest of the dancers on account of not hearing the beats, mostly during the transitions from one song to another, leading to mild laughter among onlookers, and even pejorative expressions or ridicule.

> A lady sitting and watching us laughed and said, '*Sur taal na sambhlaay enathi garbo kyaan gavaay?*' ('How can one who cannot hear the beat of the dhol—the drum—or the rhythm and tune played by the band match the garba steps?') I simply cannot forget the humiliation I felt at that moment, although I covered it up with a smile as though I'd not heard what she said.

Women with visual impairments such as low vision or blindness mostly report being protected from the garba festivities because of possible concern from their parents or families that they might collide with the dancers and hurt themselves. They mention that in their childhood, they were given more freedom to participate, often being at the centre of the circle of dancers where they danced without worry under the watchful eye of their mothers or neighbours.

> I feel really excited even today when I hear the beats of the dhol. I feel like dancing. But the dance steps of today such as the *dodhiyu* and the *popat* are intricate and complex and I cannot do these. Blind girls

find it simpler to do the traditional *be taal* (two beats or steps) and *teen taal* (three steps or beats).

Another young woman says, 'I like to dress up in all finery for garba.' But many young girls narrate the hurt they feel when their families give them hand-me-down *chaniya-cholis*, sometimes not getting any, not even second-hand ones.

Fiona Kumari Campbell writes of an 'abled imaginary' that 'relies upon the existence of an unacknowledged imagined shared community of able-bodied/minded people, held together by a common ableist homosocial world view that asserts the "preferability" of the norms of ableism' (cited in Ghai 2018). Such ableist trajectories, she states, 'erase differences in the ways humans express our emotions, use our thinking and bodies in different cultures and different situations' (Gahi 2018). Silvers discusses how society privileges 'the functional capabilities and social roles characteristic of "normal" women' to the extent that 'they become standards of womanhood against which disabled women shrink into invisibility' (1998). The idea of young disabled women in this context is the nondisabled female body and they crave it. But they can never achieve this goal and so they start perceiving themselves as lacking. Allport states that in the face of ideologies of normality, when self-worth diminishes, it leads to strained and tense social relations, a sense of puzzlement and hurt, leading to avoidance and even withdrawal from social situations (1969). This gets manifested as, what Gordon Allport calls, 'traits of victimization' such as defensiveness, passivity, shame, diminished self-esteem and sexual identity, especially when faced with debasement and diminution of the body (cited in Linton 2006). A large number of disabled women in this study mention stereotypical and dehumanising assumptions about their capabilities and oppressive prejudices of the community around them, whether it's natal families, neighbours or the broader social kinship network. Their internalisations of disabling prejudices of the able-bodied community around them, subliminal cues received from their surroundings, may result in a tendency to imagine the reactions of the nondisabled world towards their non-participation in the garba celebrations. This is seen, for instance, in Rukmini's case when she imagines what people around her at a garba venue might have thought when they saw her sitting on one side by herself. She states, 'People around must have thought, "Everybody is doing the garba. But Rukmini has this *khod khaapad* (defective body) or problem (*takleef*), so she isn't joining in." But I didn't feel upset.' The sharpness and clarity of the memory seem to show a tendency towards avoidance of the shame she perceives with respect to her body and the invalidation of disability. The profound damaging impact of disabling experiences on their selfhood and self-concept constructed and mediated through their embodiment in this specific social-cultural context are seen to be long-ranging.

Some studies in India report that families of disabled women usually fail to perceive the need to provide them with adequate emotional support and psychological care. Hans and Patri point out that the disabled girl 'ceases to exist as a person and is excluded from being recognised as a woman in the fullest sense because she does not fit in with the model of women defined by society and dear to the collective imagination' (Hans and Patri 2003). Navaratri, as it is celebrated, is embedded in multiple cultural discourses of bodily aesthetics, social imagery and embodiment and implicated in polyphonic constructions of disability. It adversely impacts the self-esteem of disabled women and highlights the de-feminisation of disabled women and, on the other hand, there prevails ignorance or lack of attention on the part of the parents about the psychosocial aspects of their personalities. It is how their families, their neighbours and others react to them that determines how their impairment results in their social exclusion. It is the discriminatory behaviour and heightened devaluation that results in a sense of being disabled, which becomes the most pervasive aspect of their identities. Years of such experiences, of the socialisation process, of internalising the reactions of others to them, the accumulated perceptions of their desirous selves to how others see them as undesirable, including during Navaratri, and of comparing themselves with the 'beauty' and 'normalcy' standards of nondisabled women result in young women acquiring a poor body image, which leads to a very low self-concept. On festive occasions, when entire families are dancing together, for a disabled woman to be unable to be part of the community merriment or dance in the fullest way, or to not be permitted by their parents to go out to garba venues may cause a great deal of emotional distress and feelings of desperation and hopelessness. Recalling these incidents brings up painful memories even years later when they have internalised and accepted the fact that culture typically denies them some traditional locations.

It is important to mention in this context that the physical body (*sthula sharira*) of disabled women and its embodiment gets embroiled with the thick religious tissue of disability as moral retribution and with their *karma phal*, or fruits of the cosmic order of *karma*, that has profound ramifications on their *sukshma sharira* (intangible body) as well. The Indian mind, which has apprehended the world since Vedic times as a weary place and human existence as a millstone around its neck, is destined to eternally harbour a philosophy of life that is ploughed through the indeterminate soil of myth, beliefs and history. This is the philosophy of *karma* that looks at an individual's life as the predetermined and immutable effect of her/his past actions in an earlier life. *Karma* holds sway through the eternal circuit of births, deaths and rebirths and offers the justification for any life at the margins (such as of the disabled) as being part of the preordained scheme of things—the morass of one's fate, and hence, hopeless (Das 2010). Hetal mentions how a 'well-meaning' neighbour, on seeing her sitting on one side in her housing colony watching the garba dance, remarked, '*Bon, karma thi kon bachi shake chhe? Tara paachla janam nu kar chhe*' ('Who can escape the cruel clutches of *karma*? You are paying off the debt of your previous birth'). What is more oppressive than the prevalence of the negative cosmologies of disability is that disabled people and their families from most faiths in India subscribe to and internalise this philosophy of *karma* with stoicism and weary resignation, sometimes imposing a debilitating sense of hopelessness and at others, with a means of succour to their embodiment.

Disabled women look at different ways of dealing with the nine nights of revelry. Only a small number mention that they sat around year after year watching others do the garba in their housing colonies or at nearby party plots. Several young women with locomotor disabilities mention that they stay away from the celebrations in their own neighbourhoods and give different reasons for doing so. Some state that they would not like to draw unsolicited attention towards themselves or foreground their disability in any way. Others stay away to save themselves from awkward questions, patronising remarks, sympathetic looks or dehumanising stares. 'They will think I am a *bichaari* and someone to be pitied. Why invite such a situation for myself? *Maare alag nathi padvu* (I do not wish to stand out among the others).'

A few participants in this study mentioned that they overcame their emotional anguish about their non-participation in the celebrations years ago and now when their siblings, cousins or friends are out dancing during Navaratri, they spend 'a normal evening' at home following their routine and bedtime. Many young women say that they spend the time when they are by themselves at home 'indulging in activities they are interested in or feel passionate about'. Some read, some paint or sketch and and engage in other creative activities or other means of recreation. A young woman said, 'I watch a film on television at a loud volume to drown out the garba music from the party plot near my house. I enjoy being on my own.' Some women make productive use of the time to deeply engage with their school or college studies. A young girl who is in a higher secondary school said,

I make myself popcorn or noodles at home and sit down to study. Since one cannot sleep in this entire din, might as well make gainful use of time for my board exams. That way, I can make some headway in my studies while the rest of my classmates are out dancing and socialising with friends or boyfriends.'

Bela says,

My body may not be beautiful like other girls my age, but my mind is sharp. God has compensated me with intelligence and a good memory. The body includes the mind too, doesn't it? So, I now focus on my college studies during the nine days of Navaratri instead of wasting time feeling vulnerable or sorry for myself.

This is in consonance with Ghai's dilemma about whether to situate herself 'as a positive mind or a negative body' (Ghai 2015).

Addlakha explains, 'Negotiations of selfhood with a disabled body may produce an alternative aesthetics with a selective focus on ability-based and moral ideals of selfhood' (2013). In this context, there is an attempt also to reconstitute the body and shift its locus to a multidimensional understanding of the body. At other times, their state of mind may stem from a very real acceptance of themselves and their disabled status. 'I am what I am,' Rukmini asserts. Immediately afterwards, follows the disclaimer: 'But I never felt upset or inadequate in any way.' It is clear that the young women who spend their time in gainful activities or in other ways during the Navaratri do so because they are not willing to be docile bodies and minds that accept received cultural representations of disability attendant with diminutive negative stereotypes. They shun self-pity and take agency and interpretive charge for their own self-representation by finding other productive or fulfilling things to do, maintaining their autonomy, thereby negotiating their feelings of self-worth and self-concept and accordingly, strategising their lives in an ability-centred manner. These may also be seen as individual acts of resistance on their part, embedded in their local contexts, which may not necessarily be part of a larger pattern but are nonetheless significant. In most cases, their aspirations and dreams focused on studies, building a good career for themselves and financial independence as a means to secure a stable future.

In select cases, I also observed the remarkable appropriation of an interstitial space or reappropriation of the garba dance during Navaratri by some disabled young women. Many of them are students at schools for the disabled, or at organisations and NGOs working in the area of disability. These organisations arrange a night or two of garba during Navaratri for the people working or studying there, including and mainly for the benefit of the disabled. Some of the young disabled women participants spoke excitedly about these celebrations. They would dress up well (or not), wear *chaniya-choli*s and faux jewellery and enjoy dancing as a community. Payal, who lives in the hostel of one such organisation away from her home in a distant town, mentioned that away from the nondisabled world's judgement of their abilities and looks, they find a way to celebrate among themselves, enjoy listening to the beats of the *dhol*, and dance in their own gratifying way at their own pace and as much as possible. 'Our teachers and seniors in the organisation encourage us to give up our shyness and associated inhibitions, our fears and apprehensions, and enjoy the moment,' she says. There are also a couple of young married disabled women in the city using wheelchairs, who do dress up and visit the party plots and enjoy being present at garba venues, participating in the merriment outside the circle of the dancers with their walking aids, crutches or wheelchairs. 'Why should we deny ourselves the joy of being present in such celebrations?' says one of them. 'Why should we depict ourselves as helpless or victims and incapable of being happily participative (*saharsh bhaag laiye*)?' said another. There is a fierce staking of their claim to full participation during the celebrations, including the assertion of 'being like the normal' in terms of participation and not impersonation of their able-bodied skills in dancing. '*Aapne navu normal banaaviye*' ('Let us create a new normal'). They show a willingness to engage in a concerted dialogue with the hegemonic able-bodied world, challenging dominant constructions of disability as *ashakt* (weak) or *daya ne patra* (pitiable), questioning the oppression of normality, opposing the normalising of their impairments, seeking to set exemplary standards for other disabled people to follow, remaining in the mainstream and positing disability aesthetics as an oppositional category of normality. Thus, what I witness is a disability cultural appropriation of the contextual culture of Navaratri leading to a changing paradigm of understanding disability and a new epistemology through shaping newer identities of disability.

The Gauri Vrat as a Site for the Foregrounding of Disability

Chakravarti mentions that the general subordination of women assumes a particularly severe form in India through the powerful instrument of religious traditions, which have shaped social practices (1993). Dube notes how, along with food and domestic or household chores, domestic rituals—the daily care of family deities are a major responsibility of women (2003). The 'rituals, worships, fasts and feasts are, in their detail, a part of the tradition of a caste' and Dube elaborates that women who play an active role in the arena of rituals gain special respect that gives them a sense of self-identity and self-esteem (2003). She adds that for most women, these practices are 'an important source of self-expression and social recognition' and are intertwined with the maintenance of family prestige. Responsibility for the preservation of traditions and control over rituals, and the task of socialisation all give women a sense of power over people and situations (Dube 2003). The Gauri Vrat or Goro as it is called is a *vrat* in Gujarat. It is 'a periodic ritual in which girls worship a certain deity standing for a certain human condition' (Gopalan 1978). It is believed that the girl who observes this *vrat* is blessed with a good husband and a happy married life. In *vrats*, women 'express their emotions of hope, rejoicing, aspirations, gratitude, and so forth, in songs. They also listen to or narrate certain traditionally circulated tales during many *vrats*.'

These tales are partly religious and partly secular in character and relate to the occasion celebrated or the deity worshipped or both. Though the *vrat* connotes vow or resolution, no such vow is taken on these occasions. There are, however, regular fasts and prayers. The ceremonial aspect of these consists of two basic elements: the ritual part and the tale-telling session. In the *Goro*, unmarried girls bathe early in the morning, dress up in all their finery and worship the goddess Gauri but no real ritual is involved. They plant some grain in a pot (*jowar*) and direct their prayers to this pot. There is no tale for the *vrat* as such. The girls who perform the *vrats* pray for a good husband. During the days of this fast, girls do not eat any cereal, vegetables, pulses, grain and salt. On the sixth day, the pots are immersed in holy river water. On the last day of the *vrat*, called *jaagran*, the girls stay up all night singing songs.

Studies in India have established that women with disabilities are often kept away even from participating in community and social occasions because of social taboos and stigma (Oniyal 2001; Ghosh 2001). Inevitably, the girls internalise these insecurities and uncertainties of their parents and families leading to a diminished sense of self-worth and tremendous loss of self-esteem (Ghai 2003). Like the socially excluding Navratri celebrations, the Gauri Vrat festival for young unmarried girls also consciously or unconsciously upholds assumptions and practices that promote the differential treatment of disabled women by re-inscribing able-bodied attitudes towards the body. The insidious manner in which ableism pervades our socio-cultural consciousness is expressed by Campbell as 'not just a matter of ignorance or negative attitudes towards disabled people', but as 'a trajectory of perfection, a deep way of thinking about bodies, wholeness and permeability' (cited in Ghai 2018). The memories of the *vrat* strike a raw nerve with many disabled women even decades later in their lives. Some disabled women mentioned how fervently their mothers and families made them observe the Gauri Vrat and other fasts in the hope of getting a good husband. 'Everything seemed to converge on my faithful observance of the ritual and how the gods would conspire to find the right match (*mooratiyo*) even for me "despite my disability". I believed wholeheartedly for years that this was true,' says

Rupal. Several disabled girls mention being marginalised in or excluded from the Gauri Vrat observances as well. In her childhood, seeing other girls dressed up to celebrate, Bhagyashree (both legs affected by polio) was upset and asked her mother why she could not join them in the festivities. When her mother explained to her that it was a futile exercise in her case (on account of her disability), Bhagyashree was anguished. 'I felt sad at that young age and understood that I was being told that no one would ever marry me with my severe disability and wondered why this (my disability) happened to me. It made me feel inferior to other girls my age.' Disabled women are in this way left out of such cultural observances and activities because of culturally legitimised representations that depict them as inadequate and expendable, reflecting asymmetric power relations within the web of their social world. Goffman says that the nature of the interaction between the stigmatised and the non-stigmatised world depends on factors such as visibility and obtrusiveness of the stigma (1963). These have an important bearing on the experiences that people with disabilities have and also their body image. Underscoring the psychosocial impact of physical disability on body image, Goffman says people with more visible physical differences are likely to have a less affirmative self-concept, and associated feelings of diminished self-worth if they have had negative experiences where society has devalued them (Goffman 1963; Mayers 1978). It is also widely accepted that a hierarchy of disabilities exist among disabled people with people with mental disabilities at the bottom and those with physically salient disabilities slightly above them. However, and significantly so, I observed that women whose disabilities are not physically salient, such as those with hearing impairment, are given greater freedom by their families to observe Goro and dance the garba. In the case of both locomotor disabilities and blindness, there is a greater avoidance on the part of parents who seem to have accepted the inevitability of their disabled daughters not making it to the marriage market even in the limited socially sanctioned options of same-impairment marriages because disabled men seem not to prefer these. Most disabled men also look at their prospective wife as being in a caregiving role and hence, reject disabled women.

Indian culture valorises both marriage and motherhood. Dube says, 'Motherhood is the highest achievement in a woman's life. Marriage is the gateway to motherhood' (2003). The legitimisation of these roles in the lives of women in India is inescapable. They 'signify good fortune and a state of bliss' (Dube 2003). Banerjee says, 'The expectations and perceptions of middle-class, higher caste, urban girls' middle-class parents have not been radically changed—marriage is still seen as the main career for women' (cited in Kapadia 2002). The emphasis on arranged marriage and the proper mechanisms and processes for the 'organisation of space and time' derive from that cultural anxiety (Dube 2003). Dube adds,

> The message that gets communicated is, however, invariably that of the immutability of the social system and that a daughter's stay in her parental home is short-lived. Moreover, not only is there something unnatural about a delay in or absence of marriage but such a situation is full of danger and risk to the reputation of the family. (2003)

Thus, the daughter is deemed a temporary member of her natal family while a son is deemed a permanent member.

Navaratri and the Gauri Vrat are contextual and symbolic systems of shared behaviour, beliefs, values, practices, customs, rituals and history in Gujarat. As mentioned earlier, the objective of the popular Gauri Vrat is to obtain a good husband. It conveys to young girls the inevitability of their leaving their natal home and family for another. Girls are socialised into believing that their lives will be substantially enhanced with marriage, and there is considerable emphasis on cultivating feminine traits such as observing fasts to acquire an ideal husband. Disabled girls grow up internalising these socialising values and norms. But find that they are deemed unsuitable for marriage as they are considered incapable of taking on sexual, reproductive and maternal roles (Fine and Asch 1988; Begum 1992; Morris 1993; Thomas 2001; Meekosha 2002; Ghai 2003) or be able to look after the marital family or do household work (Das 2019). In fact, sexuality and motherhood are distant goals for disabled girls and women. They are denied the choice to aspire to the 'goals of womanhood' due to their presumed individual incapacities (Begum 1992). As Begum states, 'We are prescribed a life of passive dependence. Our neutered sexuality, negative body-image and restricted gender roles are a direct consequence of the processes and procedures which shape the lives of women' (1992). Dhanda expresses this succinctly as 'while nondisabled women have been oppressed by the heaping of stereotypes on them, disabled women have been oppressed by exclusion from those stereotypes' of being a wife and mother (Dhanda 2008). The traditionally designated roles of wives and mothers deemed oppressive by feminists are roles they aspire to 'precisely because they are denied to them' (Addlakha 2013). Young disabled women have an overwhelming sense that 'marriage is not for us, not written in our fate and we'll never have a companion to share life with'. They are aware of all the accompanying problems of finding people to marry. Generally, disabled men also prefer to marry 'normal' or nondisabled women further devaluing them. Even educated and working disabled girls find it difficult to get life partners. So, there is oppression from both parties—the nondisabled men and disabled men (Unnati and Handicap International 2004). Tapini says with finality, 'Marriages have been difficult answers to our lives.' The girls themselves, especially those with severe disabilities, begin to understand from a very young age that they must be ready to face a life of single devalued status stemming from sexual normativity. A small number of them reported being directly or indirectly propositioned by men known to them into having sex with them. It seemed odd to them that while they were deemed unworthy for marital intimacy, they were assumed to be willing for a sexual relationship.

How do disabled women conceptualise and contest social representations, particularly the negative social messages they receive about their embodiment and sexuality, asks Addlakha and replies that they 'formulate and articulate a sense of self that straddles the slippery terrain between normative and disabled femininity' (2013). Ghosh explains, 'Disabled femininity is constructed, nurtured and contested by strategic management of the impaired body, socio-cultural pejoration of disability in general, and the pervasive normative social expectations of women' (2013). The strategy of 'passing' expressed by a few disabled respondents acquires particular significance here. Girls may try to minimise the lurch in the gait or the squint in the eyes to fit into accepted and acceptable notions of heteronormative femininity. Rather than face the disempowering and oppressive negativity of disability, they try to eclipse the material reality of their bodies and pass off as being 'normal'. This denial is what Zola calls the 'structured silence of personal bodily experiences' (cited in Ghai 2015). Shaheen exclaims, 'If I am sitting, no one will know that I am disabled. It is only when I walk that they realise I am not complete (*hum poore nahin hain*).' There are others who may completely refuse to accept their disability, or conceal it from being discovered and deny any difference. Like Navaratri, so in the case of Gauri Vrat, acts of seeking to decentre abledness and to destabilise normative cultural ideals through new narratives are seen, which uphold the right of young disabled women to redefine their physical salience and femininity for themselves on their own terms. As Bharti expresses,

In which scripture is it written that Gauri Vrat is not for us? Who determines that bodily perfection is necessary to celebrate such festivals? I may wish to observe it for my own reasons that may not necessarily have to do with finding a husband for myself. In fact, I reject the celebration. It has no business to reject me.

Disabled girls may foreground non-physical aspects of the body and demonstrating certain traits of their personality. Some of the participants in the study mentioned how their families had cloistered them initially before they crossed the thresholds of their homes to educate themselves further and later in pursuit of employment. Occupying a position in 'no woman's land' may lead disabled women to select non-traditional feminine roles by default and even personal choice. Emphasis on education and a career are ways to diminish the stigma of disability, whether it is Navaratri or the Gauri Vrat. 'Settling down' is a term often used by these young women but in the sense of getting established in a career and not in terms of marriage. They seek solace in their family structures at first but are also observed to come to terms with their disability as an indelible part of themselves, understand their own capabilities and limitations and 'help themselves' in varied ways. Examples include acquiring higher degrees in education, forming wider networks of friendships at school, college and their workplaces, seeking a community and space where they seek the support of other people, especially women, and exploring ways of dealing with the existentialist realities of their lives and seek meaning through extra-curricular or community activities, or as contributing members of society which enable them to feel empowered. With time, they begin to understand and accept that their looks and sexuality is only one aspect of their identity and that other aspects demand attention. Ghai looks at this as a resistance to normative roles and norms. As she says, 'Disabled people feel empowered as desiring subjects, capable of their re-creation, and in control not only of their bodies but also of their lives' (2015).

It is important to recognise the role of families concerning this aspect; almost all families were very encouraging when it comes to education and further studies as well as careers. Most families did not patronise or overprotect the disabled daughters; rather, they accorded them greater freedom of mobility and made them responsible for their actions.

Conclusion

The festivals of Navaratri and Gauri Vrat within the geo-specificity of Gujarat are both metaphorical of young disabled women's aspirations in Gujarat and systems of cultural practices that perpetuate the oppressive production, operation and maintenance of disablism positing a bodily based marginalisation rationale accentuating the difference of disability and shrouding young disabled women from society's collective view. Both celebrations are discriminatory, socially excluding, isolating and frequently beyond the reach of disabled women, clearly marking their 'difference' from ableist normative standards, of perceiving themselves as being non-sexual and pushing them to the precipice of emotional and psychological distress. It is in the dialogic and dynamic relation with cultural activities and practices in the immediate environment, such as Navaratri and Gauri Vrat, and the resultant ontological violence, that the subjectivities of the disabled women are constructed, shaped and mediated through their embodiment, and they comprehend the disjunct between themselves and the world around them. The invalidating cultural meanings and values associated with these festivals implicate an essential and enforced able-bodiedness and serve to enact disablism as a social and psychological process that permanently marks the ontologies, corporeality and embodiment of young disabled women. They also lead to the internalisation of ableism with a profound and long-term damaging impact on their self-concept. Disability materialises in this meeting of bodies, contextual discursive practices and accumulated cultural myths and prejudices related to physical impairment. The case of psychosocial and developmental disabilities can only be imagined in this context and merits a separate study. However, the narratives and personal accounts of young disabled women reveal how disability is complexly embodied so that even as the identities of these young women are socially constructed by the nondisabled world, the women wrestle with the everyday realism of the body, recognise the oppression inherent in social meanings ascribed to their 'disabled' bodies—such as desexualised and post-desire—struggle for their emotional well-being and rescript their embodiment and identities towards greater sexual cohesion from the perspective of strength and empowerment. They articulate their identity on their own terms, often in a form of the reconstitution of the body itself where the mind and all that it envelopes is as important as the physical apparatus, thereby reconfiguring ways of reading disability and positing alternate and transforming identities that point towards challenging of pessimistic victim-oriented narratives of disability, a mode of resistance and the formation of political consciousness among disabled young women in Gujarat. Most significantly, it leads to newer disability epistemologies.

References

Addlakha, Renu. 'Nisha: Who Would Marry Someone Like Me?' In *Unmad: Findings of a Research Study on Women's Mental and Emotional Crisis: The Voice of the Subject,* edited by Abha Bhaiya and Lynn F. Lee, 100–113. New Delhi: Jagori, 1998.

———. 'Gender, Subjectivity and Sexual Identity: How Young People with Disabilities Conceptualise the Body, Sex and Marriage in Urban India',

Occasional Paper no. 46, Centre for Women's Development Studies, New Delhi, 2007

Addlakha, Renu (ed.). *Disability Studies in India: Global Discourses, Local Realities.* London, New York, New Delhi: Routledge, 2013.

Arvind, Kavita, Shilpa Das and Tarun Deep Girdher. 'Strategic Behaviour-Change Communications Campaign for Disability Prevention and Care in Rural Areas of Gujarat. Findings from the Field'. Unpublished Report, Handicap International, Government of Gujarat and National Institute of Design, Ahmedabad, 2005.

Begum, Nasa. 'Disabled Women and the Feminist Agenda'. *Feminist Review*, 40 (Spring 1992): 70–84.

Campbell, Fiona Kumari. 'Refocusing and the Paradigm Shift: From Disability to Studies in Ableism'. In *Disability in South Asia: Knowledge and Experience*, edited by Anita Ghai, 38–57. New Delhi: Sage Publications, 2018.

Campling, Jo (ed.). *Images of Ourselves: Women with Disabilities Talking*, London: Routledge and Kegan Paul, 1981.

Chakravarti, Uma. 'Conceptualising Brahmanical Patriarchy in Early India: Gender, Caste, Class and State'. *Economic and Political Weekly*, 28, no. 14 (1993): 579–85. http://www.jstor.org/stable/4399556 (accessed on 3 March 2014).

Chib, Malini. 'Does She Take Sugar in Her Tea?' *Humanscape*, VIII, no. VI (July 2001). http://www.humanscape.org/Humanscape/new/july01/doesshe.htm (accessed on March 5, 2015).

———. *One Little Finger.* New Delhi: Sage Publications, 2011.

———. 2015. 'I Feel Normal Inside, Outside My Body Isn't!' In *Disability, Gender and the Trajectories of Power*, edited by Asha Hans, 93–112. New Delhi: Sage Publications, 2015.

Das, Shilpa. 'Hope for the Invisible Women of India: Disability, Gender and the Concepts of *Karma* and *Shakti* in the Indian *Weltanschauung*'. In *Hope against Hope: Philosophies, Cultures and Politics of Possibility and Doubt*, edited by Janet Horrigan and Ed Wiltse. Amsterdam, New York: Rodopi Press, 2010.

———. 'Gendered Disability, Stigma and Self-Concept: A Study of Disabled Women in Ahmedabad City'. Unpublished PhD Thesis, Tata Institute of Social Studies, Mumbai, 2015.

———. 'Gendered Disability in India'. In *Gender and Work: International Perspectives*, edited by Sita Vanka, Rekha Pande and Bharat Chillakuri, 66–76. Jaipur: Rawat Publishers, 2019.

Davis-Kean, P.E. and H.M. Sandler. 'A Meta-Analysis of Measures of Self-Esteem for Young Children: A Framework for Future Measures'. *Child Development*, 72 (2001): 887–906.

Dhanda, Amita. 'Sameness and Difference: Twin Track Empowerment for Women with Disabilities', *Indian Journal of Gender Studies*, 15, no. 2 (2008): 209–32.

Dube, Leela. 'Caste and Women'. In *Gender and Caste*, edited by Anupama Rao, 223–48. New Delhi: Women Unlimited and Kali for Women, 2003.

Fine, Michelle and Adrienne Asch. *Women with Disabilities: Essays in Psychology, Culture, and Politics.* Philadelphia: Temple University Press, 1988.

Franco, Fernando, Jyotsna Macwan and Suguna Ramanathan. In *Sexualities*, edited by Nivedita Menon. New Delhi: Women Unlimited and Kali for Women, 2007.

Ghai, Anita. 'Disabled Women: An Excluded Agenda of Indian Feminism', *Hypatia*, 17, no. 3 (2002): 49–66.

———. *(Dis)embodied Form: Issues of Disabled Women*. New Delhi: Shakti Books, 2003.

———. 'Disability and the Millennium Development Goals: A Missing Link', *Journal of Health Management*, 11 (2009): 279. https://www.researchgate.net/publication/278666836 (accessed on 7 December 2019).

———. *Rethinking Disability in India*. New Delhi: Routledge, 2015.

———. (ed.). *Disability in South Asia: Knowledge and Experience*. New Delhi: Sage Publications, 2018.

Ghosh, Deepshikha. '"Disability" Muddle Disables Census Staff', *Equity*, 3, no. 4 (2001): 13.

Ghosh, Nandini. '*Bhalo Meye*: Cultural Construction of Gender and Disability in Bengal'. In *Disability Studies in India: Global Discourses, Local Realities*, edited by Renu Addlakha. London, New York, New Delhi: Routledge, 2013.

———. *Impaired Bodies Gendered Lives: Everyday Realities of Disabled Women*. New Delhi: Primus Books, 2016.

———. 'Experiencing the Body: Femininity, Sexuality and Disabled Women in India'. In *Disability in South Asia: Knowledge and Experience*, edited by Anita Ghai, 101–17. New Delhi: Sage Publications, 2018.

Goffman, Erving. *Stigma: Notes on the Management of a Spoiled Identity*. New Jersey: Penguin Books, 1963.

Gopalan, V. Gopalan. 'Vrat: Ceremonial Vows of Women in Gujarat, India', *Asian Folklore Studies*, 37, no. 1 (1978): 101–29.

Hans, Asha and Annie Patri (eds). *Women, Disability and Identity*. London: Sage Publications, 2003.

Hans, Asha (ed.). *Disability, Gender and the Trajectories of Power*. New Delhi: Sage Publications, 2015.

Kapadia, Karin. 'Introduction: The Politics of Identity, Social Inequalities and Economic Growth'. In *The Violence of Development: The Politics of Identity, Gender and Social Inequalities in India*, edited by Karin Kapadia. New Delhi: Kali for Women, 2002.

Linton, Simi. 'Reassigning Meaning'. In *The Disability Studies Reader*, edited by Lennard J. Davis. New York: Routledge, 2006.

Lonsdale, Susan. *Women and Disability: The Experience of Physical Disability among Women*. London: The Macmillan Press, 1990.

Mayers, K.S. 'Sexual and Social Concerns of the Disabled: A Group-Counselling Approach', *Sexuality and Disability*, 1, no. 2 (1978): 100–11.

Mehrotra, Nilika. 'Women, Disability and Social Support in Rural Haryana', *Economic and Political Weekly*, 39, no. 52 (2004): 5640–44.

———. 'Negotiating Gender and Disability in Rural Haryana'. *Sociological Bulletin*, 55, no. 3 (2006): 406–26.

Menon, Nivedita (ed.). *Sexualities: Issues in Contemporary Indian Feminism*. New Delhi: Women Unlimited and Kali for Women, 2007.

Meekosha, Helen. 'Body Battles: Bodies Gender and Disability'. In *The Disability Reader*, edited by Tom Shakespeare, 163–80. London and New York: Cassell, 1998.

———. 'Virtual Activists? Women and the Making of Identities of Disability', *Hypatia*, 17, no. 3 (2002): 67–88.

Merleau-Ponty, Maurice. *Phenomenology of Perception*, translated by Colin Smith. London: Routledge and Kegan Paul, 1962 (1945).

Morris, Jenny. 'Feminism and Disability', *Feminist Review*, 43, no. 1 (1993): 57–70.

———. (ed.). *Encounters with Strangers: Feminism and Disability*. London: Women's Press, 1996.

———. 'Feminism, Gender and Disability', Seminar Paper, Sydney, 1998. http://www.leeds.ac.uk/disabilitystudies/archiveuk/morris/gender%20and%20disability.pdf (accessed on 18 January 2010).

Oniyal, Devyani. 'Census Miracle: How the Disabled Have Disappeared', *Equity*, 3, no. 4 (2001): 12.

Silvers, Anita. 'Disability'. In *A Companion to Feminist Philosophy*, edited by Alison Jagger and Iris Marion Young. Oxford: Blackwell, 1998.

Shildrick, Margaret and Janet Price (eds). *Feminist Theory and the Body: A Reader*. Edinburgh: Edinburgh University Press, 1999.

Slade, P.D. 'What is Body Image?' *Behaviour Research and Therapy*, 32 (1994): 497–502.

Smith, R. 'Identity Crisis', *Nursing Mirror*, 158 (1984): i–vi.

Taleporos, George and Marita P. McCabe. 'Body Image and Physical Disability: Personal Perspectives'. In *Disability and Society: A Reader*, edited by Renu Addlakha, Stuart Blume, Patrick Devlieger, Osamu Nagase and Myriam Winance. Delhi: Orient Blackswan Pvt. Ltd., 2009.

Teal, J.C. and G.T. Athelstan. 'Sexuality and Spinal-Cord Injury: Some Psychosocial Considerations', *Archives of Physical Medicine and Rehabilitation*, 56 (1975): 264–68.

Thapan, Meenakshi. *Living the Body: Embodiment, Womanhood and Identity in Contemporary India*. Los Angeles, London, New Delhi, Singapore: Sage Publications, 2009.

Thomas, Carol. 'Feminism and Disability: The Theoretical and Political Significance of the Personal and the Experiential'. In *Disability, Politics and the Struggle for Change*, edited by Len Barton, 48–58. London: David Fulton, 2001.

Unnati and Handicap International. 'Understanding Disability: Attitude and Behaviour Change for Social Inclusion', Report. Unnati, Ahmedabad, 2004.

Wendell, Susan. 'Toward a Feminist Theory of Disability', *Hypatia* 4.2, *Feminist Ethics and Medicine* (1989): 104–24, 113.

———. *The Rejected Body: Feminist Philosophical Reflections on Disability*. New York and London: Routledge, 1996.

4

(RE)DEFINING METAPHORICAL ADDRESS: FEMALE DISABILITY, EMBODIMENT AND AGENCY IN JERRY PINTO'S *EM AND THE BIG HOOM*

Smriti Verma

Alice Hall, in her discussion of the negative media reaction to the statue titled *Alison Lapper Pregnant* (2005), depicting a disabled female body, by Marc Quinn, raises the question of qualification in terms of aesthetic representation. Hall, in her book *Literature and Disability*, writes, 'the image of Lapper, an artist born without arms and with shortened legs, is sculpted in smooth, white marble' an image which becomes representative of an 'uncompromising display of a pregnant disabled body'. This 'uncompromising' quality of the statue is mirrored in the reaction to the statue, which 'provoked uproar in the British media' and was seen as 'political correctness gone mad' (Hall 2016, 44). Another critic, Millett-Gallant, saw the statue as an 'anti-monument': its very portraiture was rooted in challenging and hence subverting the conventional, whole, able, heroic bodies of public monuments and memorials by giving spatial significance to one that opposed the norm. The subversion could further create a 'disability aesthetics' which could aid the 'rethinking and re-reading (of) social settings, cultural representations, critical theories and normalising discourses' (Hall 2016, 44), by presenting an alternative representation of a body worthy of occupying public space: Marc Quinn himself saw Lapper as a subject for representing 'a different kind of heroism' ('Alison Lapper'). To understand this process of subversion in the literary form, I turn to the genre of the novel, specifically Jerry Pinto's *Em and the Big Hoom*.

The form of the novel, signified through its appeal in the domain of popular culture, has more or less come to symbolise the bridge that ties social concerns with aesthetic confrontation. Not only has the novel form heralded aesthetic value in mass culture but allowed the same to become an object of public approval or disapproval through the rate of its success in the market. In doing so, the expression of the majoritarian 'norm' in the novel occurs both as a cause and a consequence—the norm informs the 'aesthetic popular'[1] and the aesthetic popular informs the norm. Such a mutual relation leads to the novel, intentionally or unintentionally, reproducing what Lennard Davis terms 'the semiologically normative signs surrounding the reader' (2006, 11), wherein the average becomes the defining element of the signs whose identification permits the readers to 'read'. Reading, hence, symbolises the act of recognising normativity in a form where the ab-normative occurs only as a functionary to access the former. In such a theorisation, reading the ab-normative in the literary mode is a practice ridden with cultural meaning, whose exploration is central to imploding the very category of the aesthetic popular.

The sense of marginalisation attributed to the feminine disabled body separates it from the domain of the aesthetic popular—its variance from the normative not only symbolises its significance in raising issues of aesthetic merit but also creating an implosion of the normative. The statue, as a signifier of the same, establishes an avenue for the investigation of the category of aesthetic value by occupying the space of the normative. When the 'other' replaces the norm as the centre of expression, the very category of representation and its method of meaning-making is opened up to scrutiny. Similarly, the subjective form of the literary narrative in cultural discourse allows a deeper investigation of the marginalised subject through the very use of the descriptive and the metaphorical—the two forms of address, hence, empower the reconfiguration and vindication of the space occupied by the marginalised other in literary narratives. Looking into the same perhaps enables us to formulate an answer to Hall's central question concerning the Alison Lapper statue: 'What constitutes aesthetic value?' (2012, 1).

This chapter takes Hall's discussion vis-à-vis the Alison Lapper statue as a point of departure to ground the depiction of female disabled subjects in socio-cultural representation by exploring the same through the lens of Jerry Pinto's *Em and the Big Hoom*. This reworking will not only be in their role as subjects which disrupt the cultural normative but also as subjects of aesthetic representation which signify wider unease and anxiety about the entry of personal narratives of disabled bodies into the cultural public space.

Pinto's *Em and the Big Hoom*, published in 2012, qualifies as a literary form determining the aesthetic through its international critical acclaim. In doing so, the text relegates the centrality of narrative preoccupation to the figure of Em or Imelda Mendes—the mentally disabled mother of the narrator, whose spatial positioning in the narrative creates a vital foray into the field of feminist disability literature, the instrument of metaphorical address and complex disability embodiment, and linking the two to move beyond simply employing disability for what David

Mitchell and Sharon Snyder termed as 'narrative prosthesis' (2013) in the literary form. This chapter explores the same in the aforementioned areas to draw a connection between a feminist disabled enquiry of the text and its potential for expression in the form of the metaphor, which allows the disabled figure to unpack its trauma through creative meaning-making potentialities and express its agency or ability to action in terms of Tobin Siebers' theory of complex embodiment. The chapter formulates a clear correlation between the two through the novel, whose literary mode sanctions the female-gendered subject to access the nuance of the embodied self by employing the metaphor as an area of creative, revelatory potential.

Female Disability, Motherhood and the Family

Rosemarie Garland-Thomson, in her work 'Integrating Disability, Transforming Feminist Theory', invokes the integration of disability studies in the larger project of feminist theory to produce a feminist disability enterprise that not only investigates 'how culture saturates the particularities of bodies with meaning' (Garland-Thomson 2013, 335) but also introduces the ability/disability binary as a socially constructed category in the sphere of gender. In doing so, one can say that the very focus of her project inculcates not only an interdisciplinarity between the two fields but a sociological examination that probes the constructed-ness that lies at the heart of the two categories. This intersectionality generates a space for the erosion of gender as a monolithic structure, wherein disability as an identity marker disrupts what she calls 'the unity of the category "woman"' (Garland-Thomson 2013, 335). It is this fragmentation of a unified perspective that will further construct a space for an enquiry that is collaborative and by extension, inclusive.

Em and the Big Hoom examines this junction of gender and mental disability through the figure of Em, whose bipolar disorder renders her vulnerable to episodes of mania, depression and suicidal tendencies. Her manic-depressive state attempts to take up 'every inch of her' (Pinto 2012, 62), a state of being wherein her mental faculties are not only beyond the control of her agency but beyond the bounds of what may be defined sociologically as sanity. Her mental disability, hence, renders her in the space of the non-normal, wherein her gendered experiences as a female and as a mother often overlap and coincide with her experiences as a mentally disabled person. Her disability is rendered metaphorically in the narrative through the use of analogies—she describes her bipolar disorder as 'a tap of black drip filling her up' (17) which opened at the birth of the narrator, her son. In doing so, the narrative converges Em's identity as a female, as a mother and as a mentally disabled person, thus diversifying and complicating the identity markers that define her.

Within the space of the text, Em's figure comes to represent the intersection of disability and feminist studies in a literary idiom and allows an investigation of the degrees to which Em's disability defines her position within the unit of the family, within the larger narrative of motherhood and the overarching framework of ability and able-bodiedness. Pinto, through the figure of Em, fashions a merging of the two disciplines and creates an intersectional politics wherein societal labels are examined in conjunction with each other.

In doing so, motherhood emerges as the central area of contention in the novel, wherein Em's position and abilities as a disabled mother are constantly scrutinised by the narrator's—her son's—nondisabled male gaze and the multiple facets of the same. The notion of motherhood is intrinsically tied to Em's relation to her sexuality, wherein the non-linear narrative moves from her proclaiming that the Big Hoom—her husband—was always tempting her 'to sin' to earlier in their relationship when she wished to not engage in the act since she was 'not much interested in the whole business of copulation' (154). The very first opening scene of the novel begins interestingly with a discussion concerning abortion between Em, her daughter Susan, and her son. It is in the purview of this discussion that Em casually remarks of the 'twenty-six' she had to give away, an offhanded acknowledgement of the 26 times she found herself pregnant and proceeded to jump from a set of six stairs five times 'to shake those little mites from their moorings' (6). The rather comical scene, however, is recalled near the end of the novel, wherein the narrator thinks of the guilt that may have occupied Em's conscience for using contraceptives, a guilt which perhaps intersected with her desire to not be a mother.

Motherhood, in the novel, is painted as an alien, foreign state of being, a landscape which Em struggles in traversing due to her mental disability. One can perhaps say that motherhood itself as a disabling condition for the female, renders Em doubly oppressed; however, to say the same would be to cement the passivity and narrative of victimhood underpinning what Ana Bê terms as 'additive analysis' (Bê 2012, 371) of intersectional marginalisation, rather than relocating the same. Em employs the term *mudd-dha* as a form of inflecting 'all the rage and contempt she felt for it (motherhood)' (Pinto 2012, 51). Her fractured relationship with motherhood is emblematic in the relationship she shares with her children, wherein numerous times, she views her disability as a marker of her incapability to be a mother. The text gives various examples of the same, the significant one being when she takes her son for a walk as an infant and begins hearing voices, because of which commotion persists and a crowd gathers around her, concluding that she is the kidnapper of the child. The incident can be read as a larger metaphor wherein Em, as a married woman, is taken hostage by the very notion of motherhood that is supposed to drive the unit of the family forward. Her position as a stable person is often doubted in the larger overarching structure of motherhood, wherein her allegiance to her earlier family is seen as an insult, as an abnormality to her present family who further define these instances in the shadow of her mental disability. In one instance, she drains her and her husband's savings account to give the money to her mother. Not only is her action seen as 'breaking the faith' (175) of motherhood, but also an action which she is not in control of. Mental disability, then, becomes a passage for excusing agency and relocating it in a disability which is seen as governing every action of the mentally disabled female subject.

Disability, hence, invades the structure of the family and disrupts the middle-class nuclear unit into one that deviates from the normative. The narrator struggles with the notion of a family since his experience contests the larger cultural connotations of what a family stands for: 'I didn't know what we were as a family,' he states (9). The same, perhaps, can be seen as an indicator to look at the way the very affliction of disability figuratively disables the systemic functioning of the family unit. One occurs as an affect reaction of the other. The novel elaborates further that the more Em is relegated to the state of incapability, the more the father is seen as the one who could be relied upon: 'This was one of my ways of dividing up the world. My mother: incapable. My father: capable' (90). In doing so, the text reinforces the incapability of the disabled, whose inability is always defined in opposition to ability. However, such a simplistic reading would be to ignore the space allowed by the text for further reflection, where the very notion of capability is viewed in conjunction with motherhood—a socially imposed role demanded of women, the shirking of which does not immediately locate Em in an idiom of non-capability but forges a path for the opening up of alternative avenues and definitions of the term. The text can be seen as relocating the very act of parenting from the figure of the responsible, subservient mother of the domestic space to a space in transition, wherein equal roles, or perhaps inverse roles, can be accorded to the father and the mother, wherein the discourse of motherhood can explore newer realms of parenting that occur in response to the ab-normative. This is perhaps made possible only due to the convergence of feminist and disability studies in reading the text.

However, the intermittent fear of having the same disability as his mother guides much of the anxiety of the narratorial figure. He weighs his pain and suffering in comparison to his mother's, declaring his despair to be puny in front of hers. The anxiety can be seen corresponding with the larger public anxiety at Marc Quinn's *Alison Lapper Pregnant*, referenced earlier, wherein the signifier of pregnancy can be seen as the disabled passing on their disability. Halfway through the novel, the narrator's father is recalled as telling his children to 'fight your genes' (78) and to maintain their sanity through work and learning, thus again cementing the father figure as the 'sensible' one in the narrative. To be sane and sensible is to continue to fight the feeling of oncoming madness, a term Em uses to describe her condition. In one instance, the narrator visits a mental hospital on a college trip, when, after witnessing the state of the patients, he says, 'It occurred to me then that the mad in India are not the mentally ill, they are, simply, mad … they have no other identity' (196). The identity of the mentally ill as a medical category is hence chipped away by inculcating sameness— all the patients are shaved, given the same clothes, and subjected to controversial electroconvulsive therapy (ECT). Sameness becomes the bridge of transitioning from being mentally ill to becoming mad, a social idiom, separate from the medicality of the former. Therapy, then, assembles a state of passive normality, normality which both defines the bounds of deviation and consolidates itself. Em's experience with ECT disrupts her collective memory, creating a fissure of passivity since the overwhelming pain of the shocks negates her active sense of agency— she comes back quieter, disoriented, unaware. The reaction is much the same as her reaction to her medication wherein she talks about how she lost her ability to concentrate and read: 'The pills took that away from me' (99). The irony of the statement subtly hides a deeper fissure in understanding mental disability and ability as socially manufactured states of being that prioritise certain behavioural traits over others and employ medication as an avenue for systematically ingraining the same.

Complex Embodiment: The Medical and the Social

Garland-Thomson traces the links of similarity between disabled and female bodies by drawing parallels in the performance of both, parallels visible in the analogous negative labels attributed to the two—both are seen as inept, dependent and incompetent in the larger cultural set-up, 'both are excluded from full participation in public as well as economic life, both are defined in opposition to a norm that is assumed to possess natural physical superiority' (Garland-Thomson 1997, 19). Therefore, to be male is to be essential, and to be essential is to be normative. The female body, hence, signifies the non-male state of being or by extension, the non-essential, which calls to mind Freud's delineation of the female child's psychosexual development in terms of castration and what he termed as 'penis envy'—a developmental state that signified his bias in placing the penis at the centre of all gendered experience. The state of being female, hence, is defined in deformity. Garland-Thomson further states that feminist theorists have argued that 'female embodiment is a disabling condition in sexist culture' (Garland-Thomson 2013, 337) wherein to be female is to be in a state of struggle.

The centrality of the body emerges as the common, collaborative factor between gender and disability studies where the relationship between the body and its larger environment forms and informs the relation of the self to society. The instability ascribed by larger societies to the category of the disabled, hence, creates a mental distance from the embodied self by locating the primary flaw in the bodies of the disabled rather than in the social systems surrounding them. Hence, the body becomes representative, definitive in cultural experience; at the same time, the sense of inferiority drives the self away from the body that bears the mark of the non-normal or the abnormal.

In *Em and the Big Hoom*, the narrator seeks to repetitively answer and wonder where his mother's disorder came from, and despite the presence of multiple potential explanations, no unified theory is drawn from them. Perhaps the answer then lies in the clues drawn from Em's life experiences. The novel locates her very origin in an idiom of loss— the chaotic movement of her family from Rangoon to Goa and then to Bombay when the Japanese began bombing Burma during the Second World War is shown not only as formative but perhaps as an early experience of loss where the jettisoning of her family's piano off the boat is a metaphor for expressing a farewell to their earlier way of life. What followed were 'years of deprivation' (Pinto 34), and large-scale experiences of 'migration, displacement and the loss of a home when she was still a girl' (128).

Consequently, Em's trajectory was charted by her mother, who instructed her to refuse to go to college when asked by her father, to become a school teacher, a student in typewriting and shorthand, and subsequently earn a steady salary for the family. Her role as the sole earner meant her paycheque went to her mother, a habit Em struggles with post-marriage as well when her husband expects her paycheque to go towards their family. These incidents within the narrative solidify the lack of decision-making accorded to the middle-class female, whose sense of belonging is separated from the individual's agential power. Em, hence, was forced into jobs as she was pressurised to marry the man she was dating, taking the onus of agency from her subjective self to larger social formations. She ultimately has to resign from her job due to her mental disability, thus dislocating and fragmenting her sense of selfhood, which has till now been defined by her ability to earn and is now socially expected to be located in her ability to bring up her children. The conflation of the lack of agency accorded to the feminine subject in a patriarchal set-up and the disabled in an ableist set-up is signified in Em, allowing us to read the two categories in a correlative manner. These also fixate Em in a state of what Tobin Seibers termed as 'complex embodiment' (2013) where the markers of her social identity as a disabled woman and mother coincide with the part of her identity which she locates in the body, in the corporeal roots of her disability.

Siebers's idea of complex embodiment blurs between what may be called as 'competing models of disability' (2013, 290). He differentiates between the medical model, which locates disability in the individual body or an idiom of corporeality, and the social model which relocates the biological underpinnings of disability by 'defining disability relative to the social and built environment, arguing that disabling environments produce disability in bodies and require interventions at the level of social justice' (290). He proposes the theory of complex embodiment as embodiment which lies at the intersection of the two—where the sense of being disabled lies not only in the self but also in the surrounding environments. It is this sense of disability which builds, according to Siebers, a form of 'human variation' where the engagement between the body and larger social mechanisms is rendered mutually reciprocal. 'Complex embodiment theorizes the body and its representations as mutually transformative,' he says to give expression to a theory of the disabled body which is both centred in its corporeality but also takes meaning from its larger performative expression (2013).

Em's sense of self locates itself in this intersectional embodiment. The unpredictability of her disability enables her embodied self to shift from a sense of normalcy to one of depression to one of mania. It is this ambivalent existence that commands her sense of being and movement, wherein the non-linear movement of the novel can be seen as a mirror of her transforming, ever-changing bipolar disorder. Pinto gives the pain that arises out of such instability a physical dimension in parts of the narrative, a pain which renders her invalid, rigid, 'gulping for air, swallowing sobs, pain that will not let up' (Pinto 61). The frequent references to 'madness' in the text as Em's state of being as well as of other mentally disabled subjects root the discussion to the way the category itself is constructed and disrupted by those who employ it. This is a construction that occurs at the level of the social, the medical as well as the legal, but also attempts to subsume these labels under a category which Hayley C. Stefan calls 'inchoate and amorphous' one where 'the mad individual dismisses a hierarchy of knowledges in which biomedical research speaks for or over lived experiential knowledge'.

Madness becomes a distrust of 'clinical language', but is at the same time a process of self-naming for Em to signify her distinctive embodied experience.

The text, thus, not only interrogates motherhood in a state of disability, but also the position of the disabled female herself whose body 'as a living entity, both vital and chaotic' (Siebers 290) finds itself at a crossroads which corresponds with each other to give the disabled agency and control over their sense of being through the creative probabilities inherent in metaphorical address. Language, as the root of metaphor, is grounded in its social contexts and in the social role it performs in the manner of communication. The possibilities of metaphor, discussed in detail in the next section, create a space for the complexly embodied experience whose very nuance allows Em to build a space of examination and discussion between her corporeal mental disability and between the larger social systems and methods of sociality where language locates itself.

Metaphorical Address and Creative Agency

The metaphor form in literary narratives aids the construction of Davis's characterisation of the novel, wherein 'signs' become symbolic of analogies that use the metaphor form to both pack and unpack cultural meaning. Its function in a literary narrative as a form of indirect appraisal is employed by Mitchell and Snyder in their conception of narrative prosthesis, explained through its functionary elements:

> Our thesis centers not simply upon the fact that people with disabilities have been the object of representational treatments, but rather that their function in literary discourse is primarily twofold: disability pervades literary narrative, first, as a stock feature of characterization and, second, as an opportunistic metaphorical device. We term this perpetual discursive dependency upon disability *narrative prosthesis.* (Mitchell and Snyder 2013, 222)

The concept, hence, attempts to root the representational value accorded to disability in literary narratives, wherein the category of disability carries a weight of meaning, whose employment in a plot of any open-ended textual narrative is dependent upon its use as a symbol. The cultural signifiers of disability thus shape it to 'represent any potent symbolic site of literary investment' (Mitchell and Snyder 224). Experience and narrative, as dynamic aspects of literary discourse, are brought together in the metaphor form where the former is expressed in the latter. The use of the corporeal body as a metaphor emerges as exemplifying a richer materiality in the literary mode by lending the very solidity lacking in abstract literary narratives. The disabled body thus harnesses specific ideologies through its materiality as a metaphor and delineates a sense of metaphorical collapse in literary text. It is the latter which is termed as opportunistic by the two critics, wherein the metaphor form in a disability narrative is seen simply as a representational category that looks at larger symbolic realities. Clare Barker, in her text *Postcolonial Fiction and Disability*, sees this as the identification of a 'paradoxical impetus' lying at the intersection of 'the transgressive possibilities of disability representation and the identity politics of disability itself' (Barker 2012, 18). Disability, hence, is reduced to a purveyor of limited deterministic ideals, where the very materiality of metaphor in Mitchell and Snyder's theorisation allows it to hold what Barker terms as 'representational sway ... shown to function, jointly in and through language, to impinge on bodies and cultures both within and outside texts' (19), and hence contribute to the very perpetuation of the oppression it seeks to challenge.

Barker, however, challenges what she sees as a simplistic reading, seeing it as a prognosis that 'homogenizes disability representation under the banner of a "problem" and effectively sentences disabled people to a future of misrepresentation' (19). Her project, then, is identified as a nuanced, complex outlook towards disability narratives and their use of metaphor, in which she sees postcolonial fiction as a space of refraction, as stories which are 'flexible in their narrative strategies, empathetic towards their disabled characters, and explore disability as a matter-of-fact and quotidian aspect of complex sociocultural formations' (20). In doing so, she sees disability representation through the instrument of metaphor as both capable of holding allegorical meaning while being sufficiently politicised—it may be 'at once, allegorical and materially grounded, symbolic and politicised' (20), and hence have the ability of being apprehended creatively, numerously and creating a sense of polyphony. The approach, then, attempts to understand metaphor beyond its tool as a narrative device or one of textual analysis in the purview of disability and postcolonial literature:

> It is equally the case that metaphors may be sensitively employed within progressive political narratives. Metaphor can enhance awareness that disability is a complex, resonant human condition and is frequently used to establish empathetic connections between characters, communities and readers. (Barker 20)

Similarly, Alice Hall, in her book *Literature and Disability*, looks at the correlation between disability, metaphor and literary analysis through a number of critics, each of which, while agreeing to the significance of narrative prosthesis, see its centrality in literary study as 'damaging in the sense that it risks limiting the ways in which literature is discussed' (Hall 2016, 38). She cites Michael Bérubé, who says that being asked to reject and/or read disability metaphors through a lens of ambivalence and figurativeness, seems 'counterintuitive' and even 'incompatible with the enterprise of professional literary study' (38). She further cites Stuart Murray, who articulates the reductivity inherent in the idea of narrative prosthesis since 'it can lead scholars to overlook the rich variety of literary representations of disability and the creative uses of metaphor that exist alongside material concerns in cultural texts' (38). In such a reading, the metaphor form can be stressed as embedded with spatial and literary value in language and narrative structures, which are formed and informed by the social consequences it holds for questions of cultural discourse.

Drawing upon the aforementioned theoretical frameworks, I will similarly attempt to argue that Pinto's *Em and the Big Hoom*, in its employment of metaphor as a literary device by the titular character Em, actively departs from using the form for the purposes of opportunistic disruptive collapse, or for signifying the 'other' as opposed to the norm. Metaphors, in the text, become tools of social expression and performativity, equipping the female disabled subject with the ability to recuperate her trauma by lending the subject the agency to express in alternative linguistic codes.

The pervasive embeddedness of metaphor in language is investigated by Lakoff and Johnson, who see the metaphor form not as a matter of literary flourish and rhetorical excess, but as one that exists fundamentally in the experiential and the conceptual. In their paper 'Conceptual Metaphor in Everyday Language', they argue that concepts are central to everyday experience, and structure 'what we perceive, how we get around in the world, and how we relate to other people' (Lakoff and Johnson 1980, 454). They further go on to employ a variety of linguistic evidence and codes to prove the metaphorical reality of everyday conceptual and cognitive systems, thus concluding that experience, thought and being become very much 'a matter of metaphor' (454). Their conceptualisation of novel metaphors as those which make experiences coherent and sensible by describing one in terms of another is especially relevant since it allows us to locate the usage of metaphors in *Em and the Big Hoom* in a framework of coherence, of communicating that which cannot be articulated by employing 'entailments', which enable reality to translate through language. They establish the flow of metaphorical structure and its workings through three steps:

> (1) Metaphors have entailments through which they highlight and make coherent certain aspects of our experience. (2) A given metaphor may be the only way to ... organize coherently exactly those aspects of our experiences. (3) Through its entailments, a metaphor may be a guide for future action. Such actions will, of course, fit the metaphor ... metaphors, therefore, can be like self-fulfilling prophecies. (Lakoff and Johnson 1980, 484)

Hence, metaphorical forms not only 'provide ways of understanding one kind of experience in terms of another kind of experience' (Lakoff and Johnson 486), but produce an approximation of traumatic, inarticulate experience by giving it avenues of expression.

The very first chapter in the text renders Em's disability to the reader through a metaphor, expressed through the voice of the character herself, which stresses the sense of agency underlying the use of the analogy. Em's description of her manic-depressive disorder through analogies is central to a positive agential reading of the text: she describes her disability as 'a tap somewhere' (Pinto 2012, 11), and as 'black drip filling her up' (17), and herself as 'a standing red pen' (73) and 'a book with a bad binding' (100). Her manic-depressive attacks often involve her free-associating with language:

> Because the sky is so high and the crow shat in your left eye. I could tell you a lie but I don't see why. The world is a game and the game is a tie. The tie is around your neck and they'll string you high. (Pinto 2012, 137)

Elsewhere in the text, the narrator employs the metaphor form to represent his relationship with the mother. However, his use occurs in stark contrast to the mother's: their voices are differentiated not only through their subject positions but also their lived experiences. The narrator employs extended similes to talk of his unstable relationship with his mother as one wherein an idyllic experience is interrupted by the mother stepping 'into a patch of quicksand' (59). At another point in the text, he describes his mother as residing in a tower which personifies madness—while he himself is a 'tourist' of the same, his mother is a resident. The metaphor hence accumulates an inflection of outsider subjectivity, where the narrator curates his own subjectivity as external to the mother's and her world. In doing so, his metaphors symbolise what Amy Vidali, in her paper 'Seeing What We Know', labels as 'subtle references' to 'normal kinds of experiences' which exclude disabled bodies and their lived experience (2010, 36).

Barker sees the metaphor form as capable of holding prolific realities, each of which, diverse and creative, challenge the singularity of what she termed as a '"prosthetic" reading of texts' (2012, 21), and metaphorical reading as a way of diversifying 'the range of critical reading practices' and 'undoing the seeming hegemony of a prosthetic representation' (21), each of which view material metaphors beyond their face value assigned by Mitchell and Snyder, and access alternative methods of reading and re-recognising positive, creative disability narratives analysed by multiple critical frameworks. She further incorporates Vidali's argument, of disability metaphors being deeply embedded in our language structures that cannot simply be rooted out through a 'policing of language' (Barker 20), which sees the metaphor form as employing signification for its own symbolic ends rather than for the purposes of meaning-making.

In her paper, Vidali brings in Beth Ferri and Vivian May, who further write that the onus of agency of the disabled community lies in reordering and redeploying metaphors 'in ironic and agential ways, that disrupt the equation between disability and social death' (2010, 47). The same, when applied to the text at hand gives us two varying experiences: while Em employs metaphors brimming with creativity and flow to signify her condition, her son employs metaphors as reflections of death, madness, entrapment, each becoming a terminal movement away from the possibilities of language as opposed to towards it. The impact of both on the disabled person's subjectivity is hence an important aspect to consider and to conclude that metaphors, in the case of disability, should seek to disrupt and denaturalise that which is accepted by all as normative. Only the latter can give the disabled the possibility to exert more control over both their lived experience and its expression in language. It is this dialogue which Vidali sees as 'the resistance to tidy theories and engagement with the ambiguity that lies at the heart of disability, of language, and of knowing' (51).

The point of departure, then, from a simplistic reading, is one that actively engages and elucidates the metaphor form in 'diverse and creative ways' for the disabled subject (20).

> It is through developing the analytical tools to read for disability in material terms—rather than accepting literature's prosthetic analogies at face value—that we can access the most positive disability narratives that are present in fiction that suggest alternative, enabling trajectories for disability in postcolonial cultural locations. (Barker 21)

The mother's metaphors, hence, can be similarly seen as employing disability metaphors not for the purpose of packing meaning for opportunistic symbolic use, but to unpack the very reading of experience itself. The metaphor form thus formulates a newer approach wherein the text is empowered to reveal experience, as opposed to concealing it, and as a result accord brimming possibilities of creative agency to the female disabled subject and a text featuring the latter as the central character. Em's agency is rooted in her play with language and the hermeneutic potentiality of disability metaphors. Each signifies a mode of agential articulation—whether she describes herself as a 'standing red pen' or a 'book with a bad binding' (Pinto 2012, 73, 100) in both situations it is her voice that is representing her living of reality—more vivid perhaps, in the numerous scribbles she does all over her books and her letters. These metaphors go on to become a marker of what Ato Quayson terms as 'aesthetic nervousness' in the text, where they allow a reforging of experiences and relationships both within the levels of the text, between the characters themselves, as well as beyond it, in the relationship of the reader with the literary text. This can be conceptualised as a relationship which both challenges and realigns the reader's identification and engagement with the norms of reality.

The first section of this chapter dealt with the systems of oppression Em went through both covertly and overtly, where the possibilities of agential action were taken away through the institution of the family and of medical science. However, as discussed, its recuperation takes place in the form of the metaphor. Creative metaphors, hence, open up the space of interpretative chaos and allow the self a creative medium, an act rendered perhaps more vitally significant when employed by Em. Metaphors mould a bridge between the individual self to the social, and Em countlessly performs the self in a social idiom by employing metaphors to express her individual experience. This is an experience which remains abstract and separate from the sphere of communication until an attempt is made to manifest it in language. Language begets creativity, and creativity begets agency. In doing so, the text attempts to explore the social conception of Em as a manic-depressive patient, belonging in an ambivalent state of being where the self constantly flits from states of ability to states of disability, in the form of the metaphor itself. In its function of social performativity, the metaphor form can be seen as mirroring Em's nuanced sense of complex embodiment (Siebers) and an avenue of expression for the same, where disability, both as a materially embodied experience as well as a metaphoric resonance, gain space and value. Mental disability, from a corporeal and medical reality, is deeply connected to its social living for Em, who uses the metaphor form to build a channel that connects the former to the latter.

Conclusion

As a social and aesthetic instrument, the novel vis-à-vis its representation of disability attempts to 'short-circuit' what Ato Quayson terms as the 'dominant protocols of representation within the literary text' (2007, 32). In his text *Aesthetic Nervousness: Disability and the Crisis of Representation*, he locates the presence of disability to a pervasive crisis in narratorial function wherein its very representation is played out in a disruptive, disturbed framework. This disruptiveness is visible across the 'levels of the text' and signifies an aesthetic departure grounded in uneasiness and anxiety of narrative. The primary level involves interactions between a disabled and nondisabled character(s), the secondary focuses on 'the disposition of symbols and motifs, the overall narrative or dramatic perspective, the constitution and reversals of plot structure' (32) and finally the relationship between the reader and text, influenced by the presence of aesthetic nervousness. Pinto's *Em and the Big Hoom* can be seen as corresponding to these levels of rhetoric that reformulate an experience that is usually viewed in stereotypes. Em's interactions with her family members, her usage of metaphors, and finally, the reader's apprehension of these elements signify the three levels on which aesthetic nervousness functions in the text.

However, Barker, in challenging a prosthetic reading of narrative, sees Quayson's formulation as primarily a textual device which may see disability metaphors as signifying symbolic meaning, unease and apprehension at the level of aesthetics, rather than as an 'integral aspect of a human narrative' which is built on empathy (Barker 20). *Em and the Big Hoom*, in using the genre of the novel, allows a rescue of the passive, traumatised, female disabled subject by employing linguistic codes and metaphors to transition trauma from passivity into an idiom of revelatory action, creating empathetic spaces of understanding. In doing so, the text neither roots disability in its socio-cultural understanding, nor the medical one, but generates an intricate polyphony out of the nuanced interaction of the two.

The figure of the disabled woman, rendered in portraiture in Marc Quinn's statue, is perhaps allowed not only to speak but also to play with creativity in the form of the novel. While *Alison Lapper Pregnant*, in its challenging of popular aesthetic norms, remained limited to a muted subversion and protest, Jerry Pinto in *Em and the Big Hoom* is able to create a greater space for contention by giving vocalisation to the figure of the disabled woman. It is here where the degree of rescue becomes vital, and the form of the novel central in challenging the norm more fully and with a wider impact. Em speaks, renders her thoughts in language, plays with their metaphorical power, and ultimately, builds bridges of understanding between herself and those who do not understand her. Her attempts, hence, subvert what Ana Bê terms as the constructionist nature of our environments (Bê 2012, 371).

While writing about Susan Wendell's work in the field of feminist disability theory, Bê theorises that not only are environments definitive of its most normative participants—which further define the realm of power dynamics—but environments themselves are constructed to fit this power play, the central actor being a 'young adult, nondisabled, male paradigm of humanity' (Bê 2012, 368). A redefining of environmental markers requires an investigation not only of the social sphere but also of the corporeal body as rooted in Siebers and a proliferation of internal diversities that mirror the hermeneutic chaotic realities of metaphorical address. It is in the proliferation of meaning, as seen in Garland-Thomson's ideation of feminisms as opposed to the unity of the category woman, wherein agency can be restored to the ab-normal marginalised figure. A similar proliferation in the internal diversity of disability can aid in the formation of a correlation between agency and creative expression, rendered in the literary mode.

Note

1   The term attempts to conflate the defining characteristics of the literary novel form by bringing together its aesthetic merit and its popular connotations as a signifier as well as determinant of larger cultural value.

References

'Alison Lapper 2000–2012'. *Marcquinn.com.* marcquinn.com/artworks/alison-lapper.

Barker, Clare. *Postcolonial Fiction and Disability: Exceptional Children, Metaphor and Materiality.* London and New York: Palgrave Macmillian, 2012.

Bê, Ana. 'Feminism and Disability: A Cartography of Multiplicity'. In *Routledge Handbook of Disability Studies,* edited by Nick Watson, Alan Roulstone and Carol Thomas, 363–75. London and New York: Routledge, 2012.

Barker, Clare. *Postcolonial Fiction and Disability: Exceptional Children, Metaphor and Materiality.* London and New York: Palgrave Macmillian, 2012.

Davis, Lennard J. 'Constructing Normalcy: The Bell Curve, the Novel, and the Invention of the Disabled Body in the Nineteenth Century'. In *The Disability Studies Reader,* edited by Lennard J. Davis, 3–16. London and New York: Routledge, 2006.

Garland-Thomson, Rosemarie. *Extraordinary Bodies: Figuring Physical Disability in American Literature and Culture.* New York: Columbia University Press, 1997.

Garland-Thomson, Rosemarie. 'Integrating Disability, Transforming Feminist Theory'. In *The Disability Studies Reader*, edited by Lennard J. Davis, 333–53. London and New York: Routledge, 2013.

Hall, Alice. *Disability and Modern Fiction*. London and New York: Palgrave Macmillian, 2012.

———. *Literature and Disability*. London and New York. Routledge, 2016.

Lakoff, George and Mark Johnson. 'Conceptual Metaphor in Everyday Language'. *The Journal of Philosophy*, 77, no. 8 (1980): 453–86.

Mitchell, David and Sharon Snyder. 'Narrative Prosthesis'. In *The Disability Studies Reader*, edited by Lennard J. Davis, 222–35. London and New York: Routledge, 2013.

Pinto, Jerry. *Em and the Big Hoom*. New Delhi: Aleph Book Company, 2012.

Quayson, Ato. *Aesthetic Nervousness: Disability and the Crisis of Representation*. New York: Columbia University Press, 2007.

Siebers, Tobin. 'Disability and the Theory of Complex Embodiment—For Identity Politics in a New Register'. In *The Disability Studies Reader*, edited by Lennard J. Davis, 278–97. London and New York: Routledge, 2013.

Stefan, Hayley C. 'A (Head) Case for a Mad Humanities: Sula's Shadrack and Black Madness'. *Disability Studies Quarterly*, 38, no. 4 (2018).

Vidali, Amy. 'Seeing What We Know: Disability and Theories of Metaphor'. *Journal of Literary and Cultural Disability Studies*, 4, no. 1 (2010): 33–54.

5

DISMEMBERED BODIES IN A DISABLING CULTURE: GENDERED PERCEPTION OF DISABILITY IN INDIAN MYTHS

Tayyaba Rizwan

Amidst the compelling sub-stories within the epic *Ramayana* lies a shockingly gruesome tale of disabling violence as the heroic figure of Lord Rama grabs demoness Surpanakha in response to her amorous overtures and commands a resounding order to his brother, Lord Lakshmana, 'Mutilate this ugly, unvirtuous, extremely ruttish, great-bellied raksasi' (17.19-20). Omnipotent in authority, Lakshmana slices through her nose with a sword, attacking her corporeality and sexual autonomy. Thereby, literally and symbolically thrusting her out of the ethical and aesthetic social order. An unarmed victim, she can only let out a blood-curdling scream of bafflement—a shriek whose reverberations are still felt in Indian disability and gender discourses. Her dismembered face continues to arraign the authoritarian powers of the great epic and questions their social imagination of body and punishment. What is the significance behind using disability as a punitive tool? What kind of socio-judicial equilibrium does it justify? How does this discourse situate the personal body in the public sphere of socially constructed meanings? More importantly, how have such culturally interiorised mythologies affected our processes of meaning construction?

The chapter is an attempt to understand the intricate machinery of meaning-making and internalisation, or what one could term technologies of language and their socially agreed definitions of disability and ability; morality and immorality; beauty and grotesque in Indian Hindu mythologies, from a gendered lens. For the same, it undertakes semiotic readings of anatomical disabilities, namely mutilation of nose, ears, breast and hunchbacked mythological female figures, to argue that their corporeal variations are considered markers of subversions, rightfully punished through judicial orders or cosmic interventions. The chapter goes on to trace the schematic objectives of ableist signifiers behind such meanings and problematise the same.

Embodied Self in Indian Hindu Philosophy

Philosophical discourses regarding the embodied self-escape an uncontested linear conception in Hinduism, owing to its polyphonic traditions and diverse theological corpus. Lacking a singular doctrinal nucleus, as in monolithic religions, along with a history of contending interpretative literature, Hinduism itself has been appraised as an impossible definition. In her magisterial work, the oft-quoted Indologist, Wendy Doniger defines Hindu metaphysics in its very 'polythitic', a plurality marked by the absence of a deterministic centre (2009). Despite such professed and admitted liberalism, popular beliefs and majoritarian strands have historically adhered to certain themes that have actively engineered accepted 'master-images' of normative subjectivities, both spiritually and corporeally (Appadurai 1990). One of these themes, the tripartite paradigm of 'karma, dharma and moksha'— driven from relatively orthodox Hindu textual authorities, such as the *Vedas*, the ancient anthology of religious incantations; the *Upanishads*, detailed philosophical enquiries into the *Vedas*; and the *Manusmriti*, a 2nd-century parochial manual on Hindu ontology—has been subjected to repeated critiques in the Indian disability epistemology (Anees 2014; Miles 1995).

Karma, etymologically driven from the Sanskrit root '*kr*', refers to an act of 'doing' (Donahue 2016), and is ensconced within the layered imagination of 'moral causations and transmigration of soul', as postulated in the *Upanishads* and the *Manusmriti* (Ghai 2015). These theological edicts propose a phenomenology of reincarnation, wherein the moral purity of *karma*s in preceding lives determines the condition of the next, thereby arresting ontology within a tautological circuit of moral actions–moral rebirths, immoral actions–immoral rebirths. As per the *karmic* cycle, bio-socio stations of individuals are assumed to be calculated consequences of moral checks and balances carried forward from preceding births, albeit unwitnessed and unverifiable at present.

Bestowed by cosmic orders, the philosophy demands strict adherence to these allotted stations through the concept of *dharma* or a predefined, allegedly natural duty allocated to each, configured according to their gender, able-bodiedness and other identity markers. As per the dictates of orthodox texts such as the *Manusmriti*, a woman's *dharma*, in the domain of her relational identity, is being a loyal wife, a devoted mother and a submissive daughter, and if she ever risks subverting these predetermined *dharma*s, she would be forcing a violation onto her *karmic* cycle, consequently risking courting an inferior reincarnation in a subsequent birth.

At the convergence of *dharma* and *karma*, there emerges a convenient technology of arresting the status quo. In facilitating a collision of socio-religious demands with fatalistic determinism, this point of confluence predefines the social imagination of the self and the other. By postponing change to succeeding births, whose access alludes to the limit of human memory, it invites a belief beyond rationality and objectivity, divorcing autonomy of choice over one's actions and intent from within its domain. The duties accorded to different beings face further complications once they are situated within the *varna* system, the much-contested discriminatory classification of society within Hindu religiosity, that percolates its fabric of social-cultural exchange to date. Theorised within the mythological sacrifice of the primordial originary Being, which sparked the beginning of life and emanated the reality as we see today, the *varna* system hierarchises life in an invidious order of privilege. 'The Brahmana was his mouth, the Rajanya was made his arms; the being called the Vaishya, he was his thighs; the Shudra sprang from his feet' (Ambedkar 1946).

Within the system, Brahmin-borns, transpired from the symbolically and literally higher head of the originator are assumed to be always already marked by an amassed moral superiority from preceding births, while Shudras perpetually branded by foul denigrations. Regardless, each position coalesces with other social identities to engineer different *dharma*s and their different performativity, whose adherence is the sole mechanism to rectify non-*dharmic karmas*, such that each rebirth elevates ontological and spiritual status, giving a chance to prove loyalty towards assigned duty, before the soul is relieved of the bodily prison to attain *moksha* or eternal salvation—generally understood as the conclusive purpose of Hindu metaphysics.

The completion of these recurrent cyclical rebirths is contingent on rigid imaginations of a certain completeness of the body, in adherence to a corporeal reality circumscribed within a single, parochial understanding of anatomy and ontology. This reality apprehends the exterior body as a mere palpable appraisal of the non-palpable *atma* or soul, such that depreciation in *karmas* is informed to the latter through increasingly less desirable outer covers, marred by subordinate positions, of which disability remains the most conspicuous one. Hence, *Manusmriti* explicitly warns the discerning *atma*

> Thus in consequence of a remnant of (the guilt of former) crimes, are born idiots, dumb, blind, deaf, and deformed men, who are (all) despised by the virtuous. (translated by Buhler 1998)

Such cultural and religious values reiterate the treacherous notion of 'vile bodies, vile minds' while giving an illusion of agency over one's external appearance.

The understanding of sin and its manifestation in body further the dangerous coalescence between moral ambiguity and external form, for sin or *papam* is understood to be having a certain haptic quality. The customs of expiations, such as purificatory water, believed to be endowed with the potency of 'washing away of sins' (Ganguli 1926), attach immorality of the soul with cleanliness of the external form, such that inner *papam* or sin, becomes a foulness in body that may be washed away with an outer cleanliness. Such expiating rituals have textual validations in religious edicts, for instance, the *Rigveda* contains within itself a hymn singularly devoted to water deified:

> YE, Waters, are beneficent: so help ye us to energy
> we may look on great delight
> Give us a portion of the sap, the most auspicious that ye have,
> Like mothers in their longing love. (translated by Griffith 1986)

The hymn goes on to beseech waters for an able-ment, in body and soul:

> O Waters, teem with medicine to keep my body safe from harm,
> So that I long may see the Sun.
> Whatever sin is found in me, whatever evil I have wrought,
> If I have lied or falsely sworn, Waters, remove it far from me. (Griffith 1986)

By implying that a less desirable cover, in the form of a disabled body, is a manifestation of sin, whose suffering owes to deviance from social morality or ecclesiastical proclamations, it risks their exclusion from social participation. It is within this context that the *Manusmriti* proceeds to suggest royal councils of court, a carefully calibrated removal of the disabled from secret councils, lest they betray private council in public,

> At the time of consultation let him cause to be removed idiots, the dumb, the blind, and the deaf, animals, very aged men, women, barbarians, the sicks, and those deficient in limbs. (translated by Buhler 1998)

It goes on to elucidate discriminatory legal treatment of the disabled in inheritance laws:

> Eunuchs and outcasts (outside of the caste-system), (persons) born blind or deaf, the insane, idiots and the dumb, as well as those

deficient in any organ (of action or sensation), receive no share. (trans. by Buhler 1998)

Cause-and-effect frameworks, of *dharma*, *karma* and *moksha*, attract submissive acceptance because they disentangle the baffling philosophical enquiries around selfhood and diversity, power and domination, beauty and justice into utterly simplified causal dynamics, expounded in linear and logical mathematics. It deadens the cacophony of contending phenomenology of living in and with variegated bodies, by translating hierarchy and inferiority into a natural as well as a deserved way of address. Rather than demanding a complex comprehension of the world, which eternally provides mere evasive answers, it eradicates thought by doing away with the concept of difference as the rule. Bhatt views this accepted inerrancy of deterministic ontology as a fatalism that has been,

> instrumental in depriving the disabled of their inherent right to lead an independent life .... (Karmic philosophy) believed that the disabled were reaping what they had sowed in lives bygone and any attempt to ameliorate their lot would, therefore, interfere with this divine justice. (1963)

These notions find perilous championing in the discourse surrounding judiciary and punishment as well, which in ancient Hindu philosophies was thought to be either directly 'inflicted divinely judgements, penance imposed by the priest, or divinely informed orders of the king' (Hopkins 1924). For instance, there is a recurrent use of disability and disfigurement as a punitive technologies in *Manusmriti*, which directs wise twice-born (Brahmin) men to marry only those 'women who are free from bodily defects' (Sarkar 2016). Among other things, it also suggests amputating 'two fingers' of women with broken vaginas (Sarkar 2016). Anita Ghai thereby insists that disability within a Hindu context is necessarily and 'deeply embedded in the ... notion of *dukkha* or suffering or unhappiness' (2015). This notion of suffering finds homologous correspondence within the metaphysics of punishment in judicial dictates as well, for the painful journey of punishment symbolises an expiation of sin.

> *Mahabharata* says that the king should free them (the people) from sin by punishing them according to the law (righteousness). Besides this, Yajñavalkya enjoins that 'a person (in case of stealing) should makeover to the king a mace, proclaiming his own misdeeds. Killed or saved, he attains purification'. It is confirmed by Āpastamba and Manu, Usâna, and Samvarta. (Ganguli 1926)

In the backdrop of *karma*, expiation through punishment, including that of disablement, compensates for the requirement of corporeal de-elevation in the cyclical reincarnations, justifying impairment by authority. Evidently, both cosmic metempsychosis as well as earthly penalisation suppress subversiveness with perpetually visual mutilation: a disability that works as an elusive mirror of deception for the abled. They can look at it to revel in their self-assumed bodily wholeness and caution themselves against deviation from the norm, lest they themselves become reflective surfaces for society, thereby putting ethicality and aesthetics in a circular inferno. Such doctrines have the potential of pushing the disabled to a vulnerable space, wherein they are measured in negatives—their bodies become inherently lacking and their morals questionable.

If the disabled body is female, it becomes doubly marginalised within patriarchal and ableist hegemonies. In fact, the conflation of inhabiting a marginalised space and inheriting a belittling definition has been echoed in the feminist struggle since time immemorial. Female corporeality in a patriarchal society is reduced to a repository of all that the former fears and rejects—inadequacy in body and mind— and is consequently thrusted into the domain of 'abjected bodies, a field of deformation' (Butler 1993). Challenging this gender hierarchy, Judith Butler, in her phenomenal work, *Bodies That Matter*, examines the denial of wholeness to non-male subjects and their reduction into incomplete beings. She interrogates the rationale that privileges some and otherises the rest: 'what qualifies as bodies that matter, ways of living that count as "life," lives worth protecting, lives worth saving, lives worth grieving?' (1993)

These pertinent questions find stark resonance in disability studies as well, for discrimination on the basis of the physical form is employed to otherise disabled bodies, initiating a systematic rejection of their voices and individuality. Their lives become less deserving of protection, saving and grieving, and are hence abandoned as being deviations from the normative.

Furthering the argument, Julia Cho, in her essay 'Sideshow Freaks and Sexualized Children: Abject Bodies on Display', deconstructs the notion of 'wholeness of the human form': 'Are certain constructions of the body constitutive in this sense: that we could not operate without them, that without them there would be no "I," no "we"?' (1997). At the beginning of the essay, she investigates the fragments that culminate in the wholeness of the 'I', a wholeness that remains coveted and claimed, yet elusive. Furthering her rhetoric, she ruminates whether there is any fragment whose absence or lack takes away the essence of one's humanity, with the motive of denouncing the ableist forces for constructing impossibilities, as preconditions for dignified selfhood. Conflating the physical and philosophical 'I', she disputes the linear, narrow cultural ideas which separate, literally and symbolically, the disabled 'I' from the societal 'we'.

These notions are evidently cultural impositions that deny certain sections of the population their claims to an independent subject position in society with the underlying purpose of fuelling a hierarchisation, profiting the male able-body order. Consequently, both feminist and disability studies actively resist institutionalisation techniques that seek to concretise a linear definition of the disciplined body—a body that would fit in within the rules of the ableist, patriarchal society. In other words, they resist the norms of 'compulsory able-bodiedness' that have been internalised universally in shared consciousness (McRuer 2002).

Calibrating Disabling Cultures

Internalisation facilitates a dangerous interpellation of socio-culturally predicated significations onto the personal psyche, where the latter, more often than not, shows receptivity to dominant societal conditionalities in a bid to enjoy acceptance within the collective. The acceptance preconditions a transfer, if not fervent subservience, to dogmatic dictates of social institutions within the relatively more intimate world of sensibilities, such that the particular individual is circumscribed within censorial frontiers of conventional discourses. This transfer is of a semiotic nature, wherein the social process of meaning construction is reproduced and translated through signs and symbols, embedded in macro forces such as religio-cultural discourses, medical paradigms and state-sanctioned education, and micro-level quotidian language.

Relieving individualities from the confines of such social significations would necessitate a zealous inversion of all that is comprehensive and meaningful towards a carnival of unconfined frenzy and overflowing newness. It would require an intentional rejection of the real and present for a (non-)knowledge, resting in an embodiment that precedes the origination of social meanings—a veritable movement towards an unmarked canvas of the individual being, prior to the consciousness of social being.

To this end, of conceiving a thought outside—or rather—preceding socio-cultural technologies of language, Julia Kristeva's theoretical study of semiotics provide an invigorating and ever-expanding (non-)structure. Ensconced within radical feminist politics, her psychoanalytically informed socio-linguistics surface a fertile ground for reimagining—in all their unveiled temptations and trepidations—socially burdened bodies in their raw-naked humanity. Her study of semiotics inverts the sociality of language on its head, heralding thought defined by everything nondescript, undecipherable and incredibly emancipated from the social: everything that could be wielded in the struggle to dismember patriarchal ableist status quo.

Drawing from existing literature in psychoanalysis and structural linguistics, primarily the Lacanian triad of Imaginary-Mirror-Symbolic stages, she configures the genesis of the (in)dependent subject position through two chronological phases, namely the Semiotics and the Symbolic, spanning psychosocial stages of development, from an embryonic state of oblivion to a socially deferential, or rather successfully interpellated, silent adult. The primary stage of her psycho-structural linguistics coalesces with the Lacanian Imaginary Phase and characterises itself in a liberating non-meaning fluidity, inhabiting an indistinct particularity contingent on the maternal figure (Kristeva 1984). Akin to the Lacanian Imaginary phase, where the subject experiences a pre-language existence, distant from the universalising signifiers of socio-political order, Kristeva's subject savours an enigmatic fecundity in its fusion with the maternal creator. She discerns within the unrestricted synthesis of the female creator and the created, 'pre or translinguistic modalities of psychic inscription', a lyrical metaphor of the feminine language that ensconces in a structure-less imagination of rhythmic music and lawless poetry, verging on the meaningless and ignorant of dry cultural expectations; all the while enabling space for the non-normative to flourish in its fluid unconventionality (Kristeva 1987).

The stage ends as the embryonic life is integrated into the meaningful phase of the Symbolic with an inevitable departure from the maternal womb, and the commencement of communal life with the adoption of the universal language of patriarchal authoritarian order. This language 'constitutes itself at the cost of repressing instinctual drive and continuous relation to the mother', consequently incarcerating the temporal and spatial fluidity of the semiotic stage and reducing the infinitudes of life into finite laws and regulations (Kristeva 1980). Consequently, socio-cultural meanings eventually saturate the non-meaning poetics with laden signifiers, requisitioning a slavish compulsion to its sanctioned means of interaction and cognition; an articulation that markedly departs from the rhythms of the feminine. Life is compelled to abide by the inevitable concession of the unbridled indetermination of semiotic disorder for denotative over-determination of the symbolic order as a requisite for inclusion within the polis. This denigration into the universal coalesces parallelly with the Lacanian post-Mirror stage where the child self-identifies itself as one puzzle piece of a larger society.

Perhaps, there is a need to resurface the semiotic canvas of non-meaning fluidity to demystify socially fabricated meanings. In many of her writings, Kristeva advocates for a similar return. Arguing that the subject yearns to return to the dyadic fusion with the maternal, she proposes the 'adoption of modes of expressions that align with somatic impulses, drives and instincts' through a feminine voice that would give space to the unstructured, unconscious and unheard (Caputi 1993).

In the Indian Hindu context, where the symbolic orders of able-bodiedness and patriarchy are not merely dictated through ableist and gender binaries, but also through caste and the socio-religious triad of *karma*, *dharma* and *moksha*; able-bodied, twice-born Brahmin male authority constructs and imposes phallocentric ableist signifiers. Within the politics of punishment, even cosmetic deviations from the abled male body and its authorised norms get burdened with increasingly layered complexities, given the cosmically sanctioned litanies, favouring the inferiority of non-male genders and disablement. Such frameworks inhibit imagination of corporeality within a cognitive limit—already dictated from an inaccessible position of power—and arrest bodies in symbolic signifiers that suspend individual capacities for meaning-making. In other words, they manufacture disability as an episteme on the body.

Alexa Schriempf agrees, in her insistence on ungirding how disability is engineered, that if one wishes for corporeality to have any chance at alterity in the future, it would require a de-arrestation from the limits of social signifiers. Borrowing from Nancy Tuana's 'intersectionist' approach towards feminist disability study, Schriempf proposes a departure from 'biological reductionism' towards 'a recognition of material-semiotic' phenomenology of meaning construction, wherein discourse or symbolic signifiers are found at the fulcrum of materially perceived reality and culturally conceived meanings (2001). She proposes the necessity to adopt a collaborative intersectionist framework, where 'thoughts about the body, its sex-gender, its impairment-disability, and its eroticism are shaped by the body; as the body changes, so too does thinking about the body. As thought changes, bodily beings emerge out of these changes' (2001).

There is, in essence, a reimagination of the body in the possession of the individual, who has the autonomy to alter corporeality and thought to benefit the embodied self. This reimagination can happen only after the socially possessed disabled body is sundered from societal possession, stripped from ableist and phallocentric compartmentalisation and secured back in the non-definition of Kristeva's semiotics phase. The chapter further undertakes a similar material-semiotic reading of culturally internalised mythologies, intersecting politics of disability and gender.

Disabling Societies, Abled Bodies

One of the prominent disabled female characters in Indian legends is Manthara from Valmiki's *Ramayana*. The infamous hunchbacked servant, who had the supposed temerity of manipulating her mistress, Queen Kaikeyi to impede the coronation of her stepson, the omnipotent deity, Lord Rama and effectuating his fourteen years of exile into the forest, Manthara is the bothersome inconvenience blemishing royal affairs in the court of King Dasharatha in popular consciousness. She allegedly impinges upon their familial dynamics and instigates Kaikeyi to delude Dasharatha into replacing the investiture of the monarch with that of her own son and prince regent, Bharata. She thus transgresses her caste, gender as well as corporeal inferiority and unleashes violence upon her *dharma* and *karma*. Predictably, the myths arraign her as a disabling nuisance to be done away with, for the reconstitution of hierarchical, moral and monarchical order. Her undesirability is advocated, however, through an excessively unwarranted gaze at the 'monstrous proportion' of her disabled corporeality, such that even Kaikeyi's gratitude conspicuously reiterates her state of alterity,

> There are hunchbacks who are misshapen, crooked and hideously ugly—but not you ... And this huge hump of yours, wide as the hub of a chariot wheel—your clever ideas must be stored in it, your political wisdom and magic powers. (translated by Pollock 1986, quoted in Sutherland 1992)

Consequently, her 'deviance' is conflated with her non-normative stoop and her hunchback becomes a symbol of felony itself, amalgamating her supposed corporeal and ethical impairment in a fictitious symbiosis.

The figure of the hunchback is arrested within an unfortunate conflation with moral ambiguity, wherein disabled bodies become 'metaphorical encapsulations of the moral problematic' (Quayson 2007). In didactic Buddhist literature, the figure of hunchbacked Khujjutara becomes a telling testimony of the complex calibration of bodies and their humanity; her hunchback is a paradoxical cosmic penalisation for mocking a disabled man in her preceding birth (Miles 2000). Reprimanded with a corrective birth for her mockery and corrupted demeanour, she is condemned to survive a shameful residence within a similar form, thereby inverting the didacticism that superficially promulgated sympathy for the disabled into a conceptualisation of impairment as a fearful exhibition of cosmic punishment.

Rejecting the limiting connotations of hunchbacks and shrugging off cultural signifiers require a deconstructive reading of what a hunchback signifies. We need to shift the 'symbolic' connotations and revert to the 'semiotic canvas' of (non)meanings.

In popular consciousness, a straight spine is emblematic of man's victory in the evolutionary struggle as he progressed from a curved ape-like body to an unbending upright form. It is this symbolism that renders phrases 'walking straight' and 'head held high' as being denotations of potency, physical prowess and masculinity, equipping punitive orders such as those met by Khujjutara with an illusory perception of exclusivity and eminence—all of which suffers unceremonious psychological cognitive dissonance at the sight of an evolved human with a stoop who is seen to be thriving. It informs the abled of the futility of their signifiers, sundering their meticulously woven contrived reality. Thus, the rejected stoops of the disabled population have to be included within didactic social tales, merely as an exclusion. They serve as a foil for the self-acclaimed accepted ones who can manifest and experience their superiority singularly in the presence of a different populace. The disabled bodies serve as a foil for the abled who can experience their self-acclaimed superiority singularly in the presence of the former, in the absence of whom they would have nothing to experience their supposed superior 'distinguish-ness.' In their need for elevation, the abled-bodied evolved backs, de-elevate the dissimilar nondisabled in margins while paradoxically requiring the margins to define themselves.

Hunchbacked Manthara's successful intrusion into royal affairs similarly destabilised multiple conventional signifiers, whose dauntless subversiveness had to be concealed within the shroud of internalised prejudicial discernments of her lower-caste disabled subjectivity. What remains forgotten in her *karma*s is her undeniable political abstraction as well as her adroit flair for articulation. Kaikeyi, in her privileged world of ignorance, remains unattuned to the vulnerable position Lord Rama's enthronement could thrust her into and is equally oblivious of the possibility of her son, Bharata being the 'rightful heir, a fact verified later'[1] in the text (Sutherland 245). Manthara, apprehensive for her mistress' well-being and aware of the tragedies befalling naive gullibility in the politics of courts,[2] prompts her to claim autonomy,

> You are too simple-minded to see what is good for you and what Ràghava will be king, and then the son of Ràghava, while Bharat debarred from the royal succession altogether. Like a helpless boy,

that son of yours will be totally excluded from the royal succession
and from its pleasures as well. (translated by Sheldon 1986)

Her actions could potentially be seen as engendering a sisterhood
amidst the politics of care. This sisterhood, wherein Manthara self-
manufactures the *dharma* or the duty of a guardian protector and
a cogent planner, makes a mockery of the impositions levied on
patriarchally permissible female relationships, attesting to the power of
female solidarity and the possibility of flourishing alternate meanings
away from the bowdlerising phallocentric gaze while simultaneously
inverting the 'dependency-control divide' that necessarily assumes
the disabled to be reliant in perpetual need for an abled-whole carer.
Manthara's ingenuity and independence of thought and action reject
charitable patronisation (Lloyd 2001).

Hence, there is excessive emphasis on Manthara's physical attributes
and their corresponding signifiers in order to blur her sense of
self within a discriminatory haze. If Manthara's hunchback wasn't
repetitively referred to as an abnormality through the text, it would have
the potential of displaying the presence of the marginal amongst the
mainstream and would allow a strong vocal woman to create her own
lexicon of power and relationships. Her hunchback has been tactically
constructed as a tangible symbolic signifier of her supposedly crooked
thoughts, lest she betrays disability as a human attribute and sisterhood
as an alternate to male-dominated relationships. The concept of control
thus carries an inherent paradox—despite being an oppressor, it
continuously fears the possibility of its collapse.

This control suffers further setbacks as Manthara's sense of self
is reclaimed in modern revisions of the myths where derogatory
signifiers of being hunchbacked are confronted and coalesced into a
fluid polysemic. Celebrated Malayali writer Sarah Joseph's revision of
mythological fables of the *Ramayana* puts forward an inspiring socialist
critique of Manthara's time as a servant of the court in her short story
titled, 'Kuruthathulakal' ('Black Chinks'). Going beyond the web of
royal intrigues, this Manthara visibalises a materially informed reality
of the downtrodden, along with a resounding critique of the cavalier off-
handedness, pervading authoritarian institutions and their exploitation
of their unchecked privilege of social dictation. Articulated from
Manthara's voice, the narrative looks with an amalgamation of regret
and repugnance, at the political traps laid down by brothers against
fathers and husbands against wives in the court of King Dasharatha;
the 'world of fathers who decrees that power must be guarded, even
if that meant raising sword and axe at Mother! Oohh!' (Joseph 2005).
Manthara removes the voyeuristic gaze from her supposed impaired

hunchback to the morally impaired conspiracies and deceptions reciprocated among the power holders as she ominously prophesies the fall of Ayodhya, disintegrating every hierarchical imposition governing her inferior station into splinters,

> Dasarathan's lust and betrayal, Aswapathy's greed, ambition, and anger, all these will fall upon Ayodhya like a flaming comet, an evil omen. She, this hunchback, would be the one who ignites its tail. This woman will tear off Ayodhya's veils of falsehood before the eyes of its people. And then the people will know what kings driven by lust and anger are capable of. (Joseph 2005)

She self-assumes the position of a social critic and takes control of the societal (and/or the reader's) gaze, initiating a transformation from a conniving hunchback to an active participant in the socio-political integrities of courtly life.

Manthara's relationship with Kaikeyi also undergoes a Marxist revision as the former is reimagined as an independent proletariat, for whom spying is a surviving apparatus, rather than the selflessness that is expected of maidservants. As a lower-caste woman, she is not free to use her intellect. Unlike her royal mistress/employer, royal investitures and courtly machinations have no importance to her individual conscience and necessities, nor is she invested in abstract conceptions of divine authorities and cosmic justice, for she devotes herself to her earthly survival. Instead, she shifts the attention from Bharata's coronation to all that is human: a quest for material existence, the recognition of socio-political reality and a life dancing between cynicism and hope. She uses the textual space to articulate and investigate her escape from the prison hold of the royal palace, measuring every foot, deceiving every rampart and braving every attack on her way. Whether political powers, earthbound royalties or deified *devas*, each is pushed to the background with their insignificant dethronement and coups, and the narrative continuously beats with the singular focus on her escape: 'must escape. Must be over the border before dawn breaks' (Joseph 2005). Wielding a knife to ward off every obstacle in her way to freedom, she vehemently turns down Kaikeyi's order to escort her to the latter's maiden home: 'like the ghoul escaping, she swung away on a jungle-vine' (Joseph 2005). Her voice replaces courtly jargon with the woes of the downtrodden, replacing the cultural significations of the hunchbacks with an individuality of her own. Thus, in her complexity, she reclaims the wholeness that was denied to her in the original reading.

Manthara is not the solitary victim of such demonisation. Rather, the 'hunchback' trope has been historically thrusted with prejudicial and unwarranted significations in a near-universal spectrum. Western psychoanalytic studies discern in the arched spine, a metaphorical signifier for the phallus and by extension, an arched spine in a woman's body as a menacing symbol of aggressive female perversity that threatens the demands of patriarchal normative orders. Expanding on the same, Sutherland writes 'the hunchback and other deformed female figures ... are symbols of aggressive female sexuality and, in fact, are symbolic investments—for the patriarchal society—of the aggressive women with a phallus' (1992).

Parallelly, hunchbacked women repeatedly figure in South Asian folk tales as hideous and uncontrollable witches, or as dubbed in colloquial Hindi, *chudail*. Imagined as lustful, man-eaters with the knowledge that eludes 'normative' men, they are perceived to enjoy supernatural abilities of shape-shifting between plural embodiments, one of them being that of an old hunchbacked woman with a club foot. This figure is pervasive in oral stories and myths, so much so that town peripheries and abandoned castles are rarely unaccompanied by their rumoured sightings. Found in deserted alleys, the deformed witch exists in the absence of male corrective gaze and is associated with sacrilegious knowledge of black magic and hypnosis. The etymology of the word 'witch' can be traced to the process of deviant sciences. The noun 'witch', when derived from the 'old Teutonic' verb 'wik', refers 'to bend' and when derived from the Indo-European root 'wiek', alludes to 'religion and magic' (Jong 2017). Witchcraft then becomes the process of bending or de/reforming the world according to one's wishes, and the deliberate construction of the body as disabled facilitates societal acceptance of such signifiers. Thus, the symbolic meaning carries a tale of caution: knowledge outside the purview of an authorial abled male is bound to be crooked. It doesn't uplift humanity. Rather, it bends the world.

These symbolisms have their antithesis in feminist retellings, where the deformed and defamed witches sing their own stories. One such poem by Laurence Hope, titled, 'Lalla Radha and the *Churel*' redefines witches and their bodies by tracing their genesis to mourning mothers.

> When with her child unborn, a woman dies
> Her spirit takes the form of a churel,
> A maiden's form, with soft, alluring eyes
> Where promises of future rapture well
> Yet is her loveliness, through passing sweet,
> Marred by the backwards-turning of her feet. (Hope 1903)

In similar modern poems and orally transmuted tales, the women carry in their memory, tragic marital lives, abandonment by family or slaughter by husbands, wherein they transform themselves into reincarnations of hapless victims to reclaim the autonomy of self-definition (Bandukwala and Ansari 2020). Their rebirths, with inverted feet (akin to a clubfoot) and hunchbacks, become markers of reclamation and evidence of their laments and vengeance. The stories substitute ableist-patriarchal signifiers, with tragedies resulting from ableist patriarchy.

Mutilation: Dismembering Identities

Another recurring disabling mechanism in mythological texts is the mutilation of discernible parts, particularly the nose, ears and breasts of 'fallen' women. Penalisation through their dismemberment engenders a disability beyond corporeality. It is a symbolic impairment of their sovereignty and sexual autonomy.

A popular case in point is the mutilation of Ravana's sister, Surpanakha by Lord Rama and his brother in the *Ramayana*, as mentioned at the beginning of this chapter. Though there are various readings of the episode, the *Ramayana*'s impact on Indian sensibilities remains unparalleled. Appraised as the 'the national manual for ethics' (Khan 1965) and 'leading revealer of the pulse of Indian conviction', the epic oeuvre, dating back to the 5th century BC, has pervasive control over popular Indian Hindu thought, which is exhibited annually in its public re-enactments and adaptations in television shows, regular recitations and plays staged in religio-traditional festivity (Hindery 1976). This consequently renders the disabling penalisation of Surpanakha by a divinised authority figure, along with its symbolic significations, a vehement cultural acceptance.

Widowed Surpanakha is a demoness who propositions Rama when he enters her forest. A married man, he spurns her but goes on to make a mockery of the 'ugly, un-virtuous, extremely ruttish, great-bellied' *rakshasa* (17.19–20, quoted in Erndl 1991).[3] Humiliated, she unleashes her anger on the upholder of *dharma,* only to have her nose and ears mutilated in a violent penalising blow, that marks her double victimisation in the interaction—she is a woman who is mocked for bravely pursuing her love/lust interest and casted out for protesting against the mockery. The myth, however, escapes such accusations due to the predefined construction of Surpanakha's character as monstrously proportioned: 'His face was beautiful; hers was ugly. His eyes were wide; hers were deformed ... His countenance was pleasing; hers was repellent' (16.8–9, quoted in Erndl 1991).

Further in the epic, in yet another multiform depiction of women's mutilation, the character of Tataka, a *yakshi* princess, becomes the victim of patriarchal wrath. In the pursuit of avenging her husband's execution by Sage Agasthya, notoriously infamous for his omnipresent and volcanic rage, Tataka becomes a victim of disabling violence, as her murderous railing at the injustice impinged upon her conjugal life invites the Brahmin's rage, and he curses her with a repulsive aesthetic grotesqueness, 'The greatly enraged sage Agasthya immediately even cursed Tataka, to become one with a very ugly face and also have a distorted form' (25.12, 25.13). In the ensuing narrative, Lord Rama and Lakshmana are summonned to exterminate the demon figure only to have the former suggest disablement as a befitting punishment for the non-male subjects, in an ironic performance of clemency, 'as her being a lady is protecting her, I also am not making efforts to kill her and my intention is only to impede her strides and mobility' (26.12).

In a paradoxical understanding of *dharma*, he preserves capital punishment for men and privileges disability as appropriate castigation, a paradox that he himself inverts as he eventually assassinates her on being persuaded by his preceptor, Sage Vishwamitra—as the original sentence is becoming extremely dense (Chaitanya 2018). It was an act that divulged the tremendous power of patriarchal ableist authorities over making and unmaking *dharmic* legality and its implementation. Following a similar pattern of violence, the third chapter of Tulsidas' *Rāmcaritmānas*, also records Lakshmana dismembering the nose and ears of a female demon, Ayomukhi, when she verbalises sexual interest in the former (Narayan 2010).

Such paradoxical comprehension of justice has been reproduced in cultural secular texts as well, evidencing the profound impact of the fables discussed. A telling case is a *Panchatantra* tale titled 'Weaver's Wife'. A composition of varied Indian folk tales, *Panchatantra* claims didactic and comic undertones and is a widely read children's book. The tale in question chronicles a weaver dismembering the nose of a barber's wife, mistaking the latter to be culpable of adultery, who, in turn, frames her own husband for the crime to break free from her marital woes. However, she is met with an analogous punishment at the king's court, where he orders the mutilation of her ears for false accusation.

The terrible irony employed in this tale continues the tradition of dismembering facial organs of the ears and the nose as a punishment for women who 'subvert' their *dharmas,* inviting two principal enquiries. What does such disfigurement symbolise? What is the intent behind these signifiers?

The underlying notion behind changing body morphology of the above-mentioned characters is, in effect, an attribution of 'shame' and 'ignominy' through visibly different corporeality. The nose, for instance, has figured as an important organ in the ancient study of physiognomy in both the Western and Eastern worlds. As a protruding organ with orifices, it is said to have phallic resemblances. Simultaneously, the triangular form of the nose has been studied to be in a homological relationship with the vagina, with the clitoris corresponding to the pointed peak and the nostrils to the open vulva (Frembgen 2006). There has also been an evident close correlation between enticing fragrances and sexual pleasure, such that 'the nose, with its veiny and arterial folds connected to the cranial cavities', becomes a commonly 'preferred sensitive channel for smelling pleasures of a sensual kind' (Frembgen 2006). Jürgen Wasim Frembgen draws on Bakhtin's study of the semiotics of body and records a correlation between penis and nose in ancient folklore, 'the length of one supposedly corresponding to the length of the other, both spewing contaminating substances of similar consistency' and finds surprising correspondences symbolised in an Indian 'Mithila-painting' of 'an androgynous form of Shiva' endorsing a nose in his phallic area (2006). Similarly, ears are externally visible body parts that have been used for aesthetic and cosmetic purposes for years, through piercing and ornamentations in almost every culture.

Given the semiotics of the nose and ears as organs critical in affecting sexual impulses, their mutilation undertakes a pertinent attack on one's sexuality and sense of self, particularly since the limited societal understanding of sexuality and sexual pleasure assumes the exterior body to be the solitary interface, fallaciously rendering sexual functionality an incompatibility for disabled bodies. Margaret Lloyd, in her study on the possible 'discords' and 'synthesis' within the politics of feminism and disability, expands on such cavalier denial of the capacity of human intimacy to disabled corporeality by ableist orders: 'the primary issue for disabled women may be to establish recognition of her right to be seen as, and of her capacity to function as, a sexual being' (2001). Thus, the locus of their discrimination is not just a condescending gaze but also a jettisoning from the romantic-sexual social space. Within this context of such punitive dynamics, one finds that rhinotomy has been used as a judicial punishment for sexual transgression and adultery in women from time immemorial across cultures—from ancient Greece marking adulteress women with dismembered noses and Native North Americans and Mexican laws empowering men to 'bite off their wife's nose' if she falters in conjugal loyalty (Frembgen 2006). In parts of north India, 'losing one's nose' is a cultural phrase for disgrace and humiliation.

Thus, one can assume that the rhinotomy faced by Surpanakha, Ayomukhi and Tataka was due to their 'wrong *karmas*' of assuming the masculine role of persuaders and redefining the symbolics of a patriarchal relationship, and so is the judicial violence meted out to the barber's wife, for daring to admit marital dejection and contriving against her master patriarch. Their subversion is suppressed violently by thrusting them out of the intimate sexual station. The fact that otherisation takes place on their bodies echoes the construction of phallocentric meanings.

These phallocentric meanings have to be contested and replaced to allow plural and individual significations of womanhood and disability to exist. Sarah Joseph's short story 'Mother Clan' attempts such a redefinition. Included in the celebrated book, *Retelling the Ramayana*, the tale overturns perspectives on Surpanakha's spectacle of violence with the woman jettisoning the patriarchal gaze with her own gaze and replacing the authorial agency of ableist powers with her intimate personal tone.

She transforms herself from a 'ruttish' woman speaking out of turn to an empowered victim raising her voice against the normalisation of violence as she expresses her agonised incomprehension at the sudden ruthless slays of Lord Lakshmana's sword. Her indignation is not limited to her singular plight but encompasses a searing critique of the general denial of passion and sexual autonomy to women and bafflement at the sadistic callousness of dismemberment as a punishment. 'The tree blossoms because of passion. The forest blooms because of passion. If a woman's passion is denounced as wrong and harmful, it is the fruit-bearing earth that will suffer' (Joseph 2005). In her criticism, her victimisation assumes a sympathetic connotation and rewrites her story as a wronged woman, not a fallen one. Her dismembered nose and ears stand as testimonies of the blatant injustice of her perpetrators rather than as an evidential reminder of her disgrace.

Eventually, Surpanakha has the last laugh when she hears of Rama's assent for his wife Sita's *agnipariksha* or 'trial by fire', to prove her purity. Sita had been condemned to a life of hostage by her abductor, Ravana. She returns home after his defeat at Rama's hand. Instead of commemorating her secure return, the kingdom prepares a 'blazing coal-fire and asks her to jump into it' as a test of sexual chastity, while the omniscient patriarch concedes and looks on, as a distant spectator (Joseph 2005). In this spectacle, Surpanakha seeks the perpetrators of her punishment in naked and unblemished disgrace and dishonour. In an unexpected turn of events, she finds a double, a companion in Sita, and lets out a bitter yet victorious laugh, refocusing attention to her vigour and candour from her facial impairment. The 'sweet countenance' of the able-bodied Rama does not assist him in reconciling with his wife nor justifies the cruel indifference of his judicial edicts. Instead, another female body is put through disabling punishment for mere existence.

The mutilation of breasts is another recurrent trope in Indian myths. The semiotics of breasts are such that they are signifiers of contradictory as well as conflating significations, from feminine chastity and sexual indiscretion, submissive demands and destructive power, to nourishment and annihilation. They define the subject's relational position in society with her children, lover as well as the life-giving force of Mother Earth. In these multifarious relationships, breasts assume paradoxical connotations.

In southern Indian literature, breasts are a strong motif of women's *karpu*, an important cultural motif in Sangam literature, often translated as purity for a simplistic, reductive convenience (Zvelebil 1974). It is, however, an overarching term that envelops varied conventional qualities of obedience and subservience demanded of women, as part of their *dharma*. Generated from a supposed inherent purity of 'feminine virtuosity', *karpu* refers to an unflinching conjugal loyalty, a self-sacrificing spirit of service, modesty in demeanour and an inclination towards motherhood. In his study of ancient Indian poetry, George Hart defines *karpu* as 'a sort of asceticism, the restraining of all impulses that (are) in any way immodest', which summarises the term's germane philosophical underpinnings (1975).

Karpu is to be both revered and feared within Sangam literature, for this chastity and devotion have the potential to endow a *dharmic* woman with a litany of spiritual powers, including that of creation and apocalyptic annihilation. Predictably, various epic characters are modelled on this philosophy as an instructive guide for female audiences and as a corrective model for the deviant ones. The character of Kannagi, a virtuous woman, unwaveringly steadfast in her nuptial obligations and devotion, exemplifies the power of *karpu* in *Silapaddikaram*, a 4th-century south Indian epic. After her husband Kovalan is unjustly implicated and executed for a crime he didn't commit, she reaches the court to impugn the royal judicial system and prove her husband's innocence, eventually sentencing the entire kingdom to extermination by mutilating her left breast and flinging it towards the kingdom (Adigal, trans. by Dikshitar 1939). Her mutilated organ immolates the place in its entirety and symbolically cleanses it of corruption and injustice, making her self-imposed disability a radical symbol of protest and passion (Adigal 1939).

These actions, however revolutionary in their resistance towards the sovereign authority and ensconced in the paraphernalia of love, advocate a disabling discourse. Her self-mutilation is an evident unsexing of her widowed body. Without her male patron, she doesn't have the authority to exist as an independent earthly being. Thus, her sacrifice becomes necessary from an authorial lens. Though her mutilation is not externally imposed, she is removed from society within 15 days of her vengeance and ascends to heaven, thereby reconfiguring her disability as a means of reuniting with her husband and fulfilling the duties or *dharma* assigned to her.

Breast mutilation also occurs in southern retellings of Surpanakha's tragedy. Along with her ears and nose, her breasts are also maimed as part of her symbolic dehumanisation. Apart from an evident desexualisation, it is a disrobing of her strength and independence. An analogy can be made with Mahasweta Devi's story 'Draupadi'. A tribal Naxal woman, Dopti, is disrobed, raped and impaired multiple times by a unit of the special forces, a law enforcement agency deployed for vacating tribal lands of its indigenous inhabitants, as part of a capitalist-political state strategy. The forces deployed in these lands act with impunity, wreaking havoc in the lives of the original inhabitants, looting and raping sans consequences; and Dopti becomes one of the many casualties whose 'breasts are bitten raw (and) her nipples torn' (Devi 2014). Like Surpanakha, she is also a 'black-skinned' original inhabitant of the 'Neanderthal' darkness, left to weather mutilation by an external force of regulation (Devi 2014).

Another legend from south India records the story of a lower-caste woman, Nangeli, who protests against *mulakkaram*—the breast tax (Pillai 2017). Women of lower caste in 19th-century Kerala were not allowed to cover their breasts without paying a heavy tax for the same as it was perceived as a threat to the position of higher-caste men. As part of this system, uncovering their breast was considered disrespectful and incompatible with their status. This lack of autonomy was a brutal process of dehumanisation and was legitimised through the authoritative power of phallic meaning-making. Nangeli's tale is a chilling protest against this practice; as per the legend, she mutilates her breasts and submits them, covered in a leaf to the tax collector as her last *mulakkaram,* before bleeding to death. She disables her body in order to claim a right to it and inverts the semiotics of corporeal body parts. Her tragic dissent empowers other women and forces the authorities to repeal the tax. Paradoxically, her poor *karmas* liberate her community even when they deviate from her *dharma* of a submissive lower-caste woman.

These myths convey a resoundingly important message—that of a disabling society and fluid constructs of ability. In Nangeli's case, mutilation endows her with an almost divine ability to stand her ground. Kannagi's divinity is dictated by her acquiescence to gendered relations. On the other hand, Dopti's or Surpanakha's accounts register an authoritarian attack on women in an attempt to dismember their power and break all relational attachments that their breasts symbolise.

Conclusion

In her study of the bio-social dyad of physical impairment and social disability that characterises disabled embodiments, Alexa Schriempf infers, 'disability and impairment are both always about bodies in social situations and thus always about the material and social conditions of not just one's body and its abilities but also of one's environment' (2001). The epistemic construction that often overdetermines manifest realities, including social imagination of the self and the others, defines both the self, inhabiting the social, and the social, habituating the self. It is this very social domain that suffers an 'aesthetic nervousness', in the words of Ato Quayson marked by a 'subliminal fear' at the sight of disability (2007). It fails to perceive disability, and non-patriarchal stations, as varied yet deserving ontological normativity, for its existence depends on enclosing the temporal and spatial fluidity of life within a static and replicable authoritarian law.

It is this very social domain that Surpanakha screeches at with seething incandescence and frenzied disbelief at the beginning of the chapter. Brutally delivered a cosmetic dismemberment, she is reduced to an aesthetical reminder of penalisation and becomes an example of caution to others. Baffled at the ableism soaking the fabric of the society, she stands as none but one of the long inventories of wronged women further discussed; women who nevertheless successfully leave dents on the fatalist determinism of ableist signifiers as they move towards polysemic semiotics, rewrite themselves in contemporary revisions, and reclaim the wholeness denied to them.

At the beginning of the chapter, the research delves into the near-universally acknowledged Hindu reincarnation cycle, comprising the trifecta of *dharma*, *karma* and *moksha*, to locate the fulcrum conjoining moral religiosity with ontological disability within the otherwise, incredibly polyphonic Hindu belief system; followed by a close reading of the conflation of aesthetic and ethical embodiment in their legal treatises, such as the *Manusmriti* and the *Rigveda*. The chapter pursues the narrative of 'vile bodies, vile minds' meticulously woven through these socio-cultural artefacts, complemented with near-impenetrable historically solidified socialisation, to discover how social realities are mythologies interpellated through the creation of culturally laden signifiers disguised as language of communication, thought and being.

In all mythologies of disability and gender discussed above, the source of contention and the subsequent call for ambush emerge largely out of subversion of social, religious and judicial laws; laws that remain supreme and endowed with tremendous power of sanction, yet feel incapacitated at slight novelties in bodily configurations and gendered stations. Their survival prerequisites restricting the body within deterministic significations, whose deviations warrant an exile from aesthetics and ethics of both social and material orders. The connotations of grotesqueness artificially engineered on disabled bodies not only disengage them from certain anatomical completeness, circumscribed by pseudo-moral symbolic orders, but the haecceity of punitive slaying adversely impacts their material inclusion within institutions of sexual, familial and economic spaces. It is an attempt at dispossessing them of their 'normalcy and beauty', two forces which 'posit female and disabled bodies ... as pliable bodies to be shaped infinitely to conform to a set of standards called normal and beautiful' (Garland-Thomson 2002).

The chapter sets to dismantle these standards by perceiving the creation of symbolic order of sociality as socio-material ammunitions guarding the inflexibility of phallocentric ableism, with the intent of tracing their route back towards an unblemished, non-interpellated and reimagined possibility of being. Taking language as the medium of travel, the chapter finds that it is necessary to dismantle this medium of inheriting mythologies as/and thoughts, for which Kristeva's intimate poetical rhythms of the psychoanalytical Semiotic order provided compelling possibilities. The semiotic framework worked as a remarkably amenable and creatively fecundate (non-)structure, beguilingly replacing the barbarity of socio-judicial punitive rampage on disabled female bodies with the lawlessness of semiotic poetry, a structure-less reimagination of the language-less rhythms and an unabashed embrace of a meaningless prelinguistic cacophony.

It became the framework through which the entrancing power of voice behind Manthara's stoop was uncovered, the maternal love in infamous witches' inverted feet and hunchbacks were unveiled, the victorious laugh from Surpanakha's dismembered face rung triumphant, the uncontaminated purity gushing from Dopti's mutilated breasts was hailed, and self-reclamation through self-erasure in Nangelis' last *mulakkaram tax* was marvelled at.

As the chapter traversed from the trope of treacherous hunchbacks, desexualised mutilated nose and breasts, towards a reconception of disabled ontologies as phallocentric signifiers to individuals inhabiting variegated and autonomous corporeality, a newer space was imagined: a new semiotic canvas that is at once free and human.

Notes

1   Dasharatha sealed his conjugal ties with Kaikeyi with the promise of crowning her son as the next king. The promise was made to her father, and

contends the claim of Lord Rama as the rightful heir (Valmiki *Ramayana*, 'Ayodhyakand' 107–3).

2   Kaikeyi, despite being Dasharatha's favourite queen, had on a few instances displayed dismissiveness for her 'senior co-wife' Kausalya. As per Manthara, it placed her in a less-than-favourable position if her son, Lord Rama, was ordained as king.

3   This punishment has invited multiple debates and contentions on Rama as the epitome of *dharmic* virtuosity versus an emblem of callous punitive power. Though there are multiple tellings of this exchange, the chapter refers to the most popular one, resting within the writings of Valmiki, wherein it merits to mention that Surpanaka threatens to execute Sita after her proposal, thereby making Rama's conclusive response befitting at the outset. At the same time, Rama's order of execution does not follow the threat. It is preceded and complicated by a humiliating mockery at the expense of the *rakshasa*, as Rama proposes her to persuade Lakshmana instead, insinuating him to be an unmarried, virile man—an incorrect fact, as the latter was married to Sita's sister, Urmila. Lakshmana, in turn, spurns her proposal with visible derision, lampooning her throughout the conversation. For more, see Erndl's chapter, 'The Mutilation of Surpanakha' in *Many Ramayanas: The Diversity of a Narrative Tradition in South Asia*.

References

Adigal, Ilango. *The Silapaddikaram*, translated by V.R Ramachandra Dikshitar. London: Oxford University Press, 1939.

Ambedkar, B.R. *Who Are the Shudras*. Mumbai: Dr Babasaheb Ambedkar Source Material Publications Committee, Maharashtra, 2013. https://www.mea.gov.in/Images/attach/amb/Volume_07.pdf, pp. 9-204 (accessed on 20 January 2022).

Anees, Shabana. 'Disability in India: The Role of Gender, Family, and Religion'. *Journal of Applied Rehabilitation Counseling*, 45, no. 2 (2014): 32–38.

Appadurai, Arjun. 'Topographies of the Self: Praise and Emotion in Hindu India'. In *Language and the Politics of Emotion*, edited by Catherine A. Lultz and Lila Abu-Lughod, 93–113. Cambridge: Cambridge University Press, 1990.

Bandukwala, Nimra. 'Pakistani Folklore and Stories: The Churail—Reth & Reghistan: *Why folklore?*', 2014. https://www.sculpturalstorytelling.com/articles/2014/1/23/why-deserts-matter-too (accessed 22 November 2021).

Bandukwala, Nimra and Sadiya Ansari. 'The Witches That Terrified Me as a Kid Are Actually Feminist Heroes'. *Vice*, 2020. https://www.vice.com/en/article/pkeajm/churail-witches-that-terrified-me-as-a-kid-are-actually-feminist-heroes (accessed 22 November 2021).

Bhatt, G.H. and U.P. Shah. *Valmiki Ramayana: Critical Edition*. Vadodara: Oriental Institute, 1960.

Bhatt, Usha. *The Physically Handicapped in India: A Growing National Problem*. Mumbai: Popular Book Depot, 1963.

Buhler, G. (trans.). *Indian History Sourcebook: The Laws of Manu, c. 1500* BCE, Fordham University, New York, 1998. https://sourcebooks.fordham.edu/india/manu-full.asp.

Burnell, Arthur Coke. *The Ordinances of Manu: Translated from the Sanskrit.* London: Routledge, 2013. https://www.google.co.in/books/edition/The_Ordinances_of_Manu/AQ_-AQAAQBAJ?hl=en&gbpv=0 (accessed 21 November 2021).

Butler, Judith. *Bodies That Matter.* New York: Routledge, 1993.

Caputi, Mary. 'The Maternal Metaphor in Feminist Scholarship'. *Political Psychology,* 14, no. 2 (1993): 309–29.

Chaitanya, Sharanya. 'Rama and Lakshmana Slay the Mighty Tataka'. *New Indian Express,* 2018. https://www.newindianexpress.com/lifestyle/spirituality/2018/apr/28/rama-and-lakshmana-slay-the-mighty-tataka-1806617.html (accessed 22 November 2021).

Cho, Julio. 'Sideshow Freaks and Sexualised Children: Abject Bodies on Display'. *Critical Senses,* 5, no. 2 (1997): 18–52.

Devi, Mahashweta. 'Draupadi'. In *Breast Stories,* edited and translated by Gayatri Chakravorty, 91–105. Calcutta: Seagull Books, 2014.

Donahue, Amy. 'Hinduism and Disability'. In *Disability and World Religions,* edited by Darla Y. Schumm and Michael Stoltzfus, 37–102. Waco, Texas: Baylor University Press, 2016.

Doniger, Wendy. *The Hindu: An Alternate History.* New York: Penguin, 2009.

Erndl, Kathleen M. 'Telling as Refashioning and Opposition'. In *Many Ramayanas: The Diversity of a Narrative Tradition in South Asia,* edited by Paula Richman, 67–174. California: University of California Press, 1991. https://publishing.cdlib.org/ucpressebooks//view?docId=ft3j49n8h7&chunk.id=d0e9794&toc.depth=1&toc.id=d0e9794&brand=eschol (accessed 10 December 2021).

Frembgen, Jürgen Wasim. 'Honour, Shame, and Bodily Mutilation. Cutting off the Nose among Tribal Societies in Pakistan'. *Journal of the Royal Asiatic Society,* 16, no, 3 (2006): 243–60.

Ganguli, J.N.C. 'Hindu Theories of Punishment'. *Annals of the Bhandarkar Oriental Research Institute,* 8, no. 1 (1926): 72–92. https://www.jstor.org/stable/44028012.

Garland-Thomson, Rosemarie. 'Integrating Disability, Transforming Feminist Theory'. *Feminist Disability Studies,* 14, no. 3 (2002): 1–32. http://www.jstor.org/stable/4316922.

Ghai, Anita. *Rethinking Disability in India.* London and New York: Routledge, 2015.

Griffith, Ralph T.H. (trans.). *The Hymn of the Rigveda,* 2nd edition. Delhi: Orient Book Distributors, 1986. http://www.sanskritweb.net/rigveda/griffith.pdf.

Hindery, Roderick. 'Hindu Ethics in the *Ramayana*'. *The Journal of Religious Ethics,* 4, no. 2 (1976): 287–322.

Hope, Laurence. *Stars of the Dessert.* London: William Heinemann, 1903.

Hopkins, Edward Washburn. *Ethics of India.* New Haven: Yale University Press, 1924.

Jong, Erica. *Witches.* New York: Open Road Media, 2017.

Joseph, Sarah. 'Karuthathulakal' ('Black Chinks'), translated by J. Devika, *Frontline*, 2005. https://www.google.co.in/amp/s/frontline.thehindu. com/arts-and-culture/literature/black-chinks/article10108725.ece/amp/ (accessed 10 December 2021).

———. *Retelling the Ramayana: Voices from Kerala*, translated by Vasanthi Sankaranarayanan, New Delhi: Oxford University Press, 2005.

Khan, Benjamin. *The Concept of Dharma in Valmiki Ramayana*. New Delhi: Munshi Ram Manohar Lal, 1965. https://books.google.com/ books/about/The_Concept_of_Dharma_in_Valmiki_Ramayan. html?id=faEKvwEACAAJ (accessed 10 December 2021).

Kristeva, Julia. *Desire in Language*, translated by Thomas Gorz, Alice A. Jardin, Leon S. Roudiez, et al. New York: Columbia University Press, 1980.

———. *Revolution of Poetic Language*. New York: Columbia University, 1984.

———. *In the Beginning Was Love*. New York: Columbia University Press, 1987.

Lloyd, Margaret. 'The Politics of Disability and Feminism: Discord or Synthesis?' *Sociology*, 35, no. 3 (2001): 715–28.

McRuer, Robert. 'Compulsory Able-Bodiedness and Queer/Disabled Existence'. In *Disability Studies: Enabling the Humanities*, edited by Rosemarie Garland-Thomson, Brenda Jo Brueggemann and Sharon L. Snyder, 88–99. New York: MLA Publications, 2002.

Miles, Michael. 'Disability in an Eastern Religious Context: Historical Perspectives'. *Disability & Society*, 10, no. 1 (1995): 49–70. https://www.tandfonline.com/ doi/abs/10.1080/09687599550023723 (accessed 20 November 2021).

———. 'Disability on a Different Model: Glimpses of an Asian Heritage'. *Disability and Society*, 15, no. 4 (2000): 603–18.

Narayan, Aiyangar. *Essays on Indo-Aryan Mythology*. Whitefish, Montana: Kessinger Publishing, 2010.

Pillai, S. 'The Woman Who Cut Off Her Breasts', *The Hindu*, 2017. https://www. thehindu.com/society/history-and-culture/the-woman-who-cut-off-her-breasts/article17324549.ece (accessed 22 November 2021).

Quayson, Ato. *Aesthetic Nervousness: Disability and the Crisis of Representation*. New York: Columbia University Press, 2007.

Sarkar, Siuli. *Gender Disparity in India Unheard Wimpers*. Delhi: PHI Learning, 2016.

Schriempf, Alexa. '(Re)fusing the Amputated Body: An Interactionist Bridge for Feminism and Disability'. *Hypatia*, 16, no. 4 (2001): 53–79. https://www. jstor.org/stable/3810783 (accessed 10 November 2021).

Sheldon, Pollock. (trans.). *The Ramayana of Valmiki; An Epic of Ancient India*, Vol. II. New Jersey: Princeton University Press, 1986.

Sutherland, Sally J.M. 'Seduction, Counter Seduction, and Sexual Role Models: Bedroom Politics and the Indian Epics'. *Journal of Indian Philosophy*, 20, no. 2 (1992): 243–51.

Zvelebil, Kamil. *Tamil Literature*. Wiesbaden: Otto Harrassowitz Verlag, 1974. https:// books.google.com/books/about/Tamil_Literature.html?id=OQ33i496MsIC (accessed 22 November 2022).

6

OVERLAPPING DISCOURSES OF MONSTROSITY AND DISABILITY IN INDIA: DECODING ARYAN–DRAVIDIAN NARRATIVES IN THE *RAMAYANA* AND ITS CONTEMPORARY ITERATION IN AMISH TRIPATHI'S 'SHIVA' TRILOGY

Malvika Jayakumar

Evocations of monstrous figures in literature effectively imbue terror and apprehension in readers, not merely owing to the monster's so-called horrific appearance but also due to its diametric opposition to all laws of conduct dictated by nature. The penchant for committing blood-curdling acts of terror augments the horrendous appearance of the monster in the popular imagination. In turn, images of monstrosity become synonymous with acts of blood-letting.

It is therefore no surprise that appearances of monsters in the *Ramayana* necessarily coincide with expressions of apprehension within the narrative about the perceived potential of the monster to wreak havoc in a seemingly civilised world. The numerous narratives of monstrosity in the epic, whether it is the story of the giantess Tadaka or the tale of the headless Kabandha with hideous facial features on his torso—augur certain attitudes and preconceptions that represent the so-called demons as the deepest and most recurring images of the threatening, corporeally deviant other.

But what generally goes unnoticed and baffles a critical intellect are the subtexts of racial and spatial segregation in these epics which become evident from the specific geo-spatial location of these monstrous figures. Almost all monsters in the *Ramayana*, for instance, are located in or beyond the Dandaka forest where Rama, Lakshmana and Sita arrive during their exile down south. The distorted features of these monsters are constantly placed in opposition to the well-formed and beautiful Aryan figures of Rama, Lakshmana and Sita.

Such subtexts of spatiality and raciality, hence, suggest that the monsters in the epic serve a larger end rather than simply figuring as diabolical creatures to be slain by Rama. In this sense, the recurring encounters between gods and demons in Indian myths, specifically in an epic as widely circulated as the *Ramayana* can be easily read as an insidious process of Aryan self-fashioning when threatened by the racial 'other'.

What is even more confounding to a discerning mind is that the Aryan appropriation of the racial 'other' or the Dravidian is still prominent in contemporary retellings and reinterpretations of the epic. One prominent example is the representation of monstrosity in Amish Tripathi's 'Shiva' trilogy which reproduces the very racial geopolitics inherent in the binary opposition between normative and non-normative forms of corporealities in the *Ramayana* through the fictional conflict between the inhabitants of Meluha and the Nagas living beyond the Dandaka. This produces not just a specific iconography of the monster but also specific attitudes towards the non-normative body.

The chapter, by positing the deformed Nagas from the 'Shiva' trilogy as a reference point, explores the cultural construction of non-normative corporealities to understand how and why attitudes towards disability have been and continue to be heavily conditioned by the dynamics of self-identification and othering that ideologically structure popular narratives of monstrosity like the *Ramayana*. Since references to the terms Aryan and Dravidian suggest a history of geo-spatial conflicts and cultural othering, the essay also attempts to understand the intersectionalities between disability studies and spatial politics using Henri Lefebvre's theorisation of spatial segregation.

Further, the chapter delves into the geopolitics of discursive monstrosities through a study of the role played by print capitalism in India and the Hindu reformation in the 19th century. It suggests possibilities of dissecting monstrosity through a deconstruction of Indian myths and a study of polyphonic counter-narratives of these myths. Scholars like Ajoy K. Lahiri, A. Ganagatharam and P. Sundaram Pillai have emphasised the legitimacy of these counter-narratives undercutting the canonisation of a singular narrative. As a corollary to such notions, the chapter seeks to re-evaluate and reimagine lopsided narratives in order to diffuse the meaning of disability created through binary codes of normative and deviant corporealities and embodiments.

Drawing on the writings of Rosemarie Garland-Thomson and Margrit Shildrick on monstrosity and through the deployment of Advaita[1] philosophy as a reading strategy, this chapter attempts to deconstruct the normative–non-normative binaries by underscoring the diversity of human forms presented by the monster figure. The relevance of the monstrous 'other' within disability studies lies in the concerns about aberrant corporealities, embodiments and spatial politics inherent in the treatment of monstrosity and disability in society. These ideas would, in turn, reinforce the vibrant critical tradition around the literary representations of disability that conventional readings of the canon often overlook.

Construction of Monstrosity and Spatial Politics in Indian Myths

A fundamental rationale of culture, according to numerous literary theorists, anthropologists and psychologists, is premised upon group differentiation. One such definition of 'culture' has been proposed by the Dutch psychologist Geert Hofstede who viewed it as '… the collective programming of the human mind that distinguishes the members of one human group from those of another' (Hofstede 2011, 3).

This exercise of culture as an exclusionary practice could be found in Indian manuscripts ranging from ancient to early modern. A widely disseminated example of such a manuscript is the myth of the Indra–Vrtra conflict in the *Rigveda*. Discussing the figure of Vrtra as the natural foe of the Hindu god Indra, Ajoy Kumar Lahiri, in his thesis, 'Vedic Vrtra: A Study and a Suggested Interpretation', avers that starting from '… the earliest commentator[s] on the [Rigveda,] … [t]he Indra–Vrtra conflict has been interpreted as a symbolic struggle between the forces of darkness and those of the light' (1971, 1). What is evident here is that Lahiri does not associate the Indra–Vrtra conflict with any racial or geographical underpinnings.

On the other hand, historian Buddha Prakash in 'Vrtra: [A Study in the Impact of Aryans on Indian Culture]' recounts the Indra–Vrtra[2] myth as '… a metaphor for a young and vigorous race fresh from the mountains taking possession of the torrid plains of Northern India' wherein Indra is read as an Aryan symbol and Vrtra as the enemy of the Aryan (1949, 5). Moreover, Prakash also argues that early Vedic texts such as *Satapatha-Brahmana* and *Rigveda* have frequently described the non-Aryan community, termed Dasyus (aboriginals) as deviantly shaped for being '… snub nosed or broken nosed, dark skinned, phallus worshipping aborigines' (1949, 8).[3]

Lahiri, though, refutes such assertions of Aryan–Dravidian binaries being a given in the *Rigveda* from its earliest form and argues instead that initially the term Vrtra(s)[4] was more conceptual than pejorative in the *Rigveda*. But the term Vrtra kept developing and taken out of context from its original neuter form to increasingly involve narratives about the non-Aryan races, especially the Dravidians, which more often than not carried geo-spatial underpinnings. One such potent example of a later narrative associating monstrous connotations with a particular space is the *Ramayana*.

Cultural othering by means of monstrous attributes underpins the binary conceptions of Aryans and Dravidians in several later Vedic tales with interpretations that became ossified over time. In the *Ramayana*, in particular, the deviant space beyond the Dandaka depicts Rama's mission as not only rescuing Sita and slaying Ravana but also punishing or civilising the monsters, depending on their subservience to his cause. Like the Indra–Vrtra myth, irrespective of any historical veracity, the multiple retellings of the *Ramayana* projected the unrelenting 'other' with monstrous traits like cannibalism and multiple limbs.

This common denominator of monstrosity across various cultures of geo-spatial othering, as a result, introduces the monstrous '… as a kind of rhetorically-effective short-hand that was easily recognisable because of the ubiquity and simplicity of the monstrous' (Berg 2015). For instance, the representation of monstrosity as a convenient yardstick to demarcate elements and individuals that were anathema to the author's projection of an ideal Indian culture emerges in the numerous interpolations and varying degrees of exaggerations across the multiple retellings of the epic. A telling example is of the differences between Valmiki's *Ramayana* and its 12th-century retelling by Tamil poet Kamban. While Valmiki's Rama is depicted as a mortal and his assaults on the inhabitants of Dandaka as standard instances of Kshatriya excesses, the popularity of Vaishnavite culture during the Bhakti movement inspired its followers, like Kamban, to project Rama as an incarnation of Vishnu, granting divine justification for all of his actions. Monstrosity, in this context, became an easy marker to differentiate between the holy and the unholy.

The monster figure, according to Elizabeth B. Bearden in *Monstrous Kinds: Body, Space and, Narrative in Renaissance Representations of Disability*, reflects early '… representations of bodies, spaces and narratives,' thereby reinforcing the intimate connection between deviant spaces and monstrosity (2019, 4). Bearden further asserts that an understanding of how deviant corporealities were theorised in early textual representations of monstrosity '… not only provides us with more accurate genealogies of disability, but also helps us to nuance current aesthetic and theoretical disability formulations' (4).

Moreover, the notion that age-old attitudes towards disability and space construct each other could be substantiated through Brendon Gleeson's theory of 'geographies of disability' as employed by Bearden. According to her, Gleeson's theory reveals the synthesis of both nature and space to reflect bodies being either disabled or enabled by particular geographies (22). In fact, through Gleeson's theory, Bearden differentiates impairment and disability and explains the 'historical-geographical approach to disability' in the following terms:

[D]isability is what may become of impairment as each society produces itself socio-spatially: there is no necessary correspondence between impairment and disability. There are only historical-geographical correspondences which obtain when some societies, in the course of producing and reproducing themselves through cultural and political economic practices, oppressively transform impaired first nature as disablement. The historical-geographical view recognizes that different societies may produce environments that liberate the capacities of impaired people while not aggravating their limitations. (Bearden 2019)

In the context of the *Ramayana*, the historical-geographical approach to disability is evident in the north-south binary spelt out by upholding the Aryan as the norm and disabling the corporealities that do not adhere to it. The monsters in this epic are disabled not only due to their deformed features but also their inability to transgress their spatial boundary. The fraught space of Dandaka is a frequent witness to the consistent spatial encumberment of monsters like Tataka, whose very presence is considered a threat to the holy rituals of the sages. Given that the *Ramayana* still holds immense currency in the nation, its deployment of monstrosity to validate socio-spatial othering continues to be imported by contemporary narratives. One such instance is Amish Tripathi's 'Shiva' trilogy, which, while attempting to empathise with its disabled characters, fails to shake off the hegemony of the epic.

The trilogy is an expansive story partially inspired by the myth of the Hindu god, Shiva. The eponymous protagonist of the trilogy is the leader of a tribe invited to the impeccable kingdom of Meluha in the Sapt Sindhu[5] region to fulfil the prophecy that will relieve the Meluhans from the dire consequences of the Saraswati drying up and frequent attacks by their foes. The cause for this turbulence has been attributed to the production of Somras[6] from the waters of Saraswati, which prolongs the lifespan of Meluhans and it is for Shiva to unite all the people and see them through this crisis.

The trilogy initially creates a dichotomy between the upright Meluhans and the deviant Nagas insinuated by the paradisiacal description of Meluha and the naming of its capital city as Devagiri—the abode of Gods—while associating unknown dangers and karmic sins with the abode of the 'deformed' Nagas. But gradually, the trilogy subverts this binary by showcasing the hypocrisy of the Meluhan rulers who demonised the Nagas to hide their own exploitative practices like the overconsumption of Somras causing genetic deformities in the Nagas. However, the Nagas continue to express deference towards the intensely skewed and Aryanised legend of Rama. The trilogy's nostalgia for the pure world of Rama and disengagement from the spaces beyond the Narmada indicate that modern Indian mythological retellings are still shackled to the master narrative of the *Ramayana*.

The 'Shiva' trilogy's disengagement from the spaces beyond the Narmada could be gauged from the lack of description of the southern regions, even though it attempts to weave a pan-Indian narrative. The trilogy moves from Mansarovar, Srinagar, to the alluvial plains of the Sapt Sindhu region, eastern kingdoms like Branga and the mangroves of the Sundarbans. It does venture beyond the Narmada to reach Panchvati but does not go any further and merely hints at the possibility of kingdoms further south—a region which remains largely absent in the trilogy. This silence of the south affords spatiality larger significance in the construction of Aryan–Dravidian binaries. An example of this silence could be found in the irony that, for a trilogy with Shiva as its protagonist, it entirely disregards the strong Shaivite tradition in the south and yokes the legend of Shiva with the Vaishnavite figure of Rama. This authorial decision might be attributed to the lack of scholarly research on Sangam literature and the gradual insurgence of Brahminism in the south which established the supremacy of the *Vedas*.

The interconnections of monstrous traits and spatial politics reflected through the dichotomous representations of the idyllic kingdoms in the Sapt Sindhu region and the misinformation and enigma surrounding the spaces beyond the Narmada could be understood through the arguments of Henri Lefebvre, a major proponent of spatiality. Although Lefebvre's theories pertain to spatial politics in urban centres,[7] his ideas could be imported to understand the ideological underpinnings of marginalising non-normative individuals from certain spaces sanctioned by their deviant corporealities and embodiments. In *State, Space and World: Selected Essays*, Lefebvre argues that planners of urban centres often try to establish a certain epistemology to explain the spatial segregation in these centres entailing several privations due to which the inhabitants do not always fit into the form described by the planners without resistance.[8]

Elaborating on the above statement, this chapter avers that the contours of a space are not merely solidified through architectural structures or by demarcating a territorial unit under a specific authority, but also through the propagation of narratives binding people by instilling a sense of a common cultural consciousness and aspirations. In this regard, if the monstrous attributes used as discursive constructs for cultural commentary in various Aryanised narratives help to legitimise spatial stereotypes, then it also begs the question of why such pejorative notions sustained the test of time despite the growing interaction with distant regions of the world. An exploration of this question cannot be merely restricted to the idiomatic representation of monstrosity to uphold the 'normal' but also needs to take into account the formative role of print capitalism in fashioning and cementing stereotypical narratives of monstrosity in popular imagination. This approach would help in understanding how such specious claims about corporeal deviance became solidified in the popular culture. In this sense, the chapter also attempts to decode the role that print capitalism plays in serving the agendas of the hegemony.

Print Capitalism and Reinvention of Hindu Dharma

Modern Indian fantasy fiction is often backed by the country's rich heritage of mythologies. But, in the process of liberally borrowing elements from Indian myths, modern-day retellings and reinterpretations of these myths tend to inadvertently ingest the stereotypes and biases present in various mythological tales. Furthermore, the authoritative status of these narratives is evident through the consistent impunity with which these reproduce cultural stereotypes and biases over the ages and also attempt to efface a dynamic history of divergent perspectives and polyphonic counter-narratives of these mythological tales.

This effacement is evident in the cultural stereotypes proliferated by the *Ramayana*, which are often consumed by its readers with as much gusto as the epic itself. Despite the addition of newer perspectives and plot lines in the modern deployment of tropes from the epic, the denouement, more often than not, is the subjugation of the non-normative Dravidian by the upright Aryan. The sacramental treatment of the epic, irrespective of the contemporaneous existence of several counter-narratives, especially in languages other than Hindi and Sanskrit, leads to questions about how only particular narratives came to be codified. Is it merely because of the clout of Sanskrit or are there other politics involved?

One of the factors which played a great role in the proliferation of certain narratives over others was print capitalism. Due to the increase in dissemination, transmission and translation of several Indian narrative and didactic texts encouraged by the colonial authorities in the 19th century, these narratives often assumed almost monolithic forms. These activities were predominantly biased towards Aryanised narratives from the north Indian plains resulting in the emergence of ideological indices.

Dwelling on the reproduction and wide dissemination of these indices in 19th-century India, Vasudha Dalmia, in *The Nationalization of Hindu Traditions: Bharatendu Harishchandra and Nineteenth Century*

Banaras, maintains that the present-day monolithic form of Hindu *dharma*, rather than being a direct bequest of the ancient period, was cemented by the collusion of Hindu reformist-orientalist activities, leading to '... the retrospective projection of a religion conceptualized as monolinear' (2010, 1). While there had been common traditions and reference points of Hinduism in the past, Dalmia argues, none of those rituals enjoyed the kind of supreme authority achieved in the 19th century. The consolidation of loosely existing rites and practices of Hinduism could be partially attributed to the spurt in reformist activities by several Hindu organisations and the colonial government in the 19th century.

In this period, the reformist activities undertaken by nationalists like Bankimchandra Chatterjee, Aurobindo Ghose and Bipin Chandra Pal to modernise Hinduism were perceived as a form of Hindu renaissance. But, Dalmia problematises this epithet for the 19th-century reformulation of Hinduism by invoking the arguments of Barun De, who recognised the arbitrariness of attaching this epithet without understanding the socio-political context of this term as used in Europe. Unlike the European Renaissance, the so-called Indian renaissance did not culminate in bourgeois domination. Instead, according to De, it consisted of '... the cultural response of [the Indian] middle class to the modernizing bourgeois of Europe', as affected by the colonial government (9). Hence, the endorsement of Hindu traditions cemented in the 19th century could be viewed as an endorsement of the activities of the colonial government. In this cultural matrix, printing often became the propaganda machine for traditionalist-reformist Hindu organisations and the colonial government. The interpolations and expurgations while printing sacred texts like the *Ramayana* not only served to cement its status in the popular imagination but also shaped public opinion in favour of the ideas espoused by the stakeholders.

Dalmia elaborates this conception of printing through Benedict Anderson's view that print capitalism furthers nationalistic ideologies resulting in languages that get chosen for printing, laying the basis for national consciousness, unifying the fields of exchange and communication, imbuing a new fixity to language, and thus creating new languages of power.[9] In 19th-century India, the language favoured for printing and translation over other vernaculars, due to several vested interests and a blinkered outlook, happened to be Hindi with its Sanskritic roots. The overwhelming bias towards Hindi and Sanskrit was not simply an indigenous development but was also a result of the narrow attitudes of Western orientology.

For Dalmia, this oriental shortsightedness is evident in the historiographic capital associated with the notion of 'Aryan'. In contrast, the ancient literary productions of the Sangam[10] era have suffered from perpetual dismissal and indifference. Naturally, the justification offered for an Aryanised historiography, using the dichotomies and stereotypes in texts like the *Ramayana*, tightly secure the binary codes of the holy Aryan and the monstrous Dravidian in the cultural consciousness. An understanding of the role of print capitalism in emboldening these binary codes becomes more explicit in the context of Shildrick's observation that any monstrous birth could be called upon 'to support both political and moral exhortations', especially after the commercialisation of printing, which led to '... heavily illustrated popular texts [being] circulated with more or less fantastic versions of monster stories' (2009, 13).

Counter-Narratives of the Ramayana

The ossification of the *Ramayana* or the concept of 'Ramrajya'[11] through factors like the skewed modes of print capitalism both demonstrate a marginalising impact as well as offer a justification for spatial othering, or in Lefebvre's terms, helps in the creation of specific epistemologies. In the *Shiva Trilogy*, Ramrajya is present as the hallowed ideal around which Meluha and the Naga kingdoms are modelled and it is also the yardstick for judging the moral decadence of Meluha or the ethicality of the Nagas. The novels seem to redeem the monsters beyond the Narmada as long as they subscribe to Rama's laws, since, the Naga capital—Panchvati—is depicted as being sanctified by the banyan trees where Rama, Sita and Lakshman had rested during their exile. Despite efforts to destabilise the holy–unholy dichotomy between the normative Meluhans and the non-normative Nagas, Tripathi is unable to shake off the image of an ideal Aryanised ableism enshrined in the invocation of the Ramrajya.

The multiple references to Ramrajya in the trilogy play into those very homogenising tendencies of the ableist society of Meluha, which ostracises Naga children due to their physical aberrations. Much like the monstrous qualities foisted onto the Nagas due to their deformities, Meluha's legacy of the Ramrajya is another legitimation used by its normative citizens to propagate narratives about the malevolence of the othered beings. To enable a meaningful critique of such racially and spatially alienating concepts like the Ramrajya , there is a pressing need, first and foremost, to counter the ossification of the *Ramayana* and the entrenched stereotypes about non-normative corporealities and embodiments in the epic through a survey of a variety of subversive counter-narratives, especially those capturing the oft-silenced Dravidian perspective of the othered characters in the epic.

A. Ganagatharam's 'Epic, Episteme and Ethnicity: Re-Reading of the *Ramayana* in Modern Tamil Context', observes that in Aryanised narratives like the *Ramayana*, '… [h]yperbolic characterisations such as the three headed trisiras, the ten-headed Ravana, the ever sleepy Kumbakarna and the hideous Surpanakha expose the implacable prejudice of the Aryans' (2002, 883). Such a divergent perspective, according to Ganagatharam, helps in the development of the Dravidian ideology and in '[t]he re-assessment of traditional characters, symbolic representations, cultural statements and incidents of the epic with polemical flamboyance [which create] a rhetoric of political opposition and a means to construct alternative world views' (2002, 887). The potency of such alternative views could be gauged from the radical Jaina reading of the *Ramayana* by Vimalasuri, called *Paumacharyam* (3rd century AD), where Ravana is a staunch Jaina and renounces the Brahmins for grossly manipulating the original narrative in their favour. Vimalasuri goes on to declare '*rakshasas*' as human beings and not demons and dismisses all the disparaging statements about the Dravidian race in Valmiki's *Ramayana*.

Adding to this notion, noted late 19th-century Tamil scholar and educator P. Sundaram Pillai had also criticised the Sanskrit *Ramayana* for its Aryan bias which construed the Dravidians, with their highly advanced civilisation, in the worst possible light. Pillai's principal contention was that the normative Aryanised *devas* did not live up to the lofty ideals espoused by them, while it was often the non-normative Dravidian *asuras* who displayed more integrity. He substantiated his assertion by citing instances of amoral conduct by the Aryan characters in the *Ramayana*, like Rama's stealth attack on Bali, his alliance with the treacherous Sugriva and Vibhishana and his ruthless killing of the Shudra Shambuga for violating the *dharmic* order by conducting puja,[12] as opposed to Ravana, who always exhibited great fidelity to his personal moral codes. In this manner, Pillai disrupted the conventional binary between the holy Aryan and the unholy Dravidian by recasting the actions of Rama and Ravana into fresher perspectives. It is this novel reformulation in the various counter-narratives of age-old conventions and stereotypes which lends discursive tools for dismantling the stigmas and dichotomies directed at disability.

Reading the 'Shiva' Trilogy through Spatial Politics and
Disability Discourse

As evident from the discussion so far, the circulation of lopsided narratives becomes necessary to sustain the binary codes of normativity and non-normativity because the absorption of the othered sections seemingly poses the threat of robbing the normative spatial unit of its exclusivity and destabilising the exalted position of the normate self. Resistance, as a result, is bound to erupt from sections which do not get incorporated or are demonised in the circulating narratives.[13] To neutralise such a resistance, the creation of a certain epistemology, is evident in the trilogy, from the hollow ideals scaffolding Meluha as it practices a systematic exclusion of Naga children at birth not because of any perceived knowledge of the past sins of the Nagas, but to conceal that their deformities are produced by excessive consumption of Somras by the Meluhans. To hide this reality, the rulers and scholars of Meluha create histories that dictate spatial seclusion on the basis of physical aberrations.

Chris Butler, in *Henri Lefebvre: Spatial Politics, Everyday Life and the Right to the City*, explains that spatial segregation is governed by market-driven processes which, along with profit and efficiency, are also geared towards reproducing homogeneity in society. Even Shildrick seems to attest to Lefebvre's notion of the normate body reproducing homogeneity when she cites Canguilhem's arguments from 'Monstrosity and Monstrous', suggesting '… that what gives value to the individual life may be both the maintenance of a protective bodily integrity, and the capacity to reproduce it over time' (2009, 29). Such emphasis over reproducing uniformity in society is informed by the vulnerabilities and anxieties of the normative self-underscored by Shildrick.

The contingency of birth diffuses the strict segregation of the monstrous other from the normate society, thereby undercutting the claims of purity in several Aryanised narratives. The trilogy, too, is not innocent of these anxieties regarding reproductive purity as Meluha actively decrees the banishment of not only the deformed Naga children but also the women who bear them. Anything jarring the rose-tinted vision of a perfect society is promptly done away with in Meluha, resulting in a form of rigorous homogeneity visible in all of its citizens who look no older than twenty and remain healthy even after living for hundreds of years due to the effects of the Somras.

The presence of disabled bodies disrupts this homogeneity by exposing the exploitation that supports the lavish lifestyle of the Meluhans, painfully reminding them of the imperfections that the body could be subject to.[14] It is no wonder then that inherent in the territoriality of kingdoms in the Sapt Sindhu region are concerns about not just their sovereignty but also the vulnerabilities of the normate body in the presence of the monstrous figure. Time and again Meluhan characters betray these sentiments, especially when Nandi, Shiva's Meluhan aide, appalled at the mention of Nagas, endorses an absolutist society based on the casteist principles of Manu:

> Our land, my Lord, the land of the seven rivers. The land of the Indus,
> Saraswati, Yamuna, Ganga, Sarayu, Brahmaputra and Narmada.
> This is where Lord Manu mandated that all of us, Suryavanshis and
> Chandravanshis, live. (Tripathi 2010)

The non-normative corporealities and embodiments in the 'Shiva' Trilogy, hence, acquire ramifications of cultural and racial disability since aberrations from the normative body are employed to underscore the differences between two spaces which are, in turn, reflective of the dichotomies constructed in numerous Aryanised myths. This spatial othering is effectively summed up in the tendency of these Aryanised stereotypes to deliberately project '... abnormal features as deformed heads, elongated ears, and the marks of scarification, not just for purposes of fraud ... but for reasons of differential cultural norms' (Shildrick 2009).

The relevance of differential cultural norms construed through monster narratives in studying attitudes towards disability is potently summarised in Rosemarie Garland-Thomson's 'Freak Discourse'. In her introduction to *Freakery: Cultural Spectacles of the Extraordinary Body*, Garland-Thomson states that the disquiet stirred in the human soul by different bodies engenders enduring cultural images in the form of iconic mythical monsters like Cyclops, Goliath, werewolves and dwarfs. She elaborates that all these monstrous figures '... are perhaps the mythical explanations for the startling bodies whose curious lineaments gesture toward other modes of being and confuse comforting distinctions between what is human and what is not' (1996, 1). Thus, extraordinary bodies, Garland-Thomson asserts, are integral for making sense of the normative world. On account of these extraordinary bodies being '... rare, unique, material, and confounding of cultural categories, they function as magnets to which culture secures its anxieties, questions and needs at any given moment' (1996, 2). Such unique singular bodies, as a result, become increasingly politicised as concerns of individual and national values, and identity and directions are mapped onto the so-called monstrous body.

Building on Garland-Thomson's arguments, Shildrick deems corporeal disability '... as providing the present day coordinates of monstrosity or 'freakery', limited now to the abnormal' (2009, 23). Shildrick, in her text, *Embodying the Monster: Encounters with the Vulnerable Self*, convincingly argues that the normate defines itself in terms of what it most fears to become, that is, the monster. She further argues that the monstrous figure is not an external phenomenon to normative society, as the monster is a projection of the vulnerabilities and anxieties of the normatively embodied being. Due to these leaks and flows, the monstrous other ends up occupying a liminal space which disrupts '... both internal and external order, and overturn[s] the distinctions that set out the limits of the human subject' (2009, 4). This propensity of the monster figure to cause an ontological crisis in the construction of the normative self is a powerful reading strategy employed in disability studies to deconstruct the binary codes between disabled and nondisabled embodiments engendered by society.

The above notions shed new light on the alienation of the deformed Nagas from the kingdom of Meluha in Tripathi's trilogy. Meluha's exclusion of the Nagas is such that it is indicative of the corporeal and embodied otherness often associated with the notion of monstrosity. In the trilogy, this view of monstrosity implies that for the citizens of Meluha, it is not enough to shun the Nagas only on account of their aberrant corporeality. The societal rejection of the Nagas also requires a legitimation of the edifice of aberrant embodiments, like myths about the gruesome violence inflicted by them on the normatively constructed Meluhans, which play a significant part in their banishment from Meluha alongside their deformities. Hence, the disabilities of the Nagas, instead of being an isolated literary phenomenon, seemingly belong to a larger tradition of weaving monstrosity out of differential corporeal alignments as illustrated by Garland-Thomson and Shildrick.

Propagation of ideas of cultural superiority through the normative body results in aberrant corporealities and embodiments being determined through coordinates of monstrosity. This notion configures the monstrous as a receptacle for diverse interpretations of several phenomena. One such relevant phenomenon is disability sharing intersectionalities with monstrous representations as narratives of monstrosity and disability fuel each other due to the common baggage of deep anxieties and prejudices regarding aberrant corporealities and embodiments. The prejudicial treatment directed at disabled and monstrous figures spawns narratives of antithesis from the norm, suggesting that monstrosity and disability are as much culturally and psychologically produced as these are physically visible, placing the monstrous-disability combine in a conundrum of signification.

Presence of an Alternate Critical Tradition in Indian Mythology

The presence of counter-narratives indicates the existence of a broader spectrum of tales beyond the pale of canonised narratives, hinting that there are enough tools in Indian literature to formulate an alternative theoretical tradition to undercut the monstrous-disability combine.

For instance, Meluha remains oblivious to the highly advanced Naga knowledge system which helps the Branga kingdom, an ally, to tide over its frequent epidemics. It is in such a scenario that a re-evaluation of one's literary tradition and a reimagination of the pejorative representation of non-normative corporealities and embodiments aid in deconstructing stereotypes about culturally constructed disability. After all, the notion of ableism that Meluha upheld by disabling a certain section is not universal, as the Meluhans become incapacitated when they are persecuted by natural elements while crossing the Dandaka whereas the Nagas are resourceful.

If read against the grain, the presence of disabled bodies disrupts the stringent homogeneity of the normative body by exposing the exploitation that supports the lavish lifestyle of the Meluhans. Borrowing from Shildrick's argument, it seems the monster figure offers dynamic possibilities for projecting disabled identities as it dismantles the binaries between the self and the other by employing the monstrous to

> refigure it as an alternative, but the equally valuable, mode of being, an alterity that throws doubt on the singularity of the human and signals other less restrictive possibilities ... [T]he monster might be the promising location of a reconceived, and an ethics centred on a relational economy that has a place for radical difference. (2009, 67)

Instead of fixing the bounds of the normative body, Shildrick's reinterpretation of the monster figure as embodying the diversities of the human form is also evident in the reformulation of the normative ontology in the Indian philosophy of Advaita Vedanta, whichcritiques the Cartesian mind-body dualism.[15] Sthaneshwar Timalsina, in *Consciousness in Indian Philosophy: The Advaita Doctrine of 'Awareness Only*, has discussed non-dualism in the Advaita philosophy. According to him, Advaita professes that,

> there is ultimately no essential plurality in what exists. Through the epistemological lens, what is cognized is essentially non-dual awareness only ... The duality that is perceived, in the self-experience of different subjects, or in cognition of different objects, is the very pure consciousness manifested in various forms due to the state of not knowing reality. (2009, 3)

The presence of Advaita means that Indian philosophy contains elements countervailing the divide between the normative *devas* and the hideous *asuras* in the Vedic texts as these differences are based on dualism. The awareness of consciousness in Advaita does not recognise these differences, which, in turn, destabilises the binary between ability and disability that is suggested by the juxtaposition of *deva*s and *asura*s. In *The Secret of the Nagas,* a critique of dualism is presented when Shiva's conception of the Nagas is questioned by a Vasudeva priest who explains that the divide between good and evil is illusory and that what may be good for the majority may easily flip its nature with the winds of time.

At this juncture, is it not possible to reimagine the myth of the *Samudra Manthan*[16] construing the divergent categories of *deva*s and *asura*s? Such an overhauling of Indian literary myths holds great potential to offer effective critical tools to deconstruct the dichotomies of normative and non-normative embodiments. In the trilogy, Tripathi also seems to narrate a reimagination of the victims of the *Samudra Manthan* who, on account of their deformed selves, were bereft of the Somras—a product of a history of dispossessions and intense territorialism. As the immortality of the *deva*s and subsequent boons of holiness which distinguish them from the *asura*s are based on a simple trait of possessing the Somras, the same could be averred about space, the appropriation of which determines the contours of disability. The trilogy, from this viewpoint, could be read as a reimagination as well as subversion of the *Samudra Manthan* where the holy world of Meluha becomes the cause for plagues and deformities and the so-called diabolic Nagas possess the cure for the plagues and treasure their unique systems of knowledge.

Hence, monstrous manifestations are inherent in Aryan–Dravidian narratives, but these have to be broadcasted with a strong justification like most other majoritarian projects. The derogatory baggage associated with disability helps to dismiss a rich cultural tradition. But, more than being hapless victims, disability also lies in the inability to narrate one's story. David Bolt, in 'Social Encounters, Cultural Representation and Critical Avoidance', has spoken of disabled individuals being described through meta-narratives or cultural constructs for a lack of their own (2012, 290). Similarly, for the lack of adequate representation in terms of material evidence and vested interests in print capitalism, the hideousness of the other in the circulating narratives is a kaleidoscope which has not yet been turned.

Conclusion

The frequent association of monstrosity with disability requires an unpacking of the term. Shildrick does so by investigating the predicaments caused by the close encounter of the normate self and the other during voyages, an idea which could be applied in the reading of Tripathi's trilogy. Her views could be comprehended through these journeys that upstage the cultural superiority assumed by Meluha. The veneer of a utopia maintained by Meluha is not founded on its excellent administration but rather, on the exclusion of deformed individuals from consuming the Somras. But this farce can be sustained only through a complete segregation between the Meluhans and the Nagas. The more these two spaces collide, the more the unfounded narratives about the upright Meluhans and the monstrous Nagas are exposed.

Moreover, several bewildering truths about Meluha which initiate an ontological crisis in Shiva are revealed only after his arrival to the Naga kingdom. This development lends voice to Shildrick's observation that voyages to diverse spaces teeming with non-normative embodiments are one of the most important framing devices of the monster figure. This is because encounters with the so-called monstrous races during such explorations signal the human/animal hybridity superimposed on these races to highlight absolute otherness from the civilised races as well as the corruption of human form and being, hence revealing the dependence of the normate self on the monstrous for providing 'a complex vehicle for the expression of inner desires and anxieties' (2009, 16).

These anxieties are palpable in the trilogy during the entry of the central characters into the putatively impenetrable Dandaka forest— the route to the Naga kingdom—which portends a contact zone fraught with tensions between the normative and the deviant. As they venture deeper into terra incognita, Shiva and other Meluhan characters imagine more and more life-threatening situations in the alien space. It is with such preconceptions that Shiva is shocked by the advanced infrastructure and beauty, similar to Meluha, in the Naga kingdom. Shildrick's postulations could be germane in reading such instances in the trilogy which reflect that the normate and non-normate self are not mutually exclusive categories but constitute each other. It can be surmised that voyages highlight the artificially cultivated notion of the normate in a specific socio-political context that quickly loses steam when that context is changed, posing a danger to the so-called superiority of the normative society by the very presence of the other.

Shildrick's theory undercutting bodily dichotomies is predicated upon 'aberrant corporealities'. According to Andrew N. Sharpe, in *Foucault's Monsters and the Challenge of Law*, Shildrick's arguments ignore the role of human law in framing monstrosity and treat the concepts of the monster and the monstrous as the same. While Sharpe agrees with Shildrick in viewing the othering of disabled individuals as informed by the historical othering of the monster, he tries to extend Shildrick's arguments by tracing the genealogy of this exclusion as enshrined in the law. He refers to Foucault's *Abnormal: Lectures at the College de France (1974–1975)* to define the monster as presenting a double breach in nature and law due to which the monster's monstrosity could be 'understood in terms of morphological irregularity, and monstrous [...] in terms of transgression of the law' (2010, 32). Elaborating on this notion, Sharpe notes that merely a contravention of the laws of nature ensuring able-bodied corporeality does not constitute a monster, but rather, it is the transgression of human-made laws like civil, religious or divine laws which dictate what is monstrous in society. Otherwise, how can Meluhan subjects like Nandi assert the viciousness of the Nagas whom they have never encountered if not for the promulgation of laws prohibiting any contact with that monstrous race?

The blind faith in the monstrosity of an othered race echoes Shelly Tremain's theorisation of the Foucauldian idea of hegemony in *Foucault and the Government of Disability*, according to which 'subjects are produced who "have" impairments because this identity meets certain requirements of contemporary social and political arrangements' (2005, 10). This seems to suggest that the disabled identity is a function of political machinations instead of necessarily being of a tactile nature. Politically constructed disability, Tremain explains, occurs not only through prohibitions and punishments by the state but also through 'normalizing technologies that facilitate the systematic objectivization of subjects as deaf, criminal, mad and so on' (2005, 8). In light of Tremain's views, Nandi's uninformed comments about the Nagas seem like a telling example of Aryan.

Dravidian narratives of monstrosity being crystallised over time and broadcast as much through rumours and speculation as through state-sponsored conduits:

> They are cursed people, My Lord ... [t]hey are born with hideous deformities because of the sins of their previous births. Deformities like extra hands or horribly misshapen faces. But they have tremendous strength and skills. The Naga name alone strikes terror in any citizen's heart. They are not even allowed to live in the Sapt Sindhu. (Tripathi 2010)

Yet, the Foucauldian notion of monstrosity as a nature/law breach has been problematised by none other than Shildrick in her text *Dangerous Discourses of Disability, Subjectivity and Sexuality* for creating a distinction between monstrosity and disability on the basis of who gets absorbed into society. Putting it succinctly, Foucault's delineation of monstrosity and disability seems to view monsters as those disabled individuals who fail to get included in the legal framework. Such a distinction indicates that disabled individuals legally incorporated into society are passive about their subordinate position with no scope for subversion.

Shildrick further critiques Foucault's views through her remark that 'contemporary disability studies increasingly deploys queer theory to reopen the question of transgression across all designations of anomalous embodiment' (2010, 13). In her observation, Shildrick seems to invite other discourses to reimagine disabled embodiment as something dynamic and capable of transgression irrespective of its token integration into the social fabric. Similar to disability discourse, queer and feminist discourses also focus on individuals with non-normative embodiments boxed into monstrous categories. Since the transgressive potential of people of non-normative genders and aberrant sexualities is well documented, transgressions by individuals with non-normative corporealities also deserve as much legitimacy instead of clipping off its meaning through Foucault's definition.

By citing queer theory in particular, Shildrick shows the immense possibilities of studying disabled identities through a variety of discourses from other fields. For the lack of queer characters in the trilogy, Shildrick's integration of other discourses could be extended to the treatment of another marginalised section in the trilogy. The social alienation of Vikarma[17] women of Meluha is a case in point where, despite being unequally absorbed into society, the unfair practice of marginalising widows gets critiqued by Shiva from within the kingdom. This critique of the unfair practices against Vikarma women, in turn, opens up the possibility of critiquing the attitudes towards other non-normative embodiments like disabled individuals from within the system rather than rejecting the system or getting rejected by the law each time and allowing the social outcast to become a Foucauldian monster.

Notes

1 The term Advaita refers to *atman* or true self and deals with the pursuit of self-knowledge. This philosophy conceives the world as '*maya*' or illusion and understands cognition as essentially non-dualistic.

2 As per the *Rigveda*, Vrtra is a demon who is the natural foe of the Vedic deity Indra. Prakash corroborates his claims with several passages from the *Rigveda*, where the term 'Vrtra' is used to denote an enemy in general. In fact, the usage of this term in its plural form might even point towards a general designation of a class of people much like the Tripathi's Nagas.

3 Interestingly, Prakash also suggests that these terms were used in a neutral sense by the likes of the Mesopotamians due to trade relations between them and the Dravidians. However, it came to be associated with odium once the Dravidians were defeated by the Vedic tribes. He even dissects the term '*asura*' in Vedic texts to opine that initially, it did not imply demons but rather, people having their own religion, culture, language,

literature and science and drew anthropological and cultural affinities with Assyrians and Sumerians—kingdoms of the Mesopotamian civilisation.

4   Prakash quotes Professor Macdonell from 'Vedic Mythology' to depict how Vrtra(s) has been interpreted to mean obstructer or obstruction, as opposed to Aryans, or dasyus or foes vanquished by Indra. Therefore, Indra is often referred to as Dasyuhan or Vrtrahan, that is, slayer of Vrtras.

5   Refers to the seven rivers in northern India which play a prominent role in the *Rigeda*. These include Indus, Saraswati, Yamuna, Ganga, Sarayu, Brahmputra and Narmada.

6   Nectar of immortality/*amrit*.

7   For Henri Lefebvre, urban centres are not just political units but are also constituted by social relations.

8   Lefebvre further explains that

   [t]he old scarcities were bread, the means of subsistence, etc. In the great industrial nations there is already a concealed overproduction of those necessities of life that were formerly scarce, and whose scarcity produced horrific struggles. However, new scarcities emerge- such as water, air, light and space, over which there is an intense struggle. (2009)

9   Benedict Anderson, in *Imagined Communities: Reflections on the Origin and Spread of Nationalism* (1983), viewed the nation as growing from the roots provided by the religious communities and dynastic realms primarily by the means of print capitalism which supported nationalistic ideologies in their endeavour to associate particular languages with particular territorial units (Dalmia 11). Moreover, this idea also hints at the language debates of the nation, which might be one of the reasons for particular narratives gaining prominence.

10   Sangam refers to the assembly of Tamil scholars and artists in the ancient Tamil kingdoms resulting in seminal works of Tamil literature like *Tolkappiyam* and *Silappatikaram*. It is conjectured that three such assemblies were held but much of these details exist as myths, thus resulting in the difficulty to fix accurate dates for these ancients works.

11   The ideal society conceived by Rama.

12   Shambuga's tale happens after Rama's coronation as the ruler of Ayodhya. The *dharmic* order deified by the *Ramayana* stipulates that performance of Vedic rituals falls within the preserve of the Brahmins, while Shudras belong to the lowest rung of the order. It is this hierarchy which Shambuga tries to transgress by performing puja. By killing him, Rama upholds the exploitative *dharmic* order. Several retellings of the epic offer justifications for Shambuga's execution through claims that he was serving the demonic cult through his twisted invocation of the *Veda*s. Similar to the treatment of the Dravidian characters, Shambuga's killing also reflects how the epic and its Aryanised retellings justify the abuse and exploitation of non-normative individuals by projecting demonic/monstrous qualities onto them.

13 Lefebvre's famous slogan, 'right to the city', is reflective of the anxieties of reproducing the existing relations of production in a capitalistic society by stipulating the bounds that make an individual eligible to inhabit a socio-political space. It is an individual's right not to be expelled from the metropolitan centre through enforced dispersal to the urban peripheries, with the daily hardships that afflict these areas. The right to the city justifies the refusal to allow oneself to be removed from urban reality by a discriminative and segregative organisation. This right of the citizen proclaims the inevitable crisis of the city centres based on segregation, which rejects towards peripheral spaces all those who do not participate in political privileges (*Henri Lefebvre: Spatial Politics, Everyday Life and the Right to the City*).

14 Butler also talks of participation in the modes of production as an important factor determining an individual's access to the urban centre and due to which the ostracised milieu is deemed naturally incapable of contributing to society.

15 This split is closely associated with Rene Descartes, who understood the mind as non-physical and the body as physical.

16 A classic tale of dispossession of the hideous *asura*s from the nectar of immortality and other boons appropriated by the *deva*s.

17 In the trilogy, these are widows whose past sins are blamed for their husbands' deaths and who are expected to live out a marked life of celibacy.

References

Bearden, Elizabeth B. 'Introduction.' *Monstrous Kinds: Body, Space and, Narrative in Renaissance Representations of Disability*, 1–33. University of Michigan Press, 2019.

Bolt, David. 'Social Encounters, Cultural Representation and Critical Avoidance.' In *Routledge Handbook of Disability Studies*, edited by Nick Watson, Alan Roulstone and Carol Thomas, 287–97. London and New York: Routledge, 2012.

Butler, Chris. 'The Right to the City.' In *Henri Lefebvre: Spatial Politics, Everyday Life and the Right to the City*, 143–152. Oxfordshire, USA, Canada: Routledge, 2012.

Dalmia, Vasudha. *The Nationalization of Hindu Traditions: Bharatendu Harishchandra and Nineteenth Century Banaras*. Ranikhet: Permanent Black, 2010 (1997).

Ganagatharam, A. 'Epic, Episteme and Ethnicity: Re-Reading of the *Ramayana* in Modern Tamil Context.' *Proceedings of the Indian History Congress*, 63 (2002) : 877–88.

Garland-Thomson, Rosemarie. 'Introduction: From Wonder to Error: A Genealogy of Freak Discourse in Modernity.' *Freakery: Cultural Spectacles of the Extraordinary Body*, 1–19. New York: New York University Press, 1996.

Hofstede, Geertz. 'Dimensionalizing Cultures: The Hofstede Model in Context'. *Online Readings in Psychology and Culture*, 2011

Lahiri, Ajoy Kumar. 'A Survey of the Views of Earlier Scholars.' *Vedic Vrtra: A Study and a Suggested Interpretation*, 1–35. Australian National University, 1971

Lefebvre, Henri. *State, Space, World: Selected Essays*, translated by Gerald Moore, Neil Brenner and Stuart Elden, edited by Brenner and Elden. Minneapolis: University of Minnesota Press, 2009.

Prakash, Buddha. 'Vrtra [A Study in the Impact of the Aryans on Indian Culture]'. *Annals of the Bhandarkar Oriental Research Institute*, 30, no. 3/4 (July–October 1949): 163 –214.

Ramanujan, A.K. 'Three Hundred *Ramayana*s: Five Examples and Three Thoughts on Translation'. ZLibrary. https://book4you.org/book/1200822/7a2212.

Sharpe, Andrew N. *Foucault's Monsters and the Challenge of Law*. Abingdon: Routledge, 2010.

Shildrick, Margrit. *Dangerous Discourses of Disability, Subjectivity and Sexuality*. Palgrave Macmillan, 2009.

Timalsina, Sthaneshwar. *Consciousness in Indian Philosophy: The Advaita Doctrine of 'Awareness Only*. USA, Canada: Routledge, 2009.

Tremain, Shelly (ed.). *Foucault and the Government of Disability*. University of Michigan, 2005.

Tripathi, Amish. *The Immortals of Meluha*. Chennai: Westland Ltd, 2010.

——. *The Secret of the Nagas*. Chennai: Westland Ltd, 2011.

——. *The Oath of the Vayuputras*. Chennai: Westland Ltd, 2013.

7

DISABILITY, DISCOURSE AND METAPHOR

Karuna Rajeev

Pre-Text

In 2018, the department of English at the University of Delhi was in the process of overhauling the syllabus for the undergraduate English course that is taught across colleges affiliated with the university. Part of my own engagement with this syllabus revision exercise was to locate texts from varied periods and contexts that allow for an engagement with disability and subsequently interrogate the interstices of literary representation and culture. I went into this exercise with the assumption that the greater difficulty would be in locating texts that could speak both to the aegis of specific papers as well as offer engagements with disability that are more than surface-level reading. In the spirit of open admission, I was also prepared for a mild resistance to this positioning by some of my other colleagues involved in the exercise. However, what I had not anticipated was the ways in which I had to negotiate with a constant politics of disavowal amongst my own peers—liberal intellectuals—who espoused a rhetoric of fostering inclusion. This chapter is the result of my being attendant to conversations which were, in actuality, negotiations premised on statements that were about symbolically representing disability rather than engaging with corporeal representations and firsthand expressions of the experience of disability in literary texts. Insofar as this is concerned, the chapter is an attempt to engage with the fact that statements about inclusion are rhetoric premised on a hegemonic discourse which upholds an ableist normative order. The coordinates of the terrain, as such, make it impossible to charter an alternative discourse because there is no engagement with disability as an experiential and corporeal phenomenon. Further, the use of metaphor in the context of disability representation in literary texts is a double bind because disability is either only invoked metaphorically or is a metaphoric stand-in for something else. Therefore, disability is rarely about itself. Metaphor in such a context consequently only seemingly signifies an alterity; the assumed radicality of such metaphoric usage is compromised when one allows oneself to acknowledge the impoverishment and cruel injustice of drawing an equivalence between disparate identities[1] while disregarding their contextual and experiential frameworks, and, of course, the underlying datum: that such a linguistic act is operating from—and being attendant to—hegemonic discourse. The usage of disability metaphors is therefore reductive rather than expansive— owing to the limitations in considering disability as merely an empty signifier as opposed to engaging with its experiential reality.

Subtext

This chapter is an attempt to examine the intellectual repercussions of ableist rhetoric that suggests that disability be articulated metaphorically or that metaphors of disability be used to facilitate the idea of impairment as an understanding of marginalisation. Disability is often invoked metaphorically via impairment rhetoric within the ambit of the social justice discourse to expose the tyranny of a dominant or a hegemonic identity and its attendant discourse. For example, while statements like blind to suffering or maimed by the system allude to the injustice suffered by those who are marginalised by society on the basis of identity, be it gender, ethnicity, race or caste, such usage does not simultaneously acknowledge disability as an identity itself. The other corollary to such a rendering of disability as an expression of social disablement[2] is that disability no longer functions as a literal description but exists solely as a metaphoric performative. Cinema studies scholar Vivian Sobchack draws attention to precisely this in her consideration of the 'prosthetic' when she claims that barring disability studies, 'the literal and material ground of metaphor has been largely forgotten' (2004). As Sobchack subsequently argues, the 'primary context' of disability 'has been left behind—as has the experience and agency' (2004). Thus, to take recourse to such usage of disability metaphors should not be considered as a radical reimagining of countering hegemonic discourse since it fails to embrace and undermines the contexts of the disabled experience. The implication here is that in an attempt to counteract the essentialist underpinnings of hegemonic discourse, we are misguided twice over: one, into a position where we are limited in our capability of perceiving the use of disability as a metaphor—viewing it as solely subversive; and two, we defeat our purposes of counteracting hegemonic discourse— seemingly, participating in it—by disregarding individual identity positions by relegating them to metaphorical function.

If one abides by Lakoff and Johnson's established hypothesis in their influential work *Metaphors We Live By*, then metaphors shape and condition our thinking, perceptions and responses in ways that we are never attentive to. Lakoff and Johnson, at the outset of the book, represent the metaphor as the basis for our conceptual system. They claim:

> Our ordinary conceptual system ... is fundamentally metaphorical in nature ... Our concepts structure what we perceive, how we get around in the world, and how we relate to other people. Our conceptual system thus plays a central role in defining our everyday lives. If we are right in suggesting that our conceptual system is largely metaphorical, then the way we think, what we experience, and what we do every day is very much a matter of metaphor. (2003)

Here, Lakoff and Johnson are indicating the integral role metaphors play in our conceptual understanding of the world and how this shapes our everyday lives. Nonetheless, as Amy Vidali has discerningly argued, Lakoff and Johnson's theories of the metaphor 'are ableist in assuming that bodies have particular physical/cognitive/sensory experiences' (2020). Vidali's critique is levelled at the fact that ableist assumptions about perception, movement and mobility have dictated Lakoff and Johnson's notions of the relationship between body and metaphor. For instance, in critiquing Lakoff and Johnson's example of the metaphor happy is up/ sad is down where they equate the 'drooping' posture with a sad state and an 'erect' posture with a happy state, Vidali argues:

> The implications of this claim for disabled people are troubling—will a person who may 'droop' throughout her life not learn the metaphor *happy is up* because her body is quite literally never 'up'? (2020)

Vidali is drawing attention to the necessity of introducing 'bodily and cognitive diversity' to Lakoff and Johnson's limited and ableist assumptions about the body. Lakoff and Johnson's work is a departure from a comparative framework of understanding the metaphor to considering the metaphor as conceptual; indicating that we think metaphorically. Nevertheless, it is worthwhile to ponder what the lack of consideration of bodily and cognitive difference at the conceptual level indicate; coercing us to acknowledge that any discourse claiming alterity by taking recourse to disability metaphors is thereby attending to hegemonic discourse in its inability to recognise difference and in upholding the able body as the norm.

Thus, for us to devoid the act of acquiring metaphoric statements or of using disability metaphorically as barren of intent or causality is to move beyond being merely misguided into the slippery terrain of wilfully perpetuating an ableist rhetoric that disregards and disprivileges disabled identities. This chapter's pursuit of engaging with certain forms of ableist rhetoric seeks to posit the bad politics and intellectual poverty of such a language. At the same time, it seeks to clarify that such a gesture of attaining meaning via equivalence remains within hegemonic discourse and is not a counter-response, because the very drawing of equivalence blurs the distinction of identity positions portending insignificance. For instance, in claiming that a woman who has suffered domestic abuse represents disability or in using the well-known credo of disability discourse—'We are all disabled!'—to distance oneself from the corporeal/existential realities of disability, we are committing the violence we are attempting to counteract. While intersectional frameworks of solidarity need to be built and acknowledged, the ontological axis of different identity positions has to be maintained. In conveniently drawing gestures of equivalence, we wilfully forget the profound violence that frames individual marginalised identities. More disturbingly, we disregard the fact that such an equivocating language, which always operates from the outside, is nonetheless premised on expressing the truths inside. In laying claim to a position of authentic rendering via equivalence we commit a deeper violence than that which we seek to address, for such an act goes beyond mere tokenism into the terrain of effacing identity positions, which is the very language of hegemonic discourse.

My attempts in this chapter are twofold. On one hand, I wish to interrogate what it means to conceptually work with and through disability discourse, particularly, within the ambit of syllabus making, a prescriptive exercise that involves participation in the dissemination of discourse, where—as Derrida argues in his essay, 'Dissemination'—the 'moment is already written' and 'the spectator is less capable than ever of choosing his place' (1981). The second attempt is to uphold—in spite of the seemingly deterministic nature of such an exercise—the relevance of participating in a discourse-shaping exercise like syllabus formation.[3]

In his book, titled *Dissemination*,[4] Derrida reflects on aspects of representation and makes an appraisal of meaning and writing in Western discourse. His essay, also titled 'Dissemination' and which is a part of the book, is on the surface an engagement with French author Phillipe Soller's novel, *Numbers* (1968). However, Derrida builds on and uses Soller's work to further his own considerations on discourse and dissemination, which, for him, is both a multitude of meanings and a loss of meaning. Derrida's indication in the essay is the relevance of 'numbers' to the making of discourse and its dissemination. My own hermeneutic engagement with Derrida's text is an attempt to prescribe within it the logic of a dominant discourse (that emerges as the logic of numbers would have it from a majoritarian position) that might allow for multiple meanings (polysemy), but, nonetheless, allows for this plurality to only be attendant to hegemonic discourse. The implication here is that the dominant discourse appropriates elements of alternate positions without actually changing the order, that is, it still retains its hegemony. Dissemination, as Derrida uses it, then, has to work, unlike polysemy, not towards multiple meanings with the same referent, but, towards access to multiple meanings and multiple referents.

> The concept of polysemy thus belongs within the confines of explanation ... in the present, of meaning. It belongs to the attending discourse. Its style is that of the representative surface. It forgets that its horizon is framed. The difference between discursive polysemy and textual dissemination is precisely difference itself, 'an implacable difference'. This difference is of course indispensable to the production of meaning (and that is why between polysemy and dissemination the difference is very slight). (Derrida 1981)

For Derrida, dissemination ruptures the hegemonic centre of a text and is an attack on the idea that texts can be appropriated in the name of authority. Derrida posits dissemination as the opposite of polysemy, which is fixated on the idea of an overall truth, a contestable premise to begin with. The contours of polysemy are fixed even when it claims mutability since it allows for no other authority except one. What Derrida's own engagement with writing in the three texts that form the anthology that is *Dissemination* suggests is the irreducibility of writing solely to content, meaning or concern. The afterlife of the written text allows pluralities of engagement that permit an engagement with 'plurality of filiations'. The literary text therefore cannot be viewed as a sacred, inviolate entity that cannot be desecrated. Nor should suspicion of the intent in reading texts from a disability perspective permit one to surmise that such a reading be considered as desecration. What one needs to be attentive to is the attitude of suspicion that is harboured in such negotiations, especially since the suspicion is manifest by the majoritarian position. This suspicion frames the perpetuation of disability as metaphor. Thus, the imperative to participate in an exercise like syllabus revision is a need to acknowledge not just the erasure of disabled voices and how they frame discourse but to witness how voices exist and dialogue even from what we consider the margins of literary texts. It would be beyond hubristic to view such an enrolment as a reclaiming of disabled voices, especially because these voices do not need to be exhumed from buried spaces. To draw on a vital interjection of disability discourse, disability is not about individual impairment but how an individual is rendered disabled. As vital as it is to listen to the disabled voices speaking from these texts, it is equally vital to ask why do we not want to acknowledge them, thereby rejecting them, and when we acknowledge these voices, on whose terms are we doing so. This, for me, is the dissemination of discourse. Alterity in such a situation is not within the metaphor but in how it is framed. The critique of disability metaphors therefore has to move beyond just a reactionary exercise of political correctness that polices metaphor to an active engagement with disability metaphors. As Vidali argues:

> A disability approach to metaphor attends to how diverse bodies impact metaphor acquisition and use, which shifts disability away from something only 'used' or 'represented' by metaphor. Instead, disability interprets, challenges, and articulates metaphors. A disability approach to metaphor must engage the full range of disability; resist the desire to simply 'police' or remove disability metaphors; actively transgress disability metaphors by employing a diverse vocabulary; and artistically create and historically reinterpret metaphors of disability. (2020)

A disability approach facilitates an understanding of dissemination via an engagement with disability depiction and disabled voices in literary texts as well as the language of representation and articulation. Further, this dissemination allows for an engagement with a plurality of voices which considers 'bodily and cognitive diversity'. Therefore, the imperative is not to police disability metaphors but to interrogate the ableist underpinning of our own academic engagement and theories, particularly, the origins of our claims to inclusivity which are located in a language of equivalence. Consequently, equating the disabled experience with any other experience of marginalisation—whether that of gender, caste, ethnicity or race—does not acknowledge the primary context of any of these identity positions, remaining confirmed within a polysemic hegemonic discourse.

I, therefore, return to the previous distinction between polysemy and dissemination as it occurs in Derrida. Disregarding the corporeality of disabled experience is to continue to participate within an attending discourse drawing on different meanings without any shift in register. The plurality exemplified in such a suggestion is an act of equivalence located in a majoritarian discourse that has numbers on its side; it is not the plurality of identity positions. Simply put, all of the varied voices that claim to offer divergent perspectives operate on the same ideological plain and do not really represent diverse lived experiences—in as much as this is concerned, they merely indicate variety, not plurality.

Context

The participation within the exercise of analysis with a particular focus on looking at/for literary narratives around disability is not without the attendant anxieties of responding to 'attending discourse'. These anxieties are heightened to the point of hyper-actualisation when negotiations with those prejudiced towards disability discourse mean statements where disability is equated with other forms of marginalisation, disregarding the material embodiment of disability. To reiterate, statements like 'Disability can be invoked through ...' or 'We are all disabled' within this context are not fostered through an idea of broad inclusivity but to absolve oneself of engaging with individual identity positions like disability.

The need then in evaluating statements of equivalence or the use of disability as a metaphor is not so much to ask what these statements mean but to ask where such metaphors come from, because the exercise of asking the question is distinguished in being attentive to discourse. Within the ambit of language, a metaphor enables for a relation of equivalence between two disparate objects that enables meaning. Our understanding and use of the metaphor is implicated in the need to create meaning. As Nietzsche argues in his 'On Truth and Lies in a Nonmoral Sense':

> The drive toward the formation of metaphors is the fundamental human drive ... This drive is not truly vanquished ... by the fact that a regular and rigid new world is constructed as its prison from its own ephemeral products, the concepts. It seeks a new realm and another channel for its activity, and it finds this in myth and art generally. This drive continually confuses the conceptual categories and cells by bringing forward new transferences, metaphors, and metonymies. (1981)

Language, of course, moves beyond communication to become the very basis of subjectivisation and lays claim to voice through speech. The allusion Nietzsche makes is that we have no access to things as they are or 'pure truth', and language 'designates only the relations of things to man, and to express them one calls on the boldest metaphors' (1993). The first metaphor,[5] however, is not within language but pre-linguistic. It is a 'nerve stimulus, first transposed into an image' (1993), therefore resulting in Nietzsche's understanding of the formation of metaphor as 'the fundamental human drive'. In as much as this is concerned, there is no escaping the metaphor. Neither is this chapter a criticism of the metaphor in itself, but, an examination of our instinctive use of metaphor to arrive at meaning and a simultaneous introspection of how meanings are manufactured to constantly arrive at a given discursive position.

At this point, I would like to commit to an examination of dead metaphors.[6] Conventionally, dead metaphors are understood as metaphors that have lost their original meaning through overuse. It does not mean redundancy or obsoleteness of the word or the statement but an erasure of the original framework of unequal comparison. The process of deadening metaphors is to arrive at literariness, where statements like 'love is blind', 'fall on deaf ears', 'crippled by loss' are no longer about rendering meaning through an allusion to the presumed incapacity of disability but statements in and of themselves where our use of them exists without invoking disability.

What is in operation in the above statements is how one arrives at a position, where invoking disability as a metaphor is to not engage with the corporeal or experiential embodiment of disability but to disavow disability through non-engagement, even when faced with evocations of disability. As David Heavey does in an invocation of Rawl's paradigm of disavowal,

> 'The Disabled' is a non-disabled construction, a representational framework ... which has to contain two properties if it is to have any cathartic meaning for society ... these two 'able-bodied' cathartic needs are, (1) the ridding or disavowal of health, fitness and other physical/functional issues pertaining to the ability to work, and (2) the disavowal of the presence of death and mortality. This is how 'negative' representation serves 'able-bodied' people. (1993)

In this sense there is a need to also address what Tom Shakespeare states in his own expansion of Heavey's statement:

> Disabled people are scapegoats. It is not just that disabled people are different, expensive, inconvenient, or odd: it is that they represent a threat—either ... to order, or, to the self-conception of western human beings who, since the Enlightenment, have viewed themselves as perfectible, as all knowing, as god-like: able, over and above all other beings, to conquer the limitations of their nature through the victories of their culture. (1994)

In the context of the above, to come back to the problem of equivalence, the invocation of the possibility of expressing disability metaphorically is a gesture similar to the way in which disability is deadened in metaphors. Such a gesture suggests that disability can only be evoked through alternative registers of ableist normative discourse, and, the disabled body, when evoked, has to be reduced to only metaphoric meaning. Therefore, within this ableist and hegemonic paradigm is framed the imperative of responding to discourses of equivalence, a direct confrontation that bares the poverty of such a positioning.

Ricoeur, in his *The Rule of the Metaphor*, argues, 'The advantage of a direct attack on the phenomenon of discourse, omitting the linguistic stage, is that the traits proper to discourse are recognised in themselves without any need to contrast them with anything else' (1975). Nonetheless, it has to be considered that such a position disregards the linguistic realm, especially since the grounds for disavowal have been fostered through participation in an equivocating language of equivalence: (*i*) the disabled are with us, (*ii*) the disabled body can be indicated through an appropriation of metaphor. As Ricoeur himself argues later on, 'one cannot any longer simply disregard the relationship between discourse and language'; 'Correctness and error belong to discourse alone' and 'only within discourse does a generic term take on a singularizing function' (1975). However, what I seek to explore is the converse—how a singular term, whether 'blind' or 'cripple', is taking on a generalising function in the ambit of a discourse of the normative. Within this is also located the writing of a response to the general discourse of the normative. To recall Derrida once again in the context of this chapter: 'this writing circulates "here" in the intertext' of statement and its response; discourse and counter-discourse 'fragmented by the arbitrary violence of abstraction ...' (1981). In his engagement with metaphor and reference of meaning in a sentence, Ricoeur posits that signification occurs within language and reference is to the outside of language:

> The distinction between sense and reference is a necessary and pervasive characteristic of discourse, and collides head-on with the axiom of the immanence of language. There is no reference problem in language: signs refer to other signs *within* the same system. In the phenomenon of the sentence, language passes outside itself; reference is the mark of the self-transcendence of language. (1975)

Ricoeur's own exegesis on Frege's distinction between sense and reference is concentrated on the comprehension of metaphors, and, as such, does not delve into the production of metaphor. But such a position is vital in an examination such as this because beyond the cognitive and semantic realm of metaphor usage lies also the ways and means of acquiring this usage.

In such a consideration, what becomes vital both in the context of Nietzsche's positioning of the emergence of metaphor as pre-linguistic and in the ways that I hermeneutically read Derrida's distinction between polysemy and dissemination is that the improbability of multiple referents within an attending discourse is coded into the way we come into language. The function of culture in acquiring metaphor and its usage is something that we do not adequately consider. It is precisely to this aspect that a disability approach to metaphor directs our attention. That a normative culture upholds bodily perfection is something that disability scholarship has consistently directed attention towards. Consequently, the limitations of language are then not only its removal from the 'pure' thing in itself but in the way it is acquired as an inheritance of an ableist normative discourse. What then works towards destabilising this inheritance is moments of writing that cannot omit the linguistic stage and having to look at discourse within the ambit of the linguistic as what it has access to. As Vidali notes in calling for a disability approach to metaphor:

> A disability approach to metaphor is thus critical and activist. But rethinking the relationship of disability and metaphor must also be creative, historical, even literary. For while careful critique of theories ... serves as a critical antidote to assumptions of how bodies and metaphors work, creative engagement with disability metaphors can further complicate, or 'denaturalize,' ideas of how bodies and metaphors interact. (2020)

Such a denaturalisation of the ideas of body and metaphors is perhaps the site of resisting the normative able body that Tom Shakespeare identifies as the perfectible body upheld 'to conquer the limitations of their nature through the victories of their culture' (1994). A disability approach, therefore, makes us attentive to the circulation of the normative within hegemonic discourse, permitting us to see the structural violence indicated in our linguistic use. Because an engagement with disability metaphors, or a disability approach to metaphors, or else, consideration of disability representation in literary texts, coerces us to acknowledge the inequity that is at the heart of committing to registers of equivalence—one that, in their disavowal of disability, neglect disabled identity in the rhetoric of inclusivity.

Afterword

The final part of the chapter works towards illustrating the epistemic violence in appropriating the metaphor as a mode of disavowal. Our engagement with the idea of the metaphor thus far has led us to examine how it works within the ambit of suggestion because we are without access to the meaning that it alludes to. The metaphor is inherent in language because its references are to the hidden, unconscious aspects of our own being—within and without. In as much as this is concerned, I revisit Derrida:

> Clip out an example, since you cannot and should not undertake the infinite commentary that at every moment seems necessarily to engage and immediately to annul itself, letting itself be read in turn by the apparatus itself. *So make some incision, some violent arbitrary cut, after you recall that Numbers actually prescribes such scissions, and recommends 'beginning' with one.* (1981; emphasis mine)

At the beginning of this chapter, I stated my concern of a tokenistic regard given to the necessity of engaging with representations of disability in literature. The mode of response, to the empty politics of such a gesture and its underlying logic of drawing metaphoric equivalence, is an imperative to write on the body of the existing discourse, where, even if the 'moment is already written' (1981), one can still lay claim to a voice, because, dissemination is this very dispersal of meaning. Dissemination is a movement away from a central authoritative voice and emerges from within multiple moments of reading/engagement/critique, allowing for spatial and temporal nuances and a plurality of positions. The process of dissemination may perhaps lie in taking recourse to both the direct response and in reclaiming the dead metaphor and making it alive both in the context of usage and the pre-text of its origins. Such an act requires attentiveness to one's speech and the need to understand discourse-making as prescription as much as proscription. Then, in the act of altering, changing the angle, committing the violence of rewriting on the existing text, there perhaps exists a potential for 'the spectator' being able to choose her place. This is the imperative of reading narratives of disability and reading disability in narratives. A revisiting of, for example, the literary canon one is already familiar with via scissors that make incisions to insert varied contexts or hidden alterities does not disintegrate the text or reduce it but reveals its palimpsestic nature. To misread the prediction of such a 'moment already written' is to operate within the assumption that the violence of re-vision is the violence of the blind. The brutal ableism of such a statement is also the inability to move beyond its implicative meaning and reflect on the interplay between the literal and the metaphoric and relegate meaning to an absolute either/or, the very thing literary studies should not be wont to do. This is precisely the reason why a disability approach to metaphor provides us with interdisciplinary possibilities for interrogating metaphors as well as countering the circulation of a heteronormative discourse through creative and resistive modes of interpreting metaphors.

Notes

1   The equivalence I am suggesting is of the kind where the assumption is a certain aspect of particular identity positions can be represented by another. For instance, statements claiming that women who have experienced domestic violence can represent disability or caste oppression as a form of disability. This chapter is drawing particular attention to such statements because they become attempts to nullify the contours and the politics that shape individual identity positions and, in the guise of a non-essentialist humanist position, actually speak the very language of hegemonic discourse.

2   Owing to the deep fissures in Indian society, around caste identity in particular, disablement as a word, within the ambit of a social justice discourse, was used to connote underlying social inequalities. The allusion in such a usage was to social disablement. However, the inheritance of such a language unfortunately means that we very easily draw equivalence between identity positions such as caste and disability or gender and disability, completely absolving ourselves of the necessity in being attendant to the language embedded within these identity positions and the discourse that frames them. We therefore remain oblivious to the possibility of structural violence that effaces identity positions being coded in linguistic acts.

3   It needs explaining here that the University of Delhi is a central university that has around 91 colleges affiliated to it. Further, owing to the university's position as an institution of significance in India, its syllabus acts as a template for other colleges and universities throughout the country. Added to this is the fact that English is taught either as English honours or as electives offered to students of other disciplines and courses across the board. Therefore, unlike framing syllabi for individual courses taught by concerned faculty that is a generally accepted norm, syllabus making in the University of Delhi is a collective process that has the participation of over hundred faculty members that further has a ripple effect.

4   Derrida's *Dissemination*, published in 1972, is a collection of three essays, 'Plato's Pharmacy', 'The Double Session' and 'Dissemination'. While some of the ideas in the book overall have framed some of the thoughts in this chapter, it is 'Dissemination' that is a particular point of engagement.

5   The second metaphor for Nietzsche is an imitation of image through sound. However, in explicating this Nietzsche posits the ableist concern of whether a 'totally deaf' man 'will gaze in astonishment at Chladni's sound figures'. Does Nietzsche, in his presumption of asking if a sense of vibration can connote sound, not realise that he has no access to the way sound can be rendered to someone with auditory disability? In this gesture of metaphor that he uses to remark on the incapacity of the metaphor to correspond to the original entity, he falls in the same pit.

6   A clarification needs to be made that cognitive linguistics is critical of the categorisation of dead metaphors, decrying the importance of inherited conceptual frameworks and their validity for the ways they

affect our conscious action. There are also some other interventions like I.A. Richards's *The Philosophy of Rhetoric* (Taylor and Francis, 2001) and Gregory W. Dawes's *The Body in Question: Metaphor and Meaning in the Interpretation of Ephesians*, 5: 21–33 (Brill, 1998) that call for a need to avoid etymological fallacy where the true or proper meaning of a word is in its oldest meaning.

References

Derrida, Jacques. *Dissemination*, translated by Barbara Johnson. London and New York: Bloomsbury, 1981.

Heavey, David. 'From Self-Love to the Picket Line: Strategies for Change in Disability Representation'. *Disability, Handicap & Society*, 8, no. 4 (1993): 423–29.

Lakoff, George and Mark Johnson. *Metaphors We Live By*. Chicago: University of Chicago Press, 2003.

Nietzsche, Friedrich. 'On Truth and Lies in a Nonmoral Sense'. In *Philosophy and Truth: Selections from Nietzsche's Notebooks of the Early 1870's*, edited and translated by Daniel Breazeale, 79–91. New Jersey: Humanities Press, 1993.

Ricoeur, Paul. *The Rule of the Metaphor*, translated by Robert Czerny, Kathleen McLaughlin and John Costello. SJ. New York and London: Routledge, 1975.

Shakespeare, Tom. 'Cultural Representation of Disabled People: Dusbins of Disavowal?' *Disability & Society*, 9, no. 3 (1994): 283–99.

Sobchack, Vivian. *Carnal Thoughts: Embodiment and Moving in Image Culture*. Berkeley: University of California Press, 2004.

Vidali, Amy. 'Seeing What We Know: Disability and Theories of Metaphor'. *Journal of Literary and Cultural Disability Studies*, 4, no. 1 (2020): 33–54.

8

BLIND LIVES MATTER: METAPHOR AND MATERIALITY IN DHARAMVIR BHARATI'S *ANDHA YUG*

Deepak Kumar Gupta

The stock image of blindness is deeply rooted in the Indian socio-cultural discourse. It is often equated with darkness, foolishness, irrationality, helplessness, sin, immorality and even enigma. Yet, the oft-bandied association with blindness is due to the gaps in common knowledge, or an inability to perceive material reality of the visually impaired. The aforecited poem, 'The Education Leads a Person to Leave Aside the Blindness of Idiocy!' by Dr V.K. Kanniappan is just one among a plethora of literary representations of blindness as a negation of the illumination of knowledge. Like Kanniappan's poem, several Indian myths and tales yoke the lack of sight with a categorical loss of the capacity to acquire knowledge, evident in the case of the popular ancient Indian parable, 'The Blind Men and an Elephant'. This story projects blindness as synonymous with ignorance since the six blind men miserably fail to apprehend the so-called valid knowledge about an elephant. The blind men are positioned near different parts of an elephant and left to interpret the objective reality of the animal. Through their sense of touch, each arrives at a different conception of the elephant based on the body parts accessible to them. Their subjective interpretations are viewed as markers of their naivety and insularity, making this a parable about the dominant versions of acquiring knowledge by equating lack of sight to a lack of insight/ truth. The blind men cease to exist as men as they are reduced to mere cyphers of a moral impairment. The presence of such stories in our collective unconscious has shaped the very cognition of blindness in society, which gets framed as popular perceptions or stereotypes manifesting itself in many idiomatic phrases.[1] Some glaring examples of linguistic idioms which mould our cognition of blindness at every step of our lives are quotidian phrases and proverbs like '*andha andhe ko rasta dikhata*' ('the blind leading the blind'), '*andha banana*' ('rob somebody blind'), '*saavan ke andhe ko hara hi dikhta hai*' ('everything looks yellow to the jaundiced eye'), '*andhon ke desh me kana raja*' ('in the country of the blind, the one-eyed man is king') and so on. In almost all the references to blindness in literature and common parlance, blindness as a physical disability is deemed incomplete unless saddled with pejorative connotations. In other words, whether it is V.K. Kanniappan's poetic evocation of blindness, the fable of the six blind men or the various phrases invoking the figure of the blind, they all seem to actively encourage and promote a metaphorical reading of blindness as an analogue to a lack of insight/truth. But what is really disconcerting is the consummate ease with which the sighted world accepts the 'naturalness' of these arbitrary associations without questioning them. This speaks volumes about the ways in which blindness is lodged in the collective consciousness of the sighted world. This chapter attempts to understand and problematise the working of this consciousness through a reading of the metaphorical representation of blindness in Dharamvir Bharati's play, *Andha Yug*.

Conceptual Metaphors and Beyond

In *Andha Yug*, Bharati re-adapts the story of the final days of the battle of Kurukshetra narrated in the *Mahabharata* as a metaphor for the panic and frenzy during the Partition. The play figuratively captures and conveys the fears, apprehensions, anxieties and metaphysical bewilderment of an ill-informed population led astray by religious sentiments to participate in the hysterical carnage that followed in the wake of the partition of India, raising crucial philosophical questions about the ontological status of what it means to be human, or not human, in an irrational world characterised by moral chaos and degeneracy. To drive home these thematic concerns, the play actively invites its audience to read blindness metaphorically as an analogue to ignorance and irrationality. As the plot unfolds, *Andha Yug* increasingly appears to conform to David Mitchell and Sharon Snyder's theoretical paradigm of narrative prosthesis, as the trope of blindness in the play becomes a stock feature of characterisation, an opportunistic metaphorical device and 'a crutch upon which' the play 'lean[s] for [its] representational power, disruptive potentiality and analytical insight' (Mitchell and Snyder 2013, 49). In fact, Bharati depends entirely on the symbolic power of this trope to communicate the play's central motif to his audience, leaving one wondering how and why does the audience relate to such a pejorative evocation of blindness, how does this trope condition and shape our attitude and response to blind people and what impact does it have on the constitution of their subjectivity.

Dwelling on the figurative usages of disability in the specific context of postcolonial fiction, Clare Barker poignantly observes that the symbolic evocation of the phenomenon in this genre of literature results in a highly problematic and uncritical disassociation of the text from the materially embodied experience of disablement, effectively erasing 'disability from view, precluding its analysis as a socially significant phenomenon or a politicized aspect of identity' (Barker 2011, 3). In *Postcolonial Fiction and Disability: Exceptional Children, Metaphor and Materiality* (2011), she, therefore, lays great stress on the need to assert the materiality of the experience of disablement and unsettle the privileged status accorded to metaphors in literary representations of corporeal difference so that disability may be presented as an ontologically and socially contextualised phenomenon. Barker's argument raises a set of crucial questions with regard to the literary tendency to reduce disability to its metaphorical signification. How do tropes of disability relate to the materially embodied experience of non-normative corporeality? What role do these tropes play in the social and cultural critiques of postcolonial societies? What are the effects of these critiques on the constitution of disabled subjectivity within a newly independent nation? The underlying emphasis inherent in these questions, which form the crux of the present chapter, appears to be on the need to read 'postcolonial disability representations with attention to both its metaphorical content and material reality' (Barker 2011, 3).

However, in *Andha Yug*, Bharati reduces blindness to its metaphorical signification and uses it exclusively as a literary device, disassociating the phenomena from the material nature of its embodied experience and denying any form of agency to blind people. For this reason, the play needs to be problematised and critiqued from the perspective of recent developments in disability studies, particularly the wide-ranging debates surrounding the meaning and implication of the usage of disability metaphors in literature. Here, I would like to acknowledge the profound influence that Amy Vidali and her scholarly discussion on the subject has had on the writing of the chapter. The reference is singularly to her ground-breaking article, 'Seeing What We Know: Disability and Theories of Metaphors', in which she examines, problematises and expands upon George Lakoff and Mark Johnson's popular theories of conceptual metaphor,[2] where they underline the process through which metaphors are acquired and cognised in language and culture.

In common parlance, the metaphor is understood generally as a figure of speech based on a figurative yet apparently logical comparison and discursive substitution of one object or action by another.[3] In a sense, this literary device stands in sharp contradistinction with the literal form of expression. The theory of conceptual metaphors, however, makes a couple of significant departures from the aforementioned conception of metaphor. If, in popular imagination, what is being compared and substituted are objects and actions, in the theory of conceptual metaphors, it is one conceptual domain that becomes another. While retaining the former's emphasis on figurative resemblances and discursive substitution, Lakoff and Johnson turn the figure of speech into a mental process grounded in language and culture. Inherent in this concept, Lynne Cameron points out in *Metaphor in Educational Discourse*, is a suggestion that the 'metaphor is a basic mental operation by which we understand the world through mapping from known domains to unknown domains', in part because 'some conceptualizations are metaphorically structured in our own minds' (Cameron 2003, 19). But more relevant to our purposes here is the realisation that one of the many examples Lakoff and Johnson cite to illustrate their theory happens to be 'seeing is understanding'. Needless to say, this metaphor at once establishes and reinforces an erroneous yet commonplace ocular-centric equation between sight and understanding and, by extension, between blindness and ignorance, rendering the process of acquisition of knowledge incompatible with non-visual subjectivity. This thus occludes those with visual impairments from the epistemological processes of cognition and acquisition of wisdom. Predictably, while examining the role of the body in Lakoff and Johnson's theory of conceptual metaphor, Vidali pits the expression 'seeing is understanding' and problematises it from the perspective of blind subjectivity, concluding that their concept is 'ableist in assuming that bodies have particular physical/cognitive/sensory experiences and related metaphorical expressions' (Vidali 2010, 33).

The ableist orientation of Lakoff and Johnson's theory becomes even more apparent when, later on in the book, they proceed to examine the role that corporeality plays in the cultural process of the cognition and acquisition of metaphors, arguing that this process is deeply informed by a vast reservoir of cultural presuppositions about the body. Firmly anchored in the belief that 'no metaphor can ever be comprehended or even adequately represented independent of its experiential basis' (Lakoff and Johnson 1980, 19), this section of the book first asserts that our cultural experiences define the way metaphors are produced and used in society, and then goes on to note that 'the way we learn to reason and use metaphor is structured by the physical experiences of bodies' (1980, 38), thus inviting the reader's attention to how various material and cultural existence of human bodies affect reasoning and subjectivity, and, by extension, metaphor. But even here, unfortunately, it is normative subjectivity that takes precedence as evident in the following observation: '[O]ur common embodiment allows for common, stable truths' (6). Rather than introducing diversity of bodies, the emphasis on common embodiments and common, stable truths in the above statement privileges a normative form of embodiment. In fact, such a theoretical formulation has a profoundly damaging impact on the identity and subjectivity of disabled people. The logical extension of Lakoff and Johnson's argument is that disabled people acquire reason and, by extension, metaphors which are based on the experiences of normative bodies and then apply them in their daily lives without realising that they are undermining their own subjectivity, and that such metaphors produced on the basis of normative bodies' experiences do not match with the way they experience the world. The seeing is understanding metaphor, for instance, has been produced based on sighted people's personal experience of accessing the world and acquiring knowledge primarily through their sensory experience of sight. Blind people, then, acquire this metaphor from the sighted and use it liberally in their daily speech in expressions like 'I see what you mean and transparent ideas', without being conscious that such usages are incompatible with their very own subjectivity and their daily experience of accessing the world and acquiring knowledge through other sensory perceptions like sound, touch, smell and taste. Recognising these fundamental lacunae in Lakoff and Johnson's concept, Vidali poignantly observes:

> [w]hile it is reasonable to assume that ablebodied people profoundly influence metaphors through their physical and cultural experiences, I am dissatisfied with an approach to metaphor that assumes that the building blocks of language are formed by able bodies and are transferred to those with disabilities by contagious contact. People with disabilities, and their bodily experiences, also inform how metaphors are created and used. (Vidali 39)

She appears to be building a case for evolving a theoretical approach for the study of metaphors that accommodates corporeal diversity and inflects the process of metaphor cognition and acquisition from the perspective of a disabled embodiment. Lakoff and Johnson's theory of conceptual metaphors and Vidali's critique of it both provide us with a useful theoretical framework to better understand, thoughtfully engage with and critically resist problematic forms of disability metaphors of the kind we find in *Andha Yug*.

Figuring Blindness

Central to the plot of the *Mahabharata* is the story of Dhritarashtra and his life and experiences as a blind man. The epic persistently recounts and reveals the anxieties and exclusions that his visual impairment produces both at personal and social levels. Despite being the eldest child of his generation in the Kuru clan, it is his sighted younger brother Pandu who inherits the crown of Hastinapura from his father and the blind man is denied his legitimate claim to the throne on account of his impairment. The hysterical carnage that follows in the battle of Kurukshetra between the progenies of the two brothers is the inevitable outcome of this inexplicable act of discrimination. Integral to the epic, thus, is a critical meditation on the social and political consequences of corporeal differences. Bharati, in his postcolonial rendering of the battle of Kurukshetra, however, prefers to problematically disengage himself from the *Mahabharata*'s keen interest in the materiality of corporeally deviant embodiment and obscures the epic's exploration of the quotidian consequences of non-normative corporealities, reducing disability to its metaphorical signification. This is a striking narrative gesture. What is really compelling about such a gesture is that it is not unusual. Barker, in her seminal study of postcolonial disability narratives, reveals that the appropriation of disability as a metaphor in these narratives is a rampant worldwide aesthetic practice. According to her, there are obvious reasons why disability figures prominently as a metaphor in postcolonial narratives. Disability, she argues, has a specifically postcolonial resonance in that it figuratively evokes the epistemic violence and damage inflicted on colonised societies by colonialism. Bharati's deployment of blindness as a metaphor in *Andha Yug*, however, does not conjure a colonial past and its excesses. Its reference is, rather, postcolonial India and the moral degeneracy associated with the maddening violence of partition. The title itself, *Andha Yug*, announces this association and as the narrative unfolds, blindness becomes the central conceit of this allegory of Partition. One of the most striking instances of this arises in the exchanges between Dhritarashtra and Vidura:

> Dhritarashtra: Vidura try to understand. I was born blind. How could I have discerned the real world or recognized its social codes?

Vidura: You could have. Just as you accepted the world in spite of
your blindness

Dhritarashtra: But I had created that world out of the darkest
recesses of my own being. My senses were limited by my blindness.
They defined the boundary of my material world. I had spun an
illusory world of dreams and desires and passions out of the depths
of that darkness. My love, my hate, my law, my *dharma* had evolved
out of my peculiar world. My ethics had no other frame of reference.
(Bharati 2011, 1.12)

In the above instance, Dhritarashtra's blindness is pinpointed for his
failings as a king. These failings, especially his indecisiveness in the face
of gross injustices committed by his sons, are reasoned with his visual
impairment as if the darkness on account of his sightlessness has also
permeated his cognition and numbed his other sensory organs, leaving
him physically and mentally impotent. In other words, blindness is
also linked to a lack of reason/rationale, which symbolises disorder,
as Bharati himself opines, '[b]lindness rules this age not reason and
blindness shall prevail in the end' (2011, 7).

The crucial question here is not whether the parallel that *Andha Yug*
evokes between blindness on one hand and lack of insight, rationale and
moral degeneration on the other, successfully conveys the central motif
of the play, for there is little doubt that it definitely does. The pertinent
questions to be asked are how and why does the trope communicate
its message to the audience with consummate ease, how is blindness
positioned within this metaphor and, by extension, within this play, and
what is the impact of this positioning on the constitution of the identity
and subjectivity of blind people.

In 'Between the Valley and the Field: Metaphor and Disability',
Jay Dolmage asks, '[w]hy have metaphors of disability come to entail
all manner of negativity?' He then proposes that such metaphors are
irrevocably linked with 'objective' scientific discourses that 'hide an
individual's humanity and highlight a deficit' (2005, 112). The reference
to metaphor's association with 'objective scientific discourses' in
the above statement at once calls attention to Lakoff and Johnson's
description of metaphor as the natural extension of truth and reason
and their suggestion that cultural presuppositions based on the lived
life experiences of prototypical bodies inform the production of truth
and reason and, hence, metaphor. These observations provide us with
suitable entry points into understanding why the readers of *Andha Yug*
are able to strike an immediate chord with the metaphorical evocation
of blindness that lies at the heart of Bharati's play.

The parallel between blindness and ignorance that the play harps on is undoubtedly the logical corollary of the 'seeing is understanding' metaphor that Lakoff and Johnson discuss in their theory of conceptual metaphors. This extension of vision into the realm of knowledge acquisition is informed by certain cultural presuppositions based on the lived experiences of sighted people who are used to experiencing and accessing the world primarily if not exclusively through their eyes. What happens in the process is that blind people, whose embodiment is characterised by the absence of sight, are occluded from such a realm. Predictably, whenever this extension is metaphorically evoked in the case of sighted people, it evokes a positive connotation and whenever it is brought into play with reference to visually impaired embodiments, its implications are negative. Such a parallel from the perspective of a sighted embodiment may appear to be natural as they appear to be the natural extension of their lived life experiences. Predictably, a sighted reader of *Andha Yug* can strike an immediate chord with Bharati's evocation of blindness as an analogue for ignorance, establishing an ocular-centric communion between its author, text and reader.

However, these expressions do not neatly dovetail into the materially embodied experience of blindness. After all, blind people can and do access and experience the world through other cognitive modes of perception than the one based on sight, like those based on sound, touch, smell and taste. Vidali's article, mentioned in the previous section, makes the reader of *Andha Yug* wonder whether the association between seeing and understanding and between sightlessness and not understanding is natural at all, questioning the merit and the nature of the construction of the category of objective and scientific discourses that Dolmage associates with the disability metaphor. Are these objective and scientific discourses a fact of nature or are they arbitrary discursive constructions set into motion by prototypical embodiment? We could use a similar line of argument to critique Lakoff and Johnson's theory of conceptual metaphors as natural extensions of truth and reason. What is the true nature of truth and reason? Do non-normative embodiments not play a role at all in their constitution? Do such conceptions obstruct corporeal and cognitive diversity? There is little doubt that the association between blindness and ignorance that lies at the heart of *Andha Yug* does not align with and even disembodies the materially embodied experience of blindness. It is therefore a matter of little coincidence that unlike the original epic, in Bharati's play blindness is invoked as an overarching trope rather than a lived experience since, as an autonomous individual, the visually disabled are almost invisible in the play, which is evident in Dhritarashtra's case whose complex quotidian realities of blindness are never explored. The implication here is that metaphors based on the conception that sightlessness is equivalent to not understanding do not invoke any form of natural association. They are purely, arbitrary and even discriminatory, discursive constructions constituted by a predominantly ocular-centric society. But even then, we, blind people included, continue to use the analogy with tenacious regularity in our daily use of language in phrases like 'turn a blind eye to', 'blind to other people's arguments, murky ideas, blind spot, blind alley' and so on. We, therefore, have very little choice but to agree and lend our voices to Stephen Kuusisto who, in a totally different context, asserts that 'disability as a cognitive metaphor is always pejorative and its use as a trope represents a failure of critical and/or imaginative thinking.'

Nevertheless, throughout the play, the analogy between blindness and ignorance is repetitively evoked and elaborated in the context of the other characters as well. In the cases of Gandhari and Ashwatthama, the play's overarching metaphor is used to evoke their blind rage and denial over the loss of loved ones. Gandhari is negatively portrayed in the play as lacking intellectual sight in the face of truth. She is narrowly located in her niche from where she has no access to other realities. The playwright indicates that she is blinded not because of her blindfold but due to her blind love for Duryodhana. Her blind rage towards Pandavas for exterminating her children prompts her to make Ashwatthama's body adamantine. Similar to Gandhari, Ashwatthama is also presented as a raging blind brute proud of his possession of half-truths. He proclaims:

Ashwatthama: I shall live like a blind and ruthless beast and may Dharmaraj's prophecy come true!

Let both my hands turn into claws! Let these eyes sharp like the teeth of a carnivore tear the body of anyone they see!

From now on my only *dharma* is: 'Kill, kill, kill and kill again!' (Bharati 2011, 2.27)

The implication in the above statements is that in their blind rage, both Gandhari and Ashwatthama are incapable of comprehending the objective truth. Another conceptual metaphor to be noted here is the employment of 'blind rage', which means that one is so angry that one cannot see, reinforcing the idea 'seeing is understanding'. Even the warring parties—the Kauravas and the Pandavas—are not safe from the diabolical blindness in the play. For instance, while Duryodhana is blinded by his hatred and envy towards the Pandavas, Yuyutsu, a Kaurava fighting alongside the Pandavas, becomes a blind spirit due to being torn between the two sides. As a result, he kills himself, lamenting, 'I committed suicide and broke the adamantine doors of death only to find myself once again in the caves of darkness' (Bharati 2011, 104). This poses the question of whether an escape from darkness/blindness is tantamount to an escape from the existential trap of life. For the author, the 'blindness of the age' is so pervasive that no escape is possible. Even Sanjay, the gifted seer, finds his visionary prowess diminishing while trying to inform the blind Dhritarashtra about the war. He doubtfully remarks, '[t]rying to show the truth to the blind must I too become blind?' (2011, 68). All the above instances display the characters' inability to differentiate *dharma* from *adharma*. This metaphorical treatment of blindness divorces it from the material world, making it a convenient adjective for characters like Dhritarashtra, Gandhari or Ashwatthama who cannot delineate right from wrong. As a result, in order to depict a dark world of vices in the play, even sighted characters are rendered metaphorically blind in the face of *adharma*. A reader of *Andha Yug* would not find it easy to dismiss the poignant observation made by David Mitchell when he asserts that disability metaphors have a 'cumulative impact on cultural attitudes toward disabled people', particularly because disability serves 'primarily as a metaphor for things gone awry with bodily and social orders' (2013, 24).

Marginalising the Blind

Such myriad evocations of blindness in the play, which have a profoundly damaging impact on the constitution of blind people's identities and subjectivities, are often justified and excused on the grounds of the symbolic nature of their representation. All the characters in the play, with the exception of Krishna, are rendered metaphorically blind to make a crucial philosophical statement. The all-pervasive blindness in the play serves the hegemonic project of critiquing the vacuity of rampant bloodshed. Blindness thus becomes symbolic of the human condition. In other words, Bharati displays very little interest in the materiality of corporeally different embodiment, that is, in the quotidian realities and minute details of what it means to be blind. Even in the case of Dhritarashtra, the dramatic focus is on the metaphorical implications of his blindness, inability to understand his ignorance and his irrational behaviour. Hence, it may be argued that it does not represent blind people and their experiences per se. For this reason, it would have no adverse effect on the constitution of the identity and subjectivity of the visually impaired population. However, the absence of such a line of thinking is an awareness and consideration of the problematic nature of metaphorical expression and the way metaphors acquire signification. What we see on the stage may not be a ridiculous tableau of blind people running and bumping into one another nor a comical picture of them groping and grasping thin air, but the tropological evocation of blindness in the play at once calls attention to and even reinforces figurative stereotypes of the phenomena of the kind outlined in the introduction. Bharati himself, for example, in his 'Note to the Director', gives specific instructions that the 'stage should be as bare as possible' and the '[l]ighting should be restrained but imaginative' (Bharati 2011, 3). The rendition of such instructions on the stage mandates perpetual dim lighting in the theatrical productions of *Andha Yug*. To invoke the atmospheric blindness of the age as described in the play, there is minimal to no lighting on the stage during several crucial scenes, which incites a very uncomfortable experience for the sighted audience straining to make out the action on the stage. From the ominous dialogues between the guards and Ashwatthama raging and raving on the stage to important exchanges between characters on the battlefield, all such decisive moments in the play are shrouded in darkness, literally forcing the sighted viewers to squint their eyes. What this discomfiting experience ends up achieving is not only an effective rendition of the metaphor of blindness in Bharati's play but also a reinforcement of stereotypes of blindness that equates sightlessness with darkness and incomplete understanding, thereby instilling in the audience a sense of comfort in still having the full capacity of their eyes.

Andha Yug, in fact, through the invocation of this and other like stereotypes 'shore[s] up the normate subject position' by stigmatising blind people. Rosemarie Garland-Thomson, in *Extraordinary Bodies: Figuring Disability in American Culture and Literature* (1997), coined the term 'normate', thus mapping the contours of the 'veiled subject position of cultural self, the figure outlined by the array of deviant others whose marked bodies shore up the normate's boundaries' (1997, 8). This coinage indicates the 'constructed identity of those who, by way of the bodily configurations and cultural capital they assume, can step into a position of authority and wield the power it grants them' (1997, 8). Garland-Thomson's understanding of the normate subject-position reminds one of Krishna's role in Bharati's play. He happens to be the only figure with absolute sight to perceive objective realities and the ability to make moral choices. He is depicted as the moral epicentre amidst the bloodshed and annihilation in a world at the cusp of *kalyug*—a dark world of decadence and amorality. In fact, the play ends with Krishna's death, which is depicted as the death knell for the world of *dharma*. Even the visual imagery of the play envisages Krishna's death as the oncoming of an age of darkness. With the ideal present in Krishna, the metaphorical blindness in the play appears as a state of abnormality and instability which ultimately epitomises the normal and the stable embodied in the figure of Krishna. Here, Krishna's lofty position is reminiscent of 'the sense of an elevated status', as Garland-Thomson discusses, 'that is so ubiquitous that people often aspire desperately to accord with the normate subject position, trying to fit what constitutes a prohibitively exclusive ideal' (1997). Krishna, too, in this play, seems to present the very ideal that Garland-Thomson talks of. All the stock characterisations and symbolic meanings in the play are aimed at privileging the universally desired state of sight, stability and normality, turning Bharati's use of metaphors of blindness into a fairly tactful and opportunistic literary device to proclaim and affirm an ocular-centric epistemological and ethical worldview.

More importantly, when read from the perspective of non-visual embodiment, the reduction of blindness to its metaphorical signification becomes deeply problematic. *Andha Yug* as a dramatic enactment of narrative prosthesis seldom confronts the actual conditions of a sightless existence, obscuring blindness from view and impeding its study as a socially relevant phenomena or a politicised facet of identity. As a result, blind people are denied all forms of agency and turned into empty cyphers of signification. The materially embodied experience of blindness and blind people themselves are sacrificed in the plot in favour of a metaphysical bewilderment of a much larger section of humanity, producing in the visually impaired community a traumatic sense of being excluded from the material processes of national life. In this sense, *Andha Yug* is indicative of a process of human disqualification that blind people are subjected to in a literary composition patterned on the lines of narrative prosthesis. How then could one expect a blind person to read/watch this play and come out of it with a dignified sense of self?

A similar exclusionary gesture is to be found within the pages of the Indian Constitution, which, while addressing the issues of almost all minority groups by prohibiting discrimination on grounds of religion, race, sex, place of birth and abolished untouchability (Barker 2011, 140), blatantly ignored the voices of the disabled. Barker elaborates that 'disability remained, in legislative terms at least, the least recognized condition of social deprivation and discrimination in Indian society'; that is, while other marginalised sections like women, religious minorities and lower castes were assured protection under the law, 'disabilities continued to exist outside the gaze, and the administration, of state or social law' (2011, 140). It is a matter then of little coincidence that the Constitution of India was promulgated around the same time (only four years before) *Andha Yug* was published. Interestingly, during the early decades following India's independence, disabled people were not even recognised in our national census. It was only in 1981 that they were counted as part of the exercise but here too there was no separate category for blind people. It was only in 2011 that this separate category was created. In this sense, *Andha Yug* is not only an allegory of Partition. It is also a story about the status of blind people in newly independent India. Blind people have been rendered literally and metaphorically invisible.

Denaturalising the Metaphor

There is little doubt that the literary treatment of blindness in *Andha Yug* is both indicative and representative of the general attitude in the country towards blindness and blind people at the time of its publication. This statement should not be construed as an apologia for Bharati's pejorative evocation of blindness in his play. It is more a recognition of a possible criticism of the play. Literary commentary informed by visual-centric embodiments may accuse this paper of being anachronistic. It would not be right to approach a play written in the 1950s—a time when disability activism was yet to be born—from the perspective of recent developments in disability scholarship. The present chapter, however, believes that irrespective of the time when the literary work was written, we should approach the representation of disability in it donning the sensibility of a disability activist of the 21st century.

The intention is not to police the use of conceptual metaphors of the kind cited by Lakoff and Johnson. Such an exercise at best would be pointless and at worst abortive. After all, the figurative representations of the phenomena which equate blindness with ignorance are deeply ingrained in the ocular-centric cultural ethos of the society we live in. They, in fact, are an integral part of our collective consciousness, both arising out of and reinforcing prevalent literary compositions, folklores, legends, proverbs and so on. They are also in many ways germane and borne out by a sighted person's restricted experience of the world. But these should only be used to explain—not to excuse—such representations and the rampant use of problematic disability metaphors in literature. This is the endeavour we have undertaken so far. We further believe that instead of monitoring the usage of metaphors, we should focus our attention on the need to deconstruct such expressions, expose the arbitrariness of the association they establish and problematise them from the perspective of a visually impaired embodiment. Overtly conscious of the above objective, we now proceed to undertake this task. We have already claimed that blind people are not necessarily incapable of accessing the world and acquiring knowledge, but they do so through alternative modes of cognition based on the other four senses, of sound, touch, smell and taste. They are, therefore, not living embodiments of ignorance. It is not as if they are unable to understand their surrounding environment or just the consequences of their actions. It is a different matter that because of their over reliance on the eye, the sighted world may not be fully familiar with these modes. More importantly, we would also like to suggest that the material reality of being endowed with sight does not necessarily mean that a sighted embodiment has unrestricted access to understanding. The play under scrutiny itself pays testimony to this fact. Dhritarashtra may be physically blind and Gandhari may have blindfolded herself but all the other characters in the play with the exception of Krishna are sighted in the material sense and yet they appear to be as—if not more—ignorant and confused as Dhritarashtra and Gandhari. For this reason, they have been rendered metaphorically blind. Their blindness may be metaphorical but their ignorance is a lived reality within the play. *Andha Yug*, in this sense, points towards the disability of sight in the processes of cognition and acquisition of knowledge. So much for the esteemed assurance of sight in an ocular-centric world. This conflation of the materiality of being sighted with the metaphoricity of blindness clearly troubles an ocular-centric worldview that underscores the reliability of sight to acquire knowledge and destabilises the commonplace equation between sight and understanding and, thus, between blindness and ignorance that the play so heavily relies on to convey its central motif. *Andha Yug*, in this way, turns the metaphor it uses on its head, articulating the fragilities and arbitrariness of the analogy on which it is based. The play, therefore, complicates and denaturalises the said metaphor.

The parallels between blindness and ignorance, which acquire the privileged status of the overarching metaphor in *Andha Yug*, are unsettled by the recognition that all sighted characters in the play except Krishna are ignorant. It is also worth noting that in the various theatrical renditions of the play that we have come across, the role of Dhritarashtra has always been portrayed by sighted actors. In other words, we have yet to come across a performance of the play in which the part of the blind king has been assayed by a visually impaired person. One such theatrical production, where a sighted actor plays the role of Dhritarashtra, was by the Bharatendu Natya Akademi in Lucknow. This paradox of a sighted individual inhabiting the role of a sightless character appears to introduce a fluidity in the identities across the ability divide by allowing a sighted actor to embrace a visually impaired persona and accommodate the traits of the visually impaired king onto his sighted self. However, on closer scrutiny, one realises that instead of the divide being breached, the hierarchies between the two forms of embodiments are reinforced. It is not the character of the blind king that is in control of the sighted actor. It is, rather, the sighted actor who interprets this role to reinforce the symbolism at the heart of the play. In the case of this particular production of Bharati's play, Dhritarashtra's blindness is established through certain stereotypical gestures by the sighted actor, like mistaking people's identities, turning the ear towards the direction of the sound or passively being led by ministers or courtiers who assume a position of power over the king's vulnerable situation. Underpinning such typical gestures are problematic meanings and signification augmented by the playwright, directors and actor, rather than the role (here, Dhritarashtra's) dictating the bounds of these gestures. Hence, by making Dhritarashtra's character rudely jut out from the rest of the cast due to his aberrant body language, the play and its theatrical rendition exacerbate the discordance between sighted and sightless embodiments. For the sighted actor onstage, the blind character is just one of the plethora of roles he performs in the course of his theatrical career before discarding it for another, which means that in the long run, the persona of a visually impaired character would hardly leave an impression on the identity of the sighted actor. The meeting of the blind and sighted identities through the actor playing Dhritarashtra's role is only a temporary aberration which immediately dissolves as soon as the curtain falls on the performance. It is hard to ignore the prejudice that while a sighted actor is considered fit to ape a sightless individual, a blind actor, on the other hand, is deemed incapable of depicting the same character. David Bolt, in 'Aesthetic Blindness: Symbolism, Realism and Reality', underscores this sad reality in his observation that 'actors who have visual impairments have been and still are disqualified on account of an ocular-centric social aesthetic, illustrating that, irrespective of symbolism, the effect of aesthetic blindness remains a lived reality for many' (2013, 107).

Conclusion

Putting Bolt's observation into perspective with the hearty welcome reserved for decades, for the problematisation of men playing female roles in theatre in feminist and gender studies, the social exclusion of blind actors, frankly speaking, reeks of double standards. On one hand, critical theories on gender exclusion are lauded and canonised, while other similar efforts to formulate a critical tradition for disability studies are met with several bottlenecks due to the academic negligence and callousness with which this field is handled. Moreover, on closer observation, one can notice several intersections between theories on gender roles and disability studies since themes like stereotypes, cultural norms, power, exclusion, inequality and discrimination are as relevant to disability studies as it is to feminist and gender studies. In fact, feminist studies could not only be effectively juxtaposed with disability studies but also provide relevant theories into which disabled embodiment could be applied.

The Indian theatre scene, irrespective of its rich tradition involving women, witnessed greater curbs on female presence onstage due to the redefinition of morality and female chastity from the 19th century onwards, thus popularising the practice of cross-dressing by men for female roles in theatre.[4] The increasing presence of men as female impersonators, as a result, consolidated new norms and perceptions of Indian female subjectivity which 'enabled patriarchal power not only of the materiality of the female self but its symbolic projection' as well (Hansen 1999, 6). Eventually, these practices lost steam as women gained more visibility in theatre in the 20th century owing to, as Katheryn Hansen notes, 'a lengthy process of negotiation, wherein the performer's status and image have been reworked to incorporate the signs of Indian womanhood'[5] (6). With such theories in circulation, one might ponder whether the scenario isn't the same for disabled individuals as well. Unfortunately, there has not been a similar resistance to age-old practices in disability studies. Physically disabled characters, like in the case of Dhritarashtra in *Andha Yug*, are still mostly portrayed by sighted impersonators of sightlessness, quite similar to the proliferation of male impersonators of female characters in theatre for decades. As mentioned earlier, while discussing the exclusion of blind actors in theatre, the projection of disabled embodiment onto a normative self diffuses the divide between sighted and sightless identities as well as interprets and traps the disabled self within the normate gazes, akin to the patriarchal male gaze which reimagines and fixes the female body.

Hence, the reading of *Andha Yug* that this chapter attempts from the purview of disability studies is also, as a result, a clarion call to be awake to all forms of exclusion practised by society, beginning from something as innocuous as its linguistic idiom. That is, just like the phallic-centric linguistic idiom being shattered to replace problematic words like mankind, chairman, policeman with neutral and gender-inclusive terms like humankind, chairperson and police officer, it is high time, as Vidali herself asserts, to formulate more imaginative and inclusive modes of addressing and perceiving disabled individuals that do not rob them of the materiality of their embodiments or contain pejorative connotations. Thus, by applying such theories of exclusion into disability studies, it is possible to develop a vibrant and unique theoretical idiom to explore the complexities and problematics of disabled embodiment. This, first and foremost, necessitates an unlearning and relearning of all the problematic forms of socialisation internalised by us and then a recognition of the said exclusion around us. In terms of this chapter, *Andha Yug's* problematic engagements with blindness could be tackled in meaningful ways only when the presence of exclusionary practices towards the blind are addressed in each and every aspect of the play.

Notes

1   Cognition might be understood as the process of interpreting the world or amassing knowledge through one's sense perceptions. But our sense perceptions do not operate in a vacuum; they are shaped every moment by the very images, language and modes of socialisation they try to interpret. In terms of this chapter, popular idioms in one's native language are stark instances of language influencing the bounds of cognition. While cognition shapes our modes of expression, the cognitive process itself takes place simultaneously within the strictures of language, that is, we think in language. As a result, the stereotypes propagated by language (here, stereotypes about blindness) get entrenched in our ways of thinking and seeing and get unconsciously vocalised even without any intention to insult other individuals.

2   Lakoff and Johnson elaborate upon conceptual metaphors as follows:

conceptual metaphors are grounded in correlations within our experience … [these are] not arbitrary or just historically contingent; rather, it is shaped to a significant extent by the common nature of our bodies and the shared ways that we all function in the everyday world … [Say,] [m]any people in cultures around the world simply live their lives without being concerned about whether they are using their time efficiently. However, other cultures conceptualize time metaphorically as though it were a limited resource. The Time Is Money metaphor imposes on the time domain various aspects of resources. In doing so, it adds elements to the time domain, creating a new understanding of time. (Lakoff and Johnson 1980, 155, 245, 250, 252)

As the quote suggests, we live by various concepts in our lives which shape our thoughts, perceptions and actions, that is, our cognitive process, and give rise to and normalise certain metaphors. In the case of blindness, the notion of 'seeing is understanding' is one such conceptual metaphor arising from the perception of blindness as a defect or a lack.

3   While the Oxford English Dictionary expounds the meaning of metaphor as a 'figure of speech in which a metaphor is a potential or implied simile ... in a metaphor one side is stated but not the other word or phrase [which] is applied to an object or action to which it is not literally applicable', the Cambridge Dictionary defines it as 'an expression, often found in literature,

that describes a person or object by referring to something that is considered to have similar characteristics to that person or object'. In both cases the attempt is unmistakably to evolve a logical resemblance and similarity between two objects and to juxtapose the figure of speech with literal expression. A similar emphasis on metaphor being a figure of speech that evokes an apparently logical resemblance between two unlike objects and actions are to be found in the authoritative books on English grammar. The Nesfield Grammar, for example, defines metaphor as 'a potential simile' where 'one side is stated but not the other' (237). Similarly, Wren and Martin also interprets metaphor as 'an implied Simile' and unlike the simile does not 'state that one thing is like another or acts as another, but takes that for granted and proceeds as if the two things were one' (334).

4   In 'Women and Theatre in India', it is stated that

all communities, including the otherwise progressive Parsis, believed that the presence of real flesh and blood women in theatre groups and on stage would corrode moral values and lead to extremes of debauchery. So not only female impersonators but also editors, thespians, directors and theatre owners, all came together in blocking real women from joining commercial theatre companies and enacting female roles on stage. (Pande 1646–53)

One of the most popular actors playing female roles during the early 20th century was Bal Gandharava in Marathi theatre. Such actors, as Pande recounts, developed

intense 'sadhana' that was required of young thespians to become the perfect woman on the stage, whose 'chal dhal' (gait and graces) even women from good families secretly emulated. In fact, in Maharashtra, women copied Bal Gandharva's style of draping the nine-yard sari, and walking. Some fans of another transvestite Wasi were so overcome by emotions that they ripped their sleeves and fell in a dead faint in the aisles. (Pande 1647)

5   The greater visibility of women in theatre has been partially attributed to cinema as '[t]he relentless exposures and close ups of the cinematic image began to reassert the demand for women in women's roles' ('Women and Theatre in India', 6). From the 1930s onwards, more and more women started enacting the role of heroines in dramas. One such example is the

Kanpur Nautankis where they received better remuneration than men. Gulab Bai, a woman of the backward caste was the first women to perform in Nautanki. She performed the role of Laila in Laila-Majnun, Shirin in Shirin Farshad, Taramati in Harishchandra, Farida in Bahadur Ladki. Gulab Bai joined the theatre at an early age of twelve years and gained her fame and recognition by the late 1930s.

Unfortunately this traditional theatre coupled between its modern counterpart and the Indian cinema suffered a severe setback around this same period. But the cause of its degeneration was discreetly assigned to the arrival of women in the genre of theatre. Society stigmatized the public appearance of women and this gravely affected these female artists. Exclusively they hailed from the lower Bedia caste or deredar Muslims or from the outer circles of a respectable society. Thus all women appearing on the stage were collectively branded as 'loose women'. ('Women and Theatre in India', 7)

References

Barker, Clare. *Postcolonial Fiction and Disability: Exceptional Children, Metaphor and Materiality*. London: Palgrave Macmillan, 2011.

Bhalla, Alok. 'Defending the Sacred in an Age of Atrocities: On Translating Andha Yug'. *Manoa*, 22, no. 1 (2010): xi–xxiii.

Bharati, Dharmvir. *Andha Yug*, translated by Alok Bhalla. New Delhi: Oxford University Press, 2011.

Bolt, David. 'Aesthetic Blindness: Symbolism, Realism and Reality'. *Mosaic: An Interdisciplinary Critical Journal*, 46, no. 3 (2013): 93–108.

Cameron, Lynne. *Metaphor in Educational Discourse*. London: Continuum, 2003.

Dolmage, Jay. 'Between the Valley and the Field: Metaphor and Disability'. *Prose Studies*, 27, nos 1–2 (2005): 108–19. https://doi.org/10.1080/01440350500068973.

Hansen, Kathryn. 'Making Women Visible: Gender and Race Cross-Dressing in the Parsi Theatre'. *Theatre Journal*, 51, no. 2 (1999): 127–47. http://www.jstor.org/stable/25068647?origin=JSTOR-pdf.

Kanniappan, V. K. 'The education leads a person to leave aside the blindness of idiocy!' Translated from the Tamil 'Naanma Nik katikai' by V.K. Kanniappan, January 2020. https://www.poemhunter.com/poem/the-education-leads-a-person-to-leave-aside-the-blindness-of-idiocy/#google_vignette.

Lakoff, George and Mark Johnson. 'Conceptual Metaphor in Everyday Language'. *The Journal of Philosophy*, 77, no. 8 (1980): 453–86.

Mitchell, David and Sharon Snyder. 'Narrative Prosthesis'. In *The Disability Studies Reader*, edited by Lennard J. Davis, 222–35. London: Routledge, 2013.

Thomson, Rosemarie Garland. *Extraordinary Bodies: Figuring Physical Disability in American Culture and Literature*. Columbia University Press, 1997.

Vidali, Amy. 'Seeing What We Know: Disability and Theories of Metaphor'. *Journal of Literary & Cultural Disability Studies*, 4, no. 1 (2010): 33–54.

9

DISABILITY, TEXTUALITY AND THE HERMENEUTICS OF DISTANCE IN SRIRAM RAGHAVAN'S *ANDHADHUN*

Sanket Sakar

Introduction

'What is life? It depends on the Liver.'[1]

It is with these striking words that Sriram Raghavan's 2018 thriller, *Andhadhun*[2]—a film in which a sighted musician Akash (Ayushmann Khurrana) pretends to be blind—opens. Again, towards the end of the movie, the same words are voiced by the corrupt doctor Swami (Zakir Hussain). 'Liver' here can have two connotations. One is, of course, the literal bile-secreting organ of the body—shorthand for the material and biological components integral to the identity-formation. The other meaning refers to the 'person who lives'—the personal and experiential contexts of the identity-formation. Unfortunately, this seemingly simple dictum about identity at both the portals of the movie does not hold together what happens within the cinematic universe. It seems there are questions throughout the film that the experiential and corporeal contexts of the identity fail to answer: Why is Akash pretending to be blind in the first place? What is to be gained in the process of imitating a marginalised identity? How does he suddenly start to 'feel like' blind by having his black spectacles and wooden cane on? How does blindness strike a chord with good music? Why does the thriller focus so much on his vision that ceaselessly oscillates between the sight and its absence? After all, what indeed is the fault (*kasoor*) of the eyes (*naina*) in this oscillation of meaning?

The act of feigning blindness exhibits characteristics that seem to be rooted in factors not solely reliant on the actual lived experiences of those who are blind. The durability, adaptability, feasibility, and comprehensibility of such a 'faking' act seems to be firmly entrenched in notions beyond the tangible encounters of individuals with visual impairment. These extra-material notions, as I will contend, can be collectively called as the textuality of blindness—both in its perception and circulation through representation. The book-like textual nature of the pretending act is constructed on specific flat scripts that 'intextuates' blindness as a matter of adherence to looks and behaviours, which are mostly codified rather than experientially witnessed. As the first few parts of this chapter will discuss, Akash's rather effortless performance of blindness is a sort of rigorous writing penned with certain visual, behavioural and verbal indices which conform to the already circulated and agreed-upon 'ways of the blind'.[3] The people or the social structures with which he interacts under the garb of his textual blindness also simultaneously engage with him in certain socio-culturally prescribed methods. They usually shower an excessive amount of benevolence aimed at the correction of the 'tragic' life of the disabled individual through certain palliative measures—acts of quasi-charity which this chapter classifies under 'fringe-benefits' for the blind persons. There is a pervasive social circulation of methods of reading and writing disability that allows one to comfortably disengage with the method of close contact with the real disabled person. An extensive emphasis on flat interpretations of complex bodies further reduces a possibility of 'radical witnessing' that might provide space for experiencing what disability, actually and ambiguously, is and might be.

These methods have been adapted within modern neo-bio-capitalistic systems as set agreements regulating how citizens behave within the corporate-like socio-cultural framework to increase their productivity. Towards the latter half of the chapter, the discussion will explore the inspirations and limitations of Akash's impersonation in the movie by juxtaposing it with a newspaper report about an actual overcoming story of a blind musician in India. We will explore a push to transcend conditions and contingencies of the embodiment within the normate society as it demands one (whether they are disabled or not) to constantly occupy the place of an abstracted 'other'. To simply become extra-ordinary, beyond oneself. This formulaic push to *become better* dictates Akash's decision to fake blindness as much as it dictates that the actual blind person develops a 'divine eye'. That one cannot achieve neatly set citations of excellence by being their own messy, intuitive self is immaculately detailed in the socio-cultural book of quotations. Agreeing (or acknowledging) those abstract and disembodied terms of 'promotions' is maintaining the circulation of that book of citations. As we near the conclusion of the chapter, we discover that the suspected discrediting social judgements (stigma) about the disabled bodies force the audience to painstakingly search for deeper meanings. This pursuit sometimes prompts them to prioritise what they have learned is being represented over the factual accuracy of the representation. The present chapter will try to weave all these loose threads together to argue that there is a tight binding of disability within textuality in the contemporary ableist imagination of *Andhadhun*. To find treasures and reach maximum levels of perfection and satisfaction, the cultural artefact makes it so that the represented and the viewer follow nothing but the set map of disability. When conceiving it as the mere 'other' of the nondisabled self, this flattened map often ignores that the disability is a 'world-creating' phenomenon in itself. Whereas a performance, such as Lynn Manning's *Weights,* which tries to imagine blindness *from within,* contending with its nuances—ambiguities, instabilities, capabilities and limitations—on a personal experiential level, gives space for a 'radical witnessing' of the disabled other. As a way of conclusion, the need for this 'radical witnessing' of the Other as a mode of understanding disability is suggested against an over-reliance on textured interpretations in the extant social and medical models of disability.

Blind Performance, Blind Text

I am particularly inspired by Tanya Titchkosky's brilliant explorations of the textured nature of disability in works such as *Reading and Writing Disability Differently: The Textured Life of Embodiment* (2007) and *Looking Blind: A Revelation of Culture's Eyes* (2005). What these works saliently do by analysing various kinds of popular, experiential and administrative texts is to posit that disability is 'something that is made meaningful through the activity of writing and reading its appearance into existence' (2007, 20). In contemporary popular media, these activities of reading and writing most often resort to using disability as a 'problem'—a lifeless obstacle to overcome. These textual representations also shape the organisation of the movements of actual life for the disabled individuals: both subjective and objective. In reading and retaining the codes which construe disability as a 'problem', the rewritings about disability (such as a creative text) also end up becoming a horizontal channel for circulating the textual nature of embodiment. That we make meanings of embodiment by encoding them into the semiotic—that appearance is ever subject to interpretations, is an insight that the normate world constantly tries to ignore or suppress.

Braces, wheelchairs, white canes or hearing aids are not just devices for better accessibility; they are signs to be read and written. For example, the identity of a blind person standing on one side of the road with a white cane in their hand gets rapidly subsumed within the symbolic manifestations of the cane when the good-meaning people around them feel a temptation to help them cross the road. The instant pity evoked in others gets so charged with the sight of the cane that they do not care to ask whether the blind person actually needs assistance crossing the road. That the person with a cane *suffers from* blindness and *needs* assistance is a commonplace interpretive action shaped by our social consciousness.

Similarly, it is not hard to suppose that the person with the cane finds the proposal to help rather preposterous and says, 'I do not need your help. I have *learnt to cross roads on my own*.' This performance of self-reliance is also based on another signifying action. That blindness is a miserable mental state that they *need to come out of* by *refusing the offered help* is how they have made their disability mean in their minds. Both parties are mindful, though, one of the *need* for charity, and the other of the *need* for independence. Nevertheless, they often remain unmindful of the network of interpretations—pity and self-reliance that pans out from the symbolic import of the white cane and the proposal to help. While such symbolic interactionism is vital for a pragmatic engagement with the unknown Other, an excessive and exclusive insistence on an interpretation of bodies reduces the radical otherness of the disabled to the mere 'other' of the nondisabled self.

The performance of disability or non-disability in our inside and outside worlds is dictated by flattening their complex structures into readable surfaces without depth. 'The frenzy of knowing and the pleasure of looking,' de Certeau argues, 'reach into the darkest regions and unfold the interiority of bodies as surfaces laid out before our eyes', surfaces 'which are transformed into legible spaces' (quoted in Conquergood 2013, 30). These flat surfaces intimately resemble the kind of texts Roland Barthes talks about—texts shaped by an all-encompassing structure of meaning that dissipates, interacts and mutates through a reader-writer interaction over a social fabric. 'The unity of text is not in its origin but in its destination' (Barthes 1989, 54). There might be incomplete and ambiguous addresses to the destination. Still, texts nonetheless invite one to participate in the enchanting process of searching for the interpretation terminus to the extent that sometimes the reader might find that they have reached neurotic levels of over-coding rather than simple decoding (Barthes 1989, 43). The citationality networks look so expansive and dominating that there seems to be no way out—no rubbing off of the cultural marks over the body's skin. One keeps on over-coding as they search for closure on bodies and texts even where there is not any.

By thinking of Akash's performance of the blind man as a tissue of signs that shapes and is shaped by flat interpretations of the movie and the audience, the practice of a hermeneutics of distance and solitariness is revealed. Such a hermeneutics, as Dwight Conquergood would argue, closes its vision to 'a hermeneutics of experience, co-presence, humility, and vulnerability, listening to and being touched' (Conquergood 2013, 27) by the subject. This is a criticism that Conquergood perpetually poses against textual modes of performance analysis as well. I am deliberately relying on the concept of closed-textured performance to indicate how the movie desires to 'blur the edges, dissolve the boundary, dismantle the opposition, and close the space between text and performance' (25). To that end, the textual approach is purposely employed in this work to critique the hermeneutics of distance and solitariness for reading-writing disability.

Auslander and Sandahl also talk about the performance of disability over specific, limited and deeply entrenched 'socio-cultural scripts' and the need to overturn it through innovative performances that manipulate and transform these stereotypes (Sandahl and Auslander 2005, 3). One of the examples of such arrangements could be Lynn Manning's play, *Weights* (2000), which, by giving a taste of *new* and *wonderous* discoveries occasioned by personal experience of blindness, allows a 'radical witnessing' of disability unavailable within the normative modes of interpretations. Such innovative patterns of performances that move divergently and radically away from the surfaces tied to the fixed axis of interpretations are hard to imagine in textual-ableist culture. Within a modern neo-bio-capitalistic system, the lifeless citations that turn bodies into texts get reified within a very corporate-like agreement. As this power system controls bodies for political and capital gains, it introduces a matrix of reward and punishment for the acceptance and refusal of such social scripts that perpetuate the system. In a bid to transcend the bodily limits for maximising productivity, we are not only dematerialising but also disembodying complex embodiments into 'textuality'—the lifeless two-dimensional objects. This textuality incorporates both the subject and the object—the character and the audience—in a corporate agreement to find depths of transcendence and interpretations where it is mere flatness. The stigma of citations persists. Are there ways to 'radically witness' the animated world of the disabled bodies away from these tried and tested lifeless citations?

Assembly of Blind text

Let's focus on the movie's few introductory shots of Akash's body. His presence is first shown through his fingers that glide swiftly on the piano, producing a melodious tone. A few shots here try to capture his poorly lit room, his pet cat, as well as a window partly covered with curtains. Swiftly again, as the tempo of the music starts to rise, the close shots come back to track his meticulous fingers, following them intently until the point camera tilts above, and we get to see Akash's occluded eyes. Here, the intrusive camera almost feels like it is sizing up Akash's body as it almost cuts through his arms. Scenes then screen Akash reading time through his tactile watch and getting down the stairs with the help of a white cane and the touch of surrounding architectural structures. As he totters down the stairs out of his apartment, the presence of black eyeglasses becomes evident.

The semantic construction of these first few shots introduces the 'text' of the blind figure. The indices of a poorly lit room with partly closed curtains, a tactile watch, occluded eyes, a shining white cane, a pair of black eyeglasses, and a staggering walk are easy markers that fall within the interpretive paradigm of blindness. In their first viewing of such visual indices, the audience has already constructed him as a blind figure in the absence of the withheld knowledge that he is merely acting as a blind man. These visual indices are not coming out of a vacuum. It is not the case that Akash is creatively recreating the text of blindness afresh by choosing to present his body laden with these specific physical markers. The quality of his performance as a blind person lies not in his attention to detail on how a blind person actually is but in his ability to match the societal perception of what blindness is assumed to be. In other words, he is merely rewriting himself as the text upon the shared cultural scripts that shape the social exchanges with the blind.

Considering this performance as a text validates the rigorous dedication exhibited by Akash in meticulously assembling his act. The visual indices are interwoven with a taut narrativisation of the disability. He constructs a compact linear story around the cause of his blindness in resonance with the socio-cultural scripts, bracketing off the complex and often ambiguous ways the actual disablement could occur. Twice in the movie, he repeats his narrative of how he became blind at the age of fourteen when a cricket ball hit him, giving a debilitating blow to the optic nerve. Once to Sophie (Radhika Apte) and later to Simi (Tabu), his story is uttered as soon as someone asks what is wrong with his eyes. The unrelenting constancy of superfluous factual details such as age (14) and the type of ball (cricket) in each narration not only suggests a rehearsed accuracy but also an overcompensation of facts in his creation of the fiction. Other minute decisions such as wearing an eye mask in private and memorising the number of steps that make up the staircase of his dormitory are mental preparations taken in the spirit of faithful adherence to the socio-cultural scripts of blindness.

However, the terrain of these scripts remains too vast, dynamic and undulating to be folded into a single person's mechanistic act. At different moments, Akash is made aware of those scripts he has not yet hived off into his writing of the blindness. One of the early scenes shows Sophie asking him, '*Akele road kaise cross kar lete ho yaar? Koi guide kutta rakhna chahiye na!*'[4] ('How do you cross the road alone? You should keep a guide dog!'). Aimed at a corrective,

Sophie's reading of his textured performance is then governed by another predictable socio-cultural script. This script delineates that an accompanying guide dog, with its accessibility support, is necessary for the seamless and independent navigation of a visually impaired individual along the street. This script remains extraneous to the bank of limited scripts over which Akash rewrites his performance. He thought and made his best attempts to be interpreted as a blind man with his ensemble of prosthetics, such as a white cane and black spectacles. But the textuality of the performance belies his painstaking efforts to fabricate an all-encompassing text of blindness. Some parts of these social scripts seem to always stand outside the scope of his performance—some social perceptions remain unimitated, causing unintended lines of readings such as that of Sophie's. Personal text, therefore, is permanently stained within the social.

To put it in Barthesian terms, the meaning(s) that his textured performance generates becomes illuminated not through his personhood but through an interaction-circuit 'between' him and the readers—the society to which he wants to sell his appearance. It follows that his text must be experienced 'only in an activity, in production' (Barthes 1989, 58). He constructs his 'personal' text of the blind in his darkroom—like the solitary confinement of Frankenstein. But his constructed persona as the blind man runs amok with a lot of meaning(s) as it is read by others and himself during the processes of interaction and intimacy. Different institutions and characters of the movie, with their own peculiarities as well as the filmic structure itself, make space for different interpretations. All of these multiple and diverse readings nevertheless reveal affiliations with a sedimented narrative/story/script of the impairment already widely disseminated among the masses. These sedimented narratives do not allow looking out for those complex real-life experiences of the impairment that do not fit inside or are contrary to their organisation. One can afford to disengage with the experiential knowledge about the blind person, given the ready accessibility of these highly codified scripts. The evaporations of the personality of both the writer (blind performer) as well as the actual subject (experience of a blind individual) in this writing could be better understood by exploring what Akash calls *'andhe hone ke fayde'* ('the benefits of being blind') within the cinematic world. These supposed 'benefits' as they serve the (un-/) intended motivations behind his performance undergirds embodiment within a reductionist bio-political sphere of productivity—the ableist 'can do' value (Titchkosky 2007, 184). The text (i.e., the blind pretense) pushes hard to mimic the enigmatic vision associated with blindness. The enigmatic and divine vision, however, remains nothing but a performance or interpretation of the social scripts.

Fringe Benefits: Others Reading-Writing Akash's Blindness

Let's try and articulate a bunch of readings of Akash's text by other characters in the movie. More often than not, his interaction with them (when they are unaware of his acting) shows a level of over-generosity for him. These socially sanctioned readings of his masquerade by other characters allow Akash to enjoy what one of the scriptwriters of *Andhadhun* calls 'fringe benefits' in his everyday life (Ramnath 2018). As a financially-loaded phrase within neo-capitalist regimes of power, 'fringe benefits' obliges an employee with perks over and above their actual salary, which may take various forms: several types of insurance, gifts and compensations. Akash also (un-/)consciously manages his appearances and behaviours around social settings in such a way that he becomes eligible for receiving these 'fringe-benefits for the blind person' from society. His excellent job of creating a blind persona in coherence with social scripts is rewarded with those benefits (or so he thinks) that he would not have achieved otherwise. There is a crucial montage right at the beginning of the movie which aims to project his everyday life as a blind man and the benefits he gains thereof. One of the interesting fragments of this montage shows him sitting on the ledge of a temple. A lady comes to him, puts cash in his hand, folds her hands in front of him in a pose of reverence and goes away. Another fragment shows a beaming waitress serving his meal at the table of a restaurant where people usually self-service themselves. While he sits absentminded and absorbed in his own thoughts of music, the waitress informs him that she has brought his usual order to him.

Of course, he is bedecked with his usual repertoire of props—the black eyeglasses and white cane—that provides the visual indices for Akash's body to be interpreted as a blind man. But, the particular type of self-presentation that grants him these 'fringe benefits' in both these public spheres is also accompanied by a set of special behavioural codes. Similar to visual indices, these behaviours are also carefully placed parallel to socio-cultural expectations. His (in-/)activity with others in the social-scape is of a textual nature assembled with a focus on the act's interpretation. The montage in which the particular temple shot is ensconced cuts down the chronological time, as discrete images of his daily activities are stitched together. Within the continuity of the montage, the viewer is to share the idea that Akash goes and sits in temples regularly for a considerable amount of time. These sittings are constructed within a particular behavioural grammar. While sitting, his look remains far, wide and unfazed, giving the impression that he is unaware of the person moving towards or away from him. Even when the lady tries to put money in his hands and folds her hands in front of him, the most interaction he does is the twitching of fingers to grab the money notes given by her. Throughout, his look remains steadfast, directed toward a non-specific point in some distance. No dialogues are exchanged. This behaviour of un-registering the visuals of the immediate surroundings is a practised self-presentation that attracts a particular gaze from other participants in this social circle.

This gaze is interpretive. Upon looking at him sitting in such a way at a place of worship, his reception gets intimately keyed to the socio-religious template of the blind beggar icon. Even though he doesn't explicitly ask for such help, the visitors coming to the temple take him as a needy figure upon whom granting little monetary favours will secure them tremendous spiritual blessings in this life and beyond. He wears clothes that are anything but suggestive of penury. But the connotation of his decent dressing as a possible symbol of a prosperous economic condition is completely disregarded while gauging him as the subject of these charities. Akash's narrative aligns closely with the robust socio-religious archetype of a visually impaired beggar, leading to his immediate interpretation as a figure in need of financial assistance, despite his factual economic stability as a highly sought-after piano instructor. The interpretive frameworks of the text styled through props and postures precipitate social meanings, which can easily override the material conditions of the performer fabricating blindness.

A similar case can be traced to account for his inexpensive accommodation arrangement at a place run by a charity NGO (non-governmental organisation) for persons with disabilities. Looking blind person secures him the 'gift' of a dormitory at a meagre monthly rent of five hundred rupees. These cases reveal an inefficient inclusion of the blind within the contemporary neoliberal regimes of inclusion. The gifts, perks and fringe benefits that his fake blindness receives come out of a place of pity and not with a desire to create an equitable society. These fringe benefits assume sameness from all the blind individuals as they collapse individualities into textual generalities. Each is equally disenfranchised and needy regardless of their varied socio-economic situations. The modality of pity going into the scripts and coming out through the channels of interpretations of this performance is impervious to an individual's participation. The text shuts itself off to a person's interventions. The questions of social realities, individual capacities and limitations of both the performer as well as the performed are far removed from the surface of the text.

This system of fringe benefits does not allow the employee the freedom of choice. Here, the performer cannot choose not to receive the treatment of over-generosity. Consider this startling scene at the beginning: A patronising Sophie treats him to coffee and snacks at a café as she feels the need to compensate for the affront of bumping into him with her scooter. Akash, however, does not incur even a single scratch from the hit. The socially inspired guilt of hitting a blind person that drives her compensatory act looks exaggerated and hilariously disproportional against the mildness of the accident. The parallel is also striking. Just before the accident, at a traffic signal, she is seen as having an altercation with a car driver, raging comments like: *'Ae andha hai kya? Dikhta nahin?'* ('Hey! Are you blind? Can't you see?'). The road rage, which she seems given to, quickly morphs into multiple expressions of pity and apology as she lifts the stumbled Akash and takes him to the café as a compensation for her perceived affront. The blind performer appears disinterested and wants to leave the restaurant but Sophie's insistence on effecting the compensation makes him yield to her, though reluctantly. He had to stay and take these fringe benefits, even against his will. This sort of underpinning attitude logically follows the social contract that gets activated by the interpretation of his persona as a blind man. His partaking in the circuit of meanings is automatic with his kind of self-presentation. Managing and harmonising interpretations, which encompass the comprehension of texts extends beyond the writer's capabilities, while the act of writing itself is constrained by fixed socio-cultural frameworks. As soon as he undertakes the construction of his text—to sell himself off as a blind man—there appears to be no sight of exit from its folds, just as the employees of a company feel a 'soft' power, a curious thread of obligation, tying them to the cause of the company when they sign themselves up for receiving 'fringe benefits'. So much for the reception of his text by others. What about his desires, wishes and motivations for the textured performance in this busy environment that avoids entertaining such 'personal questions' while working on the assembly lines of productivity?

Blind Musician: Akash's Own Reading and Writing of Blindness

Let's turn to the protagonist's principal motivation for impersonating blindness. Towards almost the middle of the film, when Simi explicitly confronts him over the reason for his *'naatak'* (charade), he blurts out emphatically, 'Ma'am, it's just an experiment! As a musician, *mujhe lagta hai main jab nahin dekh paata, andar se music aur accha aata hai.* I am an artist. *Dimaag ki sanak hai, pagalpanti hai meri.* I thought it was harmless …' (As a musician, I think music flows better from inside when I cannot see. I am an artist. This is a quirk, almost a lunacy of mine. I thought this was harmless …'). These confessional lines come at a time when Akash has just removed his black spectacles, breaking the textual codes of his performance. So, notwithstanding his usual misleading comments about the nature of his blindness, reading these lines could really explain the socio-cultural contexts within which he is consciously/unconsciously constructing his text. Towards the very start of the movie, we hear a part of his his voice-over saying, *'Artist log focus ke liye kya kya nahin karte hain'* ('Artists go to any lengths to develop focus'). Admittedly, his iteration of the text of the blindness comes from a personal search for an aesthetic ideal. But one can only gloss over the underlying socio-cultural scripts at their own peril. As we have already seen, the constituents of his textured performance are never entirely his own invention; they derive their power as they shuttle between the cultural scripts of blindness.

Within the framing of his 'personal experiment' and 'artistic quirk', he carefully ingests the cultural assumption of sightlessness as a route to better music. Especially among Indian musical circles, Hemachandran Karah mentions, there is a prevalence of the popular notion of 'special talent' among the blind musicians—the 'freedom of distraction from sight' (2021, 41). Akash's fictional performance can only serve as a mirror to several real-life musical presentations, like that of K.J. Yesudas, where artists deliberately shut their eyes to keep them 'distraction-free like the blind' (Karah 2021, 41). The artistic endeavour to *be like blind* cunningly unfolds the interiority and complexity of blind embodiment as surfaces that are 'transformed into legible spaces' (quoted in Conquergood 2013, 30). The script of blindness as conducive to creating music is easily spooled over those legible-textual spaces.

Let's take a moment to examine the significance of the robust correlation between blindness and musical talent, as it energises a captivating narrative that entices a sighted individual to portray a blind character. There is a particular fascination with the blind musician figure who seem to offset their stigma of impairment through their super-ability in music within the Indian socio-cultural rubric. This fascination is disseminated and sustained through the legends of antique figures such as blind poet-singer Surdas and modern celebrated blind musicians such as Ravindra Jain. The regular appearance of blind beggars and children singing in trains and other public places in India is no anomaly to such fascination. To mull over the socio-cultural significance of such fascination, I will quote from the article published on the website of one of the top international dailies on the death of Ravindra Jain. What drives my choice of the article is the fact that an article on an internationally reputed news platform such as *The New York Times* cascades suggestions of a sedimented, universalised and 'commonsensical' belief among the masses. It starts as:

Ravindra Jain, who *overcame* lifelong blindness to achieve renown in his native India and beyond as a singer and composer, scoring more than 200 Bollywood films, died on Friday in Mumbai. (Pandya 2015, emphasis mine)

A little further down, it says:

Mr Jain was fond of reciting a poem with the lines, 'Work in such a way with closed eyes that it can open the eyes of those who can see.' (Pandya 2015)

The author writes off lifelong blindness as a mere impairment, a hurdle that needs to be overcome. If not through a medical cure, it should be alleviated through the crutch of some kind of super-ability. Essentially, to be socially recognised, a blind person needs to develop a 'special ability'— musical talent in this case—that transcends their material conditions. In this ableist metaphor (blind individuals as super-skilled professionals), their blindness is evaluated against the 'can-do' value of the normate and not against the value of interdependence that signify all human forms (Titchkosky 2007, 184). There is an assumption of superhuman transcendence from visual impairment in the author's words as he shares the text of Ravindra Jain's blindness through his words.

The socio-cultural narrative portraying blindness as a catalyst for the flourishing of musical abilities envisions an ascension that bestows upon the blind an almost divine discernment—the talent of an acute, focused and 'gifted' inner sight. With their totalising effect, these normative scripts expect all blind individuals to have this sacred 'gift' regardless of their individual propensity and skill.

Texts that centre around blindness, like Akash's, frequently rely heavily on these simplified narratives, disregarding the evolving capabilities, constraints, and intricate experiences inherent in the material embodiment of blindness. As they are frequently rewritten, these texts reveal and solidify an exhortation to be *more than* what one is bodily conditioned to be under the contemporary neoliberal bio-capitalist systems of power (Titchkosky 2019, 184). One feels compelled to follow the call of *going beyond limits*—stretching the limits of physical and mental labour for productivity—as a way to reciprocate the 'fringe benefits of blindness'. Therefore, aspiring individuals constantly navigate a perpetual journey surpassing the physical conditions of their embodiment, striving toward an abstract, disembodied ideal. So, Akash, a sighted individual, has to *be like blind* to be better as a musician because blind individuals are gifted to *be like musicians*, no matter what the material reality seems to indicate.

But there is a huge catch in the process of going beyond an existence that is more than or other to our conditions of embodiment. The

Otherness has to conform to the system. One can go beyond their bodily and individual selves only in the scripts decreed by the social and the cultural. The seemingly radical act of fleeing away from the 'confines' of the individual self has to take place in a textured space conditioned and ordered by the particular overcoming story. This overcoming story too, is heavily die-cast in sedimented socio-cultural scripts. For example, it is unimaginable in this textual-ableist space that the blind can explore different sonic dimensions of lights and shadows and become better painters or photographers. While analysing photographs from a Mumbai-based blind photographers' group, Partho Bhowmick similarly reveals how photography by blind individuals was an 'inconceivable' idea for him and his society at large before he began his research on them (Bhowmick 2013, 303). Akash might want to transcend his sightedness for an aesthetic ideal or to receive fringe benefits; that transcendence, unfortunately, remains circumscribed within the social idiom of the blind musician. A blind individual, similarly, would have to go beyond their conditions of embodiment but only by imbibing and perfecting a special eye to music that their social story directs them to be. One finds difficulty in travelling the road of excellence with their personal, fluctuating, messy and psychologised selves. They need the crutches of super-ability—the abilities, functions and behaviours that the socio-cultural books prescribe. In absence of a socially accepted overcoming story, the self, disabled or otherwise, looks lifeless and incomplete within the neoliberal bio-capitalist scheme of things. If being blind or non-blind are inherently unremarkable classifications on their own, it raises curiosity about how this widely acclaimed movie manages to derive excitement from these seemingly inert classifications. Do the mechanistic schemas of text still maintain control against filmic innovations such as open-ended conclusions and fluctuating corporeality?

Digging Vertically: The Audience's Reading-Writing of Akash's Blindness

The audience navigates through the ever-changing hues of Akash's narrative, where their interpretation of his sight oscillates rapidly between the realms of genuine blindness and a potentially affected or insincere portrayal. This oscillation creates a thrilling experience. There is a particular instance when the audience is let into Akash's secret right after the first ten or twenty minutes of the movie—the revelation that Akash is pretending to be blind for some real or perceived benefits. When Sophie leaves him near the dormitory after their first meeting, he quickly climbs up the stairs, shuts his door and sits down, removing his black spectacles and peeling off the vision-occluding contact lenses (an easy prop that made him look and 'feel' blind). Coupled with a piece of suspenseful music, camera work in this scene returns to its familiar language of close-up and extreme close-up shots—dissecting the eyes from the body for closer examination, it seems. Intruding the body, tracking down the movement closely to search for a hidden something resembles the sort of camera work in his introduction scene that we discussed above. Why are these scenes of revelation salient? Their salience lies in the fact that they direct the interpretation from horizontal surface reading (looking for apparent) to vertical reading (looking for obscure) as it goes inwards and onwards. The notion that 'Akash looks blind and therefore must be blind' becomes incredible here, as now the audience feels they have other cinematically credible information about the 'insides' of Akash—the *hidden meaning* of his textured performance. They feel that they now have the access to the 'insider' account of the difference between the real and the *fake* disability. The insight of probing deeper into the body and its mien gained from this scene helps them to connect his previous appearances as a pretension of blindness and casts aspersions over his future appearances. Overall, the logic of the movie encourages close reading of the textual codes to plumb out a secret status of the embodiment.

As Akash breaks apart the very corporate agreement of fringe benefits that his fake blind persona used to provide by making changes to his repertoire of props—by moving out and about without his vision-occluding lenses—he makes his performative text vulnerable. He becomes caught up in the vertical readings by others so much that he finds it difficult to receive his fringe benefits and exercise his super-ability of music. The audience and the movie's characters try to investigate in this vertical reading scheme for a hidden enigma inside his performance. He has to undergo several trials to prove his blindness now to characters such as Simi, Bandu (Kabir Sajjad) and Inspector Manohar (Manav Vij). The tests to check his visual sensitivity include attacking him with a knife that just misses his right ear and videotaping his domestic chores. Under the bio-capitalistic scheme, his personal limits and choices are taken for granted in order to reveal the secret: his hidden blindness/sightedness.

The quest of grappling, sizing and seizing the corporeal to unlock a new 'inside' territory of meaning is relevant to the kind of thrill *Andhadhun* tries to provide to the audience. That is, for the intricate subplots of this thriller to work smoothly, the audience and the characters of the film need to constantly claim, reclaim and un-claim the status of his vision. And, therefore, the busy plot does drastic somersaults in representing the status of Akash's vision and asks the audience to apply their vertical readings rigorously. To unlock the thrilling narrative of 'what is going to happen?', they have to readily question 'is he blind or not?'. Of course, the changing answers to the latter question at different points in the movie are heavily based on the social scrips of blindness. The dig to find the settled meaning of Akash's embodiment, apparently, never stops throughout the thriller. There are temporary breaks, such as when he actually goes blind. But the audience must return from their sojourn and get back to the duty to unearth the roots of his enigmatic corporeality. There is an obligation of interpretation for the audience, as much as there is the obligation to maintain the looks of the disabled body. There is a desire for closure through interpretations of Akash's body—reaching the 'secret' and final meaning that will unlock all the mysteries and ambiguities in the text.

In epilogue scenes, Akash meets Sophie after a long gap of two years and narrates to her the story of how, in a curious and unplanned turn of events, Simi dies in a road accident while Akash survives but his vision remains impaired. The final scene screens him coming out of the café and using his cane to navigate the streets. He is decked with blackened spectacles as he walks forward facing the camera. A discarded beverage can is lying on the path he is walking down. Without looking down and assessing the can's shape with the cane's touch, he kicks it powerfully away with his prosthesis. This can-kicking scene, which the writers of the movie deliberately wanted to keep as an open ending to the thriller about whether he is blind or not, has spurned vast possibilities of alternative closures from movie viewers on different online forums of discussion (Magan 2021; Ramnath 2018). Most of them refuse to believe that Akash is still a blind man in the last scene. Instead, in their fan theories they posit that he has already regained his temporarily-lost eyesight and is now telling a fabricated story of blindness to Sophie to win her trust again since he is good at narrativising his disability. Whereas, a section of fans does agree that his lost eyesight never came back, he indeed remains blind and the perfect strike on the beverage was just luck (Magan 2021).

The striking fact here is that the techniques of cinema in this particular scene are not promulgating that deep investigative look into the status of his vision that they fondly practice throughout the movie: there are no quizzing movements of the camera panning into extreme close-ups of Akash's eyes nor is there the background presence of suspenseful or dramatic music. It seems that the audience's interpretations of the open ending are not based on the factual representation of the scene itself. They derive their strength purely from the revealing scene of the past where audiences are advised to look firmly (that is, read vertically) into the codes of the performance and not accept the conditions of Akash's embodiment at the surface or face value. He is doomed to carry the blemish and stigma of bearing a textured (or, deep interpretation-prone) identity forever like how remedial processes do nothing but bring a minor change in disabled identity—'from someone with a particular blemish into someone with a record of having corrected a particular blemish' (Goffman 2017, 137). The stigma marks are still inscribed, if not on the body of the stigmatised, then certainly on the minds that continue treating it as a stigma. The interpretive trace maintains such a tough spectre that the reader here does not decode as much as they would over-code, and indict present embodiment in the congealed codes of the past. A phenomenon that Barthes would explain as readers being 'caught in a dialectical reversal' when the 'safety catch of the meanings' is removed (Barthes 1989, 42).

Suspecting his present coding as 'one who looks blind (again constructed on socio-cultural scripts) and therefore would be blind' also comes at the cost of disregarding the intuitive and kinaesthetic potential that human beings possess, although to different degrees. Locating the beverage can could very well be a result of a heightened sense of intuition that he might have developed over the years by enacting visual-deprivation. However, the binding interpretive framework advanced throughout the movie refuses to consider anything else than a probe into the ocular and the scripts made on visual perception. The multiple possible roots that an open ending could have presented are foreclosed over the surface where the readings are only possible in two directions: Akash being blind or not. The mental efforts to close off the open ending affirms the limitations of the kind of vertical readings this film encourages. The imposing reading-writing circuits reduce the complexities of embodiment into two neat outputs of blindness and sightedness and thus make the vertical reading fall back on the limited but already circulated, ever-legible surfaces of the text. The rigorous hermeneutics, which always suspects the explicit for an implicit 'deeper' meaning, therefore, seems incapable of contending with the radical otherness of the Other.

Conclusion: Radical Witnessing, Andhadhun, Weights and Social and Medical Models of Disability

In a co-written article on the simulations of blindness, Titchkosky argues for a more engaging, imaginative and dynamic understanding of blindness against a 'culture of sight'[5] that merely conceives blindness as the inability to see (Titchkosky et al. 2019, 135). As one of the examples, she explains the case of Lynn Manning's autobiographical play, *Weights*

(2000), where the protagonist, as an aspiring painter, prepares himself against a feared onset of blindness. He thinks it is the worst possible thing that could impair his painting skills and career. So, he starts stimulating blindness: 'I began secretly doing everyday tasks in the dark or with my eyes closed: dialling the phone, tying my shoes, washing the dishes. I had been determined that blindness would not catch me off guard' (quoted in Titchkosky et al. 2019, 135). However, the experience of blindness did catch him off-guard when, after an accident, he actually lost his vision. With his *new* found blindness, however, he started making several 'wondrous discoveries: A whole new way of knowing the world was opening up to me', and it was opening up 'through my ears, through my nose, through my feet, through my pores!' For Manning, 'light and shadow took on physical dimensions' (2019, 135).

Besides being an offshoot of the culture of sight, Manning's simulations of blindness are also textured and built on conditional clauses resembling a corporate agreement. Doing things in the dark or with eyes closed, that is, with eyesight disrupted, is not only the most 'authentic' way to feel blind within the ableist culture, but it is the most available code of knowledge about blindness. Similar to how Akash's performance of fake blindness is based on a code that lays out the impairment as a conducive route to musical excellence, Manning's earlier simulations and preparations cite those scripts that codify the impairment as a deterrent to a career in painting. They both have to learn, perform and maintain the agreements of corporate-like codes of textuality in their personal and public worlds of the daily reading-writing of blindness. In this type of 'intextuation'—making and maintaining a persona basis the text—living by the text and dying by the text—the embodiment becomes irrelevant, readily disposable. And shifting focus away from the physical contingencies and capacities of individual bodies becomes necessary for contemporary society—where the pressure is to 'go beyond limits'. Sure, a nondisabled body wants to eliminate its presumable bodily and experiential limitations by being *similar* to the disabled body and vice versa. There are offers for such transcendence as well. The non-blind individual will be able to get a *divine* eye, or they will be able to neutralise the *threat* of blindness. The blind person, on the other hand, will get recognition and acceptance by becoming an *inspiration for many*. But to achieve these fringe benefits, one must work themselves out tirelessly to match citations of 'greatness'. To cite many and to get cited by many then becomes the sole purpose of that kind of reading-writing process. As Titchkosky would argue, studying such performance also alerts us to our partaking in such mechanisms of in-text citations as we read and write materialities in our daily lives (2007, 20). And it should also alert us to the fact that how often this system of citations engenders us as we aspire for greater citations—medals of socio-cultural achievement. In a world where formulas of normativity leap into all sense-making apparatuses, these textured configurations are believed to be tried-and-tested endeavours towards highly anticipated outcomes such as 'fringe benefits'. Yet, at the end of the day, they are physiological and psychological experiments subject to contingencies. And the textual performance of visual-deprivation does suffer contingency in both these cultural artefacts.

However, while the contingency of actual blindness is re-appropriated and re-channelled through the already existing social scripts of blindness in Raghavan's movie, Manning's play opens itself up to an individual's 'radical witnessing' of its altered embodiment and consciousness. The way of understanding discovered by Manning upon being actually impaired involves an intuitive understanding of kinesics, proxemics and other types of para-language from *within* the domain of blindness. Auditory aspects such as the 'doppler effect of sounds' (Titchkosky et al. 2019, 135) illuminate him only after he acknowledges his blindness not as a mere sightlessness but as a 'world-creating' phenomenon in itself. These intricacies of embodied perception are difficult to decode within the simple and close-ended texts that govern the interpretation of blindness in the ableist world of *Andhadhun*. This textured world glosses or misses out on subtle individual and subjective nuances like an enhanced sense of proxemics or newly calibrated sense of haptics which might accompany blindness. A thousand complex negotiations that blind individuals have to perform in their daily lives within an inaccessible world are left out of the picture when we see Akash comfortably executing a kidnapping even while being blind. Instead of exploring the altered condition for its own sake, the textual system persuades shareholders to tether identities to fixed interpretive frameworks. That hermeneutic pattern always doubts what is too apparent, ambiguous or exceptional for its design. Any unique anomaly or ambiguity—wounds on the surface—has to be sutured down by the needle of citations. The textual tradition of hermeneutics quickly sublimates any individual talent because the creativity in itself gets *textual-ised.*

In their insistence on interpretations, the two extant models of knowing disability within the academic scholarship—the social and the medical—similarly miss out on the realm of individual nuances available through radical witnessing. While a medical model requires the unique experience of disability to be modified and expressed into the expertise of diagnostic and pathological treatment manuals, the social model recognises these experiences as a direct correlative of the inaccessible environments. The former suspects the 'explicit' body for a pathological meaning while the latter suspects it for a necessarily inherent 'social' meaning. Almost following the hermeneutical tradition of the 'schools of suspicion'[6] (Ricoeur 1970, 33), there is a search for a hidden meaning about disability to be unveiled, demystified and revealed within both of the above models; either through medical tools such as stethoscopes and thermometers or through academic tools such as close readings of social situations. Essential for a pragmatic understanding of and engagement with the disabled other, ordered inventories of the social and the medical models have sophisticated terminologies and toolkits to think about the impaired persons. In our textual and sociological encounters with the disabled individuals, these resources help us constantly sift through the sights, sounds and other sensations emanating from that body. We make out the invisible meanings of the impaired other by correlating, augmenting and adducing these received sensations with the social and medical implications already accumulated and deeply entrenched in our minds. Similarly, we as audience, and Akash, as a performer, are not engaging with the idea/figure of disability directly but attaching social/ medical meanings to it, and cognitively organising and responding to it based on these meanings. These examinations and readings are ways to sort out mental perceptions in a structured whole to make sense *of* the disabled other.

However, not unlike *Andhadhun*'s reading-writing strategies of the final scene, which limits the interpretive possibilities to two valences— blind or sighted—an exclusive and excessive focus on interpretation within disability studies essentially returns the 'problem' of disability to two neat outputs: 'bad' biological construction or 'bad' social construction. Their infrastructures of interpretation can turn into underpinning, textualising structures when they only look deep for expected meanings (symptoms of pathological/social diseases) hidden beneath the skin. Both of these approaches similarly prescribe textbook solutions to this 'problem' as well: bring disabled people back into the norm (re/habilitate, educate), make the normate society accessible to them, or banish them (cure/segregate) in institutional confines.

Such expert theoretical modes of thinking about disability not only presuppose a critical distance from the disabled text or body but also from individual aberrances and exceptions. Essentially grounded in a hermeneutics of distance and solitariness, interpretations in either medical or social models cannot help us much in understanding and relating to Manning's 'new' and 'wonderous' discoveries that he found while being blind. It seems that the 'radical witnessing' of blindness or any other disability as a world-creating phenomenon can only take place within the hermeneutics of vulnerability and co-experience that Conquergood talks about. It requires a great deal of vulnerability to listen to the 'radical otherness' of the 'Other'—which is not just an other modelled on the same self. One has to let go of their ego-gratifying theory in order to witness the particular nuances of the Other. Similar to Manning's radical witnessing of blindness, we need to open ourselves up and think *through* disability rather than thinking *about* it within trite methodological codes. Intimacy and vulnerability to and within bodies are required to witness the contingencies, shifting capabilities and limitations. Such a radical understanding *through* disabled sensations and situations will illuminate worlds of complexities that lie or extend beyond social and medical models. The possibilities of emancipation from oppression lie more in recognising, highlighting and celebrating how we perceive, understand and negotiate the world differently from others with our different embodiments rather than in smoothening our complex differentials to flatbeds of textualities.

Notes

1   As this analysis shows, the all-pervasive circuit of textual determinism and the hermeneutics of distance practised in the movie as well as in our ableist societies demand a reformulation of this dicta. One could rather put it as: 'What is life? It depends on Text', and it is particularly so in the context of blindness and, by extension, disability.

2   Could be translated as 'blind tune', also a play on the Hindi word, '*andhadhund*', which roughly translates to 'blitzkreig' or 'chaos'.

3   While commenting on the ways in which Aakash (the character) keeps pretending as a blind man, the chapter limits itself to a discussion of fake blindness as described in the narrative. Though out of scope for the current work, it will certainly be rewarding to view how the actual non-blind actor Ayushmann Khurrana prepared for this nuanced role and how his acting measures up against what Tobin Siebers call 'disability drag', i.e., the widespread practice in film industries where nondisabled actors essay disabled characters just to prove their acting mettle without undertaking a worthwhile understanding of everyday disabled experiences (Siebers 2004, 16–18).

4   The dialogues in this movie are exchanged in Hinglish (a portmanteau of Hindi and English)—a dialect spoken in contemporary metropolitan cities of India among the rich and the middle class. I have translated the Hindi portions of the dialogues to English semantically.

5   By 'culture of sight', authors name that ocular-centric cultural paradigm, that maintains the authority of sight in its ways of knowing, and in process, invalidates the experiential knowledge of the blind.

6   In his *Freud and Philosophy: An Essay on Interpretation*, Paul Ricoeur famously identifies Marx's, Nietzsche's and Freud's discourses as 'schools of suspicion' (1970, 28). He characterises their common key technique

as the destruction of 'sacred' meanings through the revelation of 'the whole of consciousness as 'false' consciousness (1970, 28). The 'schools of suspicions' have difficulty accepting the truth of experiential narratives as they always attempt to decode repressed or disguised meanings.

References

Andhadhun. Dir. Sriram Raghavan, Perf. Ayushmann Khurrana, Tabu, Radhika Apte, Manohar Vij, Kabir Sajjad, Zakir Hussain, etc. Matchbox Pictures, *Netflix*. 2018.

Barthes, Roland. *The Rustle of Language*, translated by Richard Howard. California: University of California Press, 1989.

Bhowmick, Partho. 'Blind with Camera: Photographs by the Visually Impaired'. In *Disability Studies in India: Global Discourses, Local Realities,* edited by Renu Addlakha, 303–30. New Delhi: Routledge, 2013.

Conquergood, Dwight. 'Beyond the Text: Toward a Performative Cultural Politics'. In *Cultural Struggles: Performance, Ethnography, Praxis,* edited by Patrick E. Johnson, 47–64. Ann Arbor: The University of Michigan Press, 2013.

Goffman, Erving. 'Selections from Stigma'. In *The Disability Studies Reader,* edited by Lennard J. Davis, 133–41. London and New York: Routledge, 2017.

Grosz, Elizabeth. 'Inscriptions and Body Maps: Representations and the Corporeal'. In *Space, Gender, Knowledge: Feminist Readings,* edited by Linda McDowell and Joanne P. Sharp, 236–47. London: Arnold, 1997.

Karah, Hemachandran. 'The Metanarrative of Blindness in India: Special Education and Assumed Knowledge Cultures'. In *Metanarratives of Disability: Culture, Assumed Authority, and the Normative Social Order,* edited by David Bolt, 30–44. London and New York: Routledge, 2021.

Magan, Shristi. '"Andhadhun" Never Really Ended, So We Imagined These Mind-Bending Alternate Endings Instead'. *ScoopWhoop,* 14 September 2021. https://www.scoopwhoop.com/entertainment/andhadhun-alternate-endings-/ (accessed 20 May 2022).

Pandya, Haresh. 'Ravindra Jain, Bollywood Film Composer, Dies at 71'. *The New York Times,* 10 October 2015. https://www.nytimes.com/2015/10/11/arts/music/ravindra-jain-bollywood-film-composer-dies-at-71.html (accessed 20 May 2022).

Ricoeur, Paul. *Freud and Philosophy: An Essay on Interpretation*, translated by Denis Savage. Connecticut: Yale University Press, 1970.

Ramnath, Nandini. '"Andhadhun" Revisited: The Twists and Turns That Resulted in One of 2018's Best Hindi Films'. *Scroll.in,* 17 December 2018. https://scroll.in/reel/905864/andhadhun-revisited-the-twists-and-turns-that-resulted-in-2018s-best-hindi-film (accessed 20 May 2022).

Sandahl, Carrie and Philip Auslander. *Bodies in Commotion: Disability and Performance.* Ann Arbor: The University of Michigan Press, 2005.

Siebers, Tobin. 'Disability as Masquerade'. *Literature and Medicine*, 23, no. 2 (2004): 1–22.

Titchkosky, Tanya. *Reading and Writing Disability Differently The Textured Life of Embodiment*. Toronto: University of Toronto Press, 2007.

Titchkosky, Tanya, Devon Healey and Rod Michalko, et al. 'Blindness Simulation and the Culture of Sight'. *Journal of Literary & Cultural Disability Studies*, 13, no. 2 (2019): 123–39.

10

SANJAY LEELA BHANSALI'S DISABILITY GAZE: LIGHTS, CAMERA AND SOUND! IN *BLACK* AND *GUZAARISH*

Priyam Sinha

Introduction

For many years, Bollywood cinema has been dismissed as a utopian lens, escapist cinema, often dramatising the urban cultural milieu and juxtaposing a lens of viewing Indianness, primarily through its stylistic song-and-dance picturisation (Banaji 2006; Iyer 2017). However, the last three decades witnessed a filmmaking culture beyond a hero's journey, underlining the nation's preoccupations with the subaltern voice, agency and positionality (Joshi 2015). Disability representation thus emerged as a critical vantage point in this dynamic topology wherein sound, songs and silences enhanced star body characterisations and the taxonomies of its display. It encompassed the culture of disablism and narrative prosthesis (Mitchell and Synder 2001) by portraying disability as an 'anomaly' within literature and cinema. Post-1980s, Bollywood has been gaining scholarly attention, proposing the importance of its imperial history (Prasad 2003), used synonymously with Indian cinema (Rajadhyaksha 2003), labelled as a politicised and melodramatic vantage point (Vasudevan 2010), described as an assemblage of a nation's preoccupations camouflaged in escapist fantasies (Joshi 2015; Rai 2009) and popularised through its performative bodies in its song-and-dance cultures (Morcom 2017).

Songs, therefore, would facilitate the audience's active engagement with the film and its stars even without watching the entire movie. Reflecting on Bollywood's journey with song and dance, its role within the cinema's narrative could be attributed to 'India's national anticolonial awakening' (Shresthova 2011, 23), essentially making it unique from other film cultures. Anna Morcom (2017) reiterates the prominence of a symbiotic relationship between songs and profits made by Bollywood, now a globally recognised genre. Also, songs guarantee a film's marketability, wherein much of the film's narrative is communicated through them. They indicated that even though the genres of songs vary based on the film's content and directorial vision, not having them would be inconceivable. This meant that strategic integration and aesthetic conceptualisation have been quintessential in generating hype over a film. A wide repertoire of these film traditions enables a film's marketing and popularity even before the release, producing new economies of consumer cultures that have globalised Indian identity.

This is suggestive that songless-ness and the absence of choreomusicological elements are strategic interventions to underline the realist film noir, a film genre's constructed outlier status or seriousness of the narratology. In a way, it exhibits the unconventionality of a film's underlying theme, narrative architecture and radical framing of characterisations. For these reasons, film journalist Chandan Mitra described 'a songless Hindi film as a contradiction'. As he candidly enquired in a suggestive tone,

> How many Hindi films do you recall that had no songs? ... Music is what distinguishes Indian cinema from the rest of the world. In fact, music is the defining characteristic of Indian, mainly Hindi cinema.[1]

In his efforts to highlight Bollywood's growing global popularity and recognition, he primarily acknowledged the role of song and dance by asserting that it promotes a *masala*[2] culture with just a handful of exceptions of songless films that emerged as commercial successes. He went on to name a few like *Bhoot* (2003), *My Wife's Murder* (2005), *Sarkar* (2005) and *Black* (2005). He asserted that the formulaic Bollywood melodrama still emphasises the role played by song, dance and romance with some variations in stylistic and genre-specific elements (Garwood 2006). Filmmakers, too, are caught up with these forms of cinematic representations, changing socio-political scenarios and audience expectations of going beyond the love–hate thraldom in heterosexual romance. Within these dominant constructions of Bollywood, disability representation has always held a prominent stature, often symbolising pitied, comic-relief and hero's sidekick characterisations. There have been shifting codes of disability representation, mainstreaming the performative and symbolic space of the disabled body with films such as *Hum Dono* (1961), *Dosti* (1964), *Koshish* (1972), *Sparsh* (1980), *Sadma* (1983), *Naache Mayuri* (1986), *Khamoshi* (1994), *Mann* (1999), *Iqbal* (2005), *Fanaa* (2006), *Taare Zameen Par* (2007), *My Name Is Khan* (2010), *Barfi* (2012), *Margarita with a Straw* (2014), *Bajrangi Bhaijaan* (2015), *Kaabil* (2017) and *Hitchki* (2018), to name a few. They revolved around gendered disability experiences, disability friendships and troubled familial relations that addressed a dramatised version of India's religious and social models of disability. While the visualisation, stylisation, narrative sequence and situatedness of star bodies within the narration are crucial in producing disability cinema, the sound, light and camera angles mediate as metaphors for voice, agency, and constructivism of gender, sexuality and disability in films. This chapter provides a discursive study of the song-and-dance picturisation, background scores, cinematography, (un)stylistic narratology, use of silences, and songless-ness to mediate a disability narrative. I foreground my insights using Sanjay Leela Bhansali's *Black* (2005) and *Guzaarish* (2010) as case points contributing to Bollywood's disability gaze and supercrip portrayals (Schalk 2016). Bhansali forayed into curating the sororal space of women's disability through songless-ness in *Black,* which was fixated on abandonment, being reduced to penury and scoffed at for leading a tragic life. Within a few years, he orchestrated a narrative foregrounding men's disability in *Guzaarish* (2010). In comparison, he was presented as relatively charismatic through his choice of frames, tonality and song picturisation.

This chapter is divided into three sections. I begin with a dialogue on how song-and-dance picturisation has been an intrinsic element of Bollywood's popularisation and discuss how they differ in Bhansali's vision of portraying disability. My point of departure is dance-choreomusicological elements infused with songless-ness in *Black,* spatiotemporal ties and cinematic sound-image in *Guzaarish* and how they reiterate the outlier status of the disabled body in a new media assemblage.

Bollywood's Music and Song Picturisation

Neepa Majumdar (2001) stated that by the 1930s, sound formed a quintessential role in determining a film's success. She further emphasised that the construction of the star body was based on the 'voice', mandating the actor's 'ability to make songs come alive', indicating the priority of the aural over the visual appeal and use of haptic codes in visuality for a film to garner popularity. The launch of RK Films in 1948 spearheaded romantic interludes between the hero and heroine/voyeurism through semi-nudity in choreographed dance numbers, supported by background dancers to amplify the star dancing. Even films across different decades romanticised intimacy and scopophilia, wherein songs functioned as a metaphor for onscreen chemistry between heterosexual couples (Somaaya 2004).

Songs were complemented by instrumentation, which replaced lengthy dialogues by taking the narrative forward, functioned as a fun element and established a unique stand-alone quality from the film's literary narration. Contrary to these views, Lalita Gopalan described 'song and dance elements' as 'interruptions' in the film sequence (2002). Asha Kasbekar commented that they serve as erotic digressions from the narrative, allowing 'areas of heightened transgressive pleasure' (2001) and the voyeuristic spectacle of the film that's tailored to its male-dominated audiences. Although Dwyer acknowledged it as the 'major attraction in the Hindi film' (2006, 291), a tool that engulfs eroticism and expression of love through visual codes, she added that the songs often disrupt the continuity of the film's realistic narration. By foregrounding the role of sound work in film production and pinning down 'singing, listening and speaking', Sundar (2023) also alerted towards the the aural, ocular and somatic elements that compliment the visual and iconographic framing of scenes eventually. They indicated that the 'director's vision' holds prominence in melodrama, wherein film songs express different moods like love, longing, vitality, fulfilment, and despair. I propose bringing these considerations of perception, narratology, form, stylisation and genre under a constellation of assemblage theories through its song-dance picturisation, which disperses ideas of the body as an assemblage.

The transition from Bombay cinema to Bollywood can be attributed to its song-and-dance picturisation, which led to the Bollywoodisation of Indian cinema (Rajadhyaksha 2003). India's first talkie, *Alam Ara* (1931), was a breakthrough moment that Ashish Rajadhyaksha and Paul Willemen (2014) called 'the mainstay of Indian cinema' due to a song-dance culture (253). Over time, systematic changes in cinematography by integrating higher budgets exclusively for item numbers, stunts and post-production marketing events to publicise the film meant that Bollywood was synonymous with its song-and-dance picturisation. Advanced editing techniques were also implemented to diversify the genre of song aesthetics. Along with these evolving filmmaking cultures, there were shifting implications in song picturisation that featured professional background dancers, stylisation and choreographed performances, and separate budgets assigned to shoot in exotic foreign locations. These factors essentialised incorporating songs in for storytelling, making it the game changer which has been 'evolving, shifting and little more than impromptu moves around tree trunks' (Gehlawat and Dudrah 2017, 103). Gulzar, a poet, lyricist and filmmaker, described how the expression of love is closely intertwined with its film songs: 'We're so stuck with the hero-heroine kind of cinema that we can't get out of the mindset ... as most of our films are love stories.'[3]

These factors can be inferred as simultaneous transitions in cinematic trends across different decades, making it imperative to deploy resources for song picturisation (Shah 1950, 97). The symbolic association between cinematic song-image and its spatio-temporalities complement the film narrative, reflects the director's hidden intentions and functions as a mediator between the cinema and the audience—who often remember a film through its song and dance—and provides the audience with a break from the film's plot. Chatterjee (1995) reminds us that no other country exuded such diversity, distinctiveness and proficiency in writing and singing. Thus, he reiterated how intrinsic songs are in earmarking Bollywood, where much thought is put into their lyrics, song picturisation, tune, and finesse to create a dream-like sequence.

Bhansali's distinct style in presenting grandness and opulence and recreating nation-state politics infused with heterosexual romance, familial conflicts, Islamicate and Marathwada cultures, 'New Wave of Muslim Social' (Bhaskar and Allen 2009) and war sequences were exhibited in *Hum Dil De Chuke Sanam* (1999), *Goliyon Ki Rasleela: Ram-Leela* (2013), *Bajirao Mastani* (2015) and *Padmaavat* (2018). The presented exhibitionism, richly expressive cinematic vocabularies, splendour and noble personages that glorified the past bolstered the historical imaginary in *Devdas* (2002). These elements of art deco, intensive image-sound, visual and musical styles and its 'excesses' are what Gilles Deleuze (2020) called cinema's sensory-motor schemata. These formats of new media assemblages varied based on the ubiquitous aesthetic style of the director. Bhansali's distinctive genre also underlined a women's exhibitionist gaze through a choice of vibrant colours, the tonality of frames, the portrayal of a rich cultural heritage in India, carefully crafted aesthetics through costume designs, strategic utilisation of props for dance picturisation, new technologies of fabrication and over hundred background dancers for the picturisation of its title tracks. The stylistic elements established how the male gaze mediates in a cinematic apparatus that picturises heterosexual intimacy and war sequences, echoing various avant-garde movements distinguishing Bhansali's cinematic assemblages. Also, these disjunctures in designs, aesthetic conceptualisations, director's vision and buffered reverberation of sound within their representation highlight the role of light and sound in framing characters (Thoraval 2000; Basu 2010).

An assemblage of these factors underlines that film songs have underrated qualities that can be political, religious, social and, therefore, thought-provoking. This also suggests that soundtracks, song picturisation and even songless-ness, enable situating the disabled body as an 'outlier'/aberration from the formula in Bhansali's work. It reiterates how sound, songs and silences play a pivotal role in constructing disability, implies cultures of abuse through gaze and stare, and frames disabled bodies within its narrative. At the same time, it juxtaposes how its absence, or a songless Bollywood, is intended to highlight its unconventionality that contributes to a radical framing of disabled sexuality. So, what are the implications of having mainstream Bollywood cinema be replaced with songless-ness in characterising the life of a disabled woman? What role does Bollywood's song-and-dance culture play in constructing an ableist imaginary and contrasting it with the disabled star body? How can we contextualise the centrality of the disability gaze in Bhansali's films through song-and-dance picturisation? 'Crip theory', a term coined by McRuer (2006), helps theorise how disability and sexuality are considered incongruent identities. This chapter aims to interrogate the conventions of disability and sexuality representation and how these experiences of disablements are shaped in Bhansali's work. Therefore, I focus on *Black* (2005) and *Guzaarish* (2010), which positioned the star body in a multilayered construct of disability assemblages within them.

Why Songless-ness? Theorising Visuality, Blindness and Sound in Black

When Sanjay Leela Bhansali was asked why he named the film *Black,* he candidly responded that 'there could not have been a more apt name as it is *Andheri Duniya*', which translates as 'a world of darkness'.[4] Although it was considered an Oscar-worthy film and appreciated for moving beyond the formulaic song-dance narrative conventions. What is particularly insightful is how its mise-en-scène, cinematography techniques and post-production design were drastically different from Bhansali's previous films, such as *Hum Dil De Chuke Sanam* (1999) and *Devdas* (2002), which strategised on promulgating the hegemony of ableist imaginaries through grandiosity of stylistic elements and extravagant dance performances that gained more popularity than the films. However, *Black* was not Bhansali's first disability-centred narrative. He forayed into disability films with *Khamoshi: The Musical* (1994), which revolved around the struggles of a deaf and mute couple in raising a nondisabled daughter who eventually became a celebrated singer. The construction of ableism was integral to the narration, as she eventually became the only breadwinner of the family, supporting her disabled parents. Also, the sudden shift to seek a social protector, a world beyond the 'confined and excluded disabled space', was foregrounded through song-dance sequences and jump cuts, which contrasted the flashback of her childhood mired in acts of social service and projected loss of innocence in overcompensating for the disability of her parents. It thus ended up fitting within the formulaic conventions of narrative prosthesis that capitalised on circulating a pathologised perception of disability. Looking back at the prominence of song-and-dance cultures in Bollywood since the 1930s and in Bhansali's cinematic idioms, Tejaswini Ganti's (2012, 79) statement holds relevance:

> Songs are perceived as the quintessential 'commercial' element in a film. Filmmakers working outside the mainstream treat songs to reach larger audiences, which is characterised by the press as either accommodating or pandering to popular tastes. The omission of songs is interpreted as an oppositional stance, a way of making a statement against the dominant form of cinema and circumscribing one's audience.

It is a pronounced declaration of the inability to perceive Bollywood without songs. Taking Ganti's argument forward, the 'absence of songs' poses questions about its narratology, stylistic elements and character development. Thus, the intentionality of songless-ness signals the melodramatic cinematic oeuvre that goes beyond its formulaic conventions. *Black,* inspired by Hellen Keller's autobiography *The Story of My Life* (1996) and set within the Indian context, forays into songless-ness to depict the journey of its central character, Michelle McNally, from girlhood to womanhood who turns blind and deaf after an illness as an infant. Rani Mukherjee took on Michelle's role, with Amitabh Bachchan playing the role of Debraj, her teacher. But a film featuring two big stars and no songs makes it atypically non-diegetic.

While reviewing contemporary films and production cultures in Bollywood, film journalist Pallavi Kharade (2005) candidly remarked, 'A Hindi film without songs? Inconceivable! Right? Wrong, say new-age filmmakers as they tread the experimentation path.'[5] Although she listed films that went on to become commercial successes without piggybacking on song and dance numbers, she noted that Bhansali's *Black* was critically lauded and acknowledged as a refreshing change in Bollywood by paying 'closer attention to the script and very good acting to hold the audience's attention'. However, this cannot negate its power to display a range of emotions through flashbacks and dream sequences, producing new realism in its complex embodiment. So, the absence of songs was intentionally created to foreground a disabled Indian life world, becoming a lens to view Bhansali's vision of framing statements about the body's materiality, sexual disillusionment and patronisation of disability.

Black also differed in its narrative architecture while curating a disability-centred dialogue mediated through its background sound, folly art, art direction, constructivism of the 'absence of male gaze' that focused on the eye level, use of close-ups and black-and-white tonalities in frame settings. What was strikingly visible was a women's disability dialogue, with stars performing deafness, muteness and Alzheimer's in a songless Bollywood melodrama. The film divulged into representing the politics of disablement in Michelle's life by showing her seeking the 'male gaze', bolstering how social attitudes lurk in a fatalistic acceptance of a tragic and lonely life, dehumanising her as divinely ordained, reducing the multiple shades of her Indian womanhood to a single attribute: disability and disillusionment of living within constructs that promote compulsory able-bodiedness. Debraj made his entry playing with a bulb in a dark room, wanting to be addressed as a 'magician', taking charge of bringing 'light' in the 'darkness of blind children', positing Michelle as his 'mission' or a target to feel validated as a special educator. The sustained exclusion of Michelle before Debraj's entry adds to his heroism as a saviour of a disabled person from the ableist world and soon transgresses into an infantilised narration of disabled womanhood, those who lead sex-deprived lives. These factors underline Foucault's (1973) argument on the constructivism of the gaze, how it exists in institutional and culturally produced praxis and manifests perceptions of being looked at differently, which is internalised, often contributing to sexual disillusionment, low sexual self-worth, self-surveillance and consciousness in social settings. Michelle, too, elucidated these elements of disability within a cripping media portrayal upon realising how her disability identity overrides other aspects of her identity.

The opening scene where Michelle sits down typing her autobiography with a voice-over demonstrates her dilemma in always being an outlier who has been leading a tragic life that is lonely and doomed in 'black'. The black screen fades after nearly a minute, followed by eerie silence, which amplifies the emotions of pathologising the performing disabled star's body and the politics of disavowal. Cultural images of disability, visuality and the use of light in framing the scenes in black and white function as a metaphorical tool for the narrative right from the opening shot. Her monologue in English, where she reflects on her struggle of being perceived as 'uncontrollable' and a nuisance while writing a letter to her teacher, sets the tone of pathos and misery with no glimmer of hope for the rest of the screenplay. The postcolonial influences are elucidated by emphasising the eloquent pronunciation of English words such as 'teacher', which depicts progress and self-sufficiency. Although the film proposes numerous possibilities, Debraj's insistence on Michelle learning English, articulating her pronunciation, dining like a 'cultured lady', exuding poise in dressing, emphasis on learning table manners, her need to graduate from university and lastly, delivering a speech upon receiving her degree mediate as lyrical properties in creating a mise-en-scène. Drawing upon distinctiveness in stylisation and characterisation, *Black* is posited as a film for the emerging middle classes, an urban India or even the transnational public, which is relatively English-speaking. The socio-culturally elevated status of the teacher who dictates Michelle's life, corrects her mannerisms and etiquette eventually blurs into the only man she feels could empathise and kiss her back.

The strategic use of sounds like the bells tied around her waist to track her movement by her parents, the breaking of plates to express emotional outbursts, anger and resentment, and a rising crescendo of music while she walks in the wrong direction suggestively highlighted her construction as a disruptive anomaly. At the same time, the fast-paced instrumental echoed her joy in feeling a snowfall and a waterfall that contrasted the slow-paced music when she sat down to type her autography, demonstrating a tussle of emotive display using sound work, cinematography techniques and folly artists. At those times, the camera often zoomed into her wide-opened teary eyes, evoking a look of despair while she sought companionship. It soon jump-cut into her walking stick, trembling feet and hands when she anxiously tries to communicate using sign language on being lost in finding her way home. These emotions are underlined through background sound, songless-ness and sudden silences, which evoke the embodied experience of constructing a performance of disability. Also, Michelle's dance upon feeling snow, the absence of lyrics and a poetic engagement through sound and instrumental music situates her as an unusual dancing body. Usha Iyer argues how 'choreomusicology', a combination of choreology and musicology, plays an intrinsic role in situating female stardom through her ability to dance and how the narrative sequence must progress (2017). In her words:

> Attention to the practices of moving and sounding bodies and to the linkages between the sensorial planes of sound and movement alerts us to how dancing bodies are instrumental in the creation, transmission, and reception of music. (2017, 131)

However, the songless-ness in Michelle's performance draws upon these elements of a cripping culture, which contrasts how scopophilia and voyeuristic pleasures are constructed for able-bodied women dancing. At the same time, a long shot of Michelle's body, followed by a musical shift when she walks down the wrong direction, reiterates the comic relief characterisation in portraying disability in cinema. Much unlike how the male gaze shapes and situates women within the cinematic realm, sound, music and dance picturisation, cine-choreographies, slow-motion producing aural effects and a close-up of her hands and legs trembling when alone are emoted through changing instrumentation and pace of folly-art music, which reiterates sexual dissonance and a euthanasia status quo without explicitly stating it. *Black* is also unconventional with its aesthetic cues and narratology as it poses a radical dialogue on women's disability and repressed sexual desires. Most importantly, gendered dysphoria, an absent discussion on the sexuality of the disabled woman, her seeking the male gaze and resultant lowered sexual self-esteem. In other words, it outlines a cripping culture where the disabled woman is subjected to infantilised treatment and adopts different narratological, figurative, aural and aesthetic tools to demonstrate being shunned from familial and general social settings.

On the one hand, *Black* establishes how commercial successes and artistic credibility do not equate to formulaic romance or song-dance sequences. On the other hand, it also curates a cripping culture that narratively defines the dominant morbid figurations of women's disability in India. It proposed ideological hierarchies of the material world and how sound, aural and visual tools complement a narrative without necessarily a formulaic song-dance, situating the centrality of the disability cinema as an aberration from Bollywood's formula films. Additionally, its narration of euthanasia disability figurations foregrounds the intensity of the subject using symbolic cues in defining the disabled woman's life as a deployed state of misfitting.[6] A semiotic reading of its narration also suggests that visuality created through handheld cameras and light-mediated sunshine and darkness are powerful tools of expression in framing her euthanasia. The multilayered constructivism of disability and femininity, stare and the absence of gaze and subjected 'othering' through narrative and symbolic cues are produced through these cinematic assemblages of sound, dance and silence. This underlines how the disability gaze for women is construed not just by how men look at and objectify women but also by how the nondisabled world looks at disabled people (Ghosh 2016, 140). Looking at the epistemological shift in disability being the central focus, Bhansali's vision of generating a dialogue on women's disability fits within the larger purview of a 'supercrip' phenomenon where social construction of the stare produces sympathy within ableist power structures.

Madhava Prasad (2011) described this emerging trend in the radical conceptualisation of disablement and centrality given to disabilities previously unheard of in Bollywood as a 'rare disease' portrayal in filmmaking. In his view, disability had always been on the periphery of commercial cinema. But now, with its mainstream recognition, Bollywood is witnessing a new genre of stars eager to enact disabilities onscreen due to its novelty in characterisation, way of coming back to cinemas, and award-winning tendencies.[7] It is pivotal to note that the portrayal of disability in cinema and the role of disabled characters as sidelined in the larger narrative of the hero's journey has not been a rarity. However, *Black* introduces how cinema mediates as a cultural apparatus to foreground the stigma, shame and social model of women's disability in India. The element of 'to be looked at ness', the absence of gaze and its substitution with a stare, has been a dominant concern among feminist disability studies scholars (Garland-Thomson 2009). A combination of these statements is apparent in the characterisation of Michelle as she reconciles with the 'absence of being looked at or even touched with love', primarily during her younger sibling's wedding. I draw on Campbell's (2009, 166) definition of how society intervenes and produces disablism to describe this phenomenon. She insists that 'regimes of ableism have produced a depth of disability negation that reaches into the caverns of collective subjectivity to the extent that the notion of disability as inherently negative is seen as a naturalised reaction to an aberration'. Overall, Michelle's characterisation and familial dynamics foray into these notions of women's disability, sexuality and sexual disillusionment and how they contribute to lowered sexual self-esteem.

Contextualising the Projected Helplessness in Guzaarish

Bhansali's next venture in portraying disability was *Guzaarish* (2010). But this time, he forayed into disability and masculinity through Ethan Mascarenhas, a role enacted by Hrithik Roshan. Narratively, its screenplay revolved around a magician who became a quadriplegic after an accident during a performance and then professionally pursued being a radio jockey. *Guzaarish,* which means 'a request' in the film's context, outlines a plea for euthanasia by a quadriplegic man, who often expresses his disgust by calling himself a 'vegetable' and 'having no control over his body'.

The film begins with the song 'Smile', with his voiceover pronouncing the song's lyrics as an inspiration. While Ethan hums the tune, the camera zooms into his teary eyes as he stares helplessly at the window adjacent to his wheelchair. The musical symphony repeatedly underlines the contrast of experiences through settings, colour and tonality of frames, sound work and visual tools assembled to distinguish a material world devoid of subjective stances in creating 'a happy ending.' It was constructed as a striking contrast to a formulaic narrative undertone in Bollywood and flamboyance associated with Bhansali's past filmography that capitalised on selling utopia, vibrance and exoticism of the upper-class India. However, there are some overlapping narrative confines of disablement in Bhansali's disability-centred narratives, such as situating the disabled in a relatively urban social-class milieu in India, an Anglo-Christian household, sexuality and family being the locus of its narrative. Also, the families in *Black* and *Guzaarish* speak fluent English and dress in relatively Western attires ranging from scarves with high-waisted skirts to monotone dresses in white, black and grey colour palettes. Painstakingly, both films put forth a different dialogue on disability and sexuality and lowered sexual self-worth while also displaying the diversity of viewing and perceiving disability in dull colours.

Even though Bhansali received mixed responses for his film, in a recent interview while promoting *Gangubai* (2022), he reflected on his journey with *Guzaarish*. He stated that it 'was an act of courage and fearlessness'. He further added, 'People felt my filmmaking was archaic and constantly moving in the same direction … I have taken a boy who is considered a Greek God in Hindi cinema who is known for dancing and action, he is lying on a bed and talking without moving a limb.' So, although the film might have failed at the box office, Hrithik Roshan's ability to transcend from a dancing star, taking on the challenging role and performing the role of a disabled person was lauded. This also resurfaced the popularity and commercial success of *Koi Mil Gaya* (2003), which he called an 'experimental film', 'a payback for flops' as he took on performing as a schoolgoing adult with a mental disability.

Guzaarish made a similar attempt to demonstrate his versatility as an actor.[8] Even though the narrative arc of *Guzaarish* revolved around the hero's journey with a disability, it also included romantic interludes and formulaic melodrama, which eulogised how disability equates to tragedy but does not imply being undesirable or dehumanised as an asexual being. What is pivotal is the portrayal of euthanasia, how the hero feels defeated, rather non-heroic, every day due to his inability to perform mundane tasks. At the same time, it capitalises on portraying a sense of diminished masculinity by foregrounding his helplessness in seeing his romantic interest (Aishwarya Rai) being tortured by her ex-husband. The characterisation of hegemonic masculinity and constructivism of heroism based on able-bodiedness being construed as central to building self-esteem (Staples 2011) forms the crux in contextualising the dialogue on men's disability and sexuality and through a cripping media portrayal.

Although the narrative starts with Ethan being considered divine and valorised for having wit and humour despite being disabled, it soon moves into euthanasia, his character arc with him appealing for euthanasia. Also, Ethan is considered heroic only if he masquerades his sadness for being celebrated as an inspirational figure for the disabled community. His ability to charm people as a jovial radio jockey contrasts with his request, which showcases him as the 'defeated hero' by the latter half of the film. These questions of disability inspiration, wherein the credit is given for the ability to look past the disability, by overcompensating for being disabled, have been a point of contention for many years among scholars of disability studies in India. Bhansali succumbed to these prejudices and weaved them within his cinematic idioms and idiosyncrasies. The inherent assumption of disability as a tragic occurrence has been shared across media portrayals, and eventually, *Guzaarish* also piggybacked on such formulaic narrations of disability (Mitchell and Snyder 2001; Sinha 2020).

Another notable difference between the two films is how *Black*'s songless melodrama induced pathos and the need to repress sexual desires, making it strikingly different from *Guzaarish*, which was built within the formulaic conventions of romance, lust, intimacy and scopophilia wherein men's disability did not equate to asexuality. The misogyny and sexism in language, relegating women with a disability as undesirable while disabled men's acknowledgement as attractive and marriageable by a nondisabled woman foregrounded the inherit gendered hypocrisies in India. In *Guzaarish*'s song picturisation, aesthetic cues and choice of frames, especially with lights focused at eye level, projected the chemistry between the leading protagonists, often in the absence of dialogues. In terms of narration, Bhansali evoked how disabled men can be considered gaze-worthy and acknowledged for their other intersectional identity markers. In a way, be classified as a charismatic person with sexual desires like anyone else. Despite underlining such emotions, *Guzaarish* also fades into a tragic narrative wherein he laments the loss of manliness, almost feels guilty about his situation of dependence and reminisces when he boastfully displayed his proficiency as a nondisabled magician who had a female fan following. An assemblage of these factors makes it another dehumanising portrayal of a quadriplegic person being dissatisfied with his life.

The flashback, somewhat back and forth in the narrative, highlights the abled past's demarcation, which is portrayed through a vibrant choice of colours. It strikingly contrasts the disabled future shown in relatively dull colours and dark frames. At this point, lights, colours, sound, song, dance and silences almost act as metaphors and take the narrative forward. For instance, the song 'Udi' orchestrates a spectatorial desire through Aishwarya Rai's dance-off on stage, constructing the male gaze in more than three levels situated within the narrative by the audience and serving Ethan's voyeuristic pleasures. Suddenly the screen goes black, and the camera bursts into action with two women with spotlights on them while on the stage. The camera moves over her bust, lingers on her chest and contrasts it with Ethan—who cries in amusement and appreciation—and his wheelchair. The figure of the Aishwarya Rai dancing thus evokes conflicting emotions of pleasure and helplessness, voyeurism and self-doubt, lust and anxiety, eventually contributing to a cripping culture about men's disability, conflicted with low sexual self-esteem. Rai's dancing produces a movement vocabulary where the heroine's sexually explicit dancing persona, make-up— especially the red lipstick—and persistent desire to remain 'covered', which Ethan frequently jokes about are strategised not to categorise her as the villainous vamp/damsel in distress but a woman mediating as the saviour of the disabled. Also, her wanting to look after and be a caregiver to Ethan meant she redeems her 'good girl' image and underlines how he constantly feels inadequate/incapable of being with her. A discursive study of their bond reveals that she often ignores his sexual puns without even reacting to his remarks about her clothing being boring and 'too covered'. Close-ups of his eyes elucidate helplessness when he sees her being beaten up by her husband while he remarks on what she sees in a disabled man. Soon, he reacts by posing self-doubt, projecting helplessness and underlining a tragic-hero characterisation under the garb of pleading euthanasia.

Close-ups play a pivotal role in the movie, wherein the camera is also fixated on the despair in his moist eyes. Many close-ups of Ethan are also accompanied by a sullen background score that underlined the culture of disablism and amplifies the complexity of disability and masculinity. When asked about the use of close-ups and the cinematography techniques in an interview Sudeep Chatterjee,[9] the cinematographer of *Guzaarish*, revealed:

> Closeups are the best way to portray emotions, and we just chose a few colours, so the storyline draws attention to the disability and sadness part. The colours played a crucial role, and so did Aishwarya Rai, who had a lot of red, which meant love and lust at the same time.

Thus, the close-ups, frames, choice of colours and tonality enabled the positioning of the disabled man as a misfit in an ableist world, accentuating its melodrama. From the vantage point of disability scholarship, media reiterates the language used to address the disabled and permeates into the religious, social and charity model of perceiving disability as 'misfit' and 'incapable' (Buckingham 2011; Longmore 1985; Connell 2011; Davis 2017). Also, it foregrounds how the disability leads to sympathy and infantilisation, symbolically indicating it as a tragic loss of personhood and agency. This reinforced stereotype of disability in the media, the portrayal of unhappiness and inadequacy is mediated through close-ups. However, the narration overlooks contextualising how disability is a socially created embodied experience rather than the medical condition of the disability itself. Mayank,[10] a 32-year-old wheelchair user in Delhi, described his experience of watching *Guzaarish* in the cinema hall. In his words:

> We are always shown as childlike, sad and helpless. I remember watching *Guzaarish* in the multiplex cinema hall, and during the interval, a girl looked at me and started crying. She then walked up to me and said she is [was] sorry about my misery.

A counterargument was also presented by Seema,[11] a 37-year-old wheelchair user in Delhi: 'A film like *Guzaarish*, even if poorly portrays the helplessness of disabled men, at least showed disabled men as capable of being loved by a nondisabled woman, unlike how women's disability is portrayed in a film like *Black*.' In her words, 'We are always shown as lonely and incapable of being married, and my family always assumed that marriage is not in my fate due to a disability.' Similar comments were passed about *Guzaarish*'s music and use of 'limited colours' and mostly 'why the narrative of women's disability displays sadness' by other participants in the study. A cursory glance at *Black* and *Guzaarish* also proposes how diametrically opposite romantic transactions are curated and exhibited among men and women with disability. On the one hand, *Black* emotes the absence of love and desperation in seeking the male gaze where the teacher sympathetically kisses Michelle, whom he presumes may never experience the touch of a man lovingly. Contrastingly, Ethan, whose nondisabled nurse is so mesmerised by his charm that she overlooks the severity of the disability.

A culmination of these curated moments outlines the deep-rooted cynicism about disability and sexuality and a socially disabling environment built on prejudices about disability and sexual culture, which has been enacted through visual and aural elements. Besides songs, light also plays a predominant role in accentuating how a disabled man, who cannot control his own body or even bowel movements, is aware of how days go by through the light falling on his face every morning. Although men's disability, a projected cripping culture and Bollywood's role in positioning the disabled body as a performance make the film multilayered, there is also a dialogue on euthanasia. It dramatises the pathologised portrayal of men's disability. While it normalises the interpretation of disability and sexuality onscreen, it also undermines the impact of society in making one plea for death. Also, the projected tragic imagery, relative infantilisation and constructed anomaly are intrinsic moments created through close-ups of the faces of those who pitifully stared at Ethan, reiterating how his struggle as a disabled man must end.

Scholars within disability studies and Bollywood cinema in India, such as Anita Ghai, Madhava Prasad, Joyojeet Pal, Shakuntala Banaji and Meenu Bhambhani, have been critical of Bollywood, especially for reiterating prejudices which subconsciously become significant contributors towards shaping people's psyche and perception about disability. *Guzaarish*, through its characterisations, stylisation, plot and melodramatic overtone, song-dance picturisation, which contrasts with sudden silences, reiterates the sexual dissonance about disablism. It underlines how self-doubt is socially produced and culturally embedded and foregrounds the desperate desire to draw a demarcation between them and us, the able-bodied imaginary and the disabled body. Therefore, the underlying vulnerabilities, heightened anxiety and sexually repressed desires of disabled masculinity portrayed in Bollywood reiterate how society views disability as suffering and not diversity (Connell 2011; Buckingham 2011).

Conclusion

It is pivotal to note that there has been an increasing trend of portraying disability in mainstream cinema with more actors willing to take on such roles. A survey also concludes that more than 200 films in Indian cinema represent the diversity of disabilities in them (Pal 2013, 109). However, most comply by highlighting that they capitalise on stereotypical characterisations of the social model of disability, which results from the vicious cycle of cinema, culture and society wherein the culture of disablism keeps circulating even in popularised media portrayals. Bhansali also fits within these preoccupations of tragedy and pathos in reiterating the 'other' or a sense of sexual disillusionment in his narratives of disability in India. At the same time, it is imperative to probe into the nuances of a film's style, content and form to situate how disability cinema has entered the mainstream due to Bhansali's work. It created a platform to question how offbeat characterisations portraying the 'star bodies' as disabled reiterates stereotypes and the role played by song and dance in accentuating the grandness, cinematic opulence and audience engagement, which is rarely attributed as a significant part of disability cinema.

A close reading of *Black* and *Guzaarish* suggests Bhansali's richly self-contradictory and narcissistic portrayal of disability as an anomaly, non-sexual, misfitting, infantilised, lonely and tragic. Furthermore, by reclaiming an existing culture of diversity even within disability cinema, he reinvents a novel stylistic element of sound cultures, musical transactions and taxonomy in the framing of the disabled body through aural and visual tools, which also displays the changing modes of conceptualisation, direction, production, circulation and exhibitionism of the disability-centred narrative. Thus, indicative of cinematic tension, the nation's preoccupation and a hegemonic construct of who is considered desirable eventually draw attention to a new cinephilia that transgresses from a formulaic hero's journey and reiterates disablism embedded in directorial vision.

Bollywood's global market and cinematic trends make it a pivotal advocate of cultural change. Offering endless figurative possibilities of embodied experiences, mainstream cinema has forayed into portraying a 'new Bollywood', which goes beyond a hero's journey and foregrounds a lens of viewing the dogmas of neoliberal development. It recognises the need to represent subaltern voices in the urban stratum that is relatable to its upper middle classes. The realism bent towards filmmaking can be perceived as an assemblage in the Deleuzian sense, echoing that cinema is dynamic, evolving and circulating in many ways. So, with the evolving media ecologies in globalising India, there have been interventions in presenting film content, style and characterisation that are closely intertwined with society and culture (Joshi 2015; Rai 2010). This thereby makes the 'production of bodily affect as a continuous multiplicity that is continuously affected, influenced and informed by outside forces, dynamism and materiality' (Rai 2010, 3). It weaves in multiple semiotic, historical and political factors that produce binaries between 'us' and 'them'. In this case, it would be 'othering' through disability narration, characterisation and stylisation through its song and dance elements. In any case, it foregrounds that the culture of disablism and the desire for being able-bodied are closely intertwined in Bollywood's disability cinema.

Notes

1   This phrase is used in an *Outlook* magazine article; see Chandan Mitra, 'Bollywood Music Collection', 26 June 2006, 56. https://magazine.outlookindia.com/issue/552 (accessed 15 March 2022). Credits: National Film Archive of India, Pune.

2   *Masala* is a term used to describe a spice mix. In the context of Bollywood cinema, the term means a fusion of multiple elements—melodrama, song and dance, lavish production and the constructed spectacle. This genre of *masala* movies now have commercial appeal mass and global audiences even beyond India.

3   Gulzar's interview with Saibal Chatterjee, 'Bollywood Music Collection', *Outlook*, 26 June 2006, 62, https://magazine.outlookindia.com/issue/552 (accessed 15 March 2022). Credits: National Film Archive of India, Pune.

4   Quote provided in *Navbharat*, 29 January 2005.

5   This phrase is used by Pallavi Kharade, *The Times of India*, 7 April 2005.

6   See *Outlook*, 24 January 2005, 61. https://magazine.outlookindia.com/issue/479 (accessed 21 March 2022). Credits: National Film Archive of India, Pune.

7   'Not the Perfect Hero', *The Times of India*, 16 March 2010, 13.

8   See https://www.hindustantimes.com/entertainment/bollywood/making-hrithik-roshan-lie-on-bed-talk-without-moving-a-limb-in-guzaarish-was-act-of-courage-says-sanjay-leela-bhansali-101646208537007.html.

9   The author interviewed Sudeep Chatterjee on 3 February 2022, who consented to be named for the study. He has been the cinematographer for many films, including Sanjay Leela Bhansali's *Guzaarish* for which he received awards from IIFA, Screen and Apsara for best cinematography. Eventually, he collaborated with Bhansali in *Padmaavat* (2018) and *Gangubai Kathiawadi* (2021).

10 Author interviewed the participant on 14 July 2022. Name of the interviewee has been change to ensure confidentiality.

11 Author interviewed the participant on 23 July 2022. Name of interviewee has been change to ensure confidentiality.

References

Addlakha, R. 'Disability, Gender and Society'. *Indian Journal of Gender Studies*, 15, no. 2 (2008): 191 207.

Banaji, S. 'Audiences and Hindi films: Contemporary Studies'. *Reading 'Bollywood': The Young Audience and Hindi Films*, 20–32. London: Palgrave Macmillan, 2006.

Basu, A. *Bollywood in the Age of New Media: The Geo-Televisual Aesthetic*. Edinburgh: Edinburgh University Press, 2010.

Bhaskar, I. and R. Allen. *Islamicate Cultures of Bombay Cinema*. New Delhi: Tulika Books, 2009.

Buckingham, J. 'Writing Histories of Disability in India: Strategies of Inclusion'. *Disability & Society*, 26, no. 4 (2011): 419–31.

Campbell, F. *Contours of Ableism: The Production of Disability and Abledness*. UK: Palgrave Macmillan, 2009.

Chatterjee, P. 'A Bit of Song and Dance + The Art of Song Picturisation in Indian Cinema'. *Indian Horizons*, 44, no. 1 (1995): 197–218.

Connell, R. 'Southern Bodies and Disability: Re-thinking Concepts'. *Third World Quarterly: Disability in the Global South,* 32, no. 8 (2011): 1369–81.

Davis, L.J. 'The Ghettoization of Disability. Paradoxes of Visibility and Invisibility in Cinema'. *Culture–Theory–Disability: Encounters between Disability Studies and Cultural Studies,* (2017): 39–49.

Dawn, R. 'The Politics of Cinematic Representation of Disability: "The Psychiatric Gaze"'. *Disability and Rehabilitation,* 36, no. 6 (2014): 515–20.

Deleuze, G. 'Cinema II: The Time-Image'. In *Philosophers on Film from Bergson to Badiou,* 177–99. London: Columbia University Press, 2020.

Dwyer, R. 'Kiss or Tell? Declaring Love in Hindi Films'. In *Love in South Asia: A Cultural History,* edited by Francesca Orsini, 289–302. New Delhi: Cambridge University Press, 2006.

Ganti, T. *Producing Bollywood: Inside the Contemporary Hindi Film Industry.* Durham and London: Duke University Press, 2012.

Garland-Thomson, R. 'Integrating Disability, Transforming Feminist Theory'. *NWSA Journal,* 14, no. 3 (2002): 1–32.

———. Staring: How We Look. New York: Oxford University Press, 2009.

Garwood, I. 'The Songless Bollywood Film'. *South Asian Popular Culture* , 4, no. 2 (2006): 169–83.

Gehlawat, A. and R. Dudrah. 'The Evolution of Song and Dance in Hindi Cinema'. *South Asian Popular Culture* , 15, nos 2–3 (2017): 103–8.

Ghai, A. 'Disabled Women: An Excluded Agenda of Indian Feminism'. *Hypatia,* 17, no. 3 (2002): 49–66.

Ghosh, N. *Impaired Bodies, Gendered Lives: Everyday Realities of Disabled Women.* New Delhi: Primus Publishers, 2016.

Gopal, S. *Conjugations.* Chicago: University of Chicago Press, 2011.

Gopal, S. and S. Moorti. 'Introduction: Travels of Hindi Song and Dance'. In *Global Bollywood: Travels of Hindi Song and Dance,* edited by Sangita Gopal and Sujata Moorti, 1–60. Minneapolis: University of Minnesota Press, 2008.

Gopalan, L. *Cinema of Interruptions: Action Genres in Contemporary Indian Cinema.* London, British Film Institute: Bloomsbury Publishing, 2002.

Iyer, U. 'Dance Musicalization: Proposing a Choreomusicological Approach to Hindi Film Song-and-Dance Sequences'. *South Asian Popular Culture,* 15, no. 2–3 (2017): 123–38.

Joshi, P. 'Bollywood's India'. In *Bollywood's India.* New York: Columbia University Press, 2015.

Kasbekar, A. 'Hidden Pleasures: Negotiating the Myth of the Female Ideal in Popular Hindi Cinema'. In *Pleasure and the Nation,* edited by R. Dwyer and C. Pinney, 248–86. New Delhi and London: Oxford University Press, 2001.

Longmore, P.K. 'A Note on Language and the Social Identity of Disabled People'. *American Behavioral Scientist,* 28, no. 3 (1985): 419–23.

Majumdar, N. 'The Embodied Voice: Song Sequences and Stardom in Popular Hindi Cinema'. In *Soundtrack Available: Essays on Film and Popular Music,* edited by Pamela Robertson Wojcik and Arthur Knight, 161–81. Duke University Press, 2001.

McRuer, R. *Crip Theory: Cultural Signs of Queerness and Disability* (Vol. 9). New York: New York University Press, 2006.

Mitchell, D.T. and S.L. Snyder. *Narrative Prosthesis: Disability and the Dependencies of Discourse.* Ann Arbor: University of Michigan Press, 2001.

Morcom, A. *Hindi Film Songs and the Cinema.* New York: Routledge, 2017.

Pal, J. 'Physical Disability and Indian Cinema'. In *Different Bodies: Essays on Disability in Film and Television,* edited by Marja Evelyn Mogk, Arthur Knight, Rick Altman and Priscilla Barlow, 109–30. North Carolina: McFarland & Company, Inc. Publishers, 2013.

Prasad, M. 'This Thing Called Bollywood'. *Seminar* (2003): 17–20.

———. 'Diverting Diseases'. In *Figurations in Indian Film,* edited by Meheli Sen and Anustup Basu, 91–100. London: Palgrave Macmillan, 2011.

Rai, A.S. *Untimely Bollywood Globalization and India's New Media Assemblage.* New Delhi: Duke University Press, 2009.

Rajadhyaksha, A. 'The "Bollywoodization" of the Indian Cinema: Cultural Nationalism in a Global Arena'. *Inter-Asia Cultural Studies,* 4, no. 1 (2003): 25–39.

Rajadhyaksha, A. and P. Willemen. *Encyclopaedia of Indian Cinema.* Routledge, 2014.

Schalk, S. 'Reevaluating the supercrip'. *Journal of Literary & Cultural Disability Studies,* 10, no. 1 (2016): 71–86.

Shah, P. *The Indian Film.* Bombay: Motion Picture Society of India, 1950.

Shresthova, S. *Is It All about Hips? Around the World with Bollywood Fance.* Sage Publications, 2011.

Sinha, Priyam. 'Margarita with a Straw: Female Sexuality, Same Sex Love, and Disability in India'. *Economic and Political Weekly Engage,* 55, no. 14 (2020).

Somaaya, B. *Cinema: Images & Issues.* New Delhi: Rupa & Company, 2004.

Staples, J. 'At the Intersection of Disability and Masculinity: Exploring Gender and Bodily Difference in India'. *Journal of the Royal Anthropological Institute,* 17, no. 3 (2011): 545–562.

Sundar, P. *Listening with a Feminist Ear: Soundwork in Bombay Cinema.* University of Michigan Press, 2023.

Thoraval, Y. *The Cinemas of India.* New Delhi: Macmillan India Limited, 2000.

Vasudevan, R. *The Melodramatic Public.* New York: Palgrave Macmillan, 2010.

Filmography

Alam Ara, director Ardeshir Irani, 1931.

Black, director Sanjay Leela Bhansali, 2005.

Black Friday, director Anurag Kashyap, 2004.

Devdas, director Sanjay Leela Bhansali, 2002.

Dosti, director Satyen Bose, 1964.

Gangubai Kathiawadi, director Sanjay Leela Bhansali, 2022.

Guzaarish, director Sanjay Leela Bhansali, 2010.

Hum Dil De Chuke Sanam, director Sanjay Leela Bhansali, 1999.

Hum Dono, director Amarjeet and Vijay Anand, 1961.

Khamoshi: The Musical, director Sanjay Leela Bhansali, 1994.
Koshish, director Gulzar, 1972.
Mann, director Indra Kumar, 1999.
My Wife's Murder, director Jijy Philip, 2005.
Naache Mayuri, director T. Rama Rao, 1986.
Sadma, director Balu Mahendra, 1983.
Sarkar, director Ram Gopal Varma, 2005.
Sparsh, director Sai Paranjpye, 1980.

11

'BEZUBAAN'[1] OR 'HUMZUBAAN'[2]: PROBLEMATISING DEAF IDENTITIES THROUGH A SELECT FEW HINDI FILMS[3]

Mansi Grover

The chapter attempts to probe Deaf[4] identities through a select few Hindi films, such as *Koshish*[5] (1972), *Khamoshi: The Musical*[6] (1996) and *Black*[7] (2005). It will examine the representation of deaf characters in these three films in their sheer materiality and not indulge in a metaphorical reading of deafness. It will investigate the complex nature of Deafness and whether it should be categorised as a disability or not. It will further try to locate the significance of Deaf ontologies and Deaf epistemologies to understand Deafness as a linguistic and body diversity.

Deafness is a condition where a person has a hearing impairment. Richard G. Brill (1974) has defined the deaf as those in whom the sense of hearing is non-functional for the ordinary purposes of life. *The Gallaudet Encyclopedia of Deaf People and Deafness* (Van Cleve and Gallaudet College 1987) defines deafness as an inability to hear and understand speech through the ear alone (Limaye 2008). It strikes at a basic human function—communication. Deafness separates people from people and creates a limitation in *understanding* between two individuals. Helen Keller, a blind-deaf woman who used to advocate for the rights of blind people, repeatedly voiced her sentiment that deafness was more debilitating than blindness. In 1929, she wrote in her text, *Midstream*, that she felt the impediment of deafness far more keenly than that of blindness:

> Lack of hearing has always been a heavier handicap to me than blindness. Sealed ears render more difficult every path to knowledge. The deaf are as hungry for a word as the blind are for a book under their fingers, yet it is harder to find people who will talk with the deaf than people who will supply the sightless with embossed books ... (1929)

In the Global South, especially for Indians, accepting deafness is by no means an immediate or easy decision. Typically, it is a conclusion that is drawn after a protracted period of adaptation, as noted by Jill Jepson. He inferred from his research that for a large number of people, deafness was no longer an abnormality that must be fixed or a tragedy that must be endured but a simple fact of existence that could be dealt with in successful ways while living a relatively regular life. Most commonly, this acceptance was voiced as a realisation that deafness was 'natural' or 'meant to be' or *'prakritic'* in Hindi. According to Jepson, the most basic proposition underlying the idea of naturalness is that deafness is not going to go away, regardless of any sort of measures taken to deal with it. This also suggests that efforts made to cure deafness are pointless. One has to accept that neither local healers nor city physicians, neither fasts nor surgery is going to change the condition of deafness. He further adds that

> This shift from active attempts to cure deafness to an acceptance of its intractability is not only a recognition of peoples' inability to deal with deafness but a decision that it *should* be left as it is. When people decide that the condition of deafness is 'meant to be', they are deciding that they lack not only the power but the right to change it. (1991)

Most importantly, it eliminates the constant need to seek medical and religious advice and frees the extravagant amounts of time and money often spent in this pursuit. In this way, the notion of 'naturalness' is liberating. The realisation that deafness is incurable should in no way be viewed as a surrender to despair or hopelessness. Jepson writes that the people he interviewed never described this realisation as a giving up of hope. Instead, it was seen as a release from a great deal of wasted effort.

On another level, the decision that deafness is incurable has a deeper meaning: It means that the condition of being deaf is neither transitory nor superficial, but real and permanent. By saying that deafness was natural, the deaf people and their families were saying that their striving to turn the deaf person into a hearing person was simply not going to work. Deafness for them was no longer an externally imposed experience but a fundamental and unchangeable part of the individual. The deaf person was no longer seen as someone afflicted with a condition but as a person whose self is partially defined by the fact of his or her deafness.

The acceptance of the naturalness of deafness could be seen in films too as there was hardly any narrative regarding 'curing' deafness. The nine decades of Hindi cinema saw many films with the blindness of a woman character finding a cure or a woman getting a prosthetic leg, but there is no film so far that discusses a cochlear implant. As Jepson observed, there is a naturalness about deafness and more or less an acceptance of a deaf way of life. But the world in which a deaf person operates is oralist and audist despite all the acceptance.

In an interview with *The Hindu* in 2004, Gulzar spoke about his film, *Koshish* (*Effort*): 'The film revolves around the theme of creating a special and separate world for the disabled, an idea which appeared to me to be very reactionary. From that time onward, I wanted to prove that the disabled are part and parcel of society.' Gulzar wrote and directed *Koshish* in 1972 with the vision of creating a story of a deaf couple in an able-bodied, hearing and oralist world. Through the film, Gulzar was able to establish respect for sign language as a way of communicating with the Deaf. The opening credits of the film showed two people, with just their hands visible, communicating through sign language that has a distinct grammar, syntax, and morphology. Gulzar was able to create a remarkable mise-en-scène with his opening credits and politicised Deafness. However, the films that were released years later, such as *Khamoshi: The Musical* (which means 'silence') and *Black*, could not create such a dialogue about Deafness as linguistic diversity; rather, these movies saw it as a defect or deficit.

Language is a principal means of knowing the world, and the assumption that language is equal to speech has burrowed itself within the fields of education, anthropology, psychology, medicine, history and philosophy of language. Therefore, any deaf person is seen with a judgemental eye that views deafness as a deficit. When it comes to deaf women, the evaluative gaze intensifies further. They have to undergo a dilemma of what is 'voice' and 'speaking out'. When the mainstream feminist movement talks about raising a voice and speaking out against something, deaf women as a community have to make sense of their position and how to speak out without speaking. They come face to face with the rhetoric of 'gaining the voice' and it is, in fact, the hegemony of 'voice' and 'speaking', that they want to 'speak out' against. Language is not limited to vocal speech alone; it is an expression of ideas through any medium available. Pierre Desloges, a deaf person who laid the rhetorical foundation of Deaf studies in the West, writes about the richness of sign language and that it is so neglected because of the 'irrationality' of the human mind. A contributing factor to this irrationality may be that hearing people don't actually see sign language, even when they look directly at it. It is not only a foreign language but a profoundly foreign concept that a language could exist outside the full presence of sound (Bauman 2008).

There is an ongoing battle for Indian Sign Language (ISL) to be recognised as a natural language of the Deaf and the struggle for recognition adds to the stigma attached to Deafness. For most deaf individuals, the spoken/written language becomes a burden to be tolerated in this oralist and audist world. Hearing or oral-dominated education systems emphasise the use of hearing aids, written language and lip-reading. Oralism depicts hearing deficit as a disability and suppresses sign language, which is seen to be an obstacle to the integration of the deaf person in society. It emphasises spoken and written language as a means of integration. Sign linguists contest the oralist paradigm. The underlying assumption of sign language is that the deaf habitually acquire a real language. These veridical languages are a vernacular that is endemic to deaf people and not just an amalgam of manual versions of oral languages of the surrounding hearing world (Lorente 2008).

Harlan Lane explores the social construction of disability at length in his essay, 'Do Deaf People Have a Disability?' (2008). Lane answers the title's question by noting that the question ultimately does not make sense, for a disability is not something to have but a label one acquires. The question then becomes whether or not Deaf people should openly acquire and accept this label. Lane proceeds to make the case for rejecting the disability label, noting that culture, like disability, is also a social construction and that Deaf people may have more power to construct the meanings of 'Deaf' in cultural ways precisely by rejecting the disability label (Bauman 2008). *Koshish* at many levels was able to achieve this. However, *Khamoshi* and *Black* further deepened the binary between the Deaf and hearing worlds, in turn, highlighting what 'normalcy' looks like.

Tom Humphries, in 1975, coined the term 'audism'—based on the Latin word *audire*, meaning 'to hear'—for the discriminatory treatment of deaf individuals throughout history. In his unpublished article 'Audism: The Making of a Word' in 1975, Humphries defined audism as 'the notion that one is superior based on one's ability to hear or behave in the manner of one who hears' (Bauman 2008). The opening scene of *Koshish* establishes sign language as an alternate way of communication for Deaf people, thus asserting Deaf culture as a subculture to the normative oralist and audist world. It attempts to advocate for this culture as linguistic diversity waiting to get recognised. However, if one looks at the opening scenes of *Khamoshi: The Musical* one may look at Deafness as a deficit and something that constantly requires appropriation according to the hearing world. It is a story of Annie, and her life with her deaf parents, Flavy and Joseph. It is narrated by Annie in a first-person narrative that goes back and forth in time. The film starts with Annie's words to her father, 'Papa, can you hear me?' (0:23) and 'But what is life without an impossible dream!' (0:27). The film is told through the eyes of Annie, a hearing daughter, living with her deaf parents in an able-bodied, hearing world. The film places the deaf parents in a tight spot for being what they are. *Khamoshi* starts where *Koshish* ends. Annie's story gives a very narrow essentialist understanding of what it is to be deaf in an ableist hearing world.

Resonating a similar tone, the first scene of *Black* depicts Michelle McNally, a deaf-blind woman, writing her autobiography. She introduces herself by saying, *'Bachi-kuchi mitti se banae gae un do logon ki kahaani'* ('The story of those two people who were made out of leftover soil'), and later, she says, *'Meri is kahaani ki duniya hi alag hai, awaaz jahaan pohochte hi dum tod deti hai aur roshni aankhein moond leti hai.'* ('The world of my story is different. The sound dies out before reaching the ears and the eyes do not see any light.') Michelle paints a pitiful picture of her life as a deaf-blind woman and one feels she is 'dysconsciously audist'.

Genie Gertz has used Joyce King's work on dysconscious racism to create the term 'dysconscious audism' to describe a phenomenon that is defined as a form of audism that tacitly accepts dominant hearing norms and privileges. Given audism's presence on the individual, institutional and ideological levels, Deaf individuals cannot help but internalise aspects of oppression, a phenomenon Gertz has labelled 'dysconscious audism'. It is not the absence of consciousness but an impaired consciousness or distorted way of thinking about Deaf consciousness. Dysconscious audism adheres to the ideology that the 'hearing' society because it is dominant, is more appropriate than the Deaf society. Such Deaf people can be characterised as not having fully developed a 'Deaf consciousness' connected to the Deaf identity, and they may still feel the need to assimilate into mainstream culture (Gertz 2008). Dysconscious audist Deaf people continue to have a kind of victimised thinking that they are responsible for their failure. Sanjay Leela Bhansali's *Khamoshi* as well as *Black* emanate similar feelings of self-victimisation and pity with Michelle calling herself made out of 'leftovers', and Flavy and Joseph (Annie's deaf parents) are made to feel like a burden or obstacle in Annie's life. One can sense under-confidence in Flavy and Joseph's identity as deaf people and as deaf parents.

The ableist hearing world creates a meta-narrative of deficit around deafness, which gets reflected in the way deaf parenthood is portrayed in films. There is a constant distrust around the idea of disabled people taking up parenting roles. Persons with disabilities are often seen as asexual and devoid of any desires. Women with disabilities are often 'locked in a perpetual adolescence' because of extreme societal taboos associated with their sexuality. Ableist society has an irrational fear that disabled people will give birth to 'defective' offspring and will be 'unfit' parents. This fear leads to a 'protective' regulation and control of their bodies, questioning the reproductive capacities of disabled women, thus creating barriers for them to form healthy social relationships and take up the roles of a wife or mother. This was seen in Aarti's case in *Koshish*, when her mother, first, told Aarti that two 'inadequate' people would not be able to have a successful marriage, and later, asked her not to consummate her marriage with Hari as they might produce more deaf children in this world. However, Aarti exercises her autonomy and marries Hari, and also conceives a child. At the hospital, Aarti is both happy and nervous and wants her mother to confirm that the offspring that she had delivered is a hearing child. Even in *Khamoshi*, Flavy asks Annie to abort her foetus as she is afraid that Annie might give birth to a deaf child just like her parents. Flavy has internalised the hegemony of the dominating hearing world. Abraham Graham Bell encouraged separating deaf people from one another in marriage, in education and in social life, thus making sign language and Deaf culture nearly impossible. He became a highly contentious figure in the history of culturally Deaf people. He believed signing to be a primitive and sub-human form of language. In concert with others, he led the campaign to suppress the use of sign language among deaf people.

This regulating and policing of deaf people is highlighted through ideologies perpetuated through films. Both *Koshish* as well as *Khamoshi* portrayed the deaf couple losing one of their children due to their inability to hear. Both the deaf couples, Aarti and Hari, and Flavy and Joseph, are made to feel 'inadequate' to take up parenting roles. Aarti and Hari are given a second chance to be parents only when they have a hearing friend, Narayan, living with them. In *Khamoshi* too, Annie and Mariamma are constantly there in the house to assist Flavy and Joseph in managing the house. The films convey that deaf people cannot operate on their own and will always require assistance from the hearing world. In *Black*, Michelle is denied any Deaf sociality, denying her any Deaf friendships or a feeling of Deaf community. She is left alone in this ableist world to 'overcome' her disabilities by obtaining a graduate degree. The entire film revolves around Michelle wearing a black graduation robe. This denial of Deaf sociality to a deaf woman is quite an injustice to her character.

Sanjay Leela Bhansali, the maker of *Khamoshi* and *Black*, could be seen as an auteur of his films. The French *auteur* translates to the English 'author'. Within the context of cinema, *auteur* is used to describe a director who exerts a high level of control across all aspects of a film. *Auteur* directors generally have a distinctive style from film to film and often fill other roles besides directing, including writing, editing and sometimes even acting in their films. They go beyond surface-level stories to ask bigger questions in a nuanced and skilful way. Bhansali is famous for his maximalism and for treating each frame with utmost care. He is believed to be involved in every aspect, from writing the story to choreography to music direction to art direction. Director François Truffaut, writing as a critic in the influential French journal *Cahiers du Cinéma* (*Cinema Notebook*), developed the concept of the *auteur* in his 1954 essay, '*Une Certaine Tendance du Cinéma Français*' ('A Certain Trend in French Cinema'). He compares and contrasts an *auteur* director and a director for hire and goes on to say that the former stamps his identity upon his film despite the commercial pressures within the studio system (Butler 2005).

When an *auteur* like Sanjay Leela Bhansali creates a film, he adds moments and emotions from his personal life into a character. Bhansali's personal life had been chaotic and he spent his childhood in poverty in a desolated house. He would often talk about his tough childhood in interviews and would assert that his past has a lot to do with the way he creates his characters and frames in the film. His cinematic style of grandeur comes from the lack of space that he witnessed during his growing years. In one of his interviews with *Film Companion,* he told the interviewer that he is not good at making friends and is a loner. His characters, especially the protagonists, would be depicted as alone and suffering, echoing the feelings of the director.

Michelle lived the life of a deaf-blind girl in loneliness. She craves love and physical intimacy. Being a disabled woman, she is deemed 'unfit' to have a partner by society and she has accepted that too. Her younger sister Sarah is an 'ideal', 'perfect' woman and gets married. While Sarah is getting ready to meet her future in-laws for the first time, she passes a comment that Michelle might never find love because of her disabled identity. Michelle becomes Sarah's bridesmaid and says, '*Dulhan naa sahi, dulhan ki behen to banungi.*' ('I may never become a bride, but I can be a bridesmaid.') Michelle's family never imagined her being a relationship with someone. It was assumed that she would be lonely all her life and her greatest achievement as a deaf-blind woman would be to acquire a graduation degree.

The position of a deaf woman vis-à-vis her privileges of class and caste defines the degree of disability she feels. Studies have shown that a disabled woman from an upper-class family background feels less disabled than a disabled woman from a poverty-stricken household. However, in Michelle's case, her intersectionality of being an upper-class disabled woman with a strong colonial influence in her family strips her of the freedom that Aarti or Flavy had over their lives and decision-making abilities. Her father strongly believes in the Western idea of asylums and insists on institutionalising Michelle before Debraj, her teacher, comes to her rescue. Aarti and Flavy's family are never shown talking about segregating them; rather these two women are reasonably active in their households and have taken up traditional feminine roles because of the lack of privilege in their lives. In a way, ironically, her class position makes her further disabled, adding psychosocial disabilities to her life. She is raised in a bungalow in Shimla and has access to domestic help for anything that she needs, making her environment highly protective. However, Aarti (*Koshish*) and Flavy (*Khamoshi*), because they belong to lower economic strata, are made to learn life skills that are missing from Michelle's life. Michelle is never shown stepping into the kitchen or helping her mother with domestic chores. Her class privilege denies her the feminine roles that would have given her a sense of being a woman enough.

Even Debraj, the private tutor hired to teach Michelle, agrees that she may never get to feel physical love. Michelle tells him that she is suffering and craving for love and wants him to kiss her as this is the only way she would know what it is to kiss a man on the lips. The moment of intimacy that two share is reduced to an act of guilt for Debraj and he leaves Michelle alone after that episode. Debraj talked about his other deaf students at the beginning of the film but never introduces any of his other students to Michelle. He was the only man who understood her as she was never introduced to any other man in her life who would know how to sign or would learn how to sign for her. She has no friends making her disability seem like an individual limitation and not a social construct. Genie Gertz writes:

> It is important that Deaf students interact with other Deaf individuals (youths and adults) early in their school career to take advantage of a critical period in language and social development. As a matter of fact, interaction with other Deaf people on just a social level does make a huge impact on their development and is a top priority; the earlier the better. (2008)

In *Koshish*, Aarti found Hari and was able to share her life with him. However, *Black* denied Michelle the sociality that she could have found in another deaf person or any other person apart from Debraj. There was no one else around her with any disability and she could never get that sense of community that Aarti found in Hari and her blind friend, Narayan. It was Narayan who *understood* them as '*humzubaan*' (speaking the same language) in contrast to Aarti's mother, who perceived them as '*bezubaan*' (having no language or being voiceless). He could understand them as they shared a sense of similarity owing to their disabilities. There was a beautiful scene in the film where Aarti, Hari and Narayan are sitting on a beach and enjoying the sunset in their own ways. Aarti and Hari are curious as to how Narayan could know that the sun was setting, to which he tells them that he could smell the setting of the sun. It is a scene that symbolises what sociality means for a disabled person.

Michelle's deaf-blindness seemed more of an individual's 'inability' to accommodate herself according to the abled society around her. Bhansali denied a community feeling to not just Michelle; Flavy and Joseph too appeared a lonely isolated couple who are shown to be possessive about their daughter Annie, as she is the only way they could interact with the hearing world. The onus of handling the barrier in communication again appeared to be on the deaf couple rather than the apathetic society they were residing in. However, Gulzar created the character of a blind friend, thus illustrating that Hari and Aarti are not alone. Bhansali, on the other hand, created his characters as lonely, pitiful and in an utterly desolate state, trying to make sense of their existence in an ableist world.

It is important to take notice of the Deaf world and its concerns. The hearing world's ignorance of deaf ways of being has had particularly deleterious effects on the majority of deaf people as they are born into hearing households and are therefore cast into a medicalised version of deafness that will indelibly mark their lives as disabled. The 'Deaf-mute voice' has been no match for the ideological megaphone of the biopower institutions designed to fix deafness and discourage the formation of a deaf variety of the human race (Bauman 2008).

Films have seen deafness as a disability but this form of artistic expression and a medium of entertainment that has a huge outreach should open dialogues contesting the normative ideas. Disability rights expert, Professor Deborah Stienstra summarises that the act of storytelling is also the making of social change, of recreating the world, with the stories of individuals who have been excluded, marginalised and constrained included (Stienstra 2008). Similarly, filmmakers should involve researchers who can highlight the multiple epistemologies that exist and study how deaf individuals truly develop and navigate the world as well as pass on the indigenous knowledge to their children, such as their sign language that comes naturally to them—and the way the deaf would perceive their other senses and make sense of an audist world through their own knowledge systems that comes either naturally to them or are imparted by the larger Deaf culture. One needs to research deaf people's distinct ontologies, or ways of being in the world, concerning their unique sensory orientations, and view deafness as a bodily variation that requires unlearning a whole lot of audist and oralist mindsets. Stienstra goes on to write about the responsibility that a researcher has—to ensure that these stories are valued and gathered and told in culturally respectful ways, recognising the potential the stories have to bring about social change. This requires culturally appropriate research methods that reflect upon majority cultural values that find their way into dominant research practices and values (2008).

Deaf people should be perceived as linguistically and culturally different from the dominant hearing world. In a way, Deaf culture is like a subculture to the hegemonic hearing culture. Deaf worlds encourage one to consider new ways of listening, new ways of thinking and new ways of seeing the world through Deaf eyes. The phonocentric world has marginalised Deafness to the peripheries, both literal and metaphorical. Ben Bahan writes:

> Deaf eyes have the uncanny ability to process simultaneous information through enhanced peripheral vision. Whereas hearing people depend on sound for information along the outskirts of their sight, Deaf people's vision pushes the boundaries of the peripheral, affording them the ability to entertain nuanced sensory input across a wide field of vision. Deaf vision…disperses the single-point perspective along a spectrum of perception, allowing the viewer to process multilayered, divergent information simultaneously. (cited in Bauman 2008)

A few scenes in *Koshish* and *Khamoshi* worth analysing were, in some sense, able to capture that epistemological shift that Deaf ontologies try to create. There is a scene in *Koshish* where Narayan is singing a lullaby for Ajit (Aarti and Hari's son), and Aarti and Hari are enjoying the visual experience of a song being sung with so much warmth. In another scene, Ajit is dancing and some music is being played on the radio. Hari makes Aarti touch the radio and feel the music through the vibrations generated. Even when Ajit sings on stage at his school's event, Hari and Aarti enjoy it through visuality and tactility. *Khamoshi* is a musical and there are numerous scenes in the film where Flavy and Joseph are shown enjoying and 'listening' to the music, in their way. Joseph N. Straus gave the concept of 'disablist hearing' in his book, *Extraordinary Measures: Disability in Music*. Deaf people practice, as Straus calls it, 'disablist hearing' which is a distinctive way to experience music, perhaps even hear things in music that even hearing people do not. Straus describes four kinds of disablist hearing: blind hearing (which is unmediated by notation), deaf hearing (which includes extensive visuality and tactility), mobility-inflected hearing (which includes atypical comportment and posture) and autistic hearing (which includes elements of neurodiversity such as a preference for 'local coherence', a proclivity for 'private association', and a talent for 'imitation' (2011). Straus is redefining the range of normative production and reception of music by reframing ways of being in the world that dominant understandings frame as pathologies and musical gifts. In short, deaf people have their own ways of listening and responding to music and other aspects of sounds.

This brings us to the question of who is writing the story of these deaf individuals. If one looks at *Khamoshi* and *Black*, they start with an autobiographical tone but are these *real* autobiographies of deaf individuals or are they written by a hearing person about deaf individuals? When Bhansali titles his film *Khamoshi*, which means silence, or *Black*, which becomes the colour of Michelle's life, is it not an ableist evaluative gaze towards a disabled person? In the guise of autobiographies, Bhansali produced characters that were produced by an ableist filmmaker for an ableist audience. *Khamoshi* could have been a woman writing about her deaf parents. It appears as a film written by a hearing person for her deaf parents with a lot of judgements regarding their deafness. The film reaches its pinnacle of ableism when, towards the end, Joseph is shaken and 'made to' call out 'Annie' to fulfil her 'impossible dream', which was hinted at the beginning. The sheer obsession of a hearing individual to make a deaf individual talk and hear like them is reflected in *Black* too when Michelle is 'tamed' by Debraj and she finally speaks the word, 'w-a-t-e-r'. The oralist audist world pressurises deaf individuals to go out of their way to speak for them.

Interestingly, Gulzar was able to capture how disabled bodies make meaning out of their disabilities and negotiate with the demands of the hearing world. There is a unique scene in *Koshish* where one end of a string is tied to Hari's leg and the other end is with Narayan who is sleeping in the next room. When Narayan hears that baby Amit is crying out of hunger, he pulls the string to alert Hari about the situation. Hari wakes up and he then wakes Aarti up to feed the baby. They lost their first child in the past because they could not hear his cries and he drowned in the rain. So, to avoid any such tragic occurrence again, they have Narayan living with them. They create a makeshift arrangement according to their needs in raising a child. They clap their hands to call out to their son. The factory where Hari works has installed a light instead of a bell for Hari. A similar setup is also observed in *Khamoshi*, where, instead of a doorbell, Joseph and Flavy install a door light. Jose Lorente uses the term 'body calligraphy' (2008) for such distinct ways of being where disabled people negotiate with their disabilities keeping in mind the expectations of the ableist world.

There are diverse ways of being, which makes it important to read deaf epistemologies and ontologies in order to delve into deaf lives. Broadly, there is a focus on knowing the world through understanding and not understanding; the (explicit) value placed on understanding is a key part of deaf people's epistemologies and ontologies. For Aarti, it is at the entry of Hari into her life that she starts getting a feeling of sociality. There is an ease of understanding she shares with him. Then, Narayan comes into their lives. Later, it is her sign language teacher from the Deaf School who becomes a confidante for her and understands Aarti's aspiration to be a mother. For a disabled woman, it becomes all the more important to take up the traditional feminine roles to be 'woman enough' as society deems disabled women 'unfit' and 'incapable' to take up the roles of wife and mother. The denial of a woman's 'traditional roles' to disabled women creates what Michele Fine and Adrienne Asch term 'rolelessness' (1988), which is a social invisibility and cancellation of femininity that can impel disabled women to pursue, however hopelessly, the female identity valorised by their given culture but denied to them because of their disability.

For Hari and Joseph, their disability contradicts the idea of masculinity that society perpetuates. Having a disability is seen as synonymous with being dependent, childlike and helpless—an image fundamentally challenging all that is embodied in the ideal male: virility, autonomy and independence. In the case of a disabled man, concerns regarding 'emasculation' are raised that see masculinity and disability as contradictory to each other. Joseph is treated like a grown-up child by Annie who needs constant assistance and is robbed of his role as a father. Towards the end, when they are all gathered at the church, Joseph makes a speech. Throughout the speech, he is apologising to Annie for ruining her childhood and that she has grown up so soon. The image of Annie selling soaps with her deaf father is something that is evoked time and again in the film to highlight the difficult life Annie had to live because of being a CODA.

Both Annie and Ajit are children of deaf adults (CODA). It was coined by Millie Brother, who founded CODA as an organisation in 1982. The hearing children of Deaf parents grow up in two cultures with two languages. They are similar to other bilingual, bicultural children in many ways but are also special. They can be in conflict between two worlds and often carry an extra burden of responsibility in functioning as a bridge between the two. Many feel that they are misfits, belonging in neither world. Others feel that they have a positive CODA identity, but again as neither a hearing person nor a Deaf person. Ajit and Annie are bimodal, bilingual language users and not identical to their parents who are Deaf native signers.

The location of Ajit and Annie could be read as a 'border crossing' as the issues surrounding communication created a border within their respective families. They grow up in two worlds and lead two lives, one as a CODA and one as a hearing person. It depends on them to choose what life they wish to live. The duality of their lives adds complexities to their identity. The CODA life in most cases is not visible as in Ajit's case. Robert Hoffmeister writes about the film *Passport without a Country* which is about the lives of CODAs, suggesting that they are subject to amorphous borders. He elaborates, 'This documentary is important in that it places CODAs in between cultures. We live on the border or we seek to move as far from the border as possible. There are these burning questions of not only where we belong, but what is our identity. Are CODAs Deaf and hearing—that is, are they bicultural' (Hoffmeister 2008)?

Annie, throughout the film, talks about the two contrasting worlds and creates a binary between the two cultures. *Black* follows a similar pattern of portraying the two worlds in binaries and not as coexisting together. Hoffmeister suggests that the binary relationship that is established by the terms 'Deaf' and 'hearing' must be depolarised. CODAs present a problem with that binary relationship. He writes, 'If we continue to maintain this binary split, understanding our many borders becomes more difficult. If we are able to remove this idea of a binary relationship between hearing and deaf, we may arrive at some useful discussion as to membership and transmission of the culture' (2008). Annie could not listen to the sounds of her deaf parents. Her understanding of communication came from the hearing world, which is oralist and audist in nature. She could not celebrate her parents the way they were, the culture they carried with themselves, and rather, saw them in binaries.

Lennard J. Davis, the famous disability studies scholar, born to deaf parents, has written a memoir about his life with his parents, *My Sense of Silence*. He writes:

> To most people, the deaf sound strange, guttural and strangulated. To me, the normal voices of the deaf are soothing, like whale sounds, cooing and arcing under the surface of the deep ... The consonants are not generally sharp enough, the vowels too open. The rising and falling tones of English are strangely absent, replaced by rising and falling that comes from the logic of breath and the length of words. This is pure poetry of sound. (2000)

Unlike Annie, he is the writer of his own story and has managed to archive lived experiences of living in a house with two deaf individuals. He does not paint a pitiful picture. One may argue that Davis acquires a privileged Global North position and his experiences would be very different from that of Annie. However, through his writings, he provides an alternate way of looking at Deafness as body diversity and not as body deficit. If a filmmaker plans to make a film about a marginalised group, it becomes imperative to read and understand the lives of the group from their standpoint. When a film is being made on Deaf lives, therefore, it becomes essential to look at deaf ontologies and epistemologies to portray them authentically. Emmanuelle Laborit, a deaf French actress, writes in her autobiography, *The Cry of the Gull*, about how the dominant hearing world has written *for* and *about* the Deaf and how important it is to write one's own story for others to read and understand Deaf worlds. She writes:

> Hearing people write books about the deaf ... Some people told me I wouldn't be able to do it ... I especially wanted to do it in your native language. The language of my parents. My adopted language. The seagull has grown up and flies with her own wings. I see just as I might hear. My eyes are my ears. I can write as well as sign. My hands speak two languages. (1998)

Notes

1   *Bezubaan* means voiceless or having no language.
2   *Humzubaan* means speaking the same language.
3   This chapter is part of a larger PhD thesis titled 'Representation of Disability in Women in Hindi Cinema Since 1970' submitted by Mansi Grover to the Department of English, Jamia Millia Islamia in September 2022.
4   The capitalised convention of Deaf is used for all Deaf people who identify themselves as being Deaf, which makes them a member of the culture. Hearing is capitalised because this is the cultural contrast group. The lower case deaf is used to denote the audiological impairment and hearing as a contrast to that.
5   *Koshish*. 1972. Directed by Gulzar. N.C. Sippy.
6   *Khamoshi: The Musical*. 1996. Directed by Sanjay Leela Bhansali. SLB Films.
7   *Black*. 2005. Directed by Sanjay Leela Bhansali. Applause Entertainment and SLB Films.

References

Bauman, H-Dirksen L. 'Introduction: Listening to Deaf Studies.' In *Open Your Eyes: Deaf Studies Talking*, edited by H-Dirksen L. Bauman, 1–32. Minneapolis and London: University of Minnesota Press, 2008.
Butler, Andrew M. *Film Studies*. Herts, UK: Pocket Essentials, 2005.

Chopra, Anupama. 'Sanjay Leela Bhansali Interview with Anupama Chopra', *Film Companion*, 2015. https://www.youtube.com/watch?v=5WMa4NOQgYo&t=121s (accessed 25 May 2020).

Davis, Lennard J. *My Sense of Silence: Memoirs of a Childhood with Deafness*. Urbana and Chicago: University of Illinois Press, 2000.

Fine, Michele and Adrienne Asch. *Women with Disabilities: Essays in Psychology, Culture and Politics*. Philadelphia: Temple University Press, 1988.

Friedner, Michele. 'Understanding and Not-Understanding: What Do Epistemologies and Ontologies Do in Deaf Worlds?' *Sign Language Studies*, 16, no. 2 (Winter 2016): 184–203.

Gertz, Genie. 'Dysconscious Audism: A Theoretical Proposition'. In *Open Your Eyes: Deaf Studies Talking*, edited by H-Dirksen L. Bauman, 219–34. Minneapolis and London: University of Minnesota Press, 2008.

Hoffmeister, Robert. 'Border Crossings by Hearing Children of Deaf Parents: The Lost History of Codas'. In *Open Your Eyes: Deaf Studies Talking*, edited by H-Dirksen L. Bauman, 189–215. Minneapolis and London: University of Minnesota Press, 2008.

Jain, Arushi. 'Streaming Guide: Gulzar Movies'. *Indian Express*, 2020. https://indianexpress.com/article/entertainment/bollywood/streaming-guide-gulzar-movies-5992646/ (accessed 25 May 2020).

Jepson, Jill. 'Some Aspects of the Deaf Experience in India'. *Sign Language Studies*, no. 73 (Winter 1991), Special Extra Length Issue: Papers on Sign Languages & Deaf Cultures: The 1990 Meetings of the American Anthropological Association in New Orleans (Winter 1991): 453–59.

Keller, Helen. *Midstream. My Later Life*. Westport CT: Greenwood Press, 1929.

Laborit, Emmanuelle. *The Cry of the Gull*. Washington, D.C.: Gallaudet University Press, 1998.

Lane, Harlan. 'Do Deaf People Have a Disability?' In *Open Your Eyes: Deaf Studies Talking*, edited by H-Dirksen L. Bauman, 277–92. Minneapolis and London: University of Minnesota Press, 2008.

Limaye, Sandhya. 'The Inner World of Adolescent Girls with Hearing Impairment: Two Case Studies'. In *Disability Studies in India: Global Discourses, Local Realities*, edited by Renu Addlakha, 263–81. New Delhi and Oxfordshire: Routledge, 2008.

Lorente, Jose Abad. 'Body/Text: Art Project on Deafness and Communication'. In *Disability Studies in India: Global Discourses, Local Realities*, edited by Renu Addlakha, 285–302. New Delhi and Oxfordshire: Routledge, 2008.

Stienstra, Deborah. 'Race/Ethnicity and Disability Studies: Towards an Explicitly Intersectional Approach'. In *Routledge Handbook of Disability Studies*, edited by Nick Watson and Simo Vehmas, 453–66. Oxon and New York: Routledge, 2008.

Straus, Joseph N. *Extraordinary Measure: Disability in Music*. New York: Oxford University Press, 2011.

12

FROM CURE TO HEALING:
COMPREHENDING DEAFNESS
THROUGH MADAN VASISHTA'S *DEAF IN DELHI*

Rimjhim Bhattacherjee

Madan Vasishta's memoir, *Deaf in Delhi*, in its representation of the acquired deafness of an 11-year-old boy from the small Himachal village of Gagret and the changed contours of his life thereof, deftly navigates several pressing concerns of the emergent field of disability studies in India. Madan's initial interpellation in and later resistance to pejorative notions associated with deafness at home and in the world propels readers to the careful contemplation of facets of everyday ableism as well as the systemic exclusion of disabled people such as Madan from the mainstream. In effect, the narrative critiques ableist modes of perceiving disability and shifts from the notion of 'cure' that characterises the earlier portions of the memoir to a sense of 'healing' in its later parts. This chapter analyses Vasishta's narrative employing a critical disability studies framework to unpack the ontological experience of deafness and posit the transgressive possibilities of Deaf[1] identity wherein it challenges its pejorative baggage and emerges as a positive, creative, and value-enhancing experience. In this, the chapter shall draw from Erving Goffman's (1963) work on stigma and Michelle Friedner's (2015) work on Deaf worlds in urban India.

Understanding Ableism, Interrogating Cure

The idea of being deaf petrified me. I shuddered at the terms *bola* in Punjabi, *behra* in Urdu, and *vadhir* in Hindi. All these are extremely offensive and derogatory words to describe someone who is not really a human ... I would hide my head in the quilt and cry silently at this bleak and miserable vision of my future. (Vasishta 2006, 5)

The excerpt records Madan's initial response to his acquired deafness, subsequent to which, he writes, 'my life changed forevermore' (1). Madan's narrative recalls how he had met only one deaf person in the first eleven years of his life, whom everybody called *bola*. The children of the village mocked him and he had purportedly been robbed of all his property by his own brother who also compelled him to work like a slave on their farm (5). As expressed in the excerpt, terror and misery gripped young Madan as he began to believe that his life too would resemble that of the only deaf person he knew. The trauma experienced by him on the realisation that he has acquired deafness can be attributed primarily to the stigma normatively linked with the 'condition' in Indian society. Madan correctly observes that almost all terms in Indian languages used to signify deafness— *bola, vadhir, behra*—have deprecatory connotations, best elucidated through an analogy with the frequently used phrase 'deaf and dumb'. Similar to how this phrase suggests lack of intellectual acumen as invariably accompanying speech and hearing impairments, the other epithets too—particularly the word bola—are products of an ableist *weltanschauung* that equates bodily impairments with abnormality and lack.

Here, the word 'ableism' may require some explanation. A commonly used term in disability studies literature, ableism can be defined as the underlying force creating and perpetuating negative constructions of disability as flaw, tragedy or lack. Through the operation of ableism, societies accord privileges of citizenship to those possessing the normative 'able body' and marginalise disabled people who are judged and found wanting by the standards of reductive notions of ability.[2] In the context of Madan's narrative, through the operation of ableist notions, deafness becomes an impairment that colonises all other attributes of the individual and becomes a sole identity—a negative one that implies subhuman status.

The ableist milieu in his Gagret home is exemplified when Madan's family and the young Madan himself struggle to accept the irreversibility of his deafness. The ambience is heavy with gloom and anxiety whereby Madan calls his deafness a 'family tragedy' (11). When met with a body that is even marginally non-normative, the usual ableist response is to attempt to 'cure' it through medical intervention. Madan's story also testifies to this bias of cure in both his family and his initial self. The narrative meticulously records manners of cure attempted both by his family and undertaken on his own volition, ranging from the village vaid and doctors at Hoshiarpur and Amritsar to faith healers and godmen; negotiations with the almighty through the chanting of mantras; and even excruciating home remedies that sometimes amuse him but, more often than not, cause him frustration and pain—both physical and psychological.

The onslaught of ableism in Madan's early life is not limited to desperate searches for a cure. It affects all aspects of his life, including his access to education—a basic right understood to be available to all. Being a very bright student, his teachers had predicted that he would grow up to be a doctor, but as there was no medium of instruction accessible for deaf children in the village or in other schools of nearby areas, the doors of formal education were apparently shut for him. This is indeed ironic since deafness—even as a medical 'condition'— does not diminish a person's intellectual acumen.[3] If Madan had the potential of becoming a doctor—an honour usually reserved only for the highest-performing students in India—then his lived experience of deafness might have enhanced his understanding of it, consequently increasing his chances of being better at 'treating' it. However, instead of utilising this potential of deafness, the ossified ableist society ostracises the deaf child from the human resource pool, ultimately robbing not only the child of a better future and several other deaf children of a role model—something that Madan himself could not find throughout his childhood—but also the scientific field from perhaps a more empathetic approach to 'conditions' such as deafness.

Instead, after managing to take the sixth-grade examination, Madan had to educate himself at home with the help of his cousins. He even had to spend six agonising years as a cowherd for his family, all the while despairing of a bright future: 'according to everyone in the village, including my family, a deaf person could do only one kind of work— manual labour' (72). At the insistence of his cousin, Madan prepared on his own for the matriculation examination, managing to clear it with first division. Despite faring well in the same and wishing to study further, he had to coerce himself into accepting that his 'career as a student was over' (60) since none of the colleges in Hoshiarpur would be willing to admit a deaf person. These realities persistently haunt him as he searches for a vocation and a quality of life that would be acceptable to him even though he attempts to appear optimistic and cheerful.[4]

Analysing the memoir from a disability studies perspective reveals the fact that the trauma Madan had to undergo on account of his impairment stemmed from his perceived lack of opportunities for deaf people in the world he inhabited. His misery stemmed not so much from the acquisition of deafness as from the empirical knowledge that the society we live and function in has been moulded by the nondisabled for the nondisabled. Deafness-as-negative identity fostered by ableism seeps into all facets of life, evidenced, in this regard, in some of the most basic public institutions and services—such as education—being inaccessible to Madan. The operation of ableism here is inherently confounding. Its reductive logic engenders deaf identity as sub-human. It is so reactionary that on encountering a deaf person who exhibits human qualities and desires, it demands that the latter submit to its rules and accept subhuman identity rather than challenge it towards the task of rectification. Disability studies, in turn, achieves just this—a revision and thereby dismantling of ableism. In the present context it enables us to acknowledge that had sign language been an officially recognised and frequently used language; had there been multiple examples of deaf people who had had access to educational and vocational fields of their choice; and had the very concept of deafness not been immersed in stigma, then Madan's acquired deafness would perhaps not have caused as much panic. It is a tired fact, albeit contextually significant, that the ableism inherent in society transforms Madan's impairment into a disability.

Furthermore, as stated before, the instilling of this ableism in nondisabled and disabled people alike warrants the location of the 'problem' of disability in the individual and seeks to 'cure' them of it through medical intervention. The failure of such 'cures', as in the case of Madan, can often trigger overwhelming feelings of vulnerability and desperation in the disabled person and those close to them. Therefore, the preliminary phase of Madan's coping with his disability as recorded in *Deaf in Delhi* becomes a narrative of 'hearing loss', wherein deafness is medically perceived in terms of a lack, an absence or a void and it becomes impossible to divorce this conception of deafness from the idea of loss (Bauman and Murray 2009, 3). The overarching motif of his experience of deafness in the small village of Gagret is thereby a failed attempt at 'cure'. The narrative lodges a critique against such a narrowly individualistic understanding of deafness, arguing instead, that at least in certain instances, structural changes in the social set-up can, to a considerable extent, mitigate psychological pain that often follows impairments.

Healing through the Deaf Community

We were using Indian Sign Language (ISL) … I became fascinated with this language. Each day, I picked up more signs, and by the end of the week, I was able to fully communicate with my two new friends and Mr. Goyle. I fell in love with sign language. It opened up a whole new world for me. (Vasishta 2006, 101)

Although not enunciated as such in the text, Madan's journey from a sense of vulnerability and powerlessness stemming from his acquired deafness to the 'new world' that it inaugurates for him (as expressed in the excerpt quoted above) is an archetypal example of shift from the normative medical notion of deafness as 'hearing loss' to that of 'Deaf gain' post his acquaintance with the Deaf community in Delhi and especially his induction into the world of sign language. The memoir records a gradual transformation of the perception of deafness as an individual 'aberration'—a 'condition' that isolates the Deaf from the rest of society by instilling in them a sense of abnormality and the conviction of a dismal future—to that of Deaf experience as shared by many: to the idea of a Deaf culture that imbues value in the lives of the Deaf and helps them envision a fruitful future for themselves.

Madan's negative discernment of his deafness begins to change once he shifts to Delhi to attend the Photography Training Institute for the Deaf (PID) run by the All India Federation of the Deaf (AIFD) on a government scholarship for disabled people. It is for the first time here that he gets to interact with the general secretary of AIFD, a 'powerful deaf person' with 'a fancy office, four assistants, and a ... peon sitting outside his office' (Vasishta 2006, 96). Seeing him in action rekindles in Madan the hope for the fruition of the future he dreamed for himself. However, his introduction to sign language through the students of the PID proved to be very significant to his development—he claims that it 'opened up a new world for me' (101). Madan gradually takes what in Deaf studies is called a 'Deaf turn' as he begins to seamlessly communicate in sign language with his new friends in Delhi's thriving Deaf world comprising its own Deaf clubs and associations.

A Deaf turn usually occurs in a deaf person through initiation into sign language which opens up means of unimpeded communication among Deaf people and inducts them into Deaf sociality. Taking the Deaf turn usually necessitates disorienting oneself from family (who cannot/do not wish to sign), reorienting oneself to the Deaf community, and depending on it for advice, support and succour (Friedner 2015, 29). For Friedner, as deaf young adults 'formally and informally learn the values of deaf [sic.] sociality and the importance of sign language', they also learn to share and communicate, not least, comprehend for themselves the differences between 'deafness' and 'normality' in ways they had never comprehended before. Once they observe that communication is possible among the Deaf and their impairment is not really an individual 'problem', they begin to critique the ableist society within which they are expected to function and to which their families are also usually unwitting accomplices.

Deaf in Delhi is replete with such instances of critique of both family and society and the author does not shy away from revealing his own initial interpellation in ableist thought and behaviour. In this, the narrative shifts from the strictly biomedical understanding of deafness to understanding it in terms of the social model of disability, which locates the 'problem' of disability not in the individual body but in socio-cultural barriers. To exemplify, Madan notes that although his family observed his finger-spelling with 'polite interest', they did not want to go to the extent of learning sign language themselves. Also, he mentions that the idea of teaching it to them or insisting that they learn it in order to communicate better never occurred to him either (Vasishta 2006, 100). This caused him—as with many other Deaf pointed out in Friedner's study—to lead a 'double life'—one he calls the 'old life' in which he lived among 'family and friends—all hearing— who communicated with me by tracing words on their palms' and the other was the 'new one: the Deaf world' (102). In the latter, he wields the confidence to traverse busy Delhi streets on a bicycle despite his family's protests. Further, it provides him with employment opportunities the likes of which had appeared impossible while in Gagret,[5] all the while encouraging and enabling him to hone his leadership skills.

In the Deaf world, Madan makes rapid strides from pupil to worker to teacher and then the leader of their association. This imbues him with such confidence that he manages not only to secure a government job where he had to interview against hearing people but also to apply to Gallaudet College in the US and finally travel there. The positive transformation of his life propelled by his induction into Deaf sociality can easily be comprehended if one browses through the chapter titles in *Deaf in Delhi* prior to and after Madan's introduction to the Deaf world. While initial chapters bear titles like 'Panic', 'Looking for a Cure', 'Careers or the Lack of Them', chapters following his induction into the Deaf world in Delhi are titled 'New Discoveries', 'Me, a Teacher!', 'Learning about Leadership' and so on, positing a clear shift in his comprehension of deafness and its implications for his future. Once his critical acumen develops as a result of Deaf sociality, he refuses to accept negative definitions of deafness in terms of 'hearing loss'. Instead, he critiques the fact that truly intelligent deaf people remain uneducated and even illiterate owing to lack of adequate educational opportunities. To exemplify, he writes, 'How a smart person like him [Madan's deaf friend Kesh] could not read and write after several years of schooling was hard for me to understand. But then, I had also met many other bright deaf men and women who were in the same boat as Kesh' (114). Therefore, he gradually realises that the 'problem' of deafness lies not in deaf individuals but in ableist society's antipathy towards structural changes. If efforts to deploy such structural changes can be realised, the Deaf can indeed participate in mainstream activities.

Deaf children, even those who have been to school, struggle to read and write because modes of instruction in most schools are not Deaf-friendly. This is echoed in Friedner's work years later in urban Bengaluru, where she observed that 'none of the normal schools offered deaf children additional services or support and that deaf children were treated just like everyone else' (2015, 39). Even in Deaf schools, the education was of 'poor quality' as most teachers were hearing and either did not know/use or used very little sign language. Therefore, the students found it difficult to follow the teacher and 'often emerged from these schools unable to read or write properly and without basic skills needed for livelihood' (39). For decades, disability scholars in India have been questioning methods of instruction for the d/Deaf in public learning institutions, having critiqued the preponderance of oralism and citing it as an explanation for the minimal presence of Deaf people in institutions of higher education and consequently in high-end professions (Broota 2005; Friedner 2015). Vasishta's observations and disability scholars' understanding of the appalling condition of Deaf education expose not the ineptitude of the Deaf students owing to 'hearing loss' but to the failure of an education system which does not accommodate sign language into curricula or enable the employment of Deaf teachers. In effect, the lack of education entraps deaf people into a vicious cycle of lack of job opportunities and poverty, dependence and financial insecurity which are its consequences. This has, for decades, led Deaf people to live as outliers of the social structure rather than as its active participants. Narratives like *Deaf in Delhi*, therefore, demonstrate how this alienation results from systemic rather than biological impairments.

The systemic alienation of the Deaf is further exposed by the narrative through its observation that the normate[6] stigmatises not only the deaf body but also the language of the Deaf, or in this case, Indian Sign Language (henceforth ISL). Sign language is considered inferior to speech by the normate and Madan is often advised, 'You speak very well. You do not need to sign like them' (Vasishta 2006, 100). An entire chapter of the narrative is, in fact, reserved to record the reactions of hearing people (unacquainted with the Deaf world) to sign language. There are first the 'glancers' who only 'look at signers for a few seconds' before moving on; then, the 'watchers' who stop in their tracks when they notice signers 'as if they are seeing a horse talking'; the 'starers' who go as close as possible to signers 'and follow [their] hands and fingers like a boy watching a butterfly that he wants to catch'. These people, Vasishta states, 'make deaf people, especially shy ones … nervous';

finally, there are the 'gawkers' who Vasishta labels 'the worst kind of sign watchers'. They not only gawk at signers but also follow them around and try to copy them (156–57).

In a culture where a majority of the populace remains unacquainted with sign language, signers become a spectacle. Through their language, they embody Garland-Thomson's 'extraordinary bodies' (1997)—essentially, bodies that are 'deviant' from the norm in any culture—and therefore become spectacle. Sign language is not considered to be a 'normal' language in India, thereby deeming its users to be 'abnormal' people, who must be stared at and gawked at. This often causes them discomfort and deters many deaf people from using ISL. According to Friedner, a similar stigma and discomfort surrounds sign language in the ableist imaginary which sometimes includes deaf people themselves. Her study mentions one young deaf girl who had two deaf sisters. Her sisters signed but this young girl refused to do so because she found it 'dirty' to sign even when one could speak (2015, 45).

The stigma associated with sign language is also engendered by a reductive, overtly medical conception of deafness as a bodily 'problem'. It ascribes to deaf people, in Erving Goffman's terms, 'spoiled identities' (1963). The associations of lack and failure with disability in the ableist imaginary are naturalised through interpellation, thereby, making normates shun disability as a contagion. Most champions of able-bodiedness are terrified of disability precisely because they grasp the fragility of the divide between 'ability' and (the biomedical understanding of) 'disability'. The power of this division rests entirely on the human body, itself always in flux, always vulnerable. The fear of disability, then, the cause for its stigma, is less the fear of probable transgressions by the disabled other, than of oneself slipping into disability, losing one's able-bodied status. Goffman, in his broad theorisation of stigma, differentiates between 'discredited' and 'discreditable' bodies. The former are individuals whose stigma is visible (in this context, people with physical impairments) while the latter refers to people whose stigma can be concealed (in this context, people with invisible impairments such as deafness). Deafness cannot usually be discerned by a mark on a person's body in the manner of most physical impairments. Therefore, ableist society instructs Deaf people to conceal their deafness and attempt to pass off as unimpaired—as possessors of 'able', non-discredited, bodies for as long as possible (Goffman 1963, 4). One of the reasons often cited against instruction in sign language is that deaf children have to function in a 'normal' society where nobody knows signs. Deaf children are expected to adapt in ways that make them acceptable to the majority (ableist) culture. Thereby, such a society breeds disavowal of Deafness. Deaf people who are interpellated with this ideology are ashamed of their deafness—what they perceive as a 'flaw' in the mechanism of their body—and try to imitate 'normal' people in their conditioned desire to fit into mainstream society. They seek to disavow both D/deafness and its language.

As opposed to this, signing implies an affirmation of Deafness and indeed a display of it. The use of sign language in the ableist world clearly transforms discreditable into discredited. Consequently, it is perceived as transgression from those on the other side, which upsets normates, both nondisabled and disabled. They would rather accept deafness as a 'discreditable' trait and look for a 'cure' or attempt to hide (from) it rather than explore the nuances of Deaf experience. They shun the unique perspectives it casts on the world we live in and also the possibilities of expression brought on by a language unlike any other in the hearing/speaking world.

In both Vasishta's memoir and Friedner's study, ISL is revealed to be much more than merely a language that the Deaf communicate in. They present ISL as one of the keystones of 'Deaf gain' in that it engenders both a being and a becoming. In its inauguration of a world of seamless communication for the Deaf where they no longer have to struggle to make themselves understood, it negates the feeling that deaf people are less than human in their inability to communicate with the hearing. Besides emphatically asserting the human status of the Deaf, ISL enables the conviction that real impairment lies not in them but in hearing people uninitiated in ISL. It is significant to recall Goffman's assertion that stigma does not reside in a person but in the interactions between an attribute and a context. In the contextual specificities of the Deaf world in Delhi, Madan's is no longer either a 'discredited' or a 'discreditable' body. It loses its stigma and functions seamlessly.

In this regard, the identity formation associated with deafness assumes a creative and critical reversal. The induction into Deaf sociality through ISL and consequent Deaf gain also confers Madan an identity accruing from his deafness. However, this is not an ableist, negative identity that denotes subhuman status, but a Deaf identity that enables him to accept his impairment, critique ableist attitudes to it and enlivens him to the creative possibilities of Deaf existence. For Friedner, often with sign language, Deaf people come to believe that 'normal people who could not sign were disabled, whereas deaf people who could sign were not disabled' (2015, 49). Such a reversal elucidates the constructedness of the ability/disability binary, wherein discerning readers are compelled to concede that the extent to which the Deaf feel disabled in Indian society at present would be significantly reduced had ISL been an official language taught in all schools and used freely in both public and private spaces. Such an awareness, garnered by Deaf people—in their alternative navigations of the world—exposes that 'the capacity to act and effectivity of action [in any particular society] is to a large extent structured by the ability to harness and utilize [sic.] matter for one's own purposes and interests' (Grosz, quoted in Mitchell and Snyder 2015, 7). Indeed, normates would feel as disabled in the Deaf world as the D/deaf do in Indian society, largely framed by the worldview of the normate.

The narrative further exposes how ironically, for most normates, ability pride rests in *not* knowing a language and therefore in an *inability*. Madan remembers of the person who advised him not to sign, 'He was hearing, he *did not know signs*, and thought signing was something inferior to speaking' (100; emphasis mine). This statement signifies his complete reorientation from the notion of his deafness as 'hearing loss' to that of 'Deaf gain', whereby he locates the deficiency in the hearing person rather than in himself and almost pities the former his inability to use ISL. Communicating through sign language thus translates into a claiming of Deafness and its language, fuelling Madan's refusal to hide behind a facade of 'normality.'

Another indication of this Deaf gain is revealed through the shift of the narrative focus from the diatribe of a 'cure' in its early chapters to 'healing', where Madan does not heal *from* his deafness; rather, *because of* it. His acquisition of deafness enables his induction into the Deaf world and thereby further enables him to comprehend the problematics of deaf/Deaf (endnote i). The Deaf world also reveals the complex ableist constructs that infuse deafness with an air of tragedy and coerce people to seek a cure, the absence of which often burdens them with despair. Deafness enables Madan to heal from this bleak and essentially narrow perception of his impairment.

The narrative attempts to heal the reader of their (commonly, often unwittingly held) ableist notions as well. Through its journey from an entrenchment in ableist modes of existence to a critique of them, it demands a more active and critical reappraisal of society. Furthermore, *Deaf in Delhi* enlightens people, nondisabled and disabled alike, about the existence of Deaf sociality by urging society as a whole to take a Deaf turn. As normates increasingly acquaint themselves with the Deaf world and its language, they shall be healed of their ableism and the better hope there shall be of Deaf inclusion in mainstream activities, not least the gradual attrition of stigma from deafness.

Taking a Deaf turn enhances an inclusive outlook and helps in the enrichment of bio-cultural diversity:

Sign language uses a different modality, and its visual, kinesthetic nature is a source of diversity. It represents a different way of perceiving the world and a different way of expressing oneself, and that is the heart of bio-cultural diversity … sign language … can expand our conceptions of the human potential for language, for expression, and for creativity. Deaf people contribute to … greater diversity … which in turn contributes to the greater health of humankind. (Bauman and Murray 2009, 4–5)

Therefore, 'Deaf gain' and the healing of Madan thereof needs to be comprehended not simply in terms of a newly gained identity for deaf people, but also as a means that introduces hearing people to a newer comprehension of the world and enables stretching of the limits of language, communication and expression. In the fostering of inclusivity through this changed worldview, a healthier, more adaptable society may be developed.

Conclusion: Forging Deaf Development

Disability narratives often lend themselves to being identified as disparate, individual narratives of 'overcome'. They therefore unwittingly bolster the ableist notion of disability residing within the individual who can, with effort and willpower, transcend their impairments to achieve great things. These narratives enable society to elide its responsibilities towards the positive development of disabled lives. Narratives like *Deaf in Delhi*, on the other hand, in their subtle shift in narrative focus from the individual to communities—both disabled and nondisabled— elucidate the responsibilities of both in forging development for disabled, D/deaf people.

The notion of development has been identified as one of the central aspirations of people in contemporary India (Pandian 2009). The term can be defined in a multitude of ways with the central idea being that of a progressive improvement of conditions of living and personal growth 'through deliberate endeavours in transformation' (Pandian 2009, 6). Madan's narrative insists that the onus of these 'deliberate endeavours in transformation' (6) rests not in disabled individuals alone but in Indian society at large. First, the narrative, in presenting Madan's healing through the Deaf community and the improved possibilities of his life thereof, emphasises the significance of community networks in Deaf development. Second, in its insistence on the necessity of diminishing the communicative divide between the Deaf and the hearing; the former's access to full participation in activities both at home and the world, as well as improvement in material aspects of their lives, it etches out society's role in the same. Thereby it challenges both the normate's complacent dissociation from disability as well as third-person 'expert' opinions on disability (as an individual problem requiring medical cure) that make their way into the everyday and pass off as 'normal'.

That ISL has not yet been recognised as an official language under the Indian Constitution despite its large D/deaf population has been a recurring concern of Deaf activists (Friedner 2015; Kothari and Bhutoria 2020). The narrative underscores the pervasive ignorance in a majority of the Indian populace of the existence of Deaf worlds and Deaf cultures as well as the abysmal state of existing educational and professional opportunities for the D/deaf. 'Deaf people therefore generally believe that the State has failed to provide them with deaf [sic] development and that their social, moral, and economic practices are invisible to outsiders' (Friedner 2015, 3).

Narratives such as *Deaf in Delhi* posit themselves against the systemic invisibility of Deaf worlds in their foregrounding of the same. Further, they enable readers to heal from an ableist biomedical comprehension of Deafness in terms of cure by reorienting their focus towards Deaf sociality and urging them to take Deaf turns (Bechter 2009; Friedner 2015). They show how taking a Deaf turn enables us to step away from reductive attempts at the exclusion of bodily 'imperfection' and the insecurities engendered by the threat of our bodies being labelled 'discredited'/'discreditable'. Deaf narratives such as Vasishta's initiate us, instead, into a more critical and meaningful understanding of diversity that enables adaptability to the innate fragility of the human body and the contingencies it inevitably has to negotiate. They posit Deaf development and requisite transformations in the social machinery as the surest way forward for ensuring positive Deaf futures, free from associations of tragedy or stigma.

Notes

1   After James Woodward, this analysis follows the D/deaf dichotomy where 'Deaf' represents a person or a group as part of a social, cultural and linguistic minority while 'deaf' is understood in terms of impairment, a biological/medical understanding of the term, see Woodward (1972, 1–7).

2   For more on this concept, see Campbell (2009).

3   As Oliver Sacks has observed, if one does notice a delay in the intellectual maturation of congenitally deaf people, it mostly owes to the non-acquisition of language, whether spoken or signed, early in life. This would also hold true for a hearing individual who does not acquire any language in childhood. Not deafness, then, but the lack of access to language, often delays cognition in deaf people, see Sacks (1989).

4   This is another characteristic of ableism. Treating disability as an individual anomaly, it then asks disabled people to not be 'self-centred', to not languish in misery but to try and look at the 'brighter side of things' even as most hindrances they face in the fruition of their lives (as evident in Madan's narrative and several other narratives of disabled people) accrue not from their impairment(s) but from ableist, socially sanctioned barriers. Ableism simply refuses to acknowledge any contrary claim that might upset its reductive (il)logic. Here, Madan seems to have internalised this dictum of ableism, assuming sole responsibility for the difficulties he experiences owing to his deafness in trying to remain 'cheerful' and 'optimistic'. He has not yet acquired the resources to call ableism out.

5   This recurrent comparison between the small village town of Gagret and the metropolis of Delhi is not to establish rural areas as 'backward' or more prejudiced against disability than urban spaces. It is to draw attention to the skewed resource/information availability between the two as far as disability is concerned. While Delhi seemed to have a thriving Deaf culture and community, not an inkling of its presence had reached Gagret, underscoring the disparity in the disability experience based on geographical location even within the same nation.

6   A particularly useful term coined by disability scholar Rosemarie Garland-Thomson, 'normate' signifies all persons who possess and/or prize above all other forms of embodiment the apparently 'whole' 'perfect' body unmarked by stigma—in this context, by any form of impairment.

References

Bauman, H-Dirksen L. and J.M. Murray. 'Reframing: From Hearing Loss to Deaf Gain'. *Deaf Studies Digital Journal*, no. 1 (Fall 2009): 1–10.

Bechter, Frank. 'The Deaf Convert Culture and Its Lessons for Deaf Theory'. In *Open Your Eyes: Deaf Studies Talking*, edited by H-Dirksen L. Bauman, 60–79. Minnesota: University of Minnesota Press, 2008.

Broota, Sakshi. 'Concerns of People with Hearing Impairment in India'. Draft Report prepared for the National Centre for Promotion of Employment for Disabled People, New Delhi, 2005.

Campbell, Fiona. *The Contours of Ableism: The Production of Disability and Abledness*. London: Palgrave Macmillan, 2009.

Ferris, Jim. 'Cripples'. In *Facts of Life: Poems*, 7. UW-Madison: Parallel Press, 2005.

Friedner, Michelle. *Valuing Deaf Worlds in Urban India*. New Brunswick: Rutgers University Press, 2015.

Garland-Thomson, Rosemarie. *Extraordinary Bodies: Figuring Physical Disability in American Culture and Literature*. New York: Columbia University Press, 1997.

Goffman, Erving. *Stigma: Notes on the Management of Spoiled Identity*. Englewood Cliffs, New Jersey: Prentice-Hall, 1963.

Grosz, Elizabeth. 'Feminism, Materialism, and Freedom'. In *New Materialisms: Ontology, Agency, and Politics*, edited by D. Coole and S. Frost, 139–57. Durham and London: Duke University Press, 2010.

Kothari, V. and S. Bhutoria. 'Government Should Give Official Recognition to Indian Sign Language (ISL)'. *India Education Diary*, 2020. https://indiaeducationdiary.in/government-should-give-official-recognition-to-indian-sign-language-isl-vaibhav-kothari/#:~:text=Though%20home%20to%20one%20of,sign%20language%20under%20the%20Constitution (accessed 2 December 2021).

Mitchell, David and S. Snyder. *The Biopolitics of Disability: Liberalism, Ablenationalism, and Peripheral Embodiment*. Ann Arbor: University of Michigan Press, 2015.

Pandian, Anand. *Crooked Stalks: Cultivating Virtue in South Asia*. Durham and London: Duke University Press, 2009.

Sacks, Oliver. *Seeing Voices: A Journey into the World of the Deaf*. Berkeley: University of California Press, 1989.

Vasishta, Madan. *Deaf in Delhi: A Memoir*. Washington, DC: Gallaudet University Press, 2006.

Woodward, James. 'Implications for Sociolinguistic Research among the Deaf'. *Sign Language Studies*, 1, no. 1 (1972): 1–7.

13

CROSSING CULTURES IN STORYING DEPRESSION: *SHADOWS IN THE SUN* AS INTERSECTION AND DIALOGUE BETWEEN DISABILITY STUDIES AND MEDICAL HUMANITIES

Kaustabh Kashyap and Rakhee Kalita Moral

Introduction

Gayathri Ramprasad's memoir, *Shadows in the Sun*, chronicles a protracted struggle with mental illness. In narrating this harrowing journey, a tedious uphill battle rife with stigma and despair, Ramprasad places her experience of depression at the crossroads of culture and medicine. Her storytelling process articulates the inarticulate sense of shock she undergoes as her illness moves her towards a state of abjection. This reordering of her life, by placing it in a narrativised chronotope, allows her to comprehend the 'biographical interruption posed by illness' (Kangas 2001). It is an account like any illness narrative in that it moves away from the meta-narrative of normativity in depicting oneself caught up in 'the night side of life' (Sontag 1978). It ruptures the link to one's old self outside illness and new stories are woven through the fabric of one's illness experience.

Arthur Frank astutely observes that such illness stories of embodiment are dual in nature, tying together the personal and the social (1997). The personal aspect of the story draws attention to one's corporeality by vocalising the non-verbal cues of the body in pain via language. One seeks meaning through one's body in the face of overwhelming distress, trying to figure out coping mechanisms or a way of alleviating one's symptoms. This is the sufferer or patient actively engaging in an epistemic enquiry of one's physiological rupture; an enquiry into personal resilience as well as fragility. The social nature of the narrative relates to the dialogic framing of the story. The narrator dips into the cultural repository, the myths and superstitions centred on the illness, apart from using the language of biomedicine as a result of one's exposure to the world of medical practitioners.

Ramprasad's story of mental illness portrays depression by viewing the individual through a cross-cultural lens. Depression is treated as an unspeakable ailment, a taboo manifesting a fear of social othering in India. Her bio-psychosocial disability[1] that starts in late adolescence finds voice much later in the US after her marriage, when a mental breakdown makes it extremely difficult for her to function without medical care. The psychiatric nature of her disability catches her in a double-bind. On the one hand, her Indian upbringing instils in her the notion of the good woman, the mythologised goddess Sita who deals with suffering in stoic silence. And on the other hand, living in the US alerts her to the possibilities of independent living and access to healthcare without the fear of stigma. It is through this irreconcilable binary that Ramprasad's narrative sparks a debate on the politics of disability discourse and the need of healthcare practitioners to engage actively with lay accounts of illness. Her experience of alterity also complicates the hostile relationship between the social-constructionist model and the medical model of disability. As a result, her text becomes an intersecting cultural point for a dialogue between disability studies and medical humanities.

Disability Studies and Medical Humanities

Before taking up Ramprasad's text for a close reading of the cross-cultural anxieties vis-à-vis her condition, it is crucial to briefly delve into the incongruent historical origins of disability studies and medical humanities. This would be useful in comprehending the juxtaposition and engagement of these two disparate disciplines as read through the text. Disability studies grew out of the civil rights movement in the West during the late 20th century. It is an academic as well as an activist-based response to the normative paradigms found in the medical ideology and jargon of health practitioners who frame 'disability as a negative form of being' (Garland-Thomson 2013). This pathological medicalisation confines disability to biology, considering it as an ontological aberration 'to be cured, fixed or ameliorated through medical intervention' (Lau 2018).

Most disability scholars—in their indictment of the reductive medical gaze that segregates people into categories of normal and divergent based on their physical and/or mental disposition, which, in a way, aids ableist norms—focus on the social model of disability. Through this, they powerfully interrogate the 'affective, sensory, cognitive or architectural barriers' that society imposes upon those it deems disabled (Hall 2016). The social model distinguishes between impairment and disability. Impairment is defined as a biological limitation resulting from a person's physiology and/or mental functioning. It can mean 'lacking part or all of a limb, or having a defective limb, organ, or mechanism of the body' (Barnes and Mercer 2003). Disability is viewed as a social phenomenon through which people with impairments are placed in the kind of environment that marginalises them and 'excludes them from participation in the mainstream of social activities' (Barnes and Mercer 2003). Scholars powerfully expose the metaphorical and material barriers that stigmatise people with disabilities and turn them into objects of pity, repulsion or fear.

In studying disability with a diachronic emphasis, the fluidity and historical contingency of stigmatising behaviour is stressed upon (Goffman 1963). Based on social laws and customs, 'stigma can be transferred to different groups at different times', implying that disability is not a fixed, natural condition but created through the friction of linguistic sign systems with socio-cultural beliefs (Hall 2016). Like race, gender, class, caste and sexual orientation, disability becomes a category of identity constructed, negotiated and destabilised against normative formulations. It becomes a discursive political category that speaks against prejudicial social and medical paradigms. Although the rise in disability studies has not progressed through a linear trajectory across the world, its impact has varied across different disciplines (Hall 2016), it is already a well-established field that engages with disability as 'a civil and human rights issue, a minority identity, a sociological formation, a historical community, a diversity group, and a category of critical analysis in culture and the arts' (Garland-Thomson 2013).

On the other hand, medical humanities began in the medical institutions of the West, mainly the USA and UK, aided by the philanthropy of physicians (Herndl 2005) as a 'response to the overstressing of technological and scientific training of many physicians' (Lau 2018). While the term 'medical humanities' originated in the USA during the 1960s, it started gaining prominence in Britain by the last decade of the 20th century (Evans and Greaves 2010). As a broad discipline aimed at studying the interrelationship between medicine and culture to foreground the ethical and moral issues of healthcare, it utilises cultural artefacts to understand human problems beyond reductive medical diagnoses based on anatomy. It draws power from the arts and humanities to educate and sensitise students of medicine towards the cultural aspects of health. It uses fiction, drama, autobiographical genres and other art forms to alert physicians to complex storylines of illness that teach them to go beyond the myopic medical gaze of biomedicine. Pointing to Foucault's accusation, David Misselbrook, a general practitioner remarks:

doctors are doctor-oriented, not patient-oriented, and thus medicine creates an abusive power structure. Medical school has taught us more about biomedicine than about patients. The medical tribe tends to dominate rather than share. We control, stick people into appointment slots, strand them in waiting rooms ... and talk above their heads. (2013)

Medical humanities aims to, at least in theory, modify the medical gaze of pathologisation and dehumanisation of patients. Narrative medicine, one of its growing subfields, seeks to inculcate in medical practitioners 'the narrative competence to recognize, absorb, interpret, and be moved by the stories of illness' (Charon 2006). This can be seen as a literary turn in healthcare that has been growing since the 1960s when academicians and activists were overtly engaging in dismantling the hegemony of grand narratives. In the post-war era, in the face of rapid technological advances in medicine and the rise of bureaucracy and profit-driven policies, clinicians were falling back on the humanities as a sort of reconnection (Whitehead 2014). Their concern with disability and illness narratives meant the doctor was starting to witness the patient's side of the story. In fact, one of Michael Balint's earlier books, *The Doctor, His Patient and the Illness*, first published in 1957, envisages what he terms 'the long interview' to take a thorough medical history of the patients by empathetically participating in their lives. The doctor 'first recognize[s] the patient as a person' (Berger and Mohr 1997) and becomes a 'compassionate witness' (Whitehead 2014) in her story of crisis.

Disciplinary Divide and Shortcomings

Both medical humanities and disability studies employ methodological frameworks to comprehend the diversity of human embodiment. Disability studies, in wresting agency and advocacy for people with disabilities, powerfully exposes the 'ways in which medicine has historically held the institutional and cultural power to determine what is normal' (Lau 2018). It interrogates the pervasive ideology of able-bodiedness (and able-mindedness) that shapes human behaviour. Medical humanities trains physicians to go beyond the rigid and reductive nature of diagnoses and situate biomedicine in a cultural context. It grounds them to empathise with the heterogeneity of the illness experience by acknowledging the productive tension between arts and medicine. In such a scenario, despite disparate origins, it is not implausible to imagine a dialogue or crossover between the two fields. However, as Diane Price Herndl has observed, there is hardly any interaction between the two fields[2] (2005). Perhaps, the refusal of either field to engage with the other stems from their conceptual framing of disability. While disability studies usually locates disability in environments driven by ableist social mores, medical humanities locates it in the human body. This almost watertight demarcation (which is problematic as will be highlighted while analysing *Shadows in the Sun*) inhibits a productive dialogue between the two fields. Disability studies' central goal is to bring changes in socio-political policies to advocate for the rights of people with disabilities. Medical humanities, on the other hand, 'seeks to improve the status quo' of doctors (Herndl 2005). Although they draw upon literature and the power of narrative to formulate their goals, both of them seem to have different ends in mind. It is only when the two disciplines are thoroughly scrutinised that the shortcomings in one seem to address the limitations in the other.

The self-reflexivity present in disability studies scholarship has led Mark Osteen, Tobin Siebers, Michael Bérubé, Alison Kafer, Bill Hughes, Kevin Paterson and Margaret Price, among others, to critique the inadequacies of the social constructionist model. Osteen has found that disabilities which are hard to detect, not visible to the naked eye, have been invisible in the field (2008). The discipline relies on a neo-Cartesian duality that crudely separates mind and body, impairment and disability, failing to 'adequately theorize suffering, impairment and pain' (Hall 2016). Siebers's 'theory of complex embodiment' (2011) comprehends disability not simply 'in terms of disabling environments' effects on people's lived experience of the body, but also how factors like chronic pain and ageing derive from the body and shape the social' (Lau 2018). Bérubé takes to task the problem of disability scholars in ignoring the 'biological materiality of the body [which] is susceptible to a finite (and sometimes severely delimited) number of constructions' (2002). Herndl agrees with him and remarks that the 'scientific disciplines' would find it hard to engage with disability studies as it is 'committed to a model of an almost infinitely malleable social construction of the body' (2005). Kafer in *Feminist Queer Crip* argues on behalf of a political/relational model that seeks a readjustment of the social and medical model of disability. It 'reincorporates lived experiences of impairment and even desires for improvement and cure' (Lau 2018). Hughes and Paterson also remark that in the understandable but outright rejection of the medical model, in the move from the materialism of the body to its discursivity, disability studies courts a 'disembodied notion of disability' (1997). Similarly, Price, in 'The Bodymind Problem and the

Possibilities of Pain' (2014), has drawn attention to the need to address mental disabilities in disability studies. Taking the cue from trauma studies, she picks up the term 'bodymind' to complicate the crude binary of body and mind seen in the field's scholarship. She remarks that as per this figuration, 'because mental and physical processes not only affect each other but also give rise to each other—that is, because they tend to act as one, even though they are conventionally understood as two—it makes more sense to refer to them together, in a single term' (2014).

Similarly, scholars working in the field of medical humanities have also drawn attention to its failings. Herndl argues that courses on literature and medicine used to train medical professionals are not very keen on exploring (poststructural and postmodern) theory (2005). This makes it 'hard to get anyone to understand what it means to locate disease or disability somewhere other than in a concrete, physical body' (2005). She also remarks, 'even such a clearly definable disease as tuberculosis is deeply affected by social constructions like whether the disease is considered romantic or nasty or the degree to which the culture determines standards of treatment that might lead to patient noncompliance and the evolution of a more virulent strain of the disease' (2005). Modern medicine has moved physicians away from the concept of healing to fixing human bodies and minds. This traps them in the meta-narrative of normativity that fails to counter the hegemony of ableism. If medical humanities is to succeed in its objectives, it has to allow the more transgressive nature of the arts to be infused within the approach to medicine. Alan Bleakley accuses the field of a 'utilitarian bias' that promotes a simplistic dichotomy between sickness and well-being (2014). It fails to embrace complex narratives of disability and/or illness that do not follow a linear trail of diagnosis, treatment and cure. The field presents the arts as a 'tame' form of entertainment to students of medicine, Paul Ulhas Macneill argues, which fails to arrest the dominance of biomedicine (2011). Others like Anne Whitehead feel that the subfield of narrative medicine, in yoking the power of literature to 'empathetic training', may simply function as an additive leg for healthcare training (2014). It would not do much in allowing physicians to question their own methodological training that promotes ableism by viewing people with disabilities through the narrative of pathology. A rigorous medical humanities training implies alerting medical staff to structural inequalities and societal oppression that can exacerbate disabilities and diseases. Further, Claire Hooker and Estelle Noonan have also accused the field to be driven (solely) by Western imperialism and discuss the need for cultural heterogeneity to accommodate non-Western experiences of health and healthcare (2011).

Storying Depression in a Bio-Cultural Framework:
Disability and Biomedicine

Shadows in the Sun, while storying depression through a cross-cultural lens, allows for intersection and dialogue between disability studies and medical humanities. It can serve as a text to dwell upon bridging the shortcomings of the two fields and bring a more nuanced, intersectional and holistic understanding of disability and/or illness. Ramprasad's narrative foregrounds the socio-cultural stigma associated with her condition and highlights the role of health practitioners in listening, comforting and empathising with the accounts of their patients. Unlike radical feminist memoirs prevalent in the Western tradition that explore women's troubled relationship with medicine/psychiatry,[3] Ramprasad's story is not nearly as counter-diagnostic or subversive. It is a more balanced take on raising mental health awareness that seeks to bridge the gap between lay accounts of illness and medically driven discourse. It belongs to a growing body of life-writing on mental illness by women in India who are gradually breaking the silence on this sensitive and taboo topic.[4] By situating herself in the tug of war between her Indian heritage and the American experience, Ramprasad portrays the corporeality of depression that begins in adolescence and consumes her through her adult life after marriage as she moves to the US.

Ramprasad depicts her upbringing in a Hindu joint family in Bengaluru where sacred customs and rituals play a significant part. She grows up 'in a world sanctified by the Hindu gods and goddesses … of otherworldly tales, castles, flickering oil lamps, and fragrant sandalwood dreams' (2014). Despite such a hold of tradition on her life, there is also a cultural diversion towards adopting Western values. Her father 'rebelled against the ancient traditions of India and worshipped all things American' (Ramprasad 2014). This becomes more prominent after the death of the family patriarch, Ramprasad's grandfather, when the family breaks down into small nuclear units and starts shifting into different rental homes. Ramprasad's father encourages her to groom herself in Western attire, develop English table manners and aspire to a life in the US. On the contrary, her mother, despite accepting this Americanisation, 'stood steadfast in inculcating all things Indian' (Ramprasad 2014). She firmly upholds rules of gender conformity and expects Ramprasad, like her other daughter, to 'grow up to be like Sita, the revered epitome of Indian womanhood' (Ramprasad 2014). She wishes to see them daily involved in worship and transform into 'pious, self-sacrificing, ever-loving women of grace' (Ramprasad 2014). This turns her life into 'a dizzying blend of two cultures, two continents, worlds apart: the ancient East, India, and the modern West, America' (Ramprasad 2014).

This dichotomy starts troubling Ramprasad once she enters late adolescence. While her father approves of her desire to step outside the traditional feminine style, her mother shows abhorrence at her fascination for bell-bottoms and sleeveless tops. Once, after tweezing her eyebrows in a particular way, her mother explodes in anger and compares her to a prostitute. This affects her deeply. Ramprasad also becomes a victim of catcalling when she steps into puberty as she falls prey to the male gaze. She remarks that 'It didn't matter if they were as old as [her] or old enough to be [her] father, [she] was fair game to their sexual fantasies' (Ramprasad 2014). Unable to open up about her sexual harassment, Ramprasad suffers in silence. Further, after turning down the romantic advances of the student body president Gopal, she is verbally threatened by him in public. Her friend Jaya informs her that Gopal could have had a hand in her failed grade as revenge for rejecting him and that he plans to rape her during the final year college excursion.

Ramprasad refuses to seek professional help or any form of intervention. She internalises her mother's unquestioning adherence to patriarchal norms and deems herself powerless to do anything. In navigating the turbulent episodes of adolescence, Ramprasad finds it difficult to turn to her parents because at her home, 'strength is measured by how well one can suppress emotions, not express them' (2014). Eventually, she falls into 'the night side of life' (Sontag 1978) and her 'crying spells spill into days and weeks' (Ramprasad 2014). 'Adolescent depression', as Ramprasad terms it in hindsight by relying on biomedical knowledge, allows her to contextualise and address her condition which her culture could not comprehend (2014). During the onset of her illness, when she loses weight, is unable to keep down food without vomiting and finds it overwhelming to do even simple daily chores, her parents lack insight into her psychosomatic ailment. They take her to physicians who, after several procedures, 'unite in their opinion that there is nothing wrong with [her]' (Ramprasad 2014). One of them sees it as 'adolescent angst' and calls her 'a drama queen asking for undue attention instead of navigating the roadbumps of life with maturity and grace' (Ramprasad 2014).

While the physicians fail to treat her, the home environment too remains ignorant of her plight. Her mother resorts to superstition by blaming it on the 'evil eye' and performs *drishti*[5] on her (Ramprasad 2014). Her father's concern turns to annoyance as she consistently throws up and is unable to fathom the mysterious bodily pangs that torment her. Ramprasad cries uncontrollably and withdraws into her private shell, longing for family support. Reading her condition from a disability studies perspective would enable the field not only to grapple with 'what able-mindedness might mean in relation to able-bodiedness', it would also open the discipline for self-scrutiny in order to take mental illness as seriously as physical disability (Kafer 2013). Ramprasad's inability to perform her daily life under the gaze of normativity makes her condition in Garland-Thomson's term, an act of 'misfitting' (2011). A feminist materialist disability studies concept, misfit 'reflects the shift in feminist theory from an emphasis on the discursive toward the material by centring its analytical focus on the co-constituting relationship between flesh and environment' (Garland-Thomson 2011). Although Garland-Thomson draws attention to madness as a historical position where disabled people have been relegated as 'misfits', she develops the concept of misfitting almost entirely for physical disabilities. It is Margaret Price who considers its potential for mental disability—emphasising how 'such disabilities are not exactly "visible" or "invisible", but *intermittently* apparent' (2014; emphasis added).

Ramprasad's condition of misfitting arises out of the interaction between the inexplicable pain in her bodymind and her culture's misrecognition of depression as adolescent rage or improper behaviour. Her parents and Indian physicians, unable to translate her call for help, blame her as 'hypersensitive, weak, ungrateful, self-centred, immature' (Ramprasad 2014). A disability studies reading that incorporates mental illness perspectives can show that although her pain is real (and disabling in itself), it is the environment's apathy towards Ramprasad's experience that worsens her situation. She is made to feel guilty for projecting her pain. However, not seeking a remedy to alleviate her pain, whether or not the environment is disabling, does not assuage her suffering one bit. Her condition, therefore, draws attention to 'the possibility that some aspects of disabled bodymind are distinctly undesirable' (Price 2014). It asks disability studies to theorise kinds of suffering that are not directly produced by social or political oppression. Granted that Ramprasad's depression can be seen in a significant way as a response to the pressures of being a conforming, docile female. But her prolonged suffering that continues to haunt her for many years post-adolescence also throws light on the 'complex web of genetic, gender, psychosocial, hormonal, and neurobiological factors that define clinical depression and anxiety' (Ramprasad 2014). When both her siblings are diagnosed with mental illness later, and her father's secret struggle with depression is also revealed, Ramprasad's consistent gauging of her illness under (Western) biomedical terminology becomes clear. In our current scenario, the last resort to unravel the meanings of a bodymind in pain is a good doctor. One who empathises with the patient and tries to find solutions without the urge of pathologisation or talking above her head.

In a way, a reading of the text grounded in medical humanities becomes essential.

Ramprasad's initial struggles are exacerbated by the fact that the doctors doggedly hold onto the belief that her illness is unreal, 'all in [her] head' (2014). They use their medical authority to dismiss the lay narrative of her bodily responses, and, unable to dig deeper into her condition, make a misdiagnosis. She is prescribed anti-nausea medication that does little to relieve her. However, she is acutely aware of her own biological disposition:

> Something is wrong with me, I know. And it is certainly not my stomach that is sick; I suspect I am going mad. I am terrified I will end up like the short, bald man living up the street behind the barbed-wire fence, pacing up and down all day, mumbling to himself. I have seen the neighborhood boys pelt stones at him, call him huccha— madman. (Ramprasad 2014)

When the doctors fail to console her, Ramprasad starts questioning her own sanity and seems to move, at least in her mind, from a state of agency to abjection. Her plea for assistance debunks the myth of seeing madness as rebellion. Mental illness becomes, 'far from being a form of contestation … a request for help, a manifestation both of cultural impotence and of political castration' (Felman 1997). Afraid of being stigmatised, her parents hide her medical history from everybody. Ramprasad plays along with their denial of her illness while suffering privately. Meanwhile, her marriage is fixed and plans are in place for settling down in the US. She goes through the marriage rituals, without informing her in-laws about her condition, under a 'façade of normalcy' and later moves to America with Ram, her husband (Ramprasad 2014).

Initially, Ramprasad is busy adjusting to life in a new country and her husband has no awareness of her past struggles. He does not know that soon after marriage when she goes back home, Ramprasad falls sick again. Her father makes her feel guilty and asks her to will herself to get better after keeping her on IV for some time. The doctor who treats her again misreads her symptoms as anxiety about leaving home in the absence of her full history. In the US, her symptoms relapse for a while. She starts becoming acquainted with the American way of life. Even though her mother had asked her to treat her husband like a god, Ramprasad's husband's modern approach to life seeks to ease her wifely duties as an Indian woman. He does not expect her to touch his feet or wake up before him and allows her to bask in her newfound independence. However, after the birth of her first child, postpartum blues set in. As the child starts growing up, Ramprasad starts losing her grip on herself. She is plagued by 'irrational questions [that] repeat themselves in [her] head' (Ramprasad 2014). There are times when the intrusive thoughts become so bothersome that she bangs her head repeatedly on the wall. She feels that doing this temporarily causes 'physical pain [that] dulls the emotional turmoil' (Ramprasad 2014). Price draws attention to this underexplored area in disability studies regarding 'mental pain so severe that self-injury appears to be the best possible response' (2014). She calls it 'exceptional experiences of disability, those that are (or seem to be) painful in and of themselves' (Ramprasad 2014). When Ram discovers her in this state, he blames the isolating and lonely life in the US and makes arrangements for his wife and child to spend some time in India.

In India, Ramprasad's condition quickly worsens. She sinks 'deeper and deeper into the growing darkness of [her] mind … mute with guilt and grief, paralyzed by a profound sadness' (Ramprasad 2014). Her parents try to turn her thoughts towards Indian spirituality, prayers and yogic chants to make her feel better but they fail. Ramprasad starts despising god, unable to fathom how someone so compassionate could give her so much pain. It is only when she is plagued with suicidal thoughts and pleads to her parents to help her end her life that they plan a visit to the psychiatrist. A medical humanities reading of her condition would show how a misconstrued application of the medical gaze, in the absence of the full patient's history, disempowered Ramprasad for so long. Her encounter with Dr Kiran, the psychiatrist, enables her for the first time in her life to understand her mysterious illness. After hearing her mother out, the doctor tells them that Ramprasad has 'clinical depression' (Ramprasad 2014). Although she is relieved to find out that her 'illness has a name', she is also in deep shock because of the 'stigma associated with depression' (2014). Dr Kiran tells her that 'depression doesn't discriminate' and that it is 'a very common mental illness—debilitating, but treatable' (Ramprasad 2014). But he comes to the diagnosis quickly without taking Ramprasad's history or digging into the social and gendered nature of her pain. He simply sees it as 'caused by chemical imbalances in the brain' and prescribes medication (Ramprasad 2014). A medical humanities training would ask the physician to show more patience and caution, locating medicine's value in an uncertain, interpretive culture, than one of authoritarian certainty. His quick jump into treatment fails to trace the material and discursive narrative of his patient from the beginnings of her illness and overwhelms her with his medical authority. However, Ramprasad does not blame the doctor squarely; she feels it was both her and her mother's ignorance that hindered them from comprehending that '[her] past trauma' which they kept from the doctor, 'is related to [her] present breakdown' (Ramprasad 2014). Contrary to expectations, medication aggravates her suicidal ideation. Ramprasad makes two suicide attempts and her condition draws attention to the limits of medicine that physicians rarely accede to accept. Labelling an illness is one thing; finding a treatment that caters holistically to the patient's needs is another. Medical humanities, in its more radical form, asks doctors to be sceptical of their own treatment, in case their prescribed remedy fails. A 'rigorous humanities teaching can develop an orientation toward uncertainty, knowledge, and action that characterizes the best physicians' (Belling 2010).

Helpless in the face of failing treatment, Ramprasad's doctor administers electroconvulsive therapy (ECT)[6] and eventually, her in-laws and her husband come to know of her condition. So far in the journey through her illness, Ramprasad views her non-normative experiences by connecting her disability with a sense of abjection. The fear and distress engendered by the taboo around mental illness discourse or rather the lack of it (in India), when Ramprasad was diagnosed, keeps her from exploring her trauma securely and openly in a safe environment. Her in-laws and her husband, much to her dismay, turn to special pujas to appease the gods for they attribute her sufferings to her previous sins.[7] When that proves futile, her mother-in-law 'summons a priest to exorcise' her who molests her in the name of curing her of her demons (Ramprasad 2014). Till this point in the narrative, in traversing the mythic, social and medical dimensions of her illness, Ramprasad evokes the strand of chaos narrative espoused by Arthur Frank. Depression throws Ramprasad's life completely out of order and 'disintegration [becomes her] encompassing reality' (2014).

Bridging Disciplines and the Uneven Road to Recovery

Mental illness, at least in a case like Ramprasad's, seems to bring both disability studies and medical humanities to a methodological impasse. She can neither claim depression as part of her identity, take pride or find joy in the condition of her bodymind, nor succeed in finding a cure in Western biomedicine. It opens the chasm where disability studies scholars need to engage in a dialogue with scholars from the medical humanities to formulate dynamic and non-Western approaches for navigating the challenges posed by mental illness. While disability studies can equip medical humanities to look beyond biomedicine and pay more attention to societal stigmas that exacerbate certain disabilities, medical humanities can, by depathologising illnesses and empathising with the patient's perspective, build more faith in people with disabilities who seek or are desperately in need of medical care. Disability studies can demonstrate that the linear nature of diagnosis does not parallel the complex and circuitous trajectory of a patient suffering from chronic illness. Medical humanities, taking this cue, can adopt practices in healthcare that are more patient-centred and flexible to patients' needs. Both fields must constantly seek to evolve and be willing to raise radical questions, given that complications arise in matters of disability and healthcare. The need to bring them into dialogue becomes more evident after Ramprasad moves back to the US again with her medical history from India and her uneven journey towards recovery starts.

The narrative of depression from this point onwards gradually starts entering both the quest phase and the restitution phase often found in illness narratives (Frank 1997). This is when the hope of getting better (restitution) dawns upon her and Ramprasad decides to take her suffering as a journey (quest) to comprehend her condition and regain her own distinct voice and her agency as she tries to bridge the gap between her Indian upbringing and American experience. The unmanageable symptoms despite medication push her towards psychotherapy which opens her towards the possibilities of a 'talking cure'. Initially, she is unsure how narrating her 'pain can be healing' but her psychotherapist Dr Lin helps her immensely in contextualising her condition. By enquiring about her life, relationships, marriage, the cultural conditioning in India and the experience of life in America, Dr Lin clinically assists her in destabilising the taboo around depression and coming to terms with it. Ramprasad remarks that Dr Lin listens to her with empathy and compassion, trying to comprehend the complications of her Indo-American life and seeks to identify the polar cultural forces that shake up her core.

When the medical gaze accommodates the lay experience of illness, biomedicine rises above the atomistic and materialistic paradigms, able to comprehend a 'more complete conception of human nature' (Macnaughton 2011). In Dr Lin, Ramprasad finds a maternal figure who empowers her to fight the stigma around mental illness in her culture and guides her to put her well-being above the need to please everyone else. She introduces her to 'cognitive-behavioural therapy (CBT)'[8] and guides her to 'identify and acknowledge emotions [she has] repressed over the years' to gain control over them (Ramprasad 2014). These newfound skills, along with exercise and progressive relaxation, enable her to feel better and she eventually decides to taper off the medications. However, after some improvement, Ramprasad relapses into an even more turbulent state.

Her inability to soothe her excruciating mental agony, the failure of medication, suicide attempts, hospitalisations, her second pregnancy and her husband's worries if they can continue living in America constantly unnerve her. But it is her mother's letter addressed to her that brings her to a complete breakdown. In it, she blames her daughter for not praying with a 'purer heart' that keeps her from getting better (2014). Maybe her mother's tone is casual but Ramprasad's state of mind finds it unnerving. In anger, she tears up the letter and tosses it at the god's altar in her kitchen. What she calls experiencing 'an utter state of dissociation' makes her head to the backyard where she starts digging the ground furiously so she can bury herself. In this dissociative state, Ramprasad forgets she has a biological mother. She identifies herself with her mother's revered Goddess Sita, 'the epitome of womanhood' who retreats 'back into the womb of her real mother—Mother Earth— at the end of her trials in life' (2014). This leads to her hospitalisation in a mental institute and therein the quest phase of her narrative starts.

Although Ramprasad initially views her confinement in the seclusion room with Foucauldian suspicion and the presence of a surveillance camera adds to her paranoia, once she moves to the unlocked ward and shares the room with another patient, her views on the disciplinary procedures change drastically. The hospital, instead of being a fearful asylum of segregation, becomes a convalescent home where she gains greater awareness of her troubled bodymind and learns coping strategies to improve her condition. In group therapy sessions she absorbs multifaceted ways of managing her symptoms and a class on religion and spirituality makes her ponder over her own relationship with god, whether her religious upbringing has liberated or confined her. Meeting people with mental health conditions helps her disrupt the ableist binary of sanity and insanity. She finds acceptance in the arms of strangers that she fails to find in her family. She meets Sanya, a patient with bipolar disorder who accepts her condition and converses about her self-admittance into the hospital several times without fear or regret. Another stranger who has been battling depression since she was eighteen gives her strength to battle her illness. Ramprasad is especially surprised by the humility of a resident doctor who transcends the doctor-patient hierarchy through small acts of kindness. She writes that 'the ordinary gesture of [Dr Scott] sitting next to [her] and partaking in [her] meal erases long-established boundaries between a physician and patient, and reminds [her] of [their] common humanity' (2014).

Ramprasad's narrative sets in motion the need for disability studies to accommodate stories where the role of medicine and healthcare services cannot be ignored. It can initiate the sciences in humanising health practices by illuminating the oppressive cultural hierarchy that has existed for centuries between physicians and patients, which has denied lay narratives much say. It can, through the more willing and radical aspect of the medical humanities, highlight the reasonable fear that people with disabilities have of health practitioners when it comes to medical treatment, given that they have been historically 'isolated, incarcerated, observed, written about, operated on, instructed, implanted, regulated, treated, institutionalized, and controlled to a degree probably unequal to that experienced by any other minority group' (Davis 2006). Ramprasad's first diagnosis of clinical depression in 1987 in India reasonably elicited panic because such a label of illness was equated with going mad in those days. Physicians cannot afford to overlook, in embracing and promoting humane healthcare regimes, the sinister history of illegal madhouses that committed the worst kinds of atrocities upon those abandoned by relatives who feared the degradation of their social status because of being associated with the mentally ill (Scull 2015). Training in disability studies can teach medical humanities scholars the powerful hold of pathological language over people with disabilities. Such language defines and ascribes them with negative qualities that robs them of their self-worth and their agency in defining themselves. Ramprasad's crisis worsens because the society she grows up in makes her either ignore her condition or exaggerate it through stigmatising notions of mental illness. She equates her spells of depression with madness and fears of being disowned by her family and ostracised by her community. When disability studies and medical humanities engage in dialogue through such narratives of illness, the unaccounted experiences of people with disabilities can aid healthcare practitioners in debunking ableist stereotypes and assist them in comprehending the cultural manifestation of bodyminds in pain. Ramprasad's culture fails to discern her trauma and a foreign culture enables her to contextualise the material nature of her mental illness.

Ironically though, it is only when Ramprasad returns to her Indian roots that her proper recovery starts. American culture familiarises her with a biomedical diagnosis that provides phenomenological explanations of her illness. It provides her with techniques to contain her illness but that only grants her temporary relief. She takes heed of an intern she meets at the hospital who advises her 'to learn to practice *pranayama*, a meditation discipline involving breath control, originating in ancient India, and transcendental meditation to heal [her] mind and foster overall well-being' (Ramprasad 2014). With the help of a teacher, she starts adopting these practices and gradually moves towards a deeper and more profound understanding of her condition. She finds it ironic that she had to travel miles away and lose her sanity and learn Indian 'life-affirming practices' from an American practitioner (Ramprasad 2014). Although Ramprasad still faces depression occasionally, her bodymind is now able to get a better grip on her condition and manage its symptoms effectively. She writes that she develops a scepticism towards Western medicine as her awareness about Eastern methods of healing grows.

Despite the side effects of Western medicine that increases her agitation, depression and suicidal ideation, she does concede to admitting that cognitive-behavioural therapy helped her in finding a temporary sense of stability. However, Western medicine, she feels, is limited by its approach of controlling symptoms alone. On the other hand, Eastern medicine's holistic approach allows for a wholesome reintegration as it embraces the connections between the mind, the body and the spirit. She bluntly goes on to state that "wellness does not come encapsulated in a pill that can be patented by pharmaceutical companies and traded for profits" (Ramprasad 2014). Metaphorically, this gesture can be interpreted as a sort of homecoming, of seeking her roots by navigating the terrains of her mental health.

Going beyond Disciplinary Limitations

Disability studies can alert medical humanities to the complex nature of disability and/or chronic conditions that cannot be explained away by reductive diagnoses. Since the bodymind is always in flux, it is more meaningful to take a nuanced approach to what counts as good health and what counts as illness, rather than using an ableist, solely medical definition to create a binary opposition between them. Some narratives of disability are not easily apparent. The question of what it means to be in unbearable pain, despite the absence of social barriers, needs to be better explored in disability studies. Medical humanities scholars and physicians can make healthcare more humane and empathetic by taking in the needs of people with disabilities and funding programmes to bring contradictory and radical voices together to find pluralistic and diverse methodologies that traditional biomedicine seems to limit. Disability studies and medical humanities together could translate theory into praxis and fight cultural stigmas centred on disabilities, enhance and amplify the stories of people in need of healthcare and make physicians more willing to participate with humility in their patients' moments of crisis. They can, together, walk the talk on exploring the complex nature of human embodiment. But there are caveats in both the fields for which answers are still forthcoming. Some of them are:

1. How will a more rounded theory of disability studies that goes beyond the neo-Cartesian duality of the bodymind look like? How far will the theory of bodymind complicate or simplify this dilemma?
2. What does a disability studies perspective that fully accommodates experiences of unbearable (and invisible) pain look like?

3. How will disability studies explore exceptional cases of self-harm or suicidal behaviour, or cases where the way towards self-sufficiency is through interdependence, whether willing or unwilling?

4. Can medical humanities actually train physicians to critique their own medical training and their practices and enable them to go beyond the confines of reductive diagnosis?

5. How can medical humanities make radical changes in healthcare to accommodate the needs and perspectives of people with illnesses that are not apparent and those who cannot advocate for themselves?

6. Can medical humanities truly make use of literary narratives like *Shadows in the Sun* and accede to the limits of Western medicine while embracing alternative paradigms of healing?

Notes

1 A bio-psychosocial approach to disability takes into account the complicated interaction of biological, physiological and social factors in comprehending the concept of health and healthcare.

2 Diane Price Herndl, in her essay *Disease versus Disability: The Medical Humanities and Disability Studies*, mentions that except for Tom Couser, most disability studies and medical humanities scholars are not citing each other, which makes her suspicious that they are not reading the same texts.

3 See Kaysen (1993); Slater (2011); Hornbacher (2009).

4 See Bhatt (2019); Bahuguna (2021).

5 An Indian ritual of ridding the evil eye believed to be brought about by a malevolent glare.

6 Electroconvulsive therapy (ECT) is done under general anaesthesia where electric currents are passed through the brain to trigger brain seizures and manage mental illness in the short term. Although it is considered inhuman by many as it is usually forced upon the patient and can result in memory disturbances, some psychiatrists still see it as a last resort to treat depression so severe that it puts the patient at risk of suicide.

7 Hinduism believes in reincarnation and attributes present life sufferings to bad actions or *karma* in past lives.

8 CBT is a kind of psychotherapeutic treatment that helps people identify and change their negative thought patterns that cause them distress and affect their day-to-day living.

References

Bahuguna, Urvashi. *No Straight Thing Was Ever Made*. India: Viking, Penguin Random House, 2021.

Balint, Michael. *The Doctor, His Patient and the Illness.* Edinburgh and London: Churchill Livingstone, 1964.

Barnes, Colin and G. Mercer. *Disability.* Cambridge, UK: Polity Press, 2003.

Belling, Catherine. 'Sharper Instruments: On Defending the Humanities in Undergraduate Medical Education'. *Academic Medicine*, no. 85 (2010): 938–40.

Berger, John and Jean Mohr. *A Fortunate Man: The Story of a Country Doctor.* New York: Vintage, 1997.

Bérubé, M. 'Afterword: If I Should Live So Long'. In *Disability Studies: Enabling the Humanities*, edited by Sharon L. Snyder, Brenda Jo Brueggemann, and Rosemarie Garland-Thomson, 337–43. New York: Modern Language Association of America, 2002.

Bhatt, Shaheen. *I've Never Been (Un)Happier.* India: Penguin eBury Press, 2019.

Bleakley, Alan. 'Towards a "Critical Medical Humanities"'. In *Medicine, Health and the Arts: Approaches to the Medical Humanities*, edited by Victorian Bates, Alan Bleakley and Sam Goodman, 17–26. Canada and New York: Routledge, 2014.

Charon, Rita. *Narrative Medicine: Honoring the Stories of Illness.* New York: Oxford University Press, 2006.

Davis, Lennard J. 'Introduction'. In *The Disability Studies Reader*, edited by Lennard J. Davis, xv–xviii. London and New York: Routledge, 2006.

Evans, Howell Martin and David Alan Greaves. '10 Years of Medical Humanities: A Decade in the Life of a Journal and a Discipline'. NCBI, 2010. https://www.ncbi.nlm.nih.gov/pmc/articles/PMC3779829/ (accessed 25 May 2022).

Felman, Shoshana. 'Women and Madness: The Critical Phallacy'. In *Feminisms: An Anthology of Literary Theory and Criticism,* edited by Robyn R. Warhol and Diane Price Herndl, 7–20. New Brunswick, New Jersey: Rutgers University Press, 1997.

Frank, Arthur W. *The Wounded Storyteller: Body, Illness and Ethics.* Chicago: The University of Chicago Press, 1997.

Garland-Thomson, Rosemarie. 'Misfits: A Feminist Materialist Disability Concept'. *Hypatia,* 26, no. 3 (2011): 591–609.

———. 'Disability Studies: A Field Emerged'. *American Quarterly,* 65, no. 4 (2013): 915–26.

Goffman, Erving. *Stigma: Notes on the Management of Spoiled Identity.* New Jersey: Prentice-Hall, 1963.

Hall, Alice. *Literature and Disability.* London and New York: Routledge, 2016.

Herndl, Diane Price. 'Disease versus Disability: The Medical Humanities and Disability Studies'. *Publications of the Modern Language Association (PMLA),* 120, no. 2 (2005): 593–98.

Hooker, Claire and Estelle Noonan. 'Medical Humanities as Expressive of Western Culture'. *Medical Humanities,* 37 (2011): 79–84.

Hornbacher, Marya. *Wasted: A Memoir of Anorexia and Bulimia.* New York: HarperCollins, 2009.

Hughes, Bill and Kevin Paterson. 'The Social Model of Disability and the Disappearing Body: Towards a Sociology of Impairment'. *Disability and Society,* 12, no. 2 (1997): 325–40.

Hurwitz, Brian. 'Medical Humanities: Lineage, Excursionary Sketch and Rationale'. *Journal of Medical Ethics,* 39, no. 11 (2013): 672–74.

Kafer, Alison. *Feminist, Queer, Crip.* Indiana: Indiana University Press, 2013.

Kangas, Ilka. 'Making Sense of Depression: Perceptions of Melancholia in Lay Narratives'. *Health,* 5, no. 1 (2001): 76–92.

Kaysen, Susanna. *Girl, Interrupted.* New York: Vintage Books, 1993.

Lau, Travis Chi Wing. 'Taking Stock: Disability Studies and the Medical Humanities', *Medical Health Humanities,* 2018. https://medicalhealthhumanities. com/2018/03/14/taking-stock-disabilitystudies-and-the-medical-humanities/ (accessed 14 May 2022).

Macnaughton, Jane. 2011. '"Medical Humanities" Challenge to Medicine'. NCBI, 2011. https://www.ncbi.nlm.nih.gov/pmc/articles/PMC4439737/ (accessed 29 May 2022).

Macneill, Ulhas Paul. 'The Arts and Medicine: A Challenging Relationship'. *Medical Humanities,* 37 (2011): 85–90.

Misselbrook, David. 2013. 'Foucault'. NCBI, 2013. https://www.ncbi.nlm.nih. gov/pmc/articles/PMC4439737/ (accessed 29 May 2022).

Montagu, M.F. Ashley. *Studies and Essays Offered to George Sarton.* New York: Schuman, 1947.

Osteen, Mark. 'Autism and Representation: A Comprehensive Introduction'. In *Autism and Representation,* edited by Mark Osteen, 1–47. New York: Routledge, 2008.

Price, Margaret. 'The Bodymind Problem and the Possibilities of Pain'. *Hypatia,* 30, no. 1 (2014): 1–17.

Ramprasad, Gayathri. *Shadows in the Sun.* Minnesota: Hazelden, 2014.

Scull, Andrew. *Madness in Civilization: A Cultural History of Insanity from the Bible to Freud, from the Madhouse to Modern Medicine.* Canada and New Jersey, USA: Princeton University Press, 2015.

Siebers, Tobin. *Disability Theory.* Michigan: The University of Michigan Press, 2011.

Slater, Lauren. *Lying: A Metaphorical Memoir.* New York: Penguin, 2011.

Sontag, Susan. *Illness as Metaphor.* New York: Farrar, Straus and Giroux, 1978.

Styron, William. *Darkness Visible: A Memoir of Madness.* New York: Open Road Media, 2010.

Whitehead, Anne. 'The Medical Humanities: A Literary Perspective'. In *Medicine, Health and the Arts: Approaches to the Medical Humanities,* edited by Victoria Bates, Alan Bleakley and Sam Goodman, 107–27. Canada and New York: Routledge, 2014.

ABOUT THE EDITOR AND CONTRIBUTORS

The Editor

Someshwar Sati is a professor in the Department of English, Kirori Mal College. He is also the coordinator of the Centre of Disability Research and Training (CDRT) of the college and the chairperson of the Indian Disability Studies Collective (IDSC). Currently, he is engaged in compiling narratives of disability in various regional Indian languages. His latest publications include *Disability in Translation: The Indian Experience* (Routledge, 2019) and *Reclaiming the Disabled Subject: Representing Disability in Short Fiction*, Volume 1 (Bloomsbury, 2022). He is a recipient of the National Award for the Empowerment of Persons with Disabilities in 2022, bestowed by the Ministry of Social Justice and Empowerment, Government of India.

The Contributors

Deepak Kumar Gupta is an assistant professor of English at Motilal Nehru College (Evening), University of Delhi. He is also a doctoral fellow in the Department of Humanities and Social Sciences, Indian Institute of Technology (IIT) Delhi. His areas of interest include literary disability studies, novels in India, Urdu poetry and Japanese language and culture. He also writes ghazals and renders poetic translations. He was conferred the Indira Award for academic excellence by the Ministry of Education of the Delhi Government. He has been part of the inter-ministerial and University Grants Commission (UGC) expert committees to ensure accessibility and inclusivity in higher education.

Karuna Rajeev teaches English at Lady Shri Ram College for Women. She completed her PhD from Jawaharlal Nehru University (JNU), New Delhi in 2021. The title of her thesis is 'The Deceits of Marie Corelli: Gender, Narrative and the Popular'. Her areas of research interest are 19th-century literature, narrative discourse, and literary and cultural disability studies. She has presented papers and published in these areas.

Kaustabh Kashyap is a UGC-JRF (University Grants Commission-Junior Research Fellow) scholar pursuing his PhD in the field of disability studies and medical humanities from Cotton University,

Guwahati. His works have been published in *The Assam Tribune*, *The Reading Hour*, *Vayavya*, *Erothanatos* and *Rupkatha*.

Malvika Jayakumar is currently a PhD scholar at IIT Bombay. She is researching the works of the Hindi author, Rahul Sankrirtyayan and as a corollary to the specific research questions in her thesis, she is also interested in travel writing and the intersections of history and literature. Apart from her research topic, Jayakumar has also delved into Fyodor Dostoevsky's works, literature in the Meiji and post-Meiji eras and disability studies. She graduated with a bachelor's degree in English literature from Hans Raj College, University of Delhi in 2019 and also achieved a master's degree in the same subject from St Stephen's College, University of Delhi in 2021. Jayakumar is also the winner of the autumn session of the Oceanvale Workshop (2019) conducted by Kirori Mal College, University of Delhi.

Mansi Grover has a doctorate from Jamia Millia Islamia, New Delhi. For her PhD, she examined the representation of women with disabilities in Hindi cinema since 1970. She also practices theatre and works with a Delhi-based theatre group. Her areas of interest include cultural studies, disability studies, feminist studies, age studies, film studies, and performance studies.

Priyam Sinha is a doctoral candidate in South Asian Studies at the National University of Singapore. Her dissertation foregrounds the production, representation, reception and circulation of a 'disability affect' in 'new' Bollywood. She provides an interdisciplinary engagement with film studies, media ethnography, affect theory, production cultures, disability studies and gender studies. Sinha's research articles have been published in *The Economic and Political Weekly*, *The Journal of Indian and Asian Studies* and *The Routledge Handbook of Exclusion, Inequality and Stigma in India*. She has forthcoming publications in *Media, Culture and Society* and *South Asian Diaspora*.

Rakhee Kalita Moral is an associate professor at the Department of English, Cotton University, Guwahati. A post-doctoral fellow in gender studies at the Nehru Memorial Museum and Library, New Delhi (2013–15), she is currently the coordinator of the Centre for Women's Studies, Cotton University. In 2017, she joined the Humanities across Borders Program of the International Institute of Asian Studies (IIAS), Leiden University, USA, which aimed at decolonising knowledge through new pedagogic interventions in universities across the world. This has led her to conduct research on women through their narratives in Northeast India. Currently, she is collaborating with Jadavpur University's School of Women's Studies (SWS), on a research project in oral histories, memories and women's movements (2019–20) as a Rashtriya Uchchatar Shiksha Abhiyan (RUSA) expert and a visiting faculty for 2020.

Rimjhim Bhattacherjee, is an assistant professor of English at Udaynarayanpur Madhabilata Mahavidyalaya, Howrah. She received her doctoral degree from the University of Calcutta, where her research focused on the representations of disabled sexualities in Indian writing in English. She has been awarded gold medals at both the BA and MA levels from Jadavpur University. With a keen interest in disability studies, gender studies, Indian writing in English and women's writing, Dr Bhattacherjee is a passionate advocate for inclusive literary analysis and social justice.

Sanket Sakar is currently a PhD research candidate in literary studies at the Department of Humanities and Social Sciences, IIT Madras. He has completed his bachelor's and master's in English literature from the University of Delhi. He has presented several papers on themes related to disability, aesthetics, cinema and affect at various national and international conferences. Sakar's intended doctoral research concerns the multisensory aesthetics of disability representation in contemporary Indian narratives.

Shilpa Das teaches at the National Institute of Design (NID), Ahmedabad. An alumna of JNU, New Delhi and the Tata Institute of Social Studies (TISS), Mumbai, she has cumulative work experience of three decades in the education, publishing and voluntary sectors. Disability studies is one of the various courses she teaches at NID and elsewhere. At NID, she has been involved in the two-year project on strategic behavioural change concerning persons with disabilities for Handicap International and the Department of Health and Family Welfare for the Government of Gujarat. She is on the advisory group of the Missing Billion Initiative & Philips Inclusive Health Facility Co-Design Project in London. (Philips and the Missing Billion Initiative are partnering to define and design an optimal inclusive healthcare facility model at the primary-care level). She is also on the board of advisors, Centre for Disability Research and Training, Kirori Mal College.

Shilpaa Anand is an associate professor in the Department of Humanities and Social Sciences at the BITS-Pilani Hyderabad Campus in India. She has a PhD in disability studies from the University of Illinois at Chicago and an MA in English from the University of Hyderabad. Her research interests include literary and cultural disability studies, the historiography of disability and culturally different concepts of corporeality. Her doctoral work explored the conceptual histories of disability in the Indian context. She moderates a lively email list called Disability Studies India and has co-edited multiple issues on disability for the web magazine *Café Dissensus*.

Smriti Verma is an incoming DPhil student at the faculty of English, University of Oxford. She has previously studied at the University of Delhi and Shiv Nadar University, where she worked as a research and teaching assistant in the Department of English. In the past, she worked at Akar Prakar as a gallery assistant and in the field of arts education with Slam Out Loud. Her current research interests involve contemporary women's auto-fiction, narrative form, literary lineage and global feminist praxis within popular culture. She has an abiding interest in poetry and creative non-fiction and works as a poetry editor for *Inklette* and *The Ideate Review*.

Tayyaba Rizwan holds a master's in English literature from JNU, New Delhi and a diploma in conflict management and peace building from Lady Shri Ram College for Women. She is deeply invested in deconstructing violence, both physical and epistemic, from the lens of semiology, psychology, philosophy and the normalised mundanity of life. She seeks a reinvention—an almost archaeological exploration—of life through a study of language employed in multiple forms of literature, pedagogical curriculums, political rhetoric and so forth, with the aim of unearthing possibilities of liberating ethics, sociality, education and life.

INDEX